Jill T. Freeze

SAMS
Teach Yourself

Computer Basics

in 24 Hours

SECOND EDITION

SAMS

A Division of Macmillan USA
201 West 103rd St., Indianapolis, Indiana, 46290 USA

Sams Teach Yourself Computer Basics in 24 Hours, Second Edition

Copyright © 2000 by Sams Publishing

International Standard Book Number: 0-672-31801-6

Library of Congress Catalog Card Number: 99-65598

Printed in the United States of America

First Printing: February 2000

02   01   00   4   3   2

Trademarks

Warning and Disclaimer

ACQUISITIONS EDITOR
Betsy Brown

DEVELOPMENT EDITORS
Jan Snyder
Damon Jordan

MANAGING EDITOR
Charlotte Clapp

PROJECT EDITOR
George E. Nedeff

COPY EDITOR
Jill Bond

INDEXER
Rebecca Hornyak

PROOFREADER
Candice Hightower

TECHNICAL EDITOR
Bill Bruns

TEAM COORDINATOR
Amy Patton

INTERIOR DESIGN
Gary Adair

COVER DESIGN
Aren Howell

COPY WRITER
Eric Borgert

PRODUCTION
Dan Harris
George Poole

Contents at a Glance

Contents

About the Author

Jill T. Freeze is a freelance management consultant who has worked with such organizations as the John F. Kennedy Center for the Performing Arts, the National Endowment for the Arts, The Smithsonian, and the White House. Having used computers extensively over the past decade for work and play, Jill finally decided to put her experience to good use writing computer books. She authored *Using Microsoft Office 97* (Que, 1997) and *Introducing WebTV* (Microsoft Press, 1997). In addition, Jill has assisted her husband, Wayne, in writing several advanced computer programming books. Her formal education includes a bachelor's degree magna cum laude from the University of Massachusetts at Amherst (in Arts Administration and Writing) and a master's degree from George Washington University (in Nonprofit Administration). For fun, Jill likes listening to music, writing fiction, surfing the Net, playing her flute, cheering for her favorite NASCAR driver, Terry Labonte, and playing with her two children, Christopher and Samantha. Jill can be reached at `Jfreeze@JustPC.com`.

Dedication

To Rick Dudley, a close friend who really saved the day for me as I worked on this book.
Take care, and thanks bunches!

—Jill

Acknowledgments

First off, I'd like to thank my readers. It's because of your enthusiasm for the first edition of this book that a second edition was even considered. Your supportive emails (and questions) mean a lot to me; keep 'em comin'!

Then there's the gang at Macmillan Computer Publishing, many of whom I've had the opportunity and good fortune to have worked with on previous book projects as well. Jan Snyder and Damon Jordan (Development Editors) and Bill Bruns (Technical Editor) have worked on my team several times, and each time I see their top-notch work, I continue to hope they'll be with me on future projects too! Jill Bond, I want to thank you for turning my words into smooth, flowing sentences! And finally, to Betsy Brown, my Acquisitions Editor for this project…it may have been our first time to work together, but I sure hope it won't be our last! George Nedeff, thanks a million for keeping the AR process running smoothly! And to all the other members of the *Sams Teach Yourself Computer Basics in 24 Hours, Second Edition* team whose names you'll see listed at the very front of the book. Thanks for making magic out of all those pages of courier fonts and style codes!

I'd also like to express my gratitude to Jennifer Bogden from ATI Technologies who gave me the opportunity to fully experience the amazing, uh, wonders of the latest ATI All-in-Wonder card. The WebTV for Windows chapter wouldn't have been the same without you! Thanks for everything!

And to my husband, Wayne Freeze, who took time out of his frantic programming book projects to help me muddle through all the software technobabble…thanks, Papabear. Now I'm free to begin helping you with YOUR book!

To my friend, Julie Smith, who I was supposed to help move into her first house but couldn't because I was frantically typing at the keyboard. I hope you can forgive me!

Finally, to my dear Wayne, Christopher, and Samantha…the three most important people in my life. Their love, hugs, kisses, and smiles make all the hard work worthwhile. I love you guys with all my heart!

Tell Us What You Think!

As the reader of this book, *you* are our most important critic and commentator. We value your opinion and want to know what we're doing right, what we could do better, what areas you'd like to see us publish in, and any other words of wisdom you're willing to pass our way.

You can fax, email, or write me directly to let me know what you did or didn't like about this book—as well as what we can do to make our books stronger.

Please note that I cannot help you with technical problems related to the topic of this book, and that due to the high volume of mail I receive, I might not be able to reply to every message.

When you write, please be sure to include this book's title and author as well as your name and phone or fax number. I will carefully review your comments and share them with the author and editors who worked on the book.

Fax: 317-581-4770

Email: `office_sams@mcp.com`

Mail: Mark Taber
          Associate Publisher
          Sams Publishing
          201 West 103rd Street
          Indianapolis, IN 46290 USA

Introduction

Welcome to Computer Basics, Second Edition!

If someone asked you to guess how many PCs one of the leading manufacturers ships each year, what would you guess? A hundred thousand? A million? Believe it or not, the answer is really between five and ten million. I can't divulge who told me that (they'd have to kill me if I did), but it's the truth, and that's just one PC manufacturer!

Each year, millions of people like you join the ranks of new PC users. Why? Maybe it's the desire to get online, or perhaps it was the irresistible offer of a $99 PC with a three-year Internet service contract. No matter the case, you're bound to want some guidance on this grand adventure, this book is here to give you just that—friendly guidance pure and simple.

If you're feeling a bit uneasy about jumping into the world of computers, just remember that you're not alone. In fact, I was terrified of computers when I first started working with them. I was convinced that one wrong keystroke would bring the world of computing to a grinding halt. Not so. As you'll see throughout this book, there's very little you can do to your PC that can't be fixed as long as you don't panic and you know how to respond. I may not be able to calm you in the midst of crisis, but I can see to it that you are armed with everything you need to recover from potential mishaps.

We (meaning the team of editors at Macmillan and I) have put a lot of time and energy into this revision of the book. We wanted it to cover everything the new user would ever want or need to know. In addition, throughout the text, I steer you toward other good books, should you decide to explore a given topic more thoroughly.

If we've fallen short of giving you the best all-in-one book we can, please email us with your suggestions and ideas at JFreeze@JustPC.com. Your thoughts and opinions do count; however, please keep in mind we have a broad audience to consider.

Likewise, if you found this book useful, please drop us a line at the same email address and let us know that, too. Your kind words will help fuel us through the all-nighters it takes to create a book like this.

Now back to business…

Who Should Read This Book?

This book was written with the new computer user in mind. If you can answer "Yes" to any of the following, then *Sams Teach Yourself Computer Basics in 24 Hours, Second Edition* is for you!

- Did you just acquire a PC and are wondering how to use it?
- Are you contemplating buying a computer, but are afraid it might be too hard to learn how to use?
- Have you spent some time surfing on WebTV and now find yourself ready to make the jump to a PC?
- Are you looking for a single volume that covers the hardware, the software, and the Internet?

How This Book is Organized

Inside the front cover of this book, you'll find a tear card with spaces for you to fill out information about your computer. Fill in as much of it as you can right now (you'll learn how to fill in the remaining blanks in Part II, "Windows"). This information will come in handy should you need to call tech support of your PCs manufacturer for help.

This book is organized into four parts that lead you smoothly and logically through the PC learning process.

- Part I: "Hardware: The Power Behind the PC" These chapters show you how to maximize and configure the hardware you have for optimum results in terms of speed and quality. You'll also take a close look at some of today's most desired computer peripherals: DVD, scanners, digital cameras, joysticks, and so on. I don't just tell you they exist; I show you how to set them up and get them ready for action.

- Part II: "Windows " When you set up your PC and turn it on, you stare right into the Windows desktop. Your journey begins by getting acquainted with the "brain" of your PC so that you can tell it what to do rather than the reverse! A working knowledge of Windows also will help you install and configure a printer and those neat computer toys that are discussed in Part I.

- Part III: "Software" Learn about the many types of software available to you, and unleash the power of Word 2000 and Excel 2000 to get organized and create professional looking documents.

- Part IV: "The Internet" Get the scoop on finding Web sites, sending email, shopping online, participating in newsgroups, building your own Web page, and other fun activities that you can take part in on the Internet. You'll even learn how to download shareware and free clip art and install it on your computer!

Finally, I've added three appendixes for your convenience. The first is written especially for those of you who have yet to purchase your computer. I present a list of things to think about before you make the big purchase. The second addresses "Getting Set Up," which offers valuable tips for unpacking and setting up your new PC. The last appendix, "When Something Goes Wrong…," is designed to give you instant access to the solutions for some of the most common PC problems. This is where you should turn before you call tech support or, worse yet, throw your PC out the window!

About the Sams Teach Yourself in 24 Hours Series

Each Sams Teach Yourself in 24 Hours title is divided into 24 one-hour lessons designed to explore a specific topic in detail. At the beginning of the hour, you'll see a bulleted list of items covered in that lesson. Then, throughout the hour, you'll be guided through the steps needed to accomplish the goals set forth at the beginning of the hour. A smattering of tips, tricks, and new term definitions inject further depth into the topic at hand.

Finally, at the end of the hour, we help you put your newfound knowledge to the test. First, you'll take a multiple-choice mini quiz to test what you've learned. Don't feel pressured—the quizzes are pretty easy, and in many cases they have significant entertainment value as well. Then there's a recommended activity. It's not a major project by any stretch, but it does require you to actually go over to your computer and try out some of the steps outlined in the hour. There's no better way to learn than by actually doing!

A Friendly Warning….

If you've read any of my books in the past, then you're fully prepared for what follows; but for those who haven't, you should be forewarned about my quirky sense of humor.

Learning needn't be stuffy and boring. In fact, literally hundreds of readers have emailed me, expressing their appreciation for my lighthearted style. One lady even went so far as to say after reading one of my books, she felt like she had known me for years! (What can I say, humor is my favorite coping strategy. As Simba in Disney's *The Lion King* said, "I laugh in the face of danger!") But seriously, learning something new can be stressful enough without having to wade through pages upon pages of pompous candor.

Lighten up and have fun getting to know the computer! After you get up and running on the Internet, surf over to my Web site at `www.JustPC.com` and leave a note saying "hi."

You'll also see a variety of special element boxes, including the following:

A **Note** presents interesting information related to the discussion.

A **Tip** offers advice or shows you an easier way of doing something.

A **Caution** alerts you to a possible problem and gives you advice on how to avoid it.

Text that you type and text that you see onscreen appear in monospace type:

```
It will look like this.
```

NEW TERM   New terms are introduced using the New Term icon.

PART I

Hardware: The Power Behind the PC

Hour

HOUR 1

Getting to Know the Brain of Your Computer

For years, the members of the technical crowd have referred to the computer's processor (the 500 MHz Pentium III thingy that powers the machine, for example) as its *brain*. I, on the other hand, tend to think of the operating system (Windows 98) as the computer's brain because without it, the computer is just a hunk of machinery capable of doing nothing. Think of Windows as a traffic cop that tells the computer what to do when.

Given the importance of Windows, I am taking a rather bold, nontraditional step by presenting that information first. Most basic computing books drone on about hardware from the very beginning. Not this book. I'll get you up and running on your new PC from the very first chapter. Then—and *only* then—when you're comfortable "doing Windows," I'll venture into discussing hardware.

In the meantime, here's what you have to look forward to in this
hour's lesson:

- Unlock the universe of personal computing with the Start button.
- Become comfortable with your pointing device.
- Learn about the shortcuts that reside on your desktop.
- Discover how the Quick Launch bar, taskbar, and system tray work as well as what they do.

Recently, my 60+ year-old father signed himself up for a computer class. So when Macmillan asked me to revise this book, it was only natural that I sought his opinion for what approach seemed to work best for new computer users.

Apparently, many students had an easier time dealing with larger tasks that were divided into smaller chunks rather than learning about computers by function. When learning about word processing, for example, the class responded better to a lesson in which they typed a letter and made it look nice as opposed to a lesson where they learned how to change font size, style, and color. Somehow, I think they found all that technical lingo intimidating; and it sure can be, especially when you just want to learn what you need to know and move on.

That's what this book is all about—learning what you need to know, and moving on. Should you want to explore a certain topic further, however, I point you in the direction of the best books to help you. Now, let's cut to the chase and jump right in!

Windows 98, Second Edition Briefing

Now that you've joined the ranks of proud computer owners everywhere, you'll need to adjust your definition of *windows*. Rather than being a mere clear pane of glass that separates you from rain, snow, bitter cold, and sweltering heat, it also now is Windows with a capital "W."

As you probably remember from the opening paragraphs of this hour, I described Windows as a brain and a traffic cop. While the analogy is quite accurate, you should be aware that the technical term for this function is *operating system*. Operating systems literally tell your machine which tasks to do when, and it's the very first piece of software installed on your machine.

After an operating system has been successfully installed, you can do all sorts of neat things with your new investment. In the vast majority of cases, the operating system is preinstalled on your new computer so that when you hook up the machine and turn it on for the first time, you'll be greeted by what's known as the Windows *desktop*.

So What's Behind the Name "Windows?"

Windows is much more than just a product name. In fact, it represents a whole new way of computing. Way back in the olden days of personal computing, machines were run by an operating system called *DOS*. With DOS, you could do only one thing at a time. If you were writing a letter and needed to reference a specific number in a spreadsheet, for example, you would have to shut down the word processing program, open the spreadsheet application to get the information you needed, shut down the spreadsheet program, and finally reopen the word processor to continue drafting your letter—a major hassle to say the least.

After much research and development time, the folks at Microsoft came up with an operating system that let users do two things at once (or multitasking as the techies like to call it). That operating system was known as *Microsoft Windows* because it literally created a separate window for each application or task you had running. That enabled you to easily hop from your word processor to the spreadsheet and back again with a few simple mouse clicks—a major improvement over text-based DOS.

Windows offered other advantages besides multitasking, however. At the time Windows was created, Macintosh computers were reputedly the most user-friendly because they relied heavily on graphics rather than esoteric keyboard commands. In other words, to print a document, you would click on a picture of a printer rather than typing in the Print command.

NEW TERM **Those gooey graphics...** When a program depends on graphics to run, the collection of graphics and resulting commands are referred to as a *graphical user interface* (or GUI, as in "My daughter Samantha just loves chewy, gooey brownies, fresh from the oven.") This is far from being a must-know term, but boy would it make impressive cocktail chatter the next time you're hanging out with your more nerdy acquaintances!

Microsoft tried to emulate this ease of use in Windows. It took a few revisions of the software to produce a viable product (and some will argue that Windows is still far from being stable), but it has evolved and improved over time to become the operating system you have on your computer today: Windows 98, Second Edition.

What's this Second Edition stuff; couldn't they get it right the first time?
Occasionally, no matter how long a product has been tested, it gets released with problems technically referred to as *bugs*. Many times, the problems are remedied with a simple fix, such as a single update file downloaded from the Internet. In some cases, however, more severe bugs warrant more dramatic action, such as a new version of the software altogether. Enter: Windows 98, Second Edition.

How Can I Tell If I Have Windows 98, Second Edition?

Many of the leading computer manufacturers, such as Gateway, started shipping their systems with Windows 98, Second Edition in mid-July, 1999. The same goes for machines sold in stores across the country. Many times the inclusion of the new operating system was a heavily advertised selling point in the mid-year advertising campaign.

If the version of Windows you have isn't clearly identified in the printed documentation included with your computer, then turn on your machine and watch it boot (start up).

When Windows is ready to launch, you'll see a screen of clouds, along with the logo for the operating system you have installed. If you have Windows 98, Second Edition, you'll know it then and there.

Even if you don't have the latest and greatest release, you'll still be able to learn a great deal from this book. In fact, the differences between Windows 95 and Windows 98 are minimal as well. And these differences typically appear in subtle things, such as in changes in the graphics as opposed to more radical variations.

What's What on the Windows Desktop

After your computer finishes booting, you'll see a screen similar to the one shown in Figure 1.1. This view is known as the Windows Desktop.

FIGURE 1.1
Crucial parts of the Windows Desktop.

Shortcut icons

Desktop

System tray

Task/Window buttons

Quick Launch bar

Show Desktop button

Start button

Taskbar

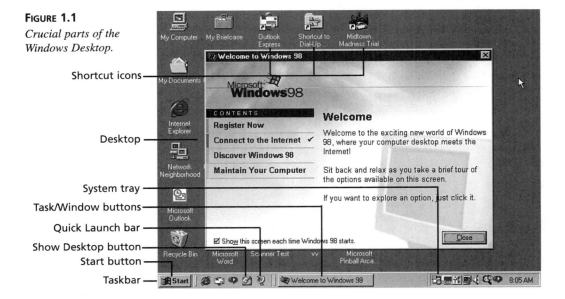

It's meant to resemble your desk at work or in your den in that it keeps the most regularly used items close at hand. In the case of Windows 98, however, those items include shortcut icons and task buttons rather than pens, scissors, and tape.

Wait a minute, you said this was going to be easy! Throughout this lesson, I occasionally use terms that may be unfamiliar to you. Don't panic! I'm not assuming you know them; rather, I'm helping you feel at ease with the lingo without bombarding you with a plethora of boring definitions. The more time you spend on your computer, the more the technical terms will become second nature to you. When you think about it, many of the terms are pretty self-explanatory anyway.

The Windows Desktop: Just Another Pretty Face

Like your desktop at work, the Windows desktop is the surface you can actually see when the desktop is clean. Instead of wood grain Formica, it's an aqua blue color that you can easily change, as you learn in the next hour.

The sole purpose of the Windows desktop is to hold all those important program buttons and icons. Believe it or not, it can get just as cluttered as your desk if you're not careful!

Taking Shortcuts

The little pictures you see dotting your Windows desktop are called *icons*. Each icon is a graphical representative of your word processing program, your Internet connection, or some other application. When you double-click an icon, the corresponding program (or document or Web site) launches.

Don't fret over how to double-click the icons properly; I'll bring you up to speed on working with your mouse in a moment.

You also should be aware that you can put your own shortcuts on the desktop. This gives you immediate access to the resources you use most. I'll show you how to create your own shortcuts in the next lesson.

Getting a Good Start in Computing

As you'll quickly discover, the Windows Start button is where it all begins. By clicking it, you open lists of everything on your computer. These lists are called *menus* because you can make a selection from the items presented to you.

The Start button also is where you shut down your computer, as you'll see at the end of this lesson.

Dealing with the Tasks at Hand

At the bottom of your screen is a narrow gray band known as the *taskbar*. This is where you'll find a button for each application you have running (or, as is the case with Microsoft Word 2000 and Excel 2000, each document you have open). Simply click the desired button, and the corresponding item appears at the front of your display.

The Windows taskbar is without a doubt the simplest way to move from one task to another.

Saving Time with the Quick Launch Bar

Unlike the shortcut icons on your desktop that you have to double-click to activate, you can open the applications in your Quick Launch bar in a single click. What's more, there's no stumbling through layers upon layers of menus to find the program you want because it's right in front of you.

While Microsoft automatically puts Internet Explorer and Outlook Express on the Quick Launch bar, you can add (or delete) any buttons you want, as you'll see in the next hour.

Show Us Your Desktop!

In the past, it used to be a major pain getting to your desktop, especially if you had multiple programs open. You had to work your way through each one to close its window. Now, thanks to the Show Desktop button, your desktop is one click away. Clicking this button simply minimizes each program window so that you can work with a fully exposed desktop.

To return to any of the applications or documents, simply click the appropriate button on the taskbar.

Presenting the Windows System Tray...

As was illustrated in Figure 1.1, the System Tray is in the lower right corner of the Windows desktop. At bare minimum, it holds the icons for screen resolution adjustment, sound volume (if a sound card is installed), and the system's clock. Other tools you may find there, depending on the software you have installed and the type of machine you're using, might include an icon to access your antivirus program; your RealPlayer plug-in that plays sounds and movies on the Web; an Internet connection monitor; and, in the case of laptops, an icon showing whether the computer is powered by electricity or its battery.

We'll revisit some of these tools in greater depth as you progress through the lessons in this book.

Telling Your PC What to Do

Working with Windows requires using a mouse—that corded two-button thing that sits next to your keyboard (see Figure 1.2), or some other pointing device such as a touch pad or trackball.

FIGURE 1.2
This little rodent will help you get all your work done in a snap.

To make things easier, I'll walk you through a fun and educational exercise that helps you get used to moving the pointer where you want it.

When a mouse isn't a mouse... You can still follow the steps below even if you're not working with a mouse. Rather than dragging the mouse in the direction indicated, touch pad users will move their index finger in the same direction across the touch pad. Likewise, trackball users will roll the little ball as indicated. No matter what type of pointing device you use, it's imperative that you grow comfortable with it.

Enough of all the talk; let's take the book over to the PC and get started!

Learning All the Moves

Perform the following steps to start getting acquainted with your pointing device of choice:

1. If you've not already done so, turn on your computer.
2. After you see a screen similar to the one shown back in Figure 1.1, jiggle your mouse around to help you find the pointer. You're looking for a small, white arrow.
3. When the arrow's in sight, try to drag it in the direction of the Start button.
4. With the arrow resting over the top of the Start button, press the left mouse button. You'll see a Start menu similar to the one shown in Figure 1.3.

FIGURE **1.3**

*The Start menu is the
first step in finding
what's been installed
on your computer.*

FIGURE **1.3**

*The Start menu is the
first step in finding
what's been installed
on your computer.*

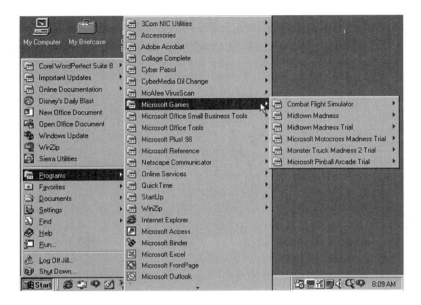

5. Move the mouse pointer up the menu until the word "Programs" is highlighted.
   The black arrow to the right of the word means another menu will appear if that
   option is selected.

6. From the resulting menu, choose Accessories, which produces yet another menu.

7. Select Games, and then choose Solitaire from the final menu. The window shown
   in Figure 1.4 appears.

FIGURE **1.4**

*Solitaire is a fun way
to learn how to control
your mouse.*

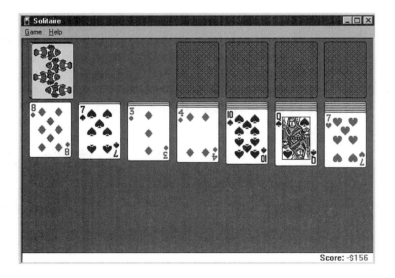

1

8. That's right, I'm actually using a game to help you practice your mouse-eye coordination! Look at the cards that are face up and see if there are any valid moves.

> **Not sure what you're doing?** For those of you who aren't familiar with the rules of solitaire, here's an oversimplification. The object is to get all the aces up top and build them up, one-by-one, according to suit. You reveal additional cards by arranging them in descending order, alternating red and black suits as you go. Don't knock yourself out trying to become a Solitaire pro; the point here is to get comfortable using Windows. I must warn you, however, Solitaire can be very addicting; it may be hard to stop playing once you start!

9. If there are any aces at the front of any of the lines of cards, simply double-click them (press the left mouse button twice in rapid succession) and they will automatically move up to one of the four slots at the top of the screen.

10. To move a card from one row to another, click on it and, with the button still pressed, drag the card to the desired location and release the button to drop it. This maneuver is referred to as *drag-and-drop*. (Big surprise, huh?)

11. After you make all possible moves, click the pile of cards on the upper left to draw a card and place it like you did the others. If it doesn't fit anywhere, draw again.

12. Keep playing until you've made all possible moves and have run out of cards in the draw pile.

13. Hooked and want to play again? See the word "Game" at the left end of the gray bar at the top of the Solitaire window? Click it to reveal a menu. Choose Deal to play another round, or Exit to end the game and close the window.

The more you play, the more at ease you should feel working with Windows and your mouse. Hey, who said learning couldn't be fun?

Summary

In this hour, you learned how to find your way around the Windows desktop. As you'll continue to discover in subsequent lessons, comfort with Windows is vital to your success with PCs.

By now, you also should feel a lot better about using a mouse. From this point on, it only gets easier! I find a lot of new computer users' progress is hampered by the ability to use a mouse effectively. The old adage, "Practice makes perfect," applies to mouse use as well. After a few hands of Solitaire, however, you'll be a pro!

In the next hour, "Customizing Windows," I'll show you how to make your desktop look the way you want it to.

Workshop

Now it's time to see just how much you learned in this lesson. I'll give you a short multiple-choice quiz to test what you learned, followed by a suggested activity designed to enhance the skills you acquired during the hour.

Quiz

Select the best answer to the questions from the choices provided, and then check your answers in the "Answers" section.

Questions

1. Which element is *not* found on the Windows desktop?

    a. Quick Launch bar

    b. Taskbar

    c. Snack bar

2. Choose the correct name of a pointing device from the following list:

    a. Rat

    b. Touch Ball

    c. Track Ball

3. What do you call it when you click on an object, drag it to a new location, and drop it into place?

    a. Drag-and-Drop

    b. Push-and-Plop

    c. Dump-and-Go

Answers

1. C is the correct choice, although you may wish it weren't during late night work sessions at the computer!

2. Again, C is the correct answer. A track ball is an alternative to a mouse—sort of like a mouse lying on its back.

3. The correct answer is A, although I guess you could argue that the others work just as well.

Activity

Grab your mouse and cruise on over to the Start button. Click it and select Programs from the menu. Finally, work your way through each of the selections to see what kind of software has been installed on your computer. Remember, the black arrows at the end of a word mean there's yet another menu to uncover. Don't open any of the programs for now; this is just an exercise.

Hour **2**

Making Your Desktop Look the Way You Want

No two people are alike, so why should your Windows desktop look (and sound) like everyone else's? Whether you're a diehard Grateful Dead fan and want your PC to reflect that, or you simply can't stand that mundane aqua background another day, you'll be happy to know all that and more can be changed.

Here are some of the topics you have to look forward to in this hour's lesson:

- Learn how to rearrange your desktop icons and make them larger.
- Make your taskbar disappear until you need it.
- Change the look of your desktop in a few quick mouse clicks.
- Create your own desktop shortcuts or add a program to the Quick Launch Bar.

Altering the appearance of your Windows desktop may seem like a frivolous waste of time at first glance, but there are times a change may be legitimately warranted.

I'm visually impaired, for example, and I'm here to tell you there are times when those larger desktop icons come in 'right handy! Or perhaps you're colorblind and could greatly benefit from a color scheme with more contrast.

Whether the changes you want to make are a necessity or just for fun, I'll show you how to get them done in the remainder of this hour.

Rearranging the Desktop Icons

If you want to move a certain shortcut from one location to another, simply click it and drag it into position, just as you dragged the Solitaire cards in the last hour.

For more global changes in the icon layout, right-click on a clean spot of the desktop and select Arrange Icons from the resulting shortcut menu. This produces a menu of choices for arranging the icons including by Name, Type, Size, or Date. Just click the desired option to rearrange your desktop in the specified order. By default, the icons are auto arranged, which means Windows automatically places them in the most space efficient, aesthetically appealing layout.

> **The quickest way to clean your desk(top).** Remember that Show Desktop button I mentioned last hour? Well, this is the perfect time to use it. One easy mouse click and your desktop is in clear view. If only cleaning my desk off were that easy...

Making It Big: Enlarging Your Desktop Icons

Small detailed icons can be a bear to see. Luckily, Windows makes it easy to enlarge them without affecting the way your programs run.

Not sure the larger size will help much? Take a look at Figures 2.1 and 2.2 to see just how big a difference the change makes. Even I can see the details on those icons!

To make your desktop icons larger, just follow these steps:

1. If you can't see a piece of your Windows desktop, click the Show Desktop button on the Windows Quick Launch Bar.

2. Right-click over the desktop to reveal the same shortcut menu you accessed to arrange your icons.

3. Select the Properties item from the menu to open the Display Properties dialog box.

FIGURE 2.1
Regular sized desktop icons.

FIGURE 2.2
Enlarged desktop icons.

2

NEW TERM **"Talk to me," said the dialog box.** While the term *dialog box* may sound a bit intimidating, the concept is quite simple. A dialog box basically is a window that opens and prompts you to provide information or answer a question.

4. The Display Properties dialog box contains a series of tabs that you can open to change various settings. Click the Effects tab to see the options in Figure 2.3.

FIGURE 2.3

The Effects tab of the Display Properties dialog box.

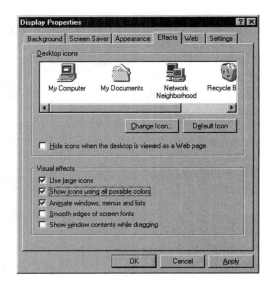

5. Under the Visual Effects section of the tab, click the Use Large Icons check box.
6. Click the OK button to exit the dialog box. In a few moments, the icons will look similar in size to the ones shown in Figure 2.2.

To return the icons to their normal size, just repeat the preceding steps. The option check boxes are like toggle buttons—clicking it turns the option to the opposite state you found it in (that is, clicking an enabled option turns it off; clicking it a second time turns it on again).

Maximize Screen Size by Hiding the Taskbar

Depending on your work style, the taskbar can occasionally take up valuable real estate onscreen that could be better allocated to your work.

If this situation describes you, then you may want to consider hiding your taskbar. When hidden, the taskbar stays out of sight until you hover the mouse pointer over the taskbar area. At that point it pops up, letting you work with it as usual.

While it increases the amount of viewing area onscreen, it has the drawback of being a royal pain when working on the bottom portion of a program window. That may not seem like a problem at first glance, but when you consider the fact that many popular word processors have buttons in that area you need to get to on a regular basis, it can potentially drive you batty.

> **A variation on the theme.** If the hiding taskbar gets in the way of your work, there's another possibility that may let you have your cake and eat it too, so to speak. Consider moving the taskbar to one side of the screen. That way you can gain the onscreen real estate without making yourself crazy. To move the taskbar, just click it and drag it toward the desired side of the screen while holding the left mouse button down. An outline of the taskbar's footprint appears in the specified location. If you like what you see, release the button to drop the taskbar into place.

To make your taskbar disappear, you'll need to do the following:

1. Make sure part of your taskbar is empty. This is crucial to getting the menu you'll need.
2. Right-click over the taskbar to open its corresponding shortcut menu.
3. Select the Properties item to launch the Taskbar Properties dialog box.
4. Verify that the Taskbar Options tab is displayed (see Figure 2.4).

FIGURE 2.4

The Taskbar Options tab of the Taskbar Properties dialog box is where you'll find the setting to hide your taskbar.

5. Click the Auto Hide check box to enable the option, and then click OK to exit the dialog box.

Here again, you can repeat the process to restore the taskbar to its previous state.

Banishing the Desktop Blues

Now for the fun part—changing your desktop's appearance. As I mentioned earlier, whether the change is a necessity or simply for fun, you'll want to know how to do it. I take you step-by-step through several ways to give your desktop a much-needed facelift.

Changing the Background Texture Using Files Provided

The simplest way to make a switch is to change the display's background using one of the files provided by Microsoft with Windows.

To do this, you'll need to perform the following steps:

1. Right-click over an uncovered portion of the desktop to open the familiar shortcut menu.

2. Choose the Properties item to launch the Display Properties dialog box.

3. Verify that the Background tab shown in Figure 2.5 is displayed.

FIGURE 2.5

Microsoft gives you a host of background textures from which to choose.

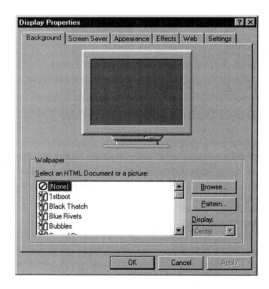

4. In the Wallpaper section of the tab, select the name of the file you want to use by clicking it. You'll see a preview of what it will look like in the monitor at the top of the tab.

5. If you like what you see, click OK to apply the design to your desktop. If it doesn't quite suit you, keep choosing from the designs available until you hit on the right one.

2

> **A neat-o, nifty desktop trick.** If you get a scanner or digital camera someday, you might be interested to know that you can even use those images for your background. Just follow the preceding steps, except rather than choosing the name of a wallpaper file, click the Browse button and surf over to the desired file (Figure A). The only gotcha' is the file needs to be in .bmp or .jpg format. Not only can you use a personal image, but you can click the black arrow next to the Display options box in the Background tab to choose an effect for the image (Figure B). As the following figures illustrate, you can stretch, center, or tile the image (Figure C).

FIGURE A

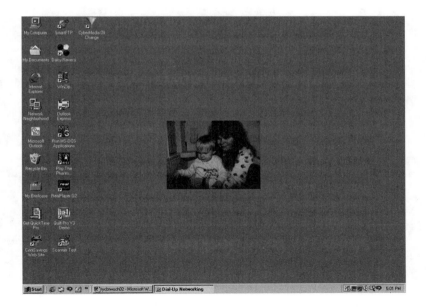

FIGURE B

FIGURE C

Coming Up with a New Scheme

Microsoft has taken the facelift thing even further by enabling you to choose a totally new color scheme for Windows as a whole. Not only can you change the desktop color, but you also can change the colors of other Windows elements, such as dialog boxes.

To apply a new color scheme, just follow these simple steps:

1. Find a clear area of your desktop and right-click it to access the shortcut menu.

2. Choose the Properties menu item to open the familiar Display Properties dialog box.

3. Click the Appearance tab and look for the Scheme option.

4. Using the down-arrow button at the end of the Scheme option, select a new color scheme for the wide variety of choices Microsoft provides. After you click the name of the chosen color scheme, you can preview it at the top of the tab, as shown in Figure 2.6.

FIGURE 2.6

You can even choose super-high contrast color schemes, as shown in the dialog box in this figure.

5. Click OK to apply your selected color scheme and exit the dialog box.

The Best of Desktop Decorating

If all the things you can do to change the appearance of your desktop impressed you, then you'd better sit down before I continue.

Okay, are you ready? Not only can you add special images to your desktop, but you can install entire desktop themes containing a wide range of sounds and animations as well. That's right, you can turn your PC into a virtual jungle complete with monkey noises, among other possibilities! Some desktop themes even include customized animated mouse pointers that change, depending on where the mouse is hovering.

Microsoft gives you a few to choose from so you can check out this neat enhancement right away. Within minutes, you too can have a funky desktop like the one shown in Figure 2.7.

FIGURE 2.7

Revisit the 60's with this groovy desktop theme.

Follow these steps to explore the wonderful world of desktop themes on your own machine:

1. Click the Start button, and then choose Settings, Control Panel from the resulting menus.

2. When the Control Panel appears, look for the Desktop Themes icon and then double-click it. That launches the dialog box shown in Figure 2.8.

3. Click the Themes dropdown arrow button to see a list of available themes. Choose one by clicking its name. You'll see it previewed in the dialog box.

4. If the theme meets with your approval, click OK to apply it and close the dialog box.

While you may not have many themes at your disposal now, just wait until you become skilled with using the Internet! If you surf over to www.themeworld.com, you'll find hundreds of desktop themes devoted to TV shows, cars, rock stars, cartoons, you name it.

Web sites with their own themes available for free download may have their own downloading and installation instructions, so be sure to read them thoroughly. Just in case they leave you hanging, however, Hour 24 of this book is dedicated to downloading such treasures from the Internet.

FIGURE 2.8

Use the drop-down box as shown here to select a theme provided by Microsoft.

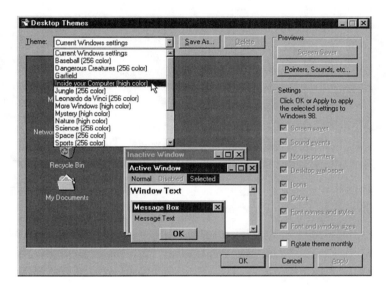

2

Hold it right there! I'll remind you of this again in Hour 24, but just in case you get overly enthusiastic...please, please, please be sure to run a virus scan on any software you download from the Internet before you install it. In the vast majority of cases, the program is clean, but it's not worth the risk. Check your PC to see whether Norton AntiVirus or McAfee AntiVirus is installed. Many computer manufacturers preinstall virus protection software on their systems.

Defining Your Own Desktop Shortcuts

The best way to define a shortcut for easy access depends on which type of file you're dealing with. If the item is a document or Web page, you can simply click on its icon and drag it to a clear space on your desktop.

When you attempt to drag-and-drop an icon, one of two things will happen. Either it appears on your desktop on the spot, or Windows launches a dialog box saying it can't move the selected item in that manner. If Windows is unable to create the shortcut on the spot, it asks you if you really intended to make a shortcut. Click the Yes button, and Windows does what it needs to build the shortcut.

> **So where do you find a file's icon?** Double-click the My Computer icon on the desktop and click your way to the desired file. This will make more sense to you after you completed Hour 4's lesson, "Getting Organized with Windows 98." In the case of Web pages, surf to the Web page you want, and then drag its icon from the Internet Explorer Address Bar to your desktop. The location of the Address Bar will be covered in Hour 20, "Web Browsing with Internet Explorer 5."

If the shortcut is intended to launch a program rather than a specific file, you'll want to complete the following steps for the best results:

1. Find a clear surface on your desktop and right-click to open the shortcut menu.
2. Choose New, then Shortcut from the menu to reveal the dialog box shown in Figure 2.9.

FIGURE 2.9

This dialog box is your key to accessing your favorite applications quickly.

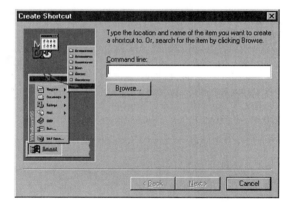

3. To make your life easier, click the Browse button.
4. Now comes the tricky part. You'll need to double-click your way to the file you want. Please note that you'll find the core programs (your word processor and such) in the Program Files folder. When you find the appropriate program, double-click it. You'll return to the dialog box shown in Figure 2.9, except this time, the file's address appears in the Command box.

> **Hey, I can't see the Program File folder!** To move through the list of files displayed, use the scroll bar tools as described in the figure below. Use the arrow buttons to move short distances, and the scroll box to move longer distances quickly.

FIGURE A

2

Click here to look left.

Or click and drag this in the desired direction.

Click here to look right.

5. Click the Next> button to continue. The first thing you'll need to do is give the shortcut a name. Note that a shorter name is more suitable for a shortcut. (In some cases, a name may be suggested. This especially is true for Microsoft applications.)

6. If the selected program doesn't have a special icon associated with it, you will be given the opportunity to choose one from several provided with Windows.

7. After you complete steps 5 and 6 as necessary, click the Finish button to save the shortcut to your desktop.

Adding an Item to the Quick Launch Bar

Adding an item to your Quick Launch Bar is similar to executing the preceding steps for creating a shortcut. Just do the following to access a program any time with a single click:

1. At the right end of the Quick Launch Bar you'll see a thick bar that separates it from the taskbar. Click it and drag it to the right to expose an empty area on the Quick Launch Bar.

2. Right-click over the newly created empty space, and choose Open from the shortcut menu. A window displaying all the icons currently residing in the Quick Launch Bar opens.

3. Click the File button near the top of the window and choose New, Shortcut from the dropdown menu.

4. Surf your way to the program you want to add to the Quick Launch Bar, and then double-click its name. Its file address now appears in the Command line box. Click Next> to proceed.

5. You then will be prompted to give the shortcut a name. In many cases, however, an acceptable suggestion will be made.

6. Click the Finish button to save the shortcut to the Quick Launch Bar.

Summary

In this hour, I introduced you to dozens of ways to personalize your Windows desktop. From reorganizing the icons to modifying the background's appearance and creating your own special shortcuts, it's all here. In many cases, tinkering with these settings is as much a necessity as it is fun. Visually impaired individuals can benefit immensely from larger icons or high contrast desktop color schemes. It can even enhance your productivity by keeping frequently used programs close to hand.

In the next hour, "Running Windows Applications," I'll help you get to know the few remaining Windows basics. You'll also take a look at some of the neat utilities included with Windows, such as the calculator, Microsoft Paint, and the Windows Address Book.

Workshop

Now it's time to see just how much you learned in this lesson. I'll give you a short multiple-choice quiz to test what you learned, followed by a suggested activity designed to enhance the skills you acquired during the hour.

Quiz

Select the best answer to the questions from the choices provided, and then check your answers in the following section.

Questions

1. Which method *cannot* be used to adjust the placement of desktop icons?

    a. Drag-and-Drop

    b. The Microsoft Telepathic Interface

    c. The Arrange Icons item on the desktop shortcut menu

2. You can use any image on your computer for a desktop background.

    a. Yes, without a doubt.

    b. Images can't be used in that way.

    c. Yes, but only if the images are in .bmp or .jpg file format.

3. What's the difference between a shortcut on your desktop and one on the Quick Launch Bar?

    a. You have to double-click the shortcut on the desktop, but only need to single click the Quick Launch Bar item.

    b. They are accessed the exact same way; the only difference is you can see Quick Launch shortcuts from anywhere on your computer because it occupies part of the taskbar space.

    c. There is no difference. Why did you waste all the book space talking about it?

Answers

1. B may sound convincing because of its fancy name, but unfortunately, Microsoft has yet to develop such a tool. If only…

2. If you chose C, you're absolutely right. Unfortunately, Windows does have some limitations on the types of images that can be used for desktop backgrounds.

3. A was the appropriate answer here. If you read the lesson thoroughly, the last two options should have been ruled out almost instantly.

Activity

Take this book over to your computer and give yourself time to experiment with the various desktop facelift possibilities.

2

HOUR 3

Running a Windows Application

As you grow more confident with your computer and start to explore various kinds of programs, you'll discover just how similar all Windows programs are. This is great news for new users because what could be perceived as radical (not to mention intimidating) differences between your word processor and a spreadsheet program, for example, have all but evaporated.

In this lesson, you'll look at common Windows application elements and take a peek at some useful programs you'll find hidden away in Windows. Here are some of the topics you have to look forward to this hour:

- Acquaint yourself with the anatomy of a basic Windows application screen.

- Learn how to change the size of your application's window.

- Try out the Windows Calculator and Address Book; they might come in handy down the road.

- Discover how to install a new program, be it on disk or a file you downloaded from the Internet.

Some Unfinished Business...

You've been introduced to the elements of the Windows desktop as well as to menus, toolbars, and dialog boxes, but there are a few more odds and ends you should know before we move on to the more advanced topics in this hour.

As was mentioned at the opening of this lesson, programs designed to run under Windows look (and behave) quite similarly. In Figure 3.1, you'll see the names of these commonly found elements, along with their placement onscreen.

FIGURE 3.1

The now familiar Solitaire screen models these common Windows program elements.

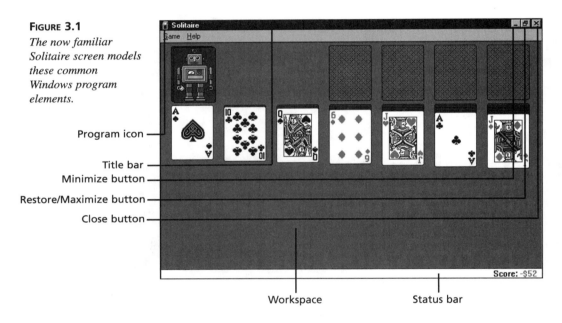

Table 3.1 presents the definition and purpose of each element illustrated in the preceding figure. While some of them may seem self-explanatory, there occasionally are subtleties that may be less obvious.

TABLE 3.1   Common Windows Program Elements and Their Functions

Element	Definition/Purpose
Title bar	This bar (which is dark blue unless you've applied your own desktop theme)across the top of your program windows displays the name of the software and open file (if applicable). This is the same information you'll see on the corresponding Windows taskbar button if the window is hidden.

Element	Definition/Purpose
Program icon	Residing at the far-left end of the title bar, the Program icon mirrors the icon shown on your Windows desktop (if you've created a shortcut for it). It also is the icon you'll see on the Windows taskbar when the program is running. Double-clicking the Program icon also exits the program.
Menu bar	This portion of the application holds a list of command types under which you'll find an assortment of items from which you can choose. Under the File menu, for example, you'd find items such as Open, Save, and so on. When you move your mouse over a selection, it turns into a button that you can click.
Minimize button	The third button in from the right end of the Title bar (the button with a single horizontal line on it) is called the Minimize button. Click it to make the program window disappear temporarily. You can reopen it by clicking the corresponding button on the Windows taskbar.
Restore/Maximize button	Each Windows application has a predefined window size. Many times, that size occupies only part of your workspace. Clicking the middle button on the right end of the title bar will either enlarge the program window to full screen size, or will restore it to the size in which it was originally intended.
Close button	Click this button on the far right of the title bar to close the application in which you currently are working.
Workspace	The largest part of the program window, the workspace, is the area in which words are typed (in the case of a word processor) or cards are moved (in the case of the Solitaire example).
Status bar	You'll find this element at the bottom of a program window. Usually, the grayish color of a typical menu bar, the status bar, gives you information about where you are in a program (such as the page number or inches down the page for a word processor) or the game's score (in the case of Solitaire's status bar). It also may contain other valuable data such as whether a certain program feature is active, error messages, and so on.

3

Resizing and Relocating Program Windows

In the preceding table, you saw how to make some basic changes to a program window's size, but you have a lot more options at your disposal. You can, for example, move windows around and narrow them so that you can see two documents at once. This may not seem like a big deal now, but it will become one as you get more comfortable working with your PC's various applications.

Moving a Program Window

Oftentimes when you launch a program, its window will be plopped in a seemingly random location on your screen. To move the window to a more convenient spot, simply drag-and-drop the program's title bar into place. You remember the old drag-and-drop maneuver, right? In this case, you click the dark blue title bar and, while keeping the left mouse button down, drag it into place, and then release the button to drop it. It's that easy!

Resizing a Program Window

Tweaking a window to the desired size is equally simple; it, too, makes use of the now familiar drag-and-drop procedure.

To adjust a window's width, move your mouse pointer over the program's left or right borderline (that thin dark line) until it turns into a double-headed east/west-like arrow (see Figure 3.2). Click on the line, and drag-and-drop it to the desired width. You can do this with both borders to achieve the results you want.

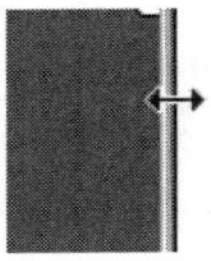

FIGURE 3.2
The resize mouse pointer lets you know you're in the right spot.

You can resize the top and bottom borders in the same manner, only this time the mouse pointer will appear as a north/south arrow when you're in the appropriate spot.

If you resize a window smaller than its original size, scroll bars might be added to the window (see Figure 3.3). These scroll bars enable you to see parts of the screen that are no longer in view.

FIGURE 3.3

These scroll bar tools help you see what you're missing.

Click here to move up the screen

Click and drag in desired direction

Click here to move to the left

Click here to move to the right

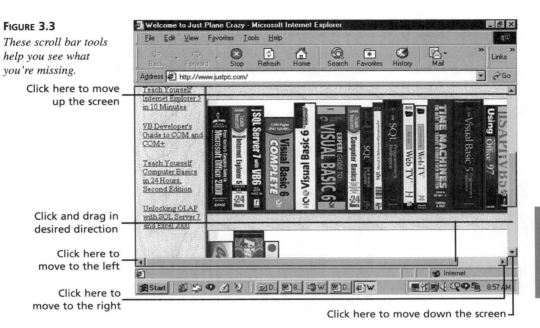

Click here to move down the screen

Click the arrow buttons on the ends of the scroll bars to move in the desired direction in small increments; or for larger jumps, click the scroll box and drag it in the appropriate direction until you see the item/text you're trying to find.

Math Made Simple with the Windows Calculator

I'm horrible at math. When I go to balance my checkbook, I usually scribble numbers on a piece of paper and work it out by hand. My husband, on the other hand, either does it in his head or cranks up Microsoft Excel and builds a full-blown spreadsheet for the occasion.

Thanks to Microsoft, there's a tool included with Windows that will help you achieve some sort of middle ground to these two extremes. Known simply as *Calculator*, it eliminates both paper waste and the complexities of spreadsheet design.

When you launch the program, you'll notice that it looks an awful lot like a standard calculator. The good news is it works like one, too! Rather than using your fingers to press keys, however, you use the mouse.

Testing the Calculator

You should seriously consider taking the time to work through the steps I'm about to present. Why? Because not only will doing so help you get to know how to use the Windows Calculator, but you'll become even more comfortable working with Windows programs in general.

Just follow these steps to start working with this handy little program:

1. To open the Calculator, click the Start button on the Windows task bar, and then choose Programs, Accessories, Calculator. The window in Figure 3.4 appears.

FIGURE 3.4

You can perform a wide variety of calculations using this nifty Windows accessory.

2. Enter the number 5,695 into the Calculator by clicking the corresponding buttons with your mouse.

There's more than one way enter a number. The Calculator gives you two alternatives to using the mouse to enter numbers. You can either use the number keys across the top of your keyboard, or you can work with the number pad at the right end of your keyboard.

3. Next, click the minus (–) sign.
4. Enter 1,592, and then click the equal (=) sign. Did you get 4,108? I hope not; the proper answer was 4,103!
5. Clear the display by clicking the C button, and then try adding the two numbers you subtracted the first time around.
6. Clear the display again, and try multiplying the numbers. See? It's just like using a "regular" calculator!

7. After you play with the program a bit, you'll be ready to move on to something else. Before you do, however, you'll need to shut down the Calculator program. The easiest way to do this is by clicking the Close (X) button in the top right corner of the Calculator's window.

The mathematicians among us might be interested to know that a full-featured scientific calculator also is available. To begin working with it, click the View item on the Menu bar, and select Scientific. A window like the one shown in Figure 3.5 opens.

FIGURE 3.5

The scientific calculator options are too numerous to mention!

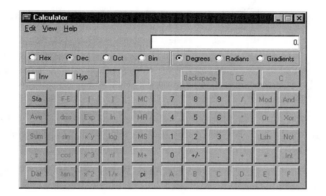

3

Staying in Touch with the Windows Address Book

While the Windows Address Book isn't the instrument that keeps you in touch, it certainly helps! The Windows Address Book helps you maintain comprehensive records on all your friends, family, and business associates. What's more, Outlook Express can easily use all that information for email. (More on that in Hour 21, "Emailing and Newsreading with Outlook Express.")

The Address Book enables you to keep track of all kinds of details, including the person's birthday, his or her Web page address, snail mail address (where mail is delivered by the U.S. Postal Service), work title/phone numbers, and so on.

Perform the following steps to create an Address Book profile for the person of your choice:

1. Open the Windows Address Book by clicking the Start button, and then pointing to Programs, Accessories, Address Book. A screen similar to the one in Figure 3.6 appears.

FIGURE 3.6

Soon, your Address Book will be populated like this one.

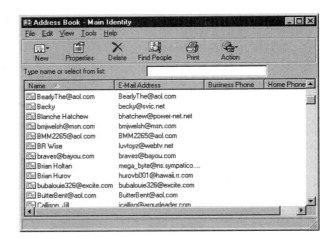

2. To enter a new profile, click the New button, and then select New Contact from the resulting menu. A tab like the one shown in Figure 3.7 appears.

FIGURE 3.7

The Name tab holds basic information about a person.

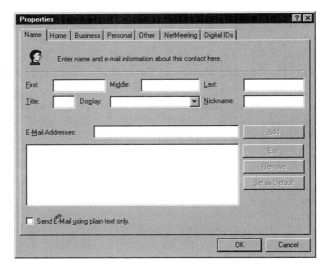

3. Click inside each blank box on the Name tab and type in the requested information. All the items are pretty straightforward, except the Display and Nickname items. The Address Book will generate a Display name from the name boxes you filled in. Others will be able to see this information, so the default Display name is a good choice. The Nickname is one to which only you will have access. For example, you might fill in your boss's full name but decide to use "Boss" as the Nickname.

NEW TERM **Fields of dreams.** The information stored in each box is technically referred to as a *field*. Specific fields help ensure that information is stored and maintained consistently.

4. Next, click the Home tab to begin filling in address, phone, and personal Web page information.

5. The Business tab is your next stop. Here, you'll provide the person's work information including job title, company, pager number, company Web page address, and so on.

6. Finally, the Personal tab is where you'll keep track of birthdays, anniversaries, spouses and children's names, and so on. Given your newness to the computer, you'll leave the remaining tabs alone.

7. Click OK to save your entry, and then either repeat the steps to add more people to your Address Book, or click the Close (X) button to exit the application.

Installing New Windows Programs

At some point down the road, you'll undoubtedly want to put some new software on your machine. Most applications today come with their own installation programs, so installing software is a fairly simple process. But before you start, check the following items:

- First, make sure you exit any programs you might be running. Because most installation programs make changes to your system files, exiting your programs will prevent any conflicts from occurring. In addition, you might need to restart your computer during the installation, so exiting your programs prevents any possible loss of data.

- If you're upgrading your software to a newer version, be sure to make copies of all your existing data, in case something happens to it during the upgrade process. You'll learn how to do this in Hour 12, "Keeping Your System Healthy Using Windows Tools." Also, be aware that some programs (but certainly not the majority) require you to uninstall the previous version before upgrading. Most, however, enable you to simply upgrade on top of the existing software. Read the installation manual before proceeding.

To install a program, follow these basic steps:

1. Insert the first installation diskette (or the CD-ROM) into its drive. CDs typically will launch a special installation program (called a wizard) to guide you through the process step-by-step. If the wizard doesn't appear, move on to Step 2.

2. Click the Start button and select Run.

3. Type the path and the filename of the installation program and click OK. To install a program from drive A:, for example, you might type something like A:SETUP or A:INSTALL. (Check with the installation manual for the exact command you need to type.) You also can click the Browse button and locate the setup file yourself.

If you downloaded a program from the Net... The last lesson in this book, Hour 24, "Downloading Treasures from the Internet," is devoted to finding programs of interest on the Internet. After you download them and checked for viruses, however, you'll be glad to know that installing them is no different than installing programs from CD or diskette. The only difference is that you'll browse to a file on your machine rather than on a disk to launch the program's installation/setup program.

4. At this point, the installation program will prompt you to make whatever selections are needed. You might, for example, be asked to select the drive and folder into which you want the program installed. If you're upgrading a previous version, make sure you select the directory in which it originally was installed. Continue to follow the onscreen prompts until the program installation is complete.

Many installations offer a choice as to the type of setup you can select. You might, for example, be offered the choices Compact, Typical, and Custom. Compact, in this case, would offer you a slimmed-down version of the program (a good choice if you're short on hard disk space), while Typical installs all the basic options. Custom enables you to select the options you want (and those you don't want).

You may save disk space, but not time. Keep in mind that you may need to have the CD in your machine to run the more watered down installations. While that may not seem like a big inconvenience, you should be aware that programs run from the CD may run more slowly. The difference in speed may not be noticeable for most productivity software, but for some games, it can be almost fatal. Games, such as flight and racing simulators, rely on speed. If speed doesn't exist, the game becomes unplayable.

The installation program creates whatever folders are needed. After checking to make sure there is enough space, it then will copy the contents of the installation diskettes or CD-ROM to your hard disk. It also will add a command for starting the program to your Start menu.

Uninstalling Software

If you've decided that you no longer need a particular program, you should remove it from the hard disk to make room for the programs you do use. To do this, perform the following steps:

1. Click the Start button and select Settings. Select Control Panel from the shortcut menu that appears.

2. Double-click the Add/Remove Programs icon. The Add/Remove Programs Properties dialog box appears, as shown in Figure 3.8.

FIGURE 3.8
Removing unwanted programs from the hard disk.

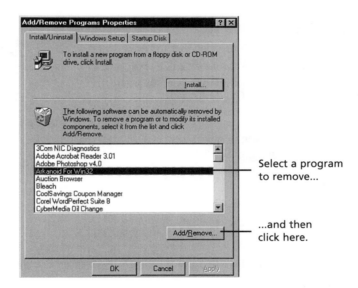

Select a program to remove...

...and then click here.

3. Select the program you want to delete and click Add/Remove.

4. You may be prompted to insert the installation diskette or CD-ROM for the program you're removing. Do so and then click OK.

5. Your application's uninstall program starts. Follow the onscreen prompts to remove the program from your hard disk.

Summary

In this hour, you learned some remaining odd and ends about Windows. In addition to learning how to move and resize program windows, you discovered some useful new tools in the Calculator and Address Book. You finished up the lesson with a quick course on installing and uninstalling programs on your computer.

In Hour 4, "Getting Organized with Windows 98, SE," we'll discuss the importance of good file management and how you can maximize your hard disk space, as well easily find what you want on your system.

Workshop

Now it's time to see just how much you learned in this lesson. I'll give you a short multiple-choice quiz to test what you learned, followed by a suggested activity designed to enhance the skills you acquired during the hour.

Quiz

Select the best answer to the questions from the choices provided, and then check your answers in the following section.

Questions

1. How do you move a program window?

    a. Send UPS to pick it up.

    b. Click the title bar and drag the window to the desired location.

    c. You can't move them; whatever the application's developer says, goes.

2. What other types of calculators will you find in the Windows Calculator?

    a. A Calorie Counter

    b. A Foreign Exchange Rate Calculator

    c. A Scientific Calculator

3. How do you remove programs you no longer want on your machine?

    a. Use the Add/Remove Program utility.

    b. You can't remove them. After they are there, you are stuck with them. When you run out of space, you'll just have to get a new hard drive and throw the full one out.

    c. Programs? What are those? I thought programs were only found on TV!

Answers

1. If you selected b, you were correct. That one should have been a "gimme" it was so easy!

2. c is the right answer. b would be like shooting at a moving target. As for a, Bill Gates has yet to team up with Richard Simmons!

3. Boy, I'm too easy on you guys! a is the correct answer for this question.

Activity

As I mentioned in the Summary, the next lesson is devoted to getting organized using Windows 98, SE. As this hour's activity, I've found the perfect segue between this lesson and the next. It's also great preparation for the email hour.

I want you to round up all the names, addresses, and numbers you have scrawled on scraps of paper, printed in your paper address book, or scribbled on the backs of business cards, junk mail envelopes, or inside matchbook covers.

Go through each item and make an entry in your electronic Address Book. Don't worry if you can't fill everything in; the objective here is to get started and throw away some of that useless clutter.

Not only will doing this activity clean off all scraps you desk, but it will make it easy to find the information you need when you need it. That's the exact premise of the next hour.

3

HOUR 4

Getting Organized with Windows 98, SE

Have you ever had the opportunity to work with or see a substantial collection of paper files up close? I'm not talking about the two lateral file cabinets you might have at work, I'm talking about the banks of ceiling high cabinets you'll find behind the counter of many doctors' offices. There literally are thousands of files crammed in there! And the file dividers go way beyond the simple A, B, and C structure—they have to, or the people who need to access them in a hurry could be there for days flipping through the folders, one-by-one! Situations like these often warrant extra subdividers, so rather than A, B, and C, you might see A, An, Ar, B, Be, Br, C, Cl, Cr, and so on.

Your computer files are no different. Right now, you may not be able to imagine the number of files on your PC getting uncontrollable, but it happens quicker than you think. When it does happen, you end up wasting valuable time plowing through dozens, if not hundreds, of files, trying to find what you want.

In this lesson, I'll show you how to get—and keep—your files under control using Windows Explorer. Here are some other topics you have to look forward to this hour:

- Discover why luck is already on your side when it comes to file management.
- Learn how to plan the document filing system that's right for you.
- Find out how to create your own set of folders in which to store your files.
- Use Windows 98's Find tool to locate a specific file.

This Is Your Lucky Day!

Okay, so maybe you didn't win the lottery, but you should still consider yourself lucky. Why? Because new computer users haven't had the time to clog up their system with years worth of misfiled data! You're not faced with the arduous task of having to open dozens of files to find an appropriate place for them after the fact. The fact that you've got this book in your hot little hands means you'll be spared a whole lot of aggravation (not to mention wasted time).

Thinking About Getting Organized

Think of the folders you'll be creating on your PC as the electronic equivalent of the "B" drawer at the doctor's office. The more you compartmentalize, the easier it should be to find what you want when you want it. Folders can have subfolders as well.

Consider this example: If I shared a PC with my family, there may be separate folders for each family member (Wayne, Jill, Christopher, and Samantha). Each person could then have his or her own group of folders. I tend to divide my Jill folder into subfolders such as Books, Fiction, Proposals, and so on. Then my Books folder may be further broken out by creating a folder for each title I write. Within that, I have folders for material submitted, author review documents, screen shot files, and so on. Each person's network of folders forms a pyramid (or hierarchy) of sorts.

Obviously, the complexity of your network of folders will vary, depending on the frequency with which you use your computer. If you use it once a month to write Aunt Linda a letter, that's one thing; but if you produce document after document for various projects at work or school, then you may benefit greatly from a highly organized system.

> **You've got mail!** Diligent file management is a good idea for your email correspondence as well. It not only enables you to find specific notes quickly, but it can be a great way to document the progress of a project or proposal.

Think about your computer use and ask yourself the following questions. Your answers should give you some valuable clues as to which type of file organization may help you most.

- **Is your machine primarily for business, personal use, or a combination of both?** Business or combined use generally would suggest a more complex filing scheme is in order. Personal use machines of people who do a lot of volunteer work also might warrant a more methodical approach.

- **In your business use of the computer, do you tend to think of items in terms of type of tasks (such as a budget, proposals, and so on), or do you plan to work on a variety of document types for various clients?** As you might guess, your answer provides tips for potential folder names.

- **Will you use the PC a lot, or just occasionally?** If you rarely save files on your computer, having a complex folder hierarchy actually might make it more time consuming to find the information you're seeking.

- **Think the way you work.** This concept is closely linked to choosing appropriate file names in that its extremely useful to have a meaningful naming scheme. Suppose that you do the newsletters for your daughter's nursery school. Rather than name each related file something outrageously long like cbcnsjan2000 (the school's initials followed by the publication date of this particular newsletter), consider creating a special CBCNS folder (or even a CBCNS Newsletters folder if you do other stuff for the school as well) and giving the files simpler names such as jan00. That way, you can find the file you need in a snap.

- **Who will be using the new computer?** If the new toy is to be shared, then you'll want to get the high-level family member folders in place as soon as possible (such as the Wayne, Jill, Christopher, and Samantha folders I used in an earlier example). That way, everyone's business is kept separate, and you won't be facing a hideously long file moving session later.

Now that you've answered some critical questions, it's time to sit down with a pen and paper and jot down a filing scheme that adequately meets your needs. I strongly urge you to take this assignment seriously and give it the time it deserves. The time you invest now will come back several times over in time saved by being able to find what you need quickly.

4

Getting to Know Windows Explorer, Filing Headquarters

While there are multiple ways to create new folders on your system, I'm going to introduce you to the way that will always be the same, no matter what other software you have installed on your machine.

By using the Windows 98 utility called *Windows Explorer*, you get a bird's eye view of the files on your computer. As you can see in Figure 4.1, Windows Explorer literally enables you to visualize how your folders are structured.

FIGURE 4.1

Click the plus sign next to a folder to reveal the folders nested underneath.

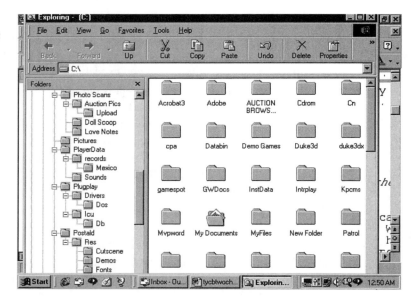

Table 4.1 gives you a quick rundown of what you can do with the various folders on your computer from within Windows Explorer. Knowing these commands will be a great help when it comes to examining your personal folder hierarchy.

TABLE 4.1   Windows Explorer folder viewing commands

Click on these folder items...	...to do the following
A folder icon	Displays information on all the files stored inside of it.
A plus (+) sign	Reveals all the subfolders within the folder immediately to the right of the plus sign.
A minus (-) sign	Makes all the subfolders underneath the folder to the right of the minus sign disappear.

There's much more you can do with Windows Explorer, as you'll see in the remainder of this hour. From this utility, you can create new folders and subfolders, move files from one folder to another, or even copy a few select files that really fit into two or more folders equally well.

Creating a New Folder

Perform the following steps to create high-level folders (also known as parent folders). Family member names are a good example of a type of parent folder you might want to create on your hard drive.

1. Launch Windows Explorer by clicking the Start button on the Windows taskbar, and then selecting Programs, Windows Explorer. Doing this launches a window similar to the one shown back in Figure 4.1.

2. Click the icon corresponding to your hard drive. You'll find it near the top of the folders pane; it's typically labeled (C:).

3. From the Windows Explorer menu bar, click File, and then point to New, Folder. A New Folder icon and label highlighted in dark blue appears at the bottom of the main viewing window (the window pane to the right of the files).

4. Click inside the highlighted area, and then type in the name you want for your new folder.

5. After you finish, click elsewhere in Windows Explorer (it doesn't really matter where, except it's wise to avoid the Enter key) to save your folder's name before it becomes inadvertently altered. Unless you perform this final step, the newly created folder will continue to be active, meaning that any keystroke potentially could add unwanted letters and/or punctuation to your folder's name.

Adding a Subfolder to the Hierarchy

The steps needed to create a subfolder mirror the steps you followed to create a parent folder, with one small exception. Rather than clicking the hard drive icon like you did in step 2, you click the folder under which you want to place the new folder.

To follow up with the example I've referred to throughout this hour, you would click on the Jill folder, and then continue with the preceding outlined steps to create a subfolder called Computer Basics to hold the files related to this book.

Renaming a Folder on Your Computer

Whether your filing needs change, or you simply think of a better name for some of the folders later on, you'll want to know how to rename them.

Renaming a folder is as simple as following these brief steps:

1. Launch Windows Explorer as you normally do.

2. Right-click the icon of the folder you want to rename. The shortcut menu shown in Figure 4.2 appears.

FIGURE 4.2

You and this Windows Explorer shortcut menu will become old friends.

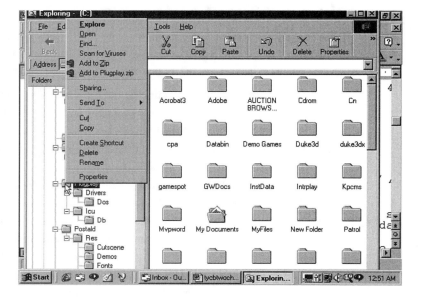

3. Choose Rename from the shortcut menu. The selected folder's name will appear highlighted in dark blue.

4. Click inside the highlights, and then type in the new name.

5. After you finish, click elsewhere in Windows Explorer to prevent altering the folder name by accident.

Deleting a Folder from Your System

There may come a day when you decide to delete a folder from your computer. Perhaps you finish your master's degree and want to archive the documents rather than take up space on your hard drive. Or maybe one of your clients moves on. Either way, you'll want to know how to delete a folder. Just follow these steps to perform the deletion:

1. Start the Windows Explorer utility, as directed earlier.

2. Right-click the icon of the folder you want to remove from your computer, and select Delete from the shortcut menu.

3. A dialog box like the one shown in Figure 4.3 opens, asking you to verify the fact that you really want to delete the selected folder and all of its contents. Click Yes or No as appropriate.

Look before you delete! Remember, the Delete command will erase not only the selected folder, but all the files within it as well. As a result, I *strongly* suggest that you click the folder to examine the files before you perform the deletion.

FIGURE 4.3

Look closely at the name of the folder about to be deleted before you make a final selection.

To archive your files, simply insert a floppy disk into your disk drive slot, and then copy the files you wish to archive onto the disk (typically the A: drive). Once the files are safely stored in another location, you can go ahead with any necessary deletions. I would, however, verify that the documents on your disk are not corrupt or otherwise damaged first. To do this, launch the application in which the document(s) was created, choose File, Open, and then click your way to your floppy drive and try to open the file(s) stored there.

Good File Naming Techniques: Another Organizational Aid

With a network of well-defined folders in place, your file names can now become shorter and more descriptive themselves.

As you create a document, be it a spreadsheet or a word processing document, think about a name for it that fully (and accurately) describes its contents. Use the following tips as a guide for coming up with that all-important document name:

- Want to be able to uncover a file just by glancing through the appropriate folder? A good file name can make a world of difference. Make the name as short yet descriptive as possible.

- Let's go back to my nursery school newsletter example. If I included the school's name in every file name as well as the document's title (such as a spreadsheet named CBCNS Budget, a Word document named CBCNS Grant Application, or so on), it would be much harder to find the file I want because they would all begin with CBCNS. A better filing strategy would be to create a special CBCNS folder; that way, you could simply call the documents Budget or Grant App. Of course, if you only use the computer for school volunteer work, there may not be a need for the school's name to be placed on the document or the folder at all.

- Consider using a date/year somewhere in the file name if it's relevant. Documents with names such as Budget, New Budget, and Projected Budget, for example, mean less than Fall 98 Budget or 99 Projected Budget.

- Name the way you work. If your work involves creating many types of documents for a single entity (such as budgets, newsletters, and grant applications for the school alone), then you'll want to emphasize the document's contents in its file name. If, on the other hand, you create a quarterly newsletter for multiple entities (the nursery school, PTA, the local animal rescue organization, and so on), you'll want the entity's name to appear prominently in the file's name. Why not create a folder for each one? Because four documents a year doesn't really warrant a separate folder. Instead, consider archiving the newsletters into folders dedicated to a specific year.

Some of these tips may seem to clash with one another at first glance. For example, how can you have a short, descriptive file name when you're trying to incorporate a date, an organization's name, and the type of document? The answer is simpler than you may think. For starters, try combining the folder and file naming strategies discussed previously. The two naming strategies are not mutually exclusive. In fact, they should—and do—work hand-in-hand to get the job done.

Remember, the goal here is to keep the number of entries in a given folder—or directory—to a minimum. Given that, it's extremely helpful if you take a long, hard look at
the way you intend to use your new computer. Every little detail, from the total number
of documents you create over the span of a year to the types of documents, influences
how you name your folders and files. While sophisticated file searching tools make finding things a lot easier than it used to be, nothing beats good file organization from the
get-go!

Once You Create It, Know Where to Store It

I'll discuss how to save files in various applications in the specific chapters dedicated to
them later on. Knowing where to place a document when you do save it, however, is a
great addition to the file management issues covered in this lesson.

The proper placement of a file in your computer's network of folders goes hand-in-hand
with the document's name when it comes to enhancing the capability to find the file
again when you need it.

Consider the following as you decide where to store a newly created document in the
computer's filing system:

4

- Don't just let all your Microsoft Office documents accumulate in the My
  Documents folder (the folder Office saves everything in unless you tell it otherwise); that's just begging for trouble!

- Do you tend to include your organization's name in a file name as well as the document's title rather than putting things into descriptive folders (such as a spreadsheet named CBCNS Budget)? Consider creating a folder for the school (in which
  case the document could simply be called Budget). Or, if that's still too broad,
  make a subfolder under the organization's folder called Finances that could then
  store the Budget document. Having large numbers of documents with similar
  names like CBCNS Budget, CBCNS Newsletter, CBCNS Reg Form, can make
  finding what you need much harder than it needs to be.

- If you know up front the types of documents you'll be generating, it may be worth
  your while to sit down and sketch out a list of appropriate folder names on paper
  before you sit down with Windows Explorer. With a little forethought, you can
  avoid having grossly unbalanced folders where some contain a handful of files, and
  others contain dozens.

- Microsoft has always made it easy to create new folders on-the-fly. So if you don't
  see a category that fits a document when you go to save it, don't hesitate to create
  a new folder on the spot. Doing so as you save the document eliminates the hassle

of having to go through scads of entries later on and manually move them to more logical locations. I'll show you how to do this from within a Microsoft Office application in Hour 14, "Word Processing Basics."

- Don't overdo it! Just because you see the logic in creating multiple folders doesn't mean it's the right thing for you. If you produce very few documents, having them stored in multiple locations can actually cost you more time than it saves.

While I'd love to give you the definitive answer when it comes to the best way to organize your files, attempting to do so would be inappropriate; everybody's situation is just too different.

You deserve the truth, and, as wishy-washy as it sounds, "it depends" really is the best answer. As long as you try to follow the preceding guidelines, however, you'll be in great shape, or at least in better shape than you would have been without them!

Relocating Files on Your Machine

We've all heard of the concept of *spring-cleaning*. Well, there are times your files may need a bit of spring-cleaning, too.

You delete a file in the same way you delete a folder—open Windows Explorer, right-click on the file you want to remove, select Delete from the shortcut menu, and then respond Yes to the question posed to you.

Moving or copying files to a second location, however, opens a whole world of new techniques. For example, you can click a file you want to move, and, while holding the mouse button down, drag it to its new folder.

Alternatively, you can right-click a file and select the appropriate option from the shortcut menu, then move to the new folder and insert it.

Because these processes are a bit trickier than they may seem on the surface, I'm going to guide you step-by-step through each method.

Dragging and Dropping a File to a New Location

"I've got drag-and-drop mastered," you may be thinking, but when it comes to using this technique in Windows Explorer, it gets a bit hairy.

So, to be on the safe side, here are the steps you'll need to follow from within Windows Explorer to drag and drop a file from one folder to another:

1. Click on the folder containing the file you want to move, then use the scroll bars in the main Windows Explorer viewing window to bring the desired file into view.

2. Now turn your attention back to the Folders pane, and use the scroll bars to locate the destination folder. But whatever you do, do *not* click the destination folder! If you do, you'll lose sight of the file you intended to move. If the destination folder is a subfolder, click the appropriate plus (+) sign to make the folder appear onscreen.

3. Finally, click the file you want to move, drag it to the destination folder, and drop it into place (see Figure 4.4).

FIGURE 4.4

It's fairly easy to see just where the selected file is being dragged.

4

When there's more than one file to be moved... Sure, you can go back and repeat the preceding steps to move additional folders, but wouldn't it be a great time-saver if you could move more than one file at a time? Well you can, assuming that the files reside in the same folder. Keep these tricks in mind, because you can use them for the next file copying/moving technique I'm about to present as well.

To move multiple files scattered throughout a folder's listing, click the first file to be moved, press the Ctrl key and hold it down (it's on the lower left side of your keyboard), and then click additional files you want to move. If the files happen to be listed in sequence, you can click the top file you want to move on the list, press and hold down the Shift key, and then click the last file on the list you want to move. All the files between the two you clicked on will be highlighted. Perform the ol' drag-and-drop as usual.

Using the Right-Click Method to Copy Files

While I prefer the drag-and-drop technique to move files, you'll need to be familiar with right-clicking to copy files. Please note that you can use these steps to move files as well, but it's a bit more cumbersome than dragging and dropping. I suggest you go this route for copying files only.

> **To complicate matters further...** When you drag and drop files from one drive to another, the files will be copied, not moved. So if you no longer want them on the original drive, you'll need to go back and delete the files manually. If you drag and drop within a drive, however, the files will be moved, not copied. That way you don't have multiple copies of a document taking up space on your machine. Of course if you want multiple copies for whatever reason, you can get them by performing the right-click and Copy command.

You'll need to do the following from within Windows Explorer to copy files to additional folders on your machine:

1. Select the files you want to copy using the tricks presented in the previous section, if necessary.
2. Right-click over any of the highlighted files, and choose Copy from the shortcut menu. (If you were moving the files, you'd choose Cut instead.)
3. Next, use the Folders pane to click your way to the folder to which you want to copy (or move) the selected files.
4. Right-click over the newly selected folder, and then select Paste from the shortcut menu. The highlighted files will be copied (or moved) to the specified folder.

Finding Files When You Need Them

Microsoft gives you more ways to locate a file than you can shake a stick at. In the sections that follow, you'll explore a variety of tools and techniques you can use to find what you need so that you can spend your valuable time doing something more important (or even fun) than hunting for documents.

The success of a lot of these methods depends on how well you followed the file naming and folder management tips presented earlier. If everything's in order on your machine, however, you should be able to find what you need in no time.

Start with the Start Menu

If you're looking for a file you've used recently but can't remember the name of it, you might want to try clicking the Windows Start button, and then pointing to Documents. Your 15 most recently accessed files will appear on the Documents list that slides into view, as shown in Figure 4.5. Just double-click an entry to launch the desired document, along with its native application. If the document doesn't appear here, don't worry; you've still got plenty of other strategies to try!

FIGURE 4.5

No matter what types of files you accessed most recently, you'll see them on this list.

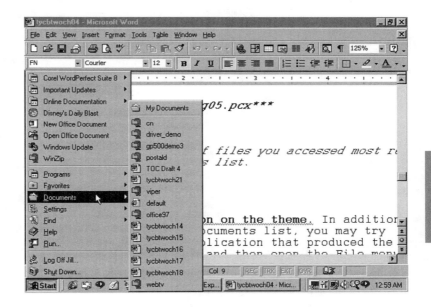

A slight variation on the theme. In addition to looking in the Documents list, you might try launching the application that produced the needed document, and then open the File menu to see the most recently created/modified files for that application. Obviously, this strategy may not be useful for Word, where you might produce dozens of documents a month. For Publisher, PowerPoint, or any of your less frequently used applications, however, you may be able to jump right to the document you're looking for.

Locating Your Files Using the Windows Find Tool

Windows 98 has a special tool designed to help you locate files. To begin using it, click the Start button and choose Find, Files or Folders... from the menu. By default, the

Name and Location tab of the Find: All Files dialog box shown in Figure 4.6 appears, but there actually are three tabs you can work with—the Name and Location tab, the Date tab, and the Advanced tab.

FIGURE 4.6

The Windows Find tool helps you find anything on your computer.

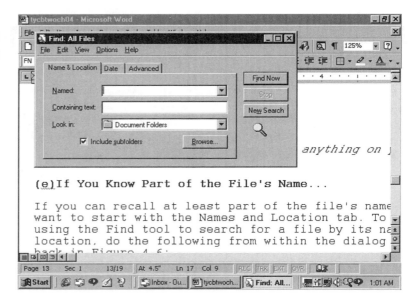

If You Know Part of the File's Name...

If you can recall at least part of the file's name, you might want to start with the Names and Location tab. To begin using the Find tool to search for a file by its name and/or location, perform the following steps within the dialog box that was shown in Figure 4.6:

1. If you know the name of the document for which you're looking, enter it in the Name text box. You can narrow the search further by adding the file extension if you know it (such as momletter.doc for a Microsoft Word document, or newsletter.pub for a Microsoft Publisher document).

2. Don't know the name of the document? You can have the Find tool search the text of the documents rather than relying only on the file names. Just enter the terms you want to search on in the Containing text field.

3. Next, you'll need to tell Find where to look using either the dropdown arrow or the Browse button. Just click your way to the folder or disk drive you want. If the selected folder has subfolders that you want searched as well, make sure that the Include Subfolders item is checked.

Give it some thought... It might, for example, be tempting to search your entire C: drive and its folders and subfolders if you really have no clue as to where the file is stored, but you should think twice before doing so, especially if you're requesting a full-text search rather than a file name search.

Setting off such a broad-scale search could take an eternity because the tool has to work its way through hundreds of program files and such in addition to your data files. Try focusing the search on a narrower area if possible, preferably a descriptive parent folder with a few subfolders at the most.

4. Click Find Now to set the search in motion. Depending on the size of the area you requested be searched, and whether the search was on a file name or document text, it could take anywhere from a few seconds to several minutes to return the results.

5. The results of your search will be returned with the following information displayed (see Figure 4.7):

- Name—The document's file name
- In Folder—Where the document was stored
- Size—The document's size
- Type—The name of the document's native application.

4

FIGURE 4.7
The status bar at the bottom left side of the Find results window tells you how many documents matched your search.

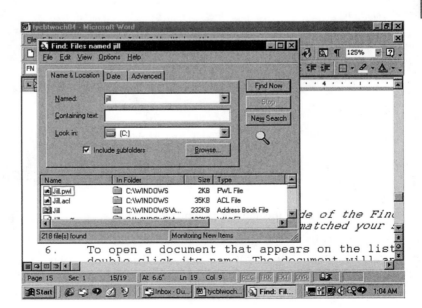

6. To open a document that appears on the list, simply double-click its name. The document will appear, along with its native application.

7. If the search did not produce the results you needed, click the New Search button and enter new search criteria.

If You Remember the Approximate Date...

If you can't remember the name of the file, perhaps an approximate date sticks in your mind. Maybe you drafted the proposal you're trying to find while staying up all night to chaperone your daughter's birthday sleepover. Or, perhaps you wrote a long letter to your sister grumbling about the fact that your husband gave you a business calculator for your first anniversary instead of something a bit more romantic. Even an approximate date can help you hone in on the file you want to retrieve.

The Date tab of the Find tool can be extremely helpful in locating files created, modified, or accessed within certain date criteria (see Figure 4.8).

FIGURE 4.8

If you want to locate a file that you worked on during a particular timeframe, the Date tab could be the answer you've been looking for!

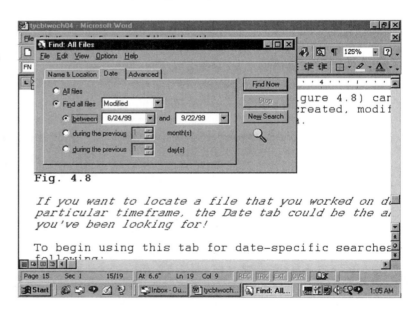

To begin using this tab for date-specific searches, perform the following steps:

1. Launch Find as described previously, and then click the Date tab.

2. Click the Find All Files item, and then use the dropdown arrow next to it to tell Find whether you want to locate files that were Modified, Created, or Last Accessed on the date you're about to provide.

3. Check one of the three items to search on any of the following date criteria:

   - **Between two dates**—Click the dropdown arrows next to each text box to reveal a calendar from which you can select the desired date.

   - **During the previous ___ months**—Use the arrow buttons to move the number up or down, as needed.

   - **During the previous ___ days**—Click the arrow buttons to shift the date up or down.

4. Click the Find Now button after you enter the information on which want to search. The results appear, as was shown in Figure 4.7.

> **Put it all together now!** You don't have to use each tab on its own. In fact, combining them can give you even more laser-focused search results. To use all the tabs (or any combination of them), just fill in the necessary information in each tab, and then click Find Now.

Other File Searching Odds and Ends

Don't be intimidated by the name of this Find tab. It's little more than a way to search by a file's type or size. While you might find the capability to search by a certain file type handy, the capability to search by size won't be used much at all by the typical user. In addition, if you know the file type's extension, you can include it in the Name box as described previously. That way, you needn't even bother with the Advanced tab.

Summary

In this hour, you were introduced to the concept of electronic file management. You took a look at some invaluable organization tips, and even learned how to find the files you need when you need them.

In the next hour, "Sharing Your Computer with Others," you'll be taken through the steps needed to create a special, customized working environment for each person who has access to your system.

Workshop

Now it's time to see just how much you learned in this lesson. I'll give you a short multiple-choice quiz to test what you learned, followed by a suggested activity designed to enhance the skills you acquired during the hour.

Quiz

Select the best answer to the questions from the choices provided, and then check your answers in the following section.

Questions

1. When is the best time to plan and define your computer's folder hierarchy?

   a. Do it only when you have a gigabyte worth of data files on your hard drive.

   b. Wait until you've used your computer for a year or two so that you know what types of folders you'll be needing.

   c. As soon as possible; sound file management practices are much easier to maintain if you start early on.

2. Which of the following is the best file naming advice?

   a. Give files short, descriptive names, and store them in well-labeled folders whenever possible.

   b. Use the longest file names possible; that way a file search is more likely to pull up the files you really want.

   c. You don't name files; Windows does it for you.

3. What is the Windows tool used to locate files?

   a. Fetch!

   b. Retriever

   c. Find

Answers

1. c is the proper answer. The longer you wait to get organized, the bigger the mess you'll have on your hands.

2. a was the answer to this one. Long file names accomplish little. As for Windows naming your files...well, let's put it this way; even if it could make up file names for you, they would more than likely be useless. After all, how much does a file name like Document 3 tell you (besides the fact it was the third document you created)?

3. All the words may have similar meaning, but only Find is a real Windows tool.

Activity

Come up with a list of five potential folder names that would be of use to you. You can either jot them on the following lines, or if you'd prefer not to deface this book, on a piece of scrap paper.

1.

2.

3.

4.

5.

4

If you're really serious about keeping all the files on your machine under control, you also should take the time to write down the types of documents you anticipate going into each folder. That will help you solidify the purpose of each folder you define so that when it comes time to save a document, you'll immediately know the best place to store it.

HOUR 5

Sharing Your Computer with Other Users

Wouldn't it be nice if every member of your family had his or her own PC? Just think, you wouldn't have to look at your daughter's Spice Girls desktop theme, and your desktop wouldn't be cluttered with icons for your husband's golf games. As for your toddler's JumpStart programs, they too, would be absent from your desktop, and you wouldn't have to worry about him getting into your Money 2000 files either. Sure, computers have gotten less expensive, but they're not *that* cheap!

In this lesson, I'll show you how to configure your computer for use by multiple people. You'll also read more about the following topics:

- Where do I begin configuring the multiple users option?
- What parts of the Windows environment can be customized for each user?
- How do users log into their customized desktop?
- Can other users see what software I've installed while in my personalized desktop?

Before I show you how to use the Windows 98, Second Edition Multi-User feature, you'll need to enable it. And as usual, Microsoft provides a handy wizard to guide you every step of the way.

To configure your computer for use by multiple people, you'll need to follow these steps:

1. Click the Start button on the Windows taskbar, and then point to Settings, Control Panel.

2. From the Control Panel, double-click the Users icon. This launches the Enable Multi-user Settings wizard shown in Figure 5.1.

FIGURE 5.1

The opening screen describes what the wizard is about to do.

3. Click the Next button to begin configuring your machine.

4. In the Add User screen shown in Figure 5.2, type in the user name by which you want to be known.

FIGURE 5.2

This is the screen in which you'll enter each user's name.

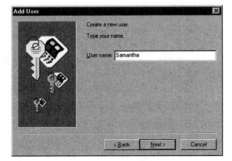

5. Click Next to move to the next screen.

6. Next, you'll want to choose a password for your private desktop (see Figure 5.3). You'll be asked to type it twice for verification. Click Next to proceed.

FIGURE 5.3

Prevent typos in your password by entering it twice.

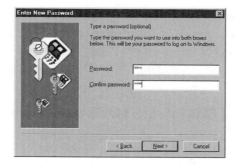

7. The Personalized Items Settings screen in Figure 5.4 opens, asking you to check off which items you want to customize for each user. The following are your choices:

- Desktop folder and Documents menu
- Start menu
- Favorites folder
- Downloaded Web pages
- My Documents folder

FIGURE 5.4

You can customize as much or as little as you want.

5

8. At the bottom of the same screen, you are asked whether you want the wizard to create copies of existing settings, or overwrite the files with new ones to save disk space. Unless you're very tight on disk space, I'd make a copy just in case.

9. Click the Next button to continue.

10 The wizard displays a message telling you that you've successfully configured a user. If you need to configure different desktops, simply repeat the preceding steps to run through the wizard as many times as you need.

After you define all the users, you'll need to log on to each account to customize the desktop and other chosen elements, as described in Hour 2, "Making Your Desktop Look the Way You Want It." Any changes made while logged on to a certain user's account will be preserved in that account only until the next time he or she logs in.

Logging on to Your Customized Windows Desktop

When you boot a computer configured for use by multiple people (or when you approach a machine that another user has logged off from), you'll see a screen with two blank text boxes, ready for your information.

Type in your user name and password, and then press Enter. Windows 98, Second Edition will start with all your settings in place. The first time you log in, however, Windows will ask you whether you want it to remember your settings for the future. Click Yes. Windows will copy a few files for you, and you'll be in business before you know it.

Logging off the Computer

To exit your Windows environment, click the Start button, and then click the Log Off [User Name]... menu item. You will be taken back to the log in screen that was shown in Figure 5.5.

Multi-User Configuration: More Than Just Aesthetics

A personalized desktop is just one reason you may want to set up your machine in this fashion, but there are many others as well.

Think back to the opening paragraph of this lesson. Now imagine the potential damage an innocent child could do to your financial software and other critical applications. Customizing a desktop especially for that child keeps your files safe while enabling the child to take full advantage of the educational value of having a computer at home.

Take my family as an example. While we don't have to share computers (thank goodness!), here is what I'd do for my children. For six year old Christopher, I'd put his educational games on his desktop; and then remove icons for My Computer, My Documents, and so on. I'd spiff the screen up with a *Star Wars* theme featuring his hero, Anakin

Skywalker, and then make my way to the Start menu and remove all shortcuts to applications I want to protect. In Internet Explorer's Favorites list, I'd put shortcuts to Web sites such as PBS, HotWheels.com, the National Zoo, a Nintendo 64 site where he can browse screenshots for up and coming games, and links to some of his favorite television shows. For five year old Samantha, *Barbie* would be the theme with the same deletions I made for Chris, and Web Favorites chosen especially for her interests. As for programs on her desktop, there's be items such as Barbie Fashion Designer, JumpStart 1st Grade, and SimTown (a SimCity-like game for kids that enables them to build and manage their own cities). When it comes to younger users, the simpler the desktop, the better.

Because older children who are good readers (or other adults in your household who might be nosey) could use DOS (or more likely Windows Explorer) to access your personal files, you might want to consider disabling DOS and Windows Explorer from their personal settings. That way, they can't surf around the hard drive looking for your personal files.

Top Ten Reasons for Choosing the Multi-User Configuration

If you're not yet convinced that configuring your computer for use by multiple people is worth it, take a look at "Jill's Top Ten Reasons You'll Want to Configure Your Computer This Way":

1. **Have your own PC—for free!**   That's right; configuring your computer for use by multiple users can give you the illusion of having your very own machine without the expense!

2. **Have it your way!**   No more putting up with your wife's George Clooney desktop, your husband's Cindy Crawford desktop, your daughter's Backstreet Boys desktop, or your son's soccer desktop. You can put any theme on your desktop you want, and no one will be able to make fun of you for it!

3. **Control clutter.**   Is your shared desktop so full of program shortcuts it takes you several minutes to find the application you need? Is the Programs menu off the Start menu so long you actually have to scroll down the menu to see everything? With multi-user configuration, you can make all the stuff you don't use disappear, making things much easier to find.

4. **Playing favorites.**   If you choose to customize the Internet Explorer Favorites folders as well, not only will the sites be a whole lot easier to organize, but they'll be easier to revisit as well.

5

5. **Protecting your programs.**   When my kids were younger, they were very good at erasing desktop shortcuts to my applications, making the applications very time-consuming to locate. If the kids have their own desktops, you can rest assured that the next time you use the computer, the icons will be exactly where you left them!

6. **No peeking!**   Because each user can have his or her own My Documents directory (where Word 2000 documents are stored unless you specify otherwise), personal letters and other documents can be kept private.

7. **Protect your files.**   Prevent others from accessing your spreadsheets and financial program files by blocking access to the applicable programs (such as Excel 2000, Money 2000, TurboTax, and so on). This helps ensure that critical files won't be erased, or that they won't be accidentally deleted.

8. **Express yourself.**   Let your individuality shine through by making your desktop and its elements look any way you want them to!

9. **Eliminate document digging.**   When you click the Start button on the Windows taskbar and point to Documents, you see a list of the most recently accessed or modified documents on the system. If you're set up for multiple users, you can have that menu item reflect only documents you've accessed or modified so that you won't have to dig through everyone else's stuff to find what you're looking for.

What's the use?—If file protection and privacy is a driving force in your decision to move to a multi-user configuration, then you'll want to be sure you tell Windows to customize *everything* for each user. If you don't, there might be an alternate route to those files you desperately want to protect. If you block someone's access to a specific application, yet you opt to share the Documents list you access via the Start menu, for example, other users could simply double-click the name of your file, which will, in turn, launch the necessary application with the chosen file already loaded.

10. **Save it for later.**   The multi-user setup also enables you to maintain a private list of Web sites that are downloaded routinely for viewing offline (without needing an Internet connection). Not only is it private, but it eliminates the need for tying up the family phone line while reading text-intensive Web content.

If that doesn't convince you, nothing will. Enjoy your new system, and happy computing!

Summary

Multi-user configuration is one of those neat Windows features that often is overlooked, yet as you saw in this lesson, there are many benefits to setting up a computer in this manner. The reasons range from pure aesthetics to security to privacy and, finally, to ease of use for younger users.

In the next hour, you'll take a look at Windows 98, Second Edition tools and utilities designed to fix your system and keep it healthy.

Workshop

Now it's time to see just how much you learned in this lesson. I'll give you a short multiple-choice quiz to test what you learned, followed by a suggested activity designed to enhance the skills you acquired during the hour.

Quiz

Select the best answer to the questions from the choices provided, and then check your answers in the following section.

Questions

1. What type of tool do you call on to set up your computer for use by multiple people?

    a. A template

    b. A dialog box

    c. The Enable Multi-User Settings wizard

2. How do you access your personalized desktop?

    a. Before you boot the computer, place a floppy disk with your name on it into the floppy drive.

    b. When you boot the machine, a little animated character appears in the bottom-right corner of the screen. When he asks for your name, say it slowly and clearly three times in a row.

    c. A log-in screen appears and asks you to type in your user name and password, if needed.

5

3. What happens if you don't log off the computer when you're done?

   a. Other users could gain access to every part of your customized Windows environment.

   b. A little animated character pops up and scolds you for wasting electricity because you didn't shut down the computer properly.

   c. Nothing happens. The keyboard analyzes the next user's fingerprints and automatically transports them to their own desktop.

Answers

1. c is the correct answer. While you make use of b along the way, it's not the primary tool used for setting up this feature.

2. It's c again. I admit it; the other two choices were the result of a 3 a.m. writing session powered by the fuel of Diet Coke and Frosted Cinnamon Pop-Tarts.

3. The a's have it! The others are funny, but are not true in the least.

Activity

Now would be a great time to sit down at your computer and enter all the necessary user profiles into the Enable Multi-User Settings wizard. Even if you don't have to share your PC, it might be useful to establish one identity for work, and one for play.

The work identity would sport a clean desktop with shortcuts to Microsoft Word 2000, Excel 2000, and other productivity applications, without the distraction of your collection of computer games.

Your "play" identity would contain not only games, but a funky desktop theme, and perhaps some hobby software such as applications for dream house designing, quilt and needlepoint design planning, baseball card collection databases, and so on.

HOUR 6

Watching While You Work

You wouldn't dream of running your car thousands upon thousands of miles without a periodic checkup, or at the very least an oil change, would you? Well the same holds true for your computer. The more often you install and uninstall software on your machine, the more often you'll need to perform maintenance on your system.

In this lesson, I'll show you how to keep your investment in tip-top shape with the help of free utilities included with Windows 98, Second Edition. You'll also find out more about the following topics:

- Which files should you save when you back up your hard drive?
- Defrag the hard drive? That's supposed to be a good thing?
- So what in the world does this blue ScanDisk screen do?
- Is there a way you can schedule some of these things?

Backing Up Your Hard Disk

To protect your valuable data, it's best to make an extra copy of it. The easiest way to do so is to back up your files onto a disk, recordable CD, Zip or Jaz drive cartridges, or tape backup unit. Then, if something happens to the original file (or worse yet, to your hard drive), you can restore the backup copy onto your hard drive.

Nipping potential confusion in the bud   In the final hour of this book, you'll be reading a lot about zip files, a file compression technique. These zip files are not the same thing as the Zip Drive mentioned here. A Zip Drive is simply a piece of hardware that uses special cartridges to store large amounts of data. The data on there can be zip files, but need not be.

When you perform a backup, it's not necessary to back up every file on your hard disk. You should primarily back up your document files (or any other files on the system you may have created and/or modified). You don't need to back up program files, however, because they can be reinstalled if needed from their original installation CDs provided with your new computer.

To back up some or all of the files on your hard disk, follow these steps:

1. Click Start, and then select Programs, Accessories, System Tools, Backup. You'll see a Microsoft Backup dialog box displayed over a Microsoft Backup window.

The System Tools folder might not be installed on your system. To install it, click the Start button on the Windows toolbar, and then choose Settings, Control Panel. Once in the Control Panel, double-click on the Add/Remove Programs icon. Click on the Windows Setup tab from the property window, and click on the check box next to the System Tools icon. You'll be prompted to insert your Windows 98 CD-ROM, and you might have to reboot your computer to complete the installation process. Given that, it might be wise to save your work and exit all of your programs before performing the installation.

2. The first time you start Microsoft Backup, it checks to see whether you have any backup devices (such as a tape drive) on your computer. If Backup can't find any such device, it asks you to confirm. If you do have a backup device (or one is not automatically detected by Windows), click Yes, and follow the directions onscreen in the Add Hardware Wizard to install or define it. If not, click No. (If you've used Microsoft Backup before, you'll jump to step 7 at this point.)

3. Next, Backup asks you if you'd like to create a set of emergency disks. You can use these disks to boot your PC and restore your most recent full backup when your PC malfunctions. Click OK.

4. To create the emergency disks, files are copied onto your startup disk (which you created when you installed Windows). If you don't have a startup disk, click Startup Disk to create one. Otherwise, insert the startup disk into its drive and click Next.

5. Insert a second disk when prompted and click OK.

6. Click Finish. A welcome dialog box appears as shown in Figure 6.1.

7. Select Create a New Backup Job and click OK.

FIGURE 6.1

Any time you deal with backup files (be it making a backup, or restoring pieces of your system), you'll see this dialog box.

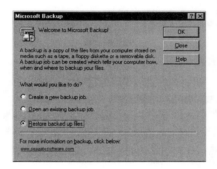

 Do I have to go through all these steps next time around? After you create a backup job, you can use it to back up the same files later. You can select Open an Existing Backup Job in place of step 7, which takes you to the main Backup screen, where you can begin the backup. You can also change the parameters of the original job if needed.

8. Select Back Up My Computer or Back Up Selected Files, Folders, and Drives. (See the dialog box shown in Figure 6.2 for what to expect.) Click Next. If you selected Back Up My Computer, skip to step 11.

9. Select the items you want backed up, using the bulleted list below as a guide. Selected files appear with a blue check mark (see Figure 6.3).

   • To back up all the files on a drive, click the check box next to a drive letter.

   • To back up all the files in a folder, click the check box next to a folder.

6

- To select only some files in a folder, double-click the folder's name to display its files in the panel on the right, and click the files you want to select. Don't forget the multiple file selection tip I shared earlier in the book (hold the Ctrl key down while selecting each file name and such)!
- To deselect a particular item, click it again to remove the check mark.

FIGURE 6.2

Decide how much or how little you want to back up.

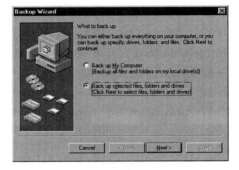

FIGURE 6.3

No matter what types of files you've created in the selected drive, you'll see them listed here.

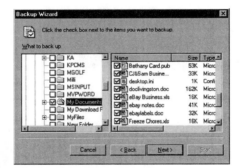

10. Click Next.

11. Select All Selected Files or New and Changed Files (as shown in Figure 6.4), and then click Next. If you select New and Changed Files, files are backed up only if they've changed since the last backup you performed. Either way, *do not use the same backup disks you used before*; try to use a new set of disks instead. This not only gives you two sets of backup material, but it prevents overwriting previous versions of a document you may have modified.

FIGURE 6.4

Choose to backup everything, or only those files that have changed since the last backup.

12. By default, backups are stored in the root directory of drive C. To select another drive or folder, click the folder icon (see Figure 6.5) and double-click the drive and folder in which you want your backup stored. Double-click the specific location to select it, and then click Next.

FIGURE 6.5

Choose exactly where you want the backup data saved.

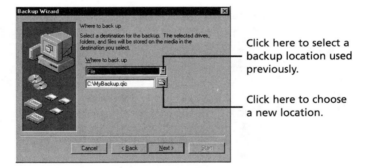

Click here to select a backup location used previously.

Click here to choose a new location.

13. Select the options you want, and then click Next:

   - **Compare Original and Backup Files to Verify Data Was Successfully Backed Up**—This option makes the backup process longer, but it does guarantee that all files are backed up successfully.

   - **Compress the Backup Data to Save Space**—This option compresses your files so that they take up less space on the backup media.

14. Type a name for this backup job as shown in Figure 6.6, such as **Full Backup**. You can later reuse this job to complete the same type of backup procedure. You'll also see a summary of the backup options you chose throughout the course of the wizard. When you're sure the summary is correct, click Start to begin the backup.

6

FIGURE 6.6

The what, where, how, and when of your backup is summarized before you continue.

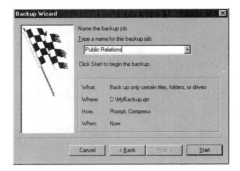

15. When the backup is complete, you'll see a message telling you so. Click OK.

16. A backup progress dialog box like the one shown in Figure 6.7 lets you know how long the backup took, how many files were copied, and how much data was transferred. Click Report to review the backup summary that should look a lot like the one shown in Figure 6.8. Be sure to maximize the Notepad window for best viewing results. You can then save or print the report as desired by accessing the File menu of the Notepad window. Click OK when you're through.

FIGURE 6.7

Keep an eye on the progress of longer backup jobs.

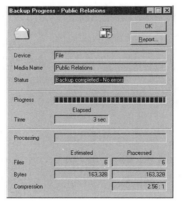

It may not be saving what you expect it to   The Windows Notepad allows you to save the report of the recently completed backup job; however, it does not save the parameters of the backup job itself. You must specifically save the job in the main Microsoft Backup Window as described in the next step.

FIGURE 6.8

*The Windows Notepad
applet makes the
backup report easy to
save or print as
needed.*

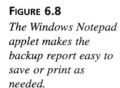

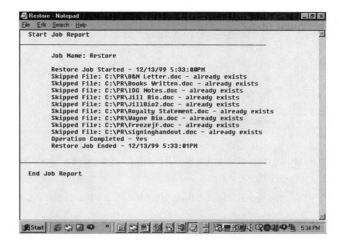

17. The main Microsoft Backup window appears. Click the Save button (the one that looks like a floppy disk) to store the job for future use, or click the Close (X) button of the Microsoft Backup Window to exit the program.

Restoring Files to Your System

If a file is accidentally deleted or damaged in some way and can't be repaired using any of the new high-tech software tools included with Microsoft applications, you can restore it from your most recent backup. You'll recognize most of these screens from the figures shown previously in this chapter, except the ones you see here will say Restore instead of Backup.

Follow these steps to restore the necessary files on your computer:

1. Click Start on the Windows taskbar, and then select Programs, Accessories, System Tools, Backup. You'll again see the Welcome to the Backup Wizard dialog box shown back in Figure 6.1.

2. Select the Restore backed up files option, and then click OK.

3. Click the folder icon, and then select the drive and folder on which your backup is stored. Click Next.

4. Select the backup set that contains the files you want to restore. Click OK.

5. Select the files you want to restore (selected files appear with a check mark as shown in Figure 6.9) and click Next.

6

FIGURE 6.9

A blue check mark indicates which files (or file) are to be restored.

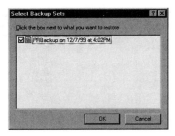

- To restore all the backed-up files on a drive, click the check box next to the proper drive letter.
- To restore all the backed-up files in a folder, click the check box next to a folder.
- To restore only some of the backed-up files in a folder, click the folder's name to display its files in the panel on the right, and click the files you want to select.
- To deselect a particular file, click it again, and the check mark is removed.

6. Select whether you want files restored to their Original Location, or an Alternate Location (another drive or folder). If you select Alternate Location, click the folder icon next to the option and double-click the drive and folder you want to use. Click Next.

7. Select the replacement option you want to use:
   - Do Not Replace the File on My Computer—Use this option if you only want to restore files that no longer exist on your hard disk.
   - Replace the File on My Computer Only If the File Is Older—This will restore all files from the backup copy, provided that they are *newer* than the files already on the hard disk.
   - Always Replace the File on My Computer—This option restores all the files on the backup, even if some of those files are older than the ones already on your hard disk. Use this option with extreme caution because it can potentially delete any recent edits you made to documents still residing on your hard drive.

8. Click Start.

9. You'll see a message asking you to get your backup files ready, which means you need to insert the backup media on which the necessary files were stored. Click OK.

10. When the restoration is complete, you'll see a message telling you so. Click OK.

11. Click Report to review the restoration summary. Click OK when you're through.

12. The main Microsoft Backup window appears. Click its Close (X) button to exit the program.

Defragmenting Your Disk

When a file is stored to a disk, it's broken into tiny chunks, and each piece is stored in the first available sector of the hard disk. After the disk starts getting full and files are deleted (making certain random sectors available here and there on the hard drive), file parts are no longer saved in adjacent sectors.

Thus, a file may be scattered (or fragmented) over the disk, which can slow down its retrieval. To improve the speed of your PC, you should *defragment* your hard disk. Defragmenting reorganizes the parts of each file so that they are once again adjacent to each other on the hard disk, eliminating excess search time.

To help you visualize this, let me share a personal story. My mother-in-law is famous for being able to cram huge amounts of stuff into her refrigerator. And she's got it down to a science, too, so much so that no one else can even help put anything away! Like your computer's hard drive, food in her refrigerator is nested and stacked in such a way as to maximize space. All the fruits and vegetables may not be in the same location, but they're all in there nonetheless, much like your files are all on your hard drive. When food is taken out, consumed, or replaced, the refrigerator's contents need to be repacked again to make sure everything fits. Likewise, as files come and go on your hard drive, you'll need to defragment it to fill some of those "holes" on your hard drive.

To defragment your hard disk and maximize storage space and search speed, follow these steps:

1. Click Start, and then select Programs, Accessories, System Tools, Disk Defragmenter. The Select Drive dialog box shown in Figure 6.10 appears.

FIGURE 6.10

Use the drop-down list box to select the drive you want to defragment.

6

2. Make sure the drive you want to defragment appears in the Which Drive Do You Want to Defragment drop-down list box, and then click OK.

> **Sleep on it**   Defragmenting your entire hard drive can take hours, especially if it hasn't been done in quite a while. You may want to consider running the defragmenter while you sleep so as not to disrupt your work. If you have a screen saver enabled on your machine, you may want to turn it off during the process to make sure the job isn't interrupted. You can learn how to do this in Hour 8, "Customizing Windows."

3. Exit all your other programs, and then return to Disk Defragmenter and click OK. Disk Defragmenter conducts its analysis.

4. After a few minutes of grinding away, the defragmentation process begins. You can work while this process continues, although you'll find that your computer is much slower than usual. To stop the defragmentation process temporarily, click Pause. Resume, of course, starts the process up again. To stop it completely, click the Stop button.

5. When the process is complete, you'll see a message telling you so. Click OK to dismiss the dialog.

6. You will then be asked whether you want to defragment another drive, or close the program. Make the appropriate choice given your circumstances.

Cleaning Your Disk

Another tool that can help you recover chewed up space on your hard drive is the Disk Cleanup utility. It analyzes the specified disk, comes back with a list of "safe" files to delete, and lets you select which ones you want removed.

The amount of space you can recover using this tool varies from a fraction of a megabyte to tens of megabytes, so the results will vary depending on the way you use your machine.

Here are the steps you'll want to take to reclaim some of your disk space:

1. To begin the Disk Cleanup process, click Start, and then choose Programs, Accessories, System Tools, Disk Cleanup. The Select Drive dialog box is displayed.

2. Select the desired drive from the Drives drop-down list box, and then click OK.

After a bit of behind the scenes work, the Disk Cleanup tab shown in Figure 6.11 opens, showing you which files you can safely delete, and how much disk space you'd regain by making the selected deletions.

FIGURE 6.11

You might be surprised by just how much space you can get back!

3. Click a file type's check box to see a description of what type of file it is. If you're not sure about deleting the files selected, simply click on the item's check box again to deselect it.

4. When you're ready to start deleting the files, click OK. The utility will ask you if you're sure about the deletion. Click Yes or No as appropriate.

A status bar appears, displaying the progress of the job. When the files have been successfully deleted, the application shuts itself down.

Scanning Your Disk

Occasionally, a file isn't stored to disk properly, and the computer loses part of it. This sometimes happens when a file is deleted, and the references to all the parts of the file aren't removed from the main file directory (File Allocation Table). In any case, it's a good idea to periodically check your hard disk for this type of error, and to let the computer fix the problems it finds.

If Windows wasn't shut down properly using the Start, Shut Down command, ScanDisk will appear on its own the next time you boot your machine. Its bright blue screen appears along with a yellow status bar that reports the progress of disk repair. Other times, you may manually need to set ScanDisk into action.

6

To scan your hard disk for errors manually, follow these steps:

1. Click Start, and then select Programs, Accessories, System Tools, ScanDisk. The ScanDisk dialog box is displayed, as shown in Figure 6.12.

2. Select the drive you want to scan.

3. Select the type of scanning you want to perform. Standard checks the hard disk for file errors. Thorough checks for errors and examines the surface of the hard disk itself.

4. If you want ScanDisk to fix any errors it finds (rather than reporting those errors to you and providing various options), select the Automatically Fix Errors check box.

5. When you're ready to scan the disk, click Start.

6. When the scanning is through, you'll see a message telling you so. Click Close.

7. You're returned to the ScanDisk dialog box. Click Close.

Scheduling Maintenance Tasks

With the Windows Maintenance Wizard, you can schedule regular maintenance tasks to be performed on your computer's hard disk. That way you never have to remember to do it! It's sort of like having someone to take your car in for an oil change for you.

The tasks you can schedule include the following:

- Scheduling programs to open when you start your PC
- Defragmenting the hard disk
- Checking the disk for errors using ScanDisk
- Deleting unneeded files

To schedule maintenance for your computer, you'll use the Maintenance Wizard. To launch the wizard for action, follow these steps:

1. Click Start, and then select Programs, Accessories, System Tools, Maintenance Wizard. The Maintenance Wizard is displayed, as shown in Figure 6.13.

FIGURE 6.13

If you want confirmation of what the wizard can do for your system, you'll see it in this dialog box.

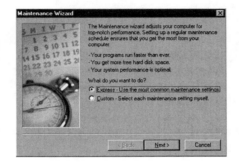

2. Select Express or Custom, and click Next.

3. Select a time period when you might want to have maintenance done (see Figure 6.14), and click Next. Remember, your system must be turned on at the time of maintenance, so schedule accordingly. If you selected Express in step 2, skip to step 8. If you selected Custom, continue to step 4.

FIGURE 6.14

There are several time slots available in which to perform maintenance.

4. A listing of the programs that are currently scheduled to run at start-up appears (see Figure 6.15). To prevent a program from running at start-up, click it to remove the check mark. Conversely, to instruct a program to launch at start-up, click its check box. Click Next to continue.

6

FIGURE 6.15

The list of applications that can start up immediately are listed here.

5. To schedule Disk Defragmenter to run automatically, click Yes, Defragment My Disk Regularly. If you want to change the time at which this occurs, click Reschedule. To change the drive to defragment (and other options), click Settings. When you're ready, click Next.

6. To schedule ScanDisk to run automatically, click Yes, Scan My Hard Disk for Errors Regularly. If you want to change the time at which this occurs, click Reschedule. To change the drive that you want scanned (among other options), click Settings. When you're done, click Next.

7. To have Windows delete files you don't need, click Yes, Delete Unnecessary Files Regularly. To change the time at which this occurs, click Reschedule. To change the types of files that are automatically deleted, click Settings. When you're done, click Next.

Summary

By now, you should be familiar with all the tools to help keep your computer in shape for years to come. Not only do you know how to call on the utilities when you need them, but you learned how to schedule the computer for routine maintenance as well.

With your fundamental understanding of Windows 98, Second Edition, you're ready to explore the topic of hardware. In the next section of the book, I'll define what a computer is, describe how your PC is different from a Mac, and introduce you to a variety of hardware add-ons that can enhance your computing experience greatly. And because you're already familiar with Windows, you'll understand how to set them up in a heartbeat.

Workshop

Now it's time to see just how much you learned in this lesson. I'll give you a short multiple-choice quiz to test what you learned, followed by a suggested activity designed to enhance the skills you acquired during the hour.

Quiz

Select the best answer to the questions from the choices provided, and then check your answers.

Questions

1. Which tool helps get rid of unwanted files on your machine?
    a. ScanDisk
    b. Disk Cleanup
    c. Disk Backup

2. What is ScanDisk?
    a. A utility that fixes disk drive errors and rearranges files to optimize system performance.
    b. A new medical device that helps doctors identify back problems like ruptured disks, and so on.
    c. The act of putting a floppy disk on a flatbed scanner and turning it into an image file.

3. Which of the following tasks is the Maintenance Wizard unable to schedule?
    a. Disk Defragmenter.
    b. Automatic system booting.
    c. ScanDisk.

Answers

1. B is undoubtedly the only tool listed for this task.

2. Of course the only acceptable answer here is a. The others simply don't exist, at least at the time this book was written. (Always gotta cover your tail, right?)

3. Your answer should have been b because the Maintenance Wizard needs to have the machine running already before it can work.

6

Activity

The best way to keep your system in good condition is to perform routine maintenance from the get-go; that way the process doesn't become too long, cumbersome, and system intensive.

As your activity for this lesson, I suggest you consider setting up the Maintenance Wizard on your system so you don't have to worry about a thing. Let it do everything— ScanDisk, disk defragmentation, and so on, so that nothing will be left behind.

PART II
Windows

Hour

HOUR 7

What Is a Computer?

As much as we might hate to admit it, we're always finding ourselves comparing what we have to what our buddy has. C'mon, fess up; it's only human nature!

This lesson gives you a good frame of reference not only for how the parts of your computer rate compared to what's available on the market, but how they all work together to give you a fully functional system. And because you know a bit about working with Windows, you'll have an even greater appreciation for how all these pieces fit together, and why certain parts affect a computer's performance more than others.

In this lesson, you'll be given a general introduction to computers as a whole. You'll also find out more about the following topics:

- Is a 600 MHz system really twice as fast as a 300 MHz system?
- What's the difference between your PC and your buddy's Macintosh?
- How do computer monitor displays differ from the flat ones found on laptops?
- How much information can a modem transfer within a second?

As you worked through the lessons dedicated to Windows 98, Second Edition in the previous section of this book, you learned that an operating system like Windows is simply a brain that tells the computer what to do. Okay, so what does this "body" that hosts the "brain" look like? To find the answer, you need look no further than your own new computer.

Like people, however, no two computers are exactly alike. An enormous number of potential combinations come together to create a totally unique package. In this lesson, I'll focus on those subtle differences and what they mean in terms of how your PC works and compares to other machines out there.

So to pull this all together once again, a computer is simply a machine designed to follow a list of instructions. The system's brain (its operating system) acts as a traffic cop, telling the computer when to execute the instructions given to it by the system's software.

Kinds of Computers

In today's market, there are two basic kinds of computers: the IBM compatible and the Macintosh (more commonly called the Mac). Both types of computers have similar parts, but because of important differences in their architecture, they run different software. Or to follow through with the human analogy, Mac software gives its instructions in a different language than the IBM compatible software.

Furthermore, IBM compatible computers usually run Microsoft Windows, whereas Mac computers have their own special operating system. This means that software written for one computer will never run on the other.

> **Hey, I bought my kid a computer game, and it says it'll work with a Mac or a PC!**   Sometimes you will find software that is listed as being both Mac and IBM compatible. This happens primarily in children's games. The CD-ROM contains separate software for both Macs and IBM Compatibles in the same disk. Each operating system is smart enough to know which software to use.

Getting Personal: The Types of Computers

There are three basic types of personal computers: Desktop computers, laptop computers, and palmtop computers.

Most computers made today are desktop computers. They consist of a number of separate parts including a monitor, a keyboard, and a case that houses the rest of the parts that make up a computer.

A laptop, on the other hand, integrates all of those components into a smaller package that you can take virtually anywhere. The cost of a laptop, however, is approximately twice that of the equivalent desktop computer, mostly because their LCD displays are so expensive to produce. Also, if speed is important to you, you should know that the fastest desktop computer is always faster than the fastest laptop. Why? Because the technological advances needed to fit the latest and greatest computer chips into the small confines of a laptop generally lag behind the introduction of a new computer chip by several months at least.

Finally, palmtop computers are the smallest of all, and generally use a lightweight version of the Windows operating system referred to as Windows CE. This means they can't run all applications designed for use with the full version of Windows, but they can usually run Web browsers, email programs, personal information managers, and scaled down word processing programs—the types of things people would most want to do on the run anyway. Like laptops, you pay a premium for their compact size, but many have found them to be extremely valuable for managing contacts and schedules.

Anatomy of a Computer

Because desktops are the most popular type of computer sold (not to mention a good reliable, sturdy, and economical choice for first time purchasers), we'll focus our attention there.

The power behind a desktop computer (and laptops and palmtops for that matter) consists of three main parts: a CPU, memory, and input/output devices (see Figure 7.1).

What Does the CPU Do?

A CPU is basically just a fancy calculator that executes a set of instructions from memory. As it performs its calculations, it retrieves and saves results into memory. In personal computers, CPUs are usually made out of a single integrated circuit or chip, hence the term CPU chip.

So What Is the Role of Memory?

Memory is simply a place to hold things for the CPU to access. There are two types of things in memory: instructions for the CPU to execute, and data that the CPU is working on. The instructions that the CPU executes are also known as programs, or software.

7

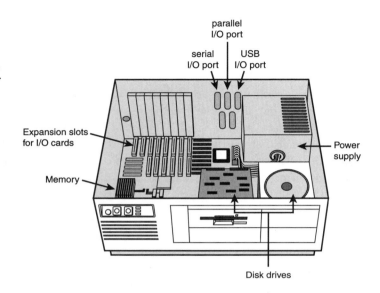

FIGURE 7.1
The CPU, memory, and input/output devices are the fundamental components of a computer.

Input/Output Devices: The Final Piece of the Computer Puzzle

The last part of the computer's power center includes its input/output devices. These devices allow the CPU to send and receive data from external sources. To interact with a human, a computer uses devices like a keyboard and a monitor for typing and reading, and devices like speakers and a microphone to speak and listen to you. Also printers, scanners, and cameras can be used to collect and display information in a form the human can read.

Input/output devices also are used to hold instructions and data for the CPU. These devices are known as disk drives. Information is loaded from a disk drive into memory and written from memory to the disk drive.

Another class of input/output devices enables one computer to communicate data with another. Although there are many different type of devices that are used to communicate between computers, the most common are a modem (which allows you to communicate with another computer over a telephone line) and a network card (which allows you to communicate with another computer over a special cable).

Putting it All Together

An IBM compatible personal computer comes equipped with a number of basic components. The typical desktop setup includes the following, which I'll cover in greater detail below:

- CPU
- Memory
- Disk drives
- Monitor and video card
- Keyboard and mouse
- Sound card and speakers
- Modem and/or network card
- Printer
- Other Input/Output devices

Now that you know the proper name and basic function of each part, let's dig a littler deeper to find out more about them. These are the sections you'll consult to see just how fast your computer chip is, or how much memory is optimal to run your computer smoothly.

The Flavors of CPU Chips

CPU chips come in many different brands and flavors. The leading brand of CPUs is Intel's Pentium line. Currently the Pentium line consists of two different types of CPU: Celeron and Pentium III. Older CPU chips produced by Intel include the Pentium II, Pentium, 486, 386, 286 and the 8088, which was used in the original IBM Personal Computer back in 1981.

Intel Inside

CPU chips are also available from other companies such as AMD with its K6-2, K6-3 and Athlon products, and Cyrix, whose products are very competitive with the corresponding Intel CPU chips.

> **Getting better with age** In the past, CPU chips from vendors other the Intel often wouldn't run various applications correctly. Thus many people recommended buying only computers with Intel CPUs. In today's market, this is no longer true. If you buy a computer with a CPU chip from AMD or Cyrix, you needn't worry about compatibility problems.

7

Measuring CPU Speed

CPU chips also come in various speeds. Generally, the faster the speed, the more work the CPU can do in a given amount of time. The speed is measured in terms of megahertz

(MHz), which indicates how many times each second that the computer can perform a simple cycle. This means that a 600 MHz Pentium III computer can perform 600,000,000 cycles in a single second.

In general if one CPU is twice the speed of another, it will run certain types of applications (games, super-large spreadsheets or databases, and so on) twice as fast. However, that assumes that the CPU is the real limiting factor. In most cases, this isn't true.

For example, if you're surfing the Internet, CPU speed is rarely the limiting factor. It's your Internet connection or Internet congestion that's the real culprit because Net surfing isn't a very CPU-intensive activity. In the case of the Internet (and even for normal word processing and spreadsheet use) the difference between a 300 MHz CPU and a 600 MHz CPU is insignificant. It's only when playing a flight simulator or other frame-rate-bound game that you'll see a noticeable improvement.

All About RAM (or Random Access Memory)

Memory (RAM more specifically) is used to hold programs and data that you are running. The more programs you want to run at the same time, the more memory you need. And the more data you want to work on (such as a large Word document or Excel worksheet), the more memory you need. Having four or five open Internet Explorer windows consumes much more memory than only one or two.

Measuring Memory

Memory is measured in terms of bytes. A single byte of memory holds 8 bits. A single bit holds a binary value consisting of either 0 or 1. Because the amount of memory in a computer is relatively large, terms like megabyte are typically used to keep the numbers simple.

> **Well actually...** If you want to get technical, one megabyte is really 1,048,576 bytes of memory. Note that value is not exactly the same as one million. One megabyte represents 2^{20}, which is approximately one million. A gigabyte of memory is 2^{30}, which is slightly more than a billion bytes.

To make it easier to install memory, memory comes in several different formats. The most popular format today is known as SDRAM. SDRAM comes in two varieties, PC-66 and PC-100. They come in various sizes ranging from 32MB to 256MB. The exact format of memory you have depends on your computer's make and model. For this, you'll need to consult the documentation that came with your computer.

Dealing with the mysteries of memory... Before you go out and buy additional memory to upgrade your system, you'll need to gather two bits of information from your PC's documentation or manufacturer. You'll need to know how many slots for memory are currently occupied on your motherboard, and how many are available for expansion. Because you don't want to throw any parts away unless you absolutely have to, this information will be vital in the purchasing decisions you make. For example, if you have a tiny amount of RAM in your computer now, and have only two slots for expansion, you'll want to buy the largest memory module you can afford. That will enable the PC to grow with you (and the most current applications you want to run). If you have a moderate amount of memory, a couple of smaller modules may be enough to get your system into that "sweet spot" where it runs smoothly.

Don't touch! Until you know what you are doing, you should not open your system console yourself in search of this information. Not only are the parts inside fragile, but in some cases there's actually a sticker over the edge of the console's opening that cracks when the console is opened, rendering your warranty null and void. Of course, if you call the manufacturer and are talked through opening the console, that's a different story.

You should also be aware that memory prices fluctuate much like the stock market. Before making a purchase, I suggest you monitor the prices for a few weeks to get a baseline for what's high, and what's low.

Virtual Memory

We've all heard the term virtual reality, right? It may be a super-realistic video game, or a Web-based video you can use to "walk" through a potential vacation home. In either case, virtual refers to something that isn't quite what it says it is. Well computers make use of something called virtual memory.

If you run out of main memory (or RAM), Windows is smart enough to move some of the stuff in main memory out to a disk drive to create some free space for other programs. The data that Windows moves out from main memory to disk is usually the oldest stuff in memory that it can find. This technique is known as virtual memory, and the place Windows stores the data it moves out of memory is called the swap file.

Eventually the program that used the data that was written to the swap file will need it again. This forces Windows to find some free space in the main memory again (probably

7

by writing another chunk of memory data to the swap file). Then it must read the original information back into main memory from the swap file.

Although your computer will run while this is going on, it might run very slowly, and you might have to wait a few seconds between tasks while Windows does its thing. From this quick discussion, you should be able to see that virtual memory is not a real substitute for main memory. If you don't have enough main memory, you need to run fewer programs at a time, or get more main memory.

You Have More Disk Drives Than You Think!

Almost all computers today have floppy disk drives, hard disk drives, and CD-ROM drives. However, many new computers have more advanced or specialized disk drives such as DVD-ROM, CD-R, CD-RW, Zip, and a few other formats. The types of disk drives can be broken down into four main groups: hard drives, floppy drives, CD-ROM drives and DVD-ROM drives, and the rest.

In the next few sections, I'll explain what some of these drives do as well as how they work.

Hard Disk Drives: The Easy Way to Store Data

Hard disks, which some people call hard drives, are the permanent storage for a computer. This is very different from RAM in that when you turn the power off, you lose anything you have in main memory, whereas the hard disk information is there for good. Also, hard disks hold hundreds of times the amount of data that you can hold in main memory. The primary disadvantage of a hard drive's memory is that a hard disk is about a thousand times slower than main memory.

In addition to the documents you create yourself, hard disks store applications that you use, such as Microsoft Word, Microsoft Excel, or various games. Windows itself is also stored on a hard disk, and various pieces of it are brought into main memory when needed.

These days, hard disk space is measured in terms of gigabytes. A gigabyte on a disk drive represents one billion bytes or 1,000,000,000 bytes. Note that this value is not the same gigabyte as used for main memory. For many years, disk drive manufacturers used the same definitions of size as the memory manufacturers, but they quickly found that their disk drives looked much bigger when measured in billions rather than using 2^{20}.

Floppy Disk Drives: Removable Storage

While the discs in a hard disk always remain inside the drive, some drives are designed to remove the disks and replace them with a different disk. These drives are known as removable disk drives. A removable drive allows you to store data on multiple disks that you can use when you need them. However, only one disk is allowed to be in the computer at any one time.

The oldest type of removable disk drive is the floppy disk drive. While over the years there have been many different types of floppy disks, only one has survived until today. This is the 3.5" High Density floppy disk. It holds about 1.44MB of data. When compared to other types of disk drives, the space available on a floppy is almost trivial. Imagine this: if Windows could be ordered on floppy disks, it would take hundreds of disks. Many software applications would take even more! It's no wonder nearly all applications come on CDs rather than floppy disks.

Floppy disks do have one unique advantage, however. Everyone who has a computer can read them or write to them. Thus a floppy disk allows you to exchange data with others, and it's small enough and reasonably priced enough to tote files to and from work or multiple machines.

Although the amount of space on a floppy is insufficient for most commercial applications, remember that you don't need to exchange an entire application with someone. You need only exchange the data the application uses (like the Word document, not Word itself). Take the following examples as a frame of reference. In most cases, a floppy will hold 10 large JPEG images, or a hundred smaller ones. And you might be able to fit five fifty-page Word documents on a single floppy. Given that, the size of a floppy isn't that much of a limitation to most people.

Got a big job?   If you need to exchange larger files, there are other types of disk drives that can be used such as writable CD-ROMs, ZIP drives, and so on. See the "Other Disk Drives You Might Encounter" section later in this chapter for more information.

So What's the Difference Between CD-ROM Drives and DVD-ROM Drives?

As you look at ads for new computers, you'll see two types of CD-ROM drives mentioned—CD-ROMs and DVD-ROMs. The difference between the two may not be obvious to those new to computers. And even those not new to computers might not know the story of how the two types of drives came to be.

The evolution of CDs goes something like this. When the stereo industry wanted to improve the quality of music, it moved to a digital format. They released albums on

7

compact discs, or CDs as they are now called. Because the compact disc stored a series of bits and bytes, it was only natural that the computer industry adopted the same physical medium, which it dubbed a CD-ROM, for Compact Disc, Read Only Memory.

A CD-ROM holds up to approximately 650MB of information on a single disk. As its name implies, you can't write to a CD-ROM. The contents of a CD-ROM are fixed when the CD-ROM is manufactured. This is ideal for software companies who could distribute their applications on a CD-ROM instead of 20 or more floppies. It actually saved many companies money in the long run because the cost to make a CD-ROM was about the same as to write three or four floppy disks.

This allowed game producers to build bigger and more complicated games with bigger and better graphics. It also became practical for encyclopedia companies to load their encyclopedias on to a CD-ROM, which made them easier to use.

Computers can also read and play music CDs in a standard CD-ROM drive. In fact I'm always playing music CDs on my computer while I write.

The video industry then saw the advantage of CD-ROMs and developed the DVD technology to allow it to distribute videos on a plastic disk rather than a videocassette. However, videos occupy much more space than sound, so the video industry increased the capacity of a DVD disk to about 5GB. Amazingly, the industry was able to do this with a disk that is the same size as the original compact disks, meaning that it is possible to design components that can play both music CDs and video DVDs.

The computer industry is presently jumping on the DVD drive bandwagon. Many high-end computers now come equipped with DVD drives. Most DVD-ROM drives will also read CD-ROMs. Just like CD-ROM drives can play CDs with music, most DVD-ROM drives will play DVD movies.

Although there isn't much software available in DVD-ROM format today, I expect that to change over the next few years. Eventually, DVD-ROMs will replace CD-ROMs in computers entirely, just as CD-ROMs have pretty much replaced floppies. That shouldn't happen for at least another three to five years, however.

Other Disk Drives You Might Encounter

Over the years, people have needed disk drives that didn't fall into any of the above categories. Some popular categories are Zip, CD-R, CD-RW, and DVD-RW drives.

Zip disks hold approximately 100MB of data. They are designed to be a floppy disk supplement or replacement, but they never really quite caught on. Laptop computer owners, to back up their disk drives and archive data for future use, mostly use them because laptop computers generally have much less hard drive space at their disposal.

Other individuals who need to exchange files that won't fit on a floppy disk also use them. Zip drives are declining in popularity as CD-R and CD-RW rise in popularity. The increased popularity of CD-R and CD-RW is due in part to their economy, both in terms of money and data storage space, which beat Zip drives hands down.

CD-R and CD-RW are specialized forms of CD-ROMs that allow you to write data. A CD-R allows you to write data to the physical disk only one time. After data has been written to a disk, it can't be rewritten. A CD that is written by a CD-R drive can be read by any CD-ROM drive, or even the compact disk player in your stereo at home.

Something may be missing... Specialized software may be necessary to create compact disks that can be played on your stereo. See the CD-R manufacturer for more information about the software needed or recommended.

A CD-RW, on the other hand, allows you to create compact disks that can be written, erased, and written on again. As with a CD-R disk, a CD-RW can be read by anything that can read a compact disk.

There are a few other disk drive devices you may encounter on the market. Some of these work like a Zip disk, others allow you to write more than 100MB of data on a special type of floppy disk, and there are even DVD-RW drives coming onto the market that will allow you to read and write DVD disks. For the most part, you should avoid these devices if you want to exchange disks with someone else, because virtually no one else uses them. Much of the technology simply hasn't been around long enough to form an accepted standard. However, if these high-tech devices fit a specific need that you have, they may be a lifesaver for you.

Monitors and Video Cards: Visual Appeal the Hard(ware) Way

When it comes to monitors and video cards, you usually get what you pay for. In other words, a cheap monitor may lack quality resolution, have a smaller viewing area, or some other downfall. Likewise, high-end video cards can give you top-notch gaming performance whereas entry-level ones may leave you with annoyingly slow screen refresh rates.

There are two basic types of monitors, conventional CRT and LCD displays. CRT displays are used in most desktop computers. They offer a large display for a comparatively reasonable price. LCD displays are typically used on laptop computers and represent a

7

big chunk of the price difference between a desktop computer and a laptop computer. Some desktop computers are now starting to come with LCD displays. Touted as wonderful space-savers, these displays can, however, be a lot more expensive than their more bulky counterparts. Both CRT and LCD displays are connected to your computer by a special hard device known as a video card.

Let's take a closer look at each of these devices.

CRT Displays

CRT displays are like TV sets—big and heavy. They are based on the same technology as television sets, though your computer monitor is far more sophisticated. Its superior resolution is partly why people find themselves watching DVD movies on their PC monitors rather than on their TVs.

If you need (or want) a large viewing area with which to work, you'll get a lot more for your money with this technology. However, a weighty 21" monitor may simply not be practical in an apartment. And its weight will surely cave in anything but the best quality, commercial grade furniture.

LCD Displays

LCD displays are typically found on laptops. The small size makes them ideal for a portable system. Considering that a laptop with a 15" display weighs less than 10 pounds whereas a 17" monitor with a similar viewing area weighs more than 50 pounds.

The primary downside to LCD displays is that they aren't as bright as a CRT monitor. Thus if you take your laptop outside on a bright day, don't expect to be able to see the display clearly. In a typical office environment, however, seeing the display isn't usually a problem.

LCD displays come in two forms, active matrix and passive matrix. *Active matrix* displays are much brighter than *passive matrix* displays and also refresh much faster, which means when the image onscreen changes, it changes more quickly and less noticeably, with a better refresh rate. The primary benefit of passive matrix displays is their lower cost. However, the price of LCD displays is dropping so rapidly that most vendors are no longer even offering the passive matrix displays.

Video Cards: Making Your Display Behave

A video card translates the bits and bytes inside a computer's memory into a signal that can be displayed on a video monitor. About five years ago, that was about all a video card needed to do. Today, video card manufacturers such as ATI Technologies build video cards that perform many different functions.

Extra hardware is included to decode DVD videos in hardware, thus freeing your CPU to do other tasks. Also, some video cards now include a TV Tuner that will let you watch (and even record) your favorite TV shows on your computer. Some even include special hardware that will let you record directly from a video camera so that you can capture pictures and movies without additional hardware!

However, one of the biggest influences in the video card industry has been the computer gaming industry. As computer game developers develop new games, they tend to push the hardware right to its limits. Video card manufacturers realized that they could improve the performance of computer games by adding special hardware support inside the video card for performing functions the game developers used to write into the software. Shifting functions to the video card did two things: the special video hardware was able to perform those functions much faster than the software could; and by moving the functions outside the CPU, it made available more CPU cycles to enhance and drive other aspects of the game.

Keyboards and Mice: Getting Places on Your Screen

Keyboards and mice are the primary way a user interacts with his or her computer. Keyboards are a relatively standard commodity these days. The primary difference between one keyboard and another is how they feel. Some have a softer touch, whereas others have a firmer touch. There are exceptions, however. Microsoft has developed a "natural" keyboard that's designed to be ergonomically better for long hours at the keyboard. And other manufacturers have made colorful keyboards with pictures on the keys so that even the youngest people can get involved in the computer age.

There are, on the other hand, a wide variety of mice available for your computer. They come in different sizes and shapes, and some (like Microsoft's IntelliMouse) have special features such as a wheel that you can spin to scroll the information on your screen. And now there are even wireless infrared mice that do away with the finicky mouse balls altogether in favor of a more high-tech solution.

Finally, some mice are really not mice at all. They're more accurately referred to as pointing devices. Many laptops have touch pads on which you move your finger to control the pointer, whereas trackballs look a whole lot like upside down mice in that you roll the ball that's usually on the bottom of your mouse with your fingers to navigate the screen.

7

Sound Cards and Speakers: Do You Hear What I Hear?

A sound card is used to generate sounds. Duh, right? You didn't need me to tell you that one! But what might not be so obvious is the fact that internally there are two different types of sounds. There are sound files that contain the complete sound you hear. These are known as .WAV (pronounced wave) files. Other sound files are known as MIDI sound files. These files contain a series of music notes and voices that are played back through virtual musical instruments in the sound card. Also, if you like to listen to music you can download .MP3 music files from the Internet and play them on your computer through your sound card and speakers.

In addition to these files, your computer also has the ability to play regular music CDs. Simply pop one in the CD-ROM drive and Windows will recognize that it contains music and will automatically begin to play it.

Just like your stereo needs speakers to play sound, so does your sound card. Depending on how you use your computer, you may want inexpensive speakers or really good speakers. In general, if you want to play games or music on your computer, a good set of speakers will be worth the investment. After all, a good subwoofer will do wonders for those explosion scenes in the movie "Top Gun"! And if quality music is a priority, don't expect the average laptop to produce anything of real quality.

Printers: What's Right for You May Not Be Right for Me!

Choosing a printer may seem like a simple task, but that couldn't be farther from the truth. In fact, the decision was a whole lot easier 10 years ago when laser printers were outrageously priced as were color printers, leaving dot matrix (and then ink jets) the only fiscally responsible option for most casual users.

In today's market, there are basically two types of printers: color inkjet printers and monochrome laser printer. Although there are other types of printers available, they are out of the price range for most users.

A more in-depth look will help you see why the decision's become so complicated.

Color Inkjet Printers

Color inkjet printers differ mostly in terms of their print speed. A few higher end color inkjet printers have a finer print resolution, which will make any photographs you print look a little crisper; or they'll have the capability to print on multiple types of material like transparencies, T-shirt transfers, paper-backed fabric, and so on. Other than these features, most color inkjet printers are nearly identical.

Inkjet printers work by spraying tiny ink bubbles on the paper from a print head as it moves across the paper. After each pass, the paper moves forward a little bit, and the print head passes back in the other direction.

Printing an average sheet of paper can take anywhere from 10 seconds to several minutes depending on what is being printed (that is, how graphically intensive the output is). Text always prints faster than graphics. A page with a couple of lines of text will print very fast, whereas a full page picture will take what seems like an eternity.

Inkjet cartridges may print anywhere from 200 to 500 pages or more before they need to be replaced. Some printers use a single ink cartridge, which use combinations of ink to produce different colors, including black. One of the downsides to a color inkjet printer is when you run out of ink for one color, you have to replace the entire cartridge, or live with strange colors in your output.

Printing text with black letters requires using all of the colors in a color cartridge, and the text doesn't look as nice as using a black cartridge. Some printers allow you to switch the color cartridge for a black cartridge, or they include a second black cartridge inside the printer that will automatically be used for printing black. That way, if you run out of one ink color (except for black of course), you can still print out text-based documents in black ink.

Replacement cartridges for color printers can get pricey, so before you purchase a printer, you may want to browse cartridge replacement prices to make sure you're getting the most for your money.

Laser Printers

Laser printers are much more expensive than inkjet printers, and only print in black (unless you have thousands of dollars to plunk down on a color laser printer). Laser printers are generally as fast or faster than inkjet printers, and produce much higher quality text output. Although toner cartridges cost more than ink cartridges, they last a lot longer too, making the laser printer much cheaper to operate over the long run.

Modems and Network Cards: Talk to Me, Baby!

7

In order to connect to the Internet, you need either a modem or a network card. Most home computers use a modem that connects to a telephone line. In addition to modems, there are several other ways to connect to the Internet. These include ISDN, ADSL, and cable modems. Network cards, are usually used to connect two or more computers in the same general area using a special cable. They may also be used to connect a computer to an ISDN, ADSL or cable modem.

Modems

Modems allow you to hook your computer to the telephone line and call other computers over your regular telephone line. Typically, you would use a modem to connect to an Internet Service Provider (ISP), which gives you access to the Internet.

Transmission speeds vary, but most modems today communicate at up to 56,000 bits per second. This translates to a maximum of about 7,000 bytes per second. Of course a less than perfect telephone connection will considerably reduce this speed. Also, most telephone companies have technical limitations that will affect the transmission speed. Even so, most connections will be made at a speed of at least 48,000 bits per second, or about 6,000 bytes per second.

The faster you can connect to the Internet, the better the Net surfing experience. At 6,000 bytes per second, a Web page that has takes up 1,000 bytes and has a dozen images at 12,000 bytes each will take 25 seconds to load. If your connection speed is half of that, you're up to nearly a minute just to view a single Web page!

Alternatives to Modems

Some telephone companies offer a service known as ISDN, which offers speeds as high as 128,000 bits per second. ISDN service is much more expensive than regular telephone service. You need a special device, similar to a modem, to connect your computer to an ISDN line.

A more practical alternative to ISDN is called ADSL. Only a few telephone companies offer the technology today, but many of the rest have plans to offer it in a year or so. ADSL operates at speeds starting at about 1,000,000 bits per second, and can reach as high as 8,000,000 bits per second. For exact speed and equipment requirements, talk to your local telephone company.

The last alternative to a modem is something called a cable modem. This is a service provided by your cable TV company that allows you to connect your computer to the Internet at speeds up to 10,000,000 bits per second. However, unlike ADSL, you have to share the connection with some of your neighbors, so the 10,000,000 bit-per-second speed can quickly drop depending how many people are using the service at a given time. Like ADSL, this service is highly dependent on the cable TV provider in your area, so check with your cable company for more information.

Network Cards

If you have two or more computers that are in the same general area, you might want to connect them together so that you can share files and printers. Doing this requires a network card and some special hardware to build a network.

Although there are many different types of networks, Ethernets are the most common. Basically all you have to do is install a network card in each computer you want on the network, and run a special cable from the network card to a small device known as a network hub.

The cost to install a network with three computers is about the same price as a nice inkjet printer. If you were thinking about buying a second printer for convenience, considering buying the hardware for a network instead.

> **So what else do I need?**   The software you need to connect the computers together is already bundled in Windows. Older operating systems often needed special software in addition to the hardware required to build the network.

After you have a network up and running, you can share files and printers. There are also a number of games that will work over a network. If you enjoyed playing Quake against the computer, imagine how much fun it would be to play against the rest of your family!

Other Input/Output Devices

Besides the hardware I've already discussed, there are some other interesting input/output devices you can attach to your computer. These devices can be attached to various I/O ports on your computer. Some common I/O ports include the game port, a USB port, a serial port, a parallel port and a keyboard port. You should check the type of ports needed by the specific devices you want to use and compare them to the ports listed in your computer's owner's manual.

Joysticks and Other Game Controls: Adding Fun to Your PC

If you want to fly an airplane on your computer, you have the option of using your keyboard and pressing various keys to turn, or you can use a joystick. A joystick is a more natural way to control a flight simulator game, for example, because the tightness of the turn depends on how much you move the stick, rather than how fast the computer responds to you hitting the keyboard.

7

In addition to the joystick, some companies also offer rudder pedals and a weapons control systems. The weapons control system allows you to control the thrust from the engine in the aircraft as well as controlling various weapons systems, landing gear, cockpit views, and so on.

As auto racing games have grown in popularity, many companies that make joysticks also make steering wheels. Although you can control your car using a joystick, a steering wheel is much more authentic. Also, some of the steering wheels come with gas and brake pedals to make the experience even more realistic.

Many other types of games such as Quake will allow you to control your character with a joystick. However, you can also purchase controls similar to what you use on your cartridge game systems. Some people prefer these types of controls for different types of games.

Scanners and Digital Cameras: Say "Cheese"!

Although printers allow you to get pictures from your computer to paper, a scanner or digital camera lets you acquire pictures and put them into your computer—kind of reverse printing, if you will.

To use a scanner, you place a photograph or sheet of paper in a device that is similar to the top part of a copier. A special program instructs the scanner to scan the image into the program's memory. From there, you can save the picture to your hard disk for use as a Windows desktop theme, or on your personal Web page.

A digital camera, on the other hand, works independently of your computer. You take pictures with it and then download them to your computer by using a special cable (or in some cases, a floppy disk that's been stored in the camera much like a roll of film in a traditional camera). After the pictures are on the computer, you can delete them from the camera's memory and shoot more pictures. Some digital cameras will save the pictures to special flash cards, which can be loaded into your computer, giving you the ability to shoot oodles of pictures on your Disney World vacation, but keep only the good ones.

Summary

I guess that was more than you ever wanted to know about hardware, huh? Understanding how all these components and devices work together as well as individually is of utmost importance in truly being able to understand computers. You now know some details about how each component works, as well as how they compare to one another.

In the next lesson, we'll focus our discussion on the skeleton of your computer—the CPU and memory, video card, and monitor. You'll learn how to tweak your computer's performance among other useful tidbits.

Workshop

Now it's time to see just how much you learned in this lesson. I'll give you a short multiple-choice quiz to test what you learned, followed by a suggested activity designed to enhance the skills you acquired during the hour.

Quiz

Select the best answer to the questions from the choices provided, and then check your answers.

Questions

1. Which is the fastest CPU?
    a. 600 gigabytes
    b. 600 megabytes
    c. 600 megahertz
2. What is virtual memory?
    a. RAM you think you have in your computer, but you really don't.
    b. Memory you can see, but can't touch.
    c. Additional short-term memory that is created temporarily on your hard disk.
3. Which of the following is true about computer monitors?
    a. CRTs are bigger and heavier than LCDs, but they're a lot less expensive, too.
    b. Monitors have horrible resolution compared to your TV. If you want a good, economical solution, buy a TV set to use as a monitor instead.
    c. LCDs are easier to see outside than are CRTs.

Answers

1. C is the answer to this one; the other two are not CPU speeds.
2. Again, c is the correct choice.
3. This question may have been a bit more challenging than usual, but a is the only correct answer. The other choices have some part that makes them false.

7

Activity

Because this hour was stuffed with information as opposed to steps to be followed, you've got an easy assignment this time. Review the tearcard in the front of this book you filled out with your system specifications. This encourages you to have the components you have on your personal system in the forefront of your mind as you go into the remaining lessons in this section of the book.

HOUR 8

Getting to Know the Bare Bones of Your Computer

Other books out there might give you more technical details about the hardware components in your system. (Hey, I'm not here to give you a snow job!) But what good are a bunch of technical facts that don't teach you anything along the way? Sure, it's great trivia material, but that's about it.

In this hour, you'll find loads of useful information about managing the main components of your computer. You'll also find out more about the following topics:

- How do you give your computer a performance checkup by yourself?
- Kernels…more than just bits of corn on a corncob!
- What's the optimal display resolution for my monitor given its size?
- How do I put one of those cool screen savers on my computer?

In the following sections, I want to focus on the core components of your computer system—the CPU and memory, video card, and monitor. (I've tossed the discussion about keyboards into the next lesson, where mice and other pointing devices are covered.) Without these components, you wouldn't have a computer.

Unlike many other computer books that talk about hardware from a hardware perspective, I want to focus on how to manage this hardware using software. This accomplishes two things: it puts your new-found hardware knowledge into a meaningful context, and it shows you how to actually do something with the software rather than just bombard you with useless facts.

Keeping Track of Your CPU and Memory

Without the CPU and memory, your computer couldn't run. Do you know how well your computer is running? Windows 98 includes a special tool called the System Monitor that allows you to see how much memory and CPU cycles are used over time. In addition to CPU and memory, it will also track information about the performance of your Internet connection.

Um, aren't I a bit out of my league here?   Many long-time computer users would consider monitoring system performance an advanced topic. But hey, you don't have to be a pro to appreciate good system performance, right? Don't let some of the technobabble you encounter intimidate you; instead, tuck it away in your memory for fun cocktail party conversation with some of your "nerdier" friends!

Using the System Monitor Utility

To start the System Monitor, click the Start button, and then choose Programs, Accessories, System Tools, System Monitor. The System Monitor program will start and display a window similar to the one pictured in Figure 8.1.

Although the System Monitor utility can track many different pieces of information, most are interesting only to techie types. However there are a few pieces of information that might be useful to you. The Kernel: Processor Usage tracks how busy your CPU is over time, whereas the Memory Manager: Page Faults are a way of monitoring memory usage. Let's take a closer look at this utility.

FIGURE 8.1

Use the System Monitor utility to track CPU usage.

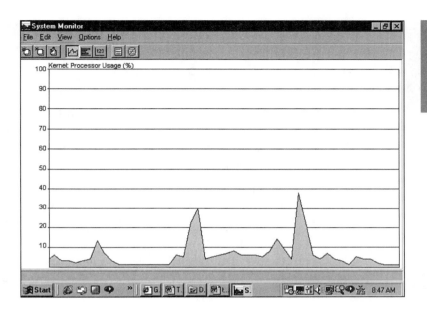

Adding a Report to the System Monitor

By default, the System Monitor utility displays only one report, the Kernel: Processor Usage report you saw back in Figure 8.1. You also can view the Memory Manager: Page Fault report.

To add this report to the System Monitor display, do the following:

1. With the System Monitor open, choose Edit, Add Item from the main menu to display the Add Item dialog box.

2. Choose Memory Manager in the Category list box. This displays a list of reports available in the Item pane (see Figure 8.2).

FIGURE 8.2

You can add the Page Fault Report to the current display by using the Add Item dialog box.

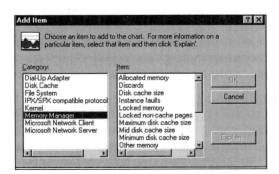

3. Choose Page Faults in the Item list box, and then click OK to add the report to the display.

Monitoring Kernel: Processor Usage

Processor Usage is expressed as a value ranging from 0 to 100 that tracks how much work the CPU is doing over time. A value of 0 means that the CPU isn't doing any work, whereas a value of 100 means that there are no CPU cycles available to do anything else. High values typically manifest themselves in sluggish system performance, which is usually your first clue something is wrong.

Each of the values is captured at a particular instant in time. Think of it as a snapshot that basically freezes what's happening at that particular moment in time. It's important to know that these usage values change quickly, and reflect only what you were doing at the time the data was captured.

There are basically two types of applications on your computer: CPU bound and I/O bound. CPU bound applications generally use every bit of CPU time available. Games like SimCity or Flight Simulator grab every CPU cycle available, so seeing 100 percent on the System Monitor while these games are running is normal and not a sign of a problem.

On the other hand, programs like Word and Excel don't use CPU cycles continuously. They spend most of their time waiting for input and generating output. These applications are called I/O bound applications (the I/O standing for input/output). I/O bound programs use CPU cycles only when performing a specific function such as loading a file or finding a particular value in the document. Most of the time, the Processor Usage chart shows a relatively low level of Processor Usage, because the program is waiting for you to type a character, click on a button, or perform some other type of task.

When's the best time to use the System Monitor? First, you should run System Monitor while no other programs are running. This will tell you what percentage of the CPU cycles that Windows uses to support itself. You can call this value *system overhead*. The remaining percentage of the CPU resource is available for use by your programs. If you notice sluggish system performance, you can call up the System Monitor as you work. If you're running an I/O bound application and aren't doing anything with it, the Processor Usage value should be just a little bit more than the overhead value.

On the other hand, if you're running a CPU bound application, don't worry about seeing a high Processor Usage value. Because these applications use every bit of the CPU you have available, they will distort this value to the point of making it meaningless.

If you are running several I/O bound applications and your system seems to be sluggish, check the Processor Usage. If it spends a lot of time at or near 100 percent, you should either try to run fewer applications at one time, or consider looking for a faster processor that more adequately meets your needs.

The Memory Manager: Monitoring Page Faults

Watching memory is a more complicated task. Windows is designed to use as much of your memory as possible. Even if you're not running any programs, Windows will still use nearly all of your memory. It keeps copies of programs you might have executed recently in memory, guessing that you might want to run them again soon.

This means you need to look at how your memory is used through more indirect means. A page fault occurs when Windows needs to load something into memory from disk, such as when Windows loads a program for the first time. A page fault also occurs when Windows has run out of memory and needs to swap something from memory to disk to make room to bring something back into memory from disk. Tracking how many page faults occur per second over time is a good way to know how your memory is performing.

When your applications are loaded into memory and you aren't starting any new ones, the page fault rate should be effectively zero. Occasionally, you will see little spikes, which aren't significant. Typically these spikes occur while switching from one application to another, although they might appear for other unknown reasons. Ah the mysteries of computers....

If the page faults never seem to reach zero, you might not have enough memory to satisfy your currently running applications. This means that Windows is spending a lot of time handling the page faults, so in effect, it is stealing memory from one application to give it to another (the old robbing Peter to pay Paul thing). Of course the obvious solution is to run fewer applications, but if that isn't possible or desirable, you might want to consider adding memory to your system.

Working with Your Display Monitor and Video Card

The display monitor/video card combination is the computer's primary way to communicate with you. Although you can tell the computer what to do with a variety of devices such as the keyboard, mouse, joysticks, and game controllers, the computer nearly always provides its response to your input via your video display (or monitor).

However, this doesn't mean that your video card and display monitor are configured optimally. Choosing the settings is a highly personal choice, and most manufacturers just choose to use the default values figuring you can easily alter them if you want to. Changing them to look the way you want them isn't difficult and is well worth your time.

Controlling Display Settings

You can modify your video card and display monitor through the Display Properties dialog box. To access this dialog box, right-click on the desktop background, and then select Properties from the resulting shortcut menu. Alternatively, you can click the Start button on the Windows taskbar, and then choose Settings, Control Panel. From there, double-click the Display icon to display the Dialog Properties dialog box (see Figure 8.3). You might recall this dialog box from an earlier lesson where you used this property window to change the wallpaper on your desktop. Now let's see what some of the other settings can do to alter your monitor's display.

FIGURE 8.3

The Display Properties dialog box is where you can change many attributes of your screen's appearance.

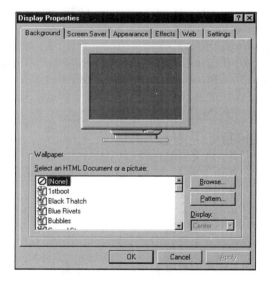

Optimizing Your Display Settings

When you turn on your computer for the first time, its manufacturer will have made a number of choices for the display settings. However, the manufacturer might not have taken the time to optimize these settings for your particular hardware configuration. The two primary configuration parameters are Screen Area and Colors. Both of these values can be set on the Settings tab of the Display Properties window (see Figure 8.4).

FIGURE 8.4

Change the color palette of your display using the Settings tab of the Display Properties dialog box.

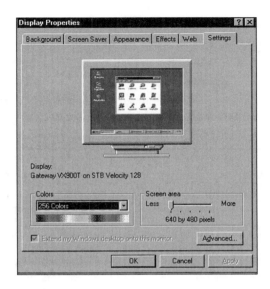

Selecting the Right Screen Area Size

The screen area displayed on your computer is measured in pixels. A pixel (which is short for picture element) is just a single dot that the computer draws on the screen. The number of dots across the screen by the number of dots from top to bottom determines the screen area. Thus if your screen displays 640 dots across by 480 vertically, the screen area (or resolution) is said to be 640×480.

Windows supports a number of standard screen area sizes, including 640×480, 800×600, 1024×768, 1280×960, and 1600×1200. The more you increase the size of the screen area, the more information you can display on your desktop. However, while the screen area increases, the size of the icons and characters shrink. Of course, the size of your display monitor will ultimately determine the size of the icons and text on your desktop, so you really need to take that into consideration when tweaking your monitor's resolution.

Table 8.1 lists various display monitor sizes and my recommendations for screen area size. Because I recognize that everyone is different, I've listed multiple choices for most of the different display monitor sizes. The first value is the one I would use, whereas other values will also generate acceptable results depending on your personal preference. You should try each of them out for a while to find the best size for you.

TABLE 8.1 Recommended Screen Area Sizes

Display Size (in Inches)	Recommended Screen Area Size
14	640×480
15	800×600, 640×480
17	1024×768, 800×600
19	1024×768, 1280×960, 800×600
21	1280×960, 1024×768, 1600×1200

Caveat emptor! Until a few years ago, CRT manufacturers used the same technique to measure displays as the television industry. Thus a 15-inch display had a cathode ray tube inside it that measured 15 inches across the diagonal. However the actual space occupied by the Windows desktop (known as the viewing area) was about 13.7 inches. A lawsuit against the major computer manufacturers forced them to change how they advertise their monitors. Most now refer to their monitors by using a model number such as SX1500, and then refer to the actual screen size of 13.7 inches in parentheses. Even so, it is still pretty easy to determine the real monitor size.

Take this into consideration... Although Windows will let you set your monitor to 640×480, you should expect to encounter a number of situations where dialog boxes and other displays won't fit on your screen. Even the appearance of some icons and screen elements can change as each of the applications competes for the available palette of colors. You should also know that most Web pages are formatted for a display resolution of 800×600; therefore, I recommend setting your display resolution to at least 800×600.

Selecting the Right Value for Colors

The other major display setting is Colors. This determines how many colors can be displayed on your screen. Typical values are 16, 256, High Color (16 bit) and True Color (32 bit). In general, you should avoid 16 colors because nearly all Windows applications will not run correctly with this setting.

But my true color option says 24 bit... Whether the 24 or 32 bit value is displayed depends on the video card you have installed. But no matter which it lists, rest assured that both options give comparable true color results.

Although using 256 colors is better, it will still cause problems when you're running multiple programs. The 256 colors displayed on the screen are chosen from a palette of over 16 million colors by each application you are running. Frequently, these applications will choose different sets of colors. This means that if you're running more than one program, you might get different colors for all but one application. This might make the other applications unusable due to the color combinations.

Both High Color (16 bit) and True Color (32 bit) resolve the color conflict problem. They also have the advantage of displaying images at near photographic quality. For most users, I recommend using either High Color (16 bit) or True Color (32 bit) to achieve the best results.

Some Advanced Settings of Interest

If you find yourself frequently changing your display settings, you might consider setting a few advanced properties. Modifying these properties makes it easier to make frequent changes.

To display these property options, click the Advanced button on the Settings tab of the Display Properties dialog box. When you do, you'll see the video card's Properties dialog box as shown in Figure 8.5. Although this window is unique to each video card, the General tab will always be the same.

FIGURE 8.5

A video card-specific Properties dialog box lets you change additional display options.

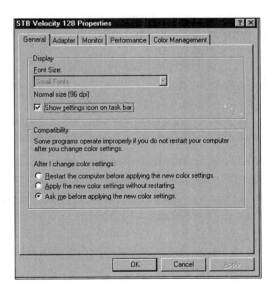

In the Compatibility section of the dialog box, you can choose how the changes are made. By default, Windows does not apply the changes until the next time you restart your computer. However, you can also choose to apply the new color settings without restarting. You can also instruct Windows to ask you if you want to change the colors, or just tell it to make the changes without asking.

 You may not have a problem, but...   Nearly all programs in Windows will work properly if you change the screen area and color settings without rebooting. However you should know that there is a small possibility that an application might not run properly if you change the settings without rebooting. If that should happen to you, simply save your work, and then shut down and restart your system to correct the problem.

Checking the Show Settings icon on the task bar option will add a shortcut icon to this tab on the in the system tray at the right end of the Windows taskbar. Double-clicking the corresponding monitor-shaped icon in the system tray will show the Display Properties window. Clicking on the icon opens a pop-up menu of display settings. You can simply choose the resolution you want, and the change will be applied according to the options you select.

To change any of the display options, make the desired modifications and click Apply to make the changes and keep the Properties dialog box open, or click OK to make the changes and close the dialog box. As always, clicking Cancel closes the window without making any changes, even if you've clicked different options during the current viewing of the dialog box.

Changing the Settings

For clarity's sake, let me recap the steps you'll need to follow to tweak your display settings. To change the display settings as shown back in Figure 8.4, choose the Settings tab of the Display Properties dialog box and then do the following:

1. On the Settings tab in the Display Properties dialog box, click on the arrow on the Colors drop-down list, and then choose the number of colors you want.

2. Drag the slider in the Screen area back and forth until you get the desired screen area size. As you move the slider, the picture in the preview monitor will change, giving you a rough idea of what the new desktop will look like.

3. When you're satisfied with both settings, click Apply or OK to make the changes. Depending on your selections for the advanced settings I described earlier, you might be prompted to verify the change and to reboot your computer.

Games, games, games.   Many computer games work only at 640×480 and 256 colors, especially those that were made before 1999 and many games designed especially for children. The better and newer games automatically switch to the needed settings, and then restore them to your specifications when you leave the game. Others will run, but leave a black border around the game, whereas others refuse to run at all. Unfortunately, there isn't an easy solution to this problem. For my son's machine, I usually set the display to 640×480 and 256 colors. I then change it for him only when needed because he's only 6 years old. However, on my machine, I change the settings as needed by clicking the Display icon in my system tray.

Flying Toilets and Swirling Colors (Screen Savers)

A long time ago (boy, am I ever starting to date myself!), computer monitors used to suffer from a problem called burn-in. Burn-in occurred when the same image was displayed on the monitor for long periods of time. Eventually, the image became etched on the phosphorus of the screen, and you would see a ghosted image of that screen on your monitor forever no matter what you did.

To prevent burn-in, screen savers were created, the primary purpose of which was to display a constantly changing picture on the monitor. A screen saver would start any time the computer hadn't been used for a few minutes, and would automatically stop anytime the user pressed a key on the keyboard or moved the mouse.

Since screen savers were first introduced, they have become an art form with many different styles and patterns available. That's where the flying toilets part of this section's title comes in. A commercially designed and marketed collection of novelty screen savers, called After Dark, fueled the trend toward bizarre screen savers like toasters with wings, flying toilets, and the like. Even today you'll find a host of funky screen savers in clearance bins at computer stores nationwide.

Windows 98, Second Edition includes a number of different screen savers that you can select and configure using the Screen Savers tab of the Display Properties window (see Figure 8.6).

You can choose a screen saver from the Screen Saver drop-down list box. After you choose one, the monitor area of the window will show you a small preview of the screen saver. You can see a full screen preview of the screen saver by clicking the Preview button. Pressing any key on the keyboard or moving the mouse will return you to the Display Properties dialog box.

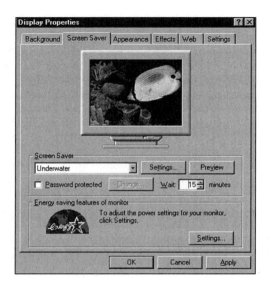

FIGURE 8.6

The Screen Saver tab helps you express yourself.

Most screen savers have a series of settings that allow you to refine how they work. These options often control values such as the object displayed, the speed with which the object moves, and the color of the object. These settings are specific to each screen saver, so I'm not going to cover them here; however, they are easy to change. Press the Settings button to display the dialog box with the screen saver's settings. After changing the settings you can test them by closing the Settings dialog box and clicking the Preview button.

Waiting and Password Protection

The Wait field allows you to specify how long the system must be idle before the screen saver kicks in. Choose the value that is best for you. Note, however, that if you make it too short, it can launch while you're simply trying to compose a sentence in your head, thus causing a major distraction and potential loss of train of thought.

Screen savers also include a password protection feature. After the screen saver has started, you must enter the correct password to stop the screen saver. This way, if you walk away from your computer, the screen saver will automatically start and prevent others from using your computer. Because the screen saver won't start immediately, you need to choose a wait time that doesn't disrupt your work, yet doesn't leave the system unprotected for too long of a time.

To enable password protection, do the following:

1. Select a screen saver on the Screen Saver tab using the drop-down list.

2. In the Wait spin box, choose the wait time that is best for you. You can either type in a number, or use the arrow buttons to make your selection.

3. Check the Password Protected check box by clicking inside of the box.

4. Click the Change button to display the Change Password dialog box. Enter your password twice (once in the New password text box, and again in Confirm new password), and then click OK to save the password.

5. Click OK in the Display Properties dialog box to make these changes and close the dialog box.

> **"You must remember this..."**   Don't forget your password. Windows encrypts the password before it stores it in your computer, so that anyone with access to your computer won't be able to find the password. Unfortunately, this also includes you. If the screen saver hasn't started, you always have the option to use the Display Properties window to change the password. But after it has started, you'll need the password to unlock your computer. Likewise, try not to choose a password that's too obvious; an unauthorized person might be able to guess it.

Tuning Your Modem

Your modem is your connection to other computers. I'll talk about how to establish a modem connection to the Internet in Hour 19, "Setting Up a Connection to the Internet." However, there are some little things you might want to do before you connect to the Internet.

A modem is short for modulator-demodulator. This is a device that converts digital signals into an analog signal, which is then transferred over a telephone wire into another modem, which finally converts the analog signal back to a digital signal.

Losing the Noise

When connecting to another modem, you will hear the dial tone, the computer dialing the other computer, and the crackling and squawking noises associated with one computer connecting to another. Personally, I find this noise bothersome, and one of the very first things I do when I get a new computer is to turn off this noise.

To bring silence to your own computer while the modem connects, follow these simple steps:

1. Click the Start button on the Windows taskbar, and then point to Settings, Control Panel to open the Control Panel.

2. Double-click on the Modems icon to display the Modems Properties dialog box. You should see your modem listed here.

3. Make sure that your modem is selected, and then click the Properties button (not to be confused with the Dialing Properties button).

4. This displays a modem-specific dialog box similar to the one shown in Figure 8.7. Although the Properties dialog box for your modem might have different tabs from the one shown, the General tab should be the same.

FIGURE 8.7

Silence at last, thanks to the Modem Properties dialog box.

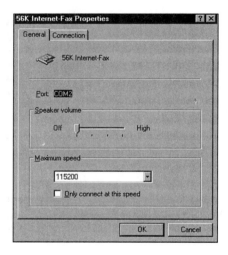

5. To disable the sounds from your modem, move the Speaker volume slider to the Off position (the farthest point on the left). If you want to hear the modem sounds while you connect, move the slider towards High.

Who'd wanna listen to all that noise, anyway?   Believe it or not, there might come a time when you'll actually want to hear all those modem noises. Sound might come in handy when troubleshooting modem-related problems. For example, you can learn whether your modem is finding a dial tone, if it's able to dial the phone number to your Internet service provider, or if the computer at the other end of the line is even answering.

8

6. When you're finished, click the OK button to close the modem-specific dialog box and click OK to close the Modems Properties dialog box.

Summary

I realize some of the sections in this lesson might have gotten a bit deeper into PCs than you might have felt ready for, but at least now you have a good grasp of how you can make your PC perform its very best, even if it's not the speediest thing on the market.

With all that behind us, we can move on to discuss the various input devices for your computer. Among them are keyboards, mice, joysticks, and a variety of specialized game controllers.

Workshop

Now it's time to see just how much you learned in this lesson. I'll give you a short multiple-choice quiz to test what you learned, followed by a suggested activity designed to enhance the skills you acquired during the hour.

Quiz

Select the best answer to the questions from the choices provided, and then check your answers.

Questions

1. What does the kernel part of the System Monitor track?

    a. How much corn you eat during a meal.

    b. How many trips you've made to KFC over the past month.

    c. The performance of your computer's processor.

2. What happens when you run your monitor at a resolution of 640×480?

    a. Your computer blows up.

    b. It might be okay on 14" monitors or smaller, but you can still expect some performance glitches and unexpected color shifts.

    c. Windows goes on strike and refuses to work.

3. What do flying toilets and computers have in common?

    a. Flying toilets can be found on screen savers that are run by computers.

    b. There's no such thing as a flying toilet! This author needs psychiatric help.

    c. Absolutely nothing; what do flying toilets have to do with the price of eggs?

Answers

1. Okay, now that I've stopped laughing at my own dumb jokes...the correct answer is c.

2. B; and I ought to know, too, because the screenshots for this book had to be captured at 640×480 on my 19" monitor. Trust me, it wasn't pretty!

3. Okay, so maybe there's an element of truth to all of the answers. Given that, I'll rank order them from best answer to worst: a, b, c (though a, c, b is also acceptable).

Activity

Go in and preview all the screen savers included with Windows. Find one you like, apply it, and then sit at your computer awhile to help yourself determine the best wait time given your personal needs and work habits.

And after you've connected to the Internet, you can surf over to www.downloads.com to retrieve even more screen saver candidates!

HOUR 9

Adding Fun and Functionality with Peripherals

When it comes to computers, there are two kinds of people—mouse people, and keyboard people. Thus far, I've talked a lot about using your mouse to complete tasks, but some people would just rather use the keyboard. Perhaps their vision precludes them from using the mouse effectively. Or maybe they simply remember keystrokes better than which commands are hidden somewhere on a menu. Whatever your preference for working with computers is, you'll find information about it on the pages that follow.

You'll find more specific information about the following topics:

- Are there any general Windows shortcuts I should know about?

- I'm a lefty; how do I convert my mouse for use?

- The instructions with my new computer game say I need to calibrate my joystick; how do I do that?

- Someone told me there are joysticks that enable you to feel what's going on in a flight combat game; is that true?

In the sections that follow, I'm going to talk about the many devices you can use to talk to your computer. This includes devices such as keyboards, mice, joysticks, game controllers, and specialized peripherals like steering wheels and rudder pedals.

Your Keyboard: You're the Simplest Way to Talk to Your PC

If the display monitor is the primary way your computer communicates with you, the keyboard is the primary way to communicate with the computer. To make it easier to use your computer, Windows allows you to control the speed of the keyboard repeat function, and the rate at which the cursor blinks.

Keyboard Settings: How Slow Can You Go?

To change the keyboard's settings click Start, and then choose Settings, Control Panel to display the Control Panel. Next, double-click on the Keyboard icon to display the Keyboard properties dialog box shown in Figure 9.1.

FIGURE 9.1

The Keyboard Properties dialog box lets you specify the character repeat rate to reflect your personal typing style.

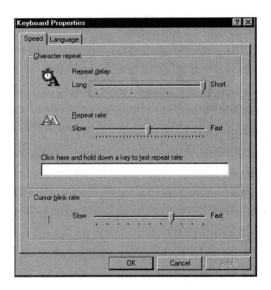

Some of us are faster typists than others. I certainly wouldn't hold any speed records, which is why I keep the repeat speed slow. Given the way I linger over the keys, most of my work would end up looking like thisssss if I didn't change the speed.

To change the repeat speed on your computer, do this:

1. Move the Repeat delay slider from Long to Short to set how long you must hold the key before the repeat function starts. If you want to restore this property to the default, move the slider all the way to the right (Short).

2. Move the Repeat rate from Slow to Fast to set how quickly the characters will be repeated. To restore this property to the default, move the slider halfway between Slow and Fast.

3. Click in the text box below both sliders and press a key to see if you are comfortable with the repeat rate.

4. To save your changes click OK. To abandon your changes, click the Cancel button.

Keyboard Shortcuts You Won't Want to Live Without

Okay, so I'm being a bit overdramatic…. But you don't need a mouse to use Windows; you can enter a sequence of key strokes that will accomplish the same thing as a mouse would. In some cases, such as resizing a window, keyboard shortcuts can be rather complicated; while in other cases, using the keyboard might be faster than using a mouse, especially when multiple steps or menus are involved.

Here is a list of some of my favorite keyboard shortcuts:

- **Getting help:** Press the F1 key. If there is help available, it will automatically be displayed. What's more, the help you get is based on the context in which you are working. For example, if you're writing a letter in Microsoft Word and press F1, you'll get the Microsoft Word help files, not some generic computer help file.

- **Closing the currently active window:** Press the Alt+F4 keys. This is the equivalent of pressing the Close button on the title bar or choosing File, Exit.

- **Undo change:** Press the Ctrl+Z keys.

- **Copy selected information:** Press the Ctrl+C keys. This will copy the selected information from the current window onto the clipboard.

- **Paste information from the Clipboard:** Press the Ctrl+V keys. This will paste whatever is in the Clipboard into the current window.

- **Selecting menu items:** Press the Alt key by itself to transfer the focus to the menu bar. Then you can use the left and right arrow keys to select the main menu option, and then press the down arrow key to select the submenu you want. Then press the Enter key to choose the menu item you want to execute or press the Esc key to move back one level. If you press the Esc key enough times, you will eventually reach the same place you were before you pressed the Alt key.

9

- **Using the Windows key:** That funny key with the Windows logo located between the Ctrl and Alt keys does the same thing as clicking on the Start button on the taskbar. From there you can use your arrow keys to select the menu item you want to execute and then press the Enter key to start it.

Moving with Mice

A mouse makes your computer easier to use, at least for some people. Although every function in Windows can be performed with a keyboard, there are many tasks that are made easier with a mouse. Just try to resize a form with your keyboard! A mouse is an indispensable tool for using Windows, one you won't want to do without.

However, using a mouse isn't always a pleasant experience for everyone. If you want to use a mouse with your left hand, for instance, the left mouse button falls under your middle finger rather than your index finger, which is uncomfortable for many people.

Likewise, you might want to adjust the double-click speed and how fast your mouse will respond to your movements by using the Mouse Properties window. To display this window, click Start, and then point to Settings, Control Panel. Next, double-click on the Mouse icon.

Left Handed Mice

While mice are generally preconfigured for use by the average right-handed person, the buttons can easily be swapped on the mouse by using the Mouse Properties dialog box (see Figure 9.2).

FIGURE 9.2

Make your mouse a lefty if necessary using the Mouse Properties dialog box.

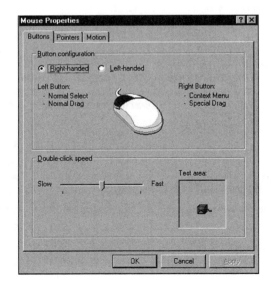

To change the mouse button's configuration, do the following:

1. Open the Mouse Properties dialog box from the Control Panel.

2. On the Buttons tab, select Left-Handed and click OK or Apply to change the setting.

Speed Clicking

Does Windows think you clicked twice on an icon, rather registering a double-click? (Yes, there is a difference.) Does Windows register two clicks as a single double-click? Then you might be interested in tweaking the double-click speed. This is done on the Buttons tab of the Mouse Properties dialog box (see Figure 9.2).

To change the amount of time between clicks for a double-click, follow these steps:

1. Open the Mouse Properties dialog box from the Control Panel.

2. On the Buttons tab, move the slider in the Double-Click Speed section toward Fast to decrease the time between clicks for a double-click, or to Slow to increase the time.

3. Then move your mouse to the test area and try clicking twice. If Windows thinks you double-clicked, the jack-in-the-box will pop out or back into the box. If you didn't click twice fast enough, the jack-in-the-box won't change positions.

4. Click the Apply or OK buttons to accept your changes.

5. To restore the default settings, move the slider halfway between Slow and Fast.

Rolling the Mice

You can adjust how much the cursor on your screen will move for a given mouse movement on the Motion tab of the Mouse Properties window (see Figure 9.3). You can also adjust the speed of mouse motion until you're comfortable with it.

Changing Mouse Properties

To change the mouse properties, follow these steps:

1. Open the Mouse Properties window from the Control Panel, and select the Motion tab.

2. In the Pointer speed frame, move the slider toward Fast to increase the distance the mouse pointer will travel on the screen for a given mouse movement, or toward Slow to decrease the distance.

3. To test the new setting, click the Apply button, or to accept the setting without testing, click the OK button.

4. To restore the original settings, move the slider halfway between Slow and Fast.

FIGURE 9.3

Need a faster mouse?
Use the Mouse
Properties dialog box
to make it so.

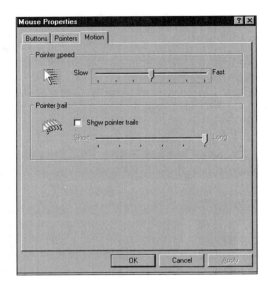

Trailing Pointers (or Mouse Tracks)

If you have difficulty trying to find your mouse pointer, you might want to set a pointer trail. A pointer trail is a series of pointer icons displayed along the path you move the mouse pointer. When you stop moving the mouse, the pointer trail disappears.

Makin' tracks   Pointer trails are very useful if you have an older laptop computer with a passive matrix display. When you move the mouse quickly with this type of display, the mouse pointer isn't always visible. The pointer trail makes it easier to find the mouse pointer and track its movement on screen.

To enable pointer trails, do the following:

1. Open the Mouse Properties window from the Control Panel, and select the Motion tab.

2. Check the Show pointer trails check box.

3. You can adjust the length of the pointer trail by moving the slider between Short and Long.

4. Click Apply to test your changes. If you're not happy with them, uncheck the Show Pointer Trails check box.

5. Click OK to save your changes and close the Properties window.

Let the Fun Begin! (Joysticks and Other Game Controllers)

When you talk to people who are buying computers for the first time, you'll hear many different reasons why they want one. Reasons like balancing their checkbook and organizing their recipes are usually spouted off, as if they have to rationalize their decision.

After the computer is home however, the computer ends up being used for two main purposes: surfin' the Internet, and playing computer games. Even if the computer was purchased to help educate their kids, game playing becomes one of the biggest ways the computer is used.

Although some games are easily played with a mouse and keyboard, most games benefit from having a specialized gaming control such as a joystick or gamepad. It helps to make the game play more realistic and more accurate than using the keyboard or mouse.

Not every game needs a joystick   SimCity, Ages of Empire, Roller Coaster Tycoon, and many other simulation games need only your keyboard and mouse for effective game play.

The Joy of Joysticks

The classic game control is the joystick. Joysticks have been used with personal computers since the 1970's. They allow you to provide accurate input to the computer in two dimensions.

Computer joysticks are modeled after the flight controls of a fighter aircraft, and often include triggers, buttons, and switches that allow you to perform many different functions. Joysticks are mostly used in flight simulator games, such as Microsoft's Flight Simulator or Falcon 4.0 by Microprose.

In a combat flying game, you don't want to spend your time hunting for keys on your keyboard; you might get shot down while you're searching for the radar key on your keyboard! The buttons on the joystick allow you to perform some of the most commonly used functions in your aircraft without looking for the correct key (or worse yet, combinations of keys) on your keyboard.

Come on over to my 'pad   Joysticks can be used in other games such as Doom and Quake, but you might want to use a gamepad instead. Driving games such as Midtown Madness and Test Drive also support joysticks, though you might find a steering wheel more enjoyable.

The Force (Feedback) be With You!

The latest trend in joysticks is to include force feedback to help you feel what's happening in the game. It builds on the concept of the rumble packs used for console games like the Nintendo 64, but provides a much more realistic experience. When you're flying a plane and get shot at, you can "feel" the bullets hit you. When you try to enter a loop, you'll feel the joystick fighting you every step of the way.

There are two downsides to a force feedback joystick. Obviously the first downside is the cost. Most force feedback joysticks (or at least the nice ones worth owning) cost more than $100. If you're a hardcore gamer with lots of flying games, this might not be out of line; but if you've got one flight simulation game in your huge collection of games, the expense might not be worth it to you.

Force feedback joysticks also make playing first person air combat games such as Microsoft Air Combat much more authentic and enjoyable because you can feel the bullets hitting your plane as you get shot, or feel your hand jerking back as you pull the trigger on your own gun.

 Who needs the distraction? Although force feedback joysticks provide a more realistic experience, they also can be distracting. You might not want to use one when your goal is to win. This is especially true if you compete against other players online.

Flight Controllers, Flight Yokes, and Rudder Pedals

A flight controller is a device that allows you to control the throttle of your airplane. In addition, flight controllers also have a number of switches and buttons. These switches and buttons allow you to perform a number of different functions such as switching from one weapon to another, raising and lowering flaps and landing gear, and switching radar modes. The switches and buttons on a flight controller complement the switches and buttons on a joystick, so you focus on what is happening in a game rather than searching for keys on your keyboard.

If your main interest is flying commercial jets or general aviation aircraft, you might want to consider a flight yoke. A flight yoke is similar to a steering wheel, but in addition to turning left or right, it also moves in and out. Most commercial aircrafts use yokes instead of joystick-like controls, making your experience a bit more authentic. Even some combat aircraft such as the P-38 Lightning used yokes instead of sticks. As far your game is concerned, a joystick and a flight yoke are identical, so which one you prefer to use is really up to you.

To complete your flight experience, a set of rudder pedals is absolutely necessary. Although you can control your virtual airplane with just a joystick or flight yoke, a real airplane also uses a set of rudder pedals. That's because an airplane moves in three dimensions, not just two. When you don't have a set of rudder pedals, most flight games will automatically control the rudder for you. Although this is fine in most situations, you do lose a little bit of the realism without them.

They're a must!   Rudder pedals are critical for any serious flight simulators that use piston powered airplanes, especially the combat oriented games.

Get Real with Steering Wheels

If you think you can beat Jeff Gordon in a NASCAR race, you've gotta have a steering wheel. A steering wheel makes your driving game much easier to play (and to win).

A steering wheel includes a gear shifter for you to control which gear you're driving in. Sometimes a steering wheel package comes with a gas and break pedal combination to make the game play more realistically. Also, some steering wheels include force feedback to make your driving experience even more realistic.

For the more unreal drive...   Many people find gamepads easier to use on some driving games, especially the games that don't try to provide a realistic driving experience.

Gamepads: Turning Your PC into a Nintendo

Gamepads are similar to the controls you find on a Nintendo 64 or Sony Playstation. They are full of buttons and pads that allow you to choose multiple directions for game movement. These buttons make it easier to play sports games such as FIFA 2000. They can also be used with many other types of games.

Before You Buy

Choosing a game controller is a highly personal matter. There are many different models and kinds to choose from. If possible, try out the controller in the store before you purchase one. While you're trying it, you should consider the following:

- See how the controller feels in your hand. Is it comfortable to hold? If you're left handed, is the joystick optimized for a right-handed person? That might make your position uncomfortable at best.

- Does the joystick base stay flat when you move the joystick to the extreme limits? In most combat flying games, you'll find yourself moving from one extreme to another. A wide, heavy base is in order here.

- Decide if the buttons and switches are easy to reach and easy to use. Try to reach buttons and switches without looking at them, because when you're playing your game, you'll be watching the screen and not your game controller.

- If you're buying a flight control system, make sure that it's compatible with your joystick. Generally, you're going to want to buy the flight control system from the same company that made your joystick.

- When buying rudder pedals or automobile pedals, are the pedals so close together that they're difficult to use? Likewise, are the pedals so far apart that they don't fit easily under you desk or table where your computer rests?

- Make sure that the controller is compatible with your system. Obviously, if you don't have a USB port on your machine, don't get a USB game controller.

- Does the joystick support the game you want to play? Although a simple joystick is supported by nearly all games, the same might be not true of your new force feedback joystick. Nothing's worse than paying a lot of money for a gizmo you can't use.

- Does DirectX support your new game controller? Although it is highly likely that the answer is yes as more and more games come to rely on DirectX support, this is an increasingly important issue. You don't want to invest in a game controller today, only to replace it in a year or two because DirectX doesn't support it.

Adding a New Game Controller to Your Machine

Windows allows you to add various game controllers to your computer via the Game Controls dialog box. You manage the game controllers on your system using the Game Controllers dialog box, which is started from the Windows Control Panel.

The following instructions show you how to install and calibrate a simple joystick on your system.

This time, ask for directions!   As with all new devices you want to add to your computer, you should review the installation instructions for your game controller prior to installing it. The game controller might include special software drivers that are necessary for it to work properly.

To add a joystick to your system, follow these steps:

1. Turn off your computer and attach the joystick to the joystick port on your computer following any instructions or diagrams that came with your joystick and your computer system.

2. Turn the computer's power back on to restart Windows.

3. When Windows is running, click Start, and then select Settings, Control Panel. Double-click the Game Controllers icon to display the Game Controllers dialog box shown in Figure 9.4.

FIGURE 9.4

The Game Controllers dialog box is where you'll begin configuring that neat new gaming device.

4. On the General Tab of the Game Controllers dialog box, click on the Add button. This will display the Add Game Controller dialog box (see Figure 9.5).

5. Choose the appropriate game controller from the list of game controllers. Note that many of the most popular game controllers are listed by name. To install a simple 2-axis, 2-button joystick, choose the first value on the list and click OK.

6. Click OK to close the Game Controllers dialog box or continue with the steps below to calibrate your joystick.

Calibrating a Joystick

Before you use your joystick for the first time, you need to calibrate it. Because joysticks are made of mechanical components, there is a slight variation between each one made. To compensate for this, Windows has a procedure that enables you to calibrate the joystick.

FIGURE 9.5
*The Add Game
Controller dialog box
is where you'll actu-
ally add the new
device.*

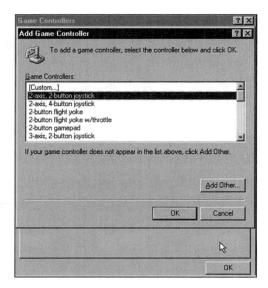

Hmm, what's going on here?   If you're playing your game and you find
your plane drifting to one side or another even with your hand off the control, it's time to recalibrate your joystick.

To calibrate your joystick, follow these steps:

1. Open the Game Controllers dialog box as explained in the previous section.

2. Select the controller you want to calibrate.

3. Click the Properties button to display the Game Controller Properties dialog box
   shown in Figure 9.6.

4. Click the Calibrate button to display the Controller Calibration Wizard shown in
   Figure 9.7.

5. Center the joystick and click one of the buttons on the joystick. This step identifies
   the center location of the joystick.

6. When you click the button on the joystick, the instructions on the wizard will
   change. These new instructions will tell you to move the joystick in a circle to its
   outer limits. This will establish the extreme limits of the joystick. When you've finished this step, click one of the buttons on the joystick to move to the next step.

7. The next set of instructions tells you center the joystick to confirm the center location. Press one of the buttons on the joystick to go to the final step.

8. Click on the Finish button to save your joystick calibration.

FIGURE 9.6

in order to get your joystick ready for action, you'll need to calibrate it using the Game Controller Properties dialog box.

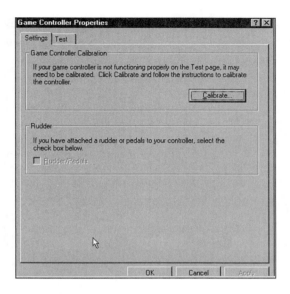

FIGURE 9.7

The Controller Calibration Wizard takes you through the process one step at a time.

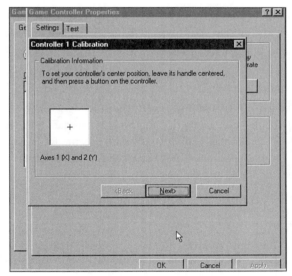

To test your joystick's calibration, follow these instructions:

1. Open the property window for your joystick and click on the Test tab (see Figure 9.8).

FIGURE 9.8

Testing your joystick's calibration is a snap if you consult the joystick's properties dialog box.

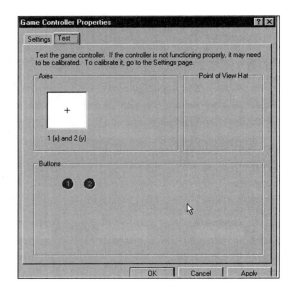

2. Verify that the crosshairs in the Axis box are in the center of the box. If they aren't, you need to calibrate your joystick using the procedure described previously.

3. Move your joystick in a full circle at its extreme limits. The cursor in the Axis box should move around the outer edge of the box. If it doesn't, your joystick needs to be recalibrated.

4. Press the buttons on the joystick. Each of the lights in the Buttons section should light up. If they don't, you might have selected the wrong type of controller. To fix this, close the Properties dialog box and click the Remove button on the Game Controller dialog box to remove this controller. Then follow steps 1 to 3 as described above to add the game controller again with changed controller type.

5. If your controller passed all these tests, it is properly calibrated.

Don't lose control!   It is very important that you calibrate your joystick before using it. When the joystick is in the center, your plane should be flying straight and level. If you don't calibrate your joystick, you might find your plane drifting to the left or right or up or down without your hand on the joystick.

Summary

With all these neat gizmos set up, you should be able to have a blast with just about any game out there. And hopefully, you've been given enough troubleshooting tips to make playing with these toys equally fun.

Next up, printers. I'll explain the various types of printers, how to select the one that's best for you, and how to set a printer up and use it.

Workshop

Now it's time to see just how much you learned in this lesson. I'll give you a short multiple-choice quiz to test what you learned, followed by a suggested activity designed to enhance the skills you acquired during the hour.

Quiz

Select the best answer to the questions from the choices provided, and then check your answers below.

Questions

1. Can you configure a mouse for use by someone who's left-handed?

   a. No; you have to buy a special lefty mouse.

   b. Yes; you taught me how in this lesson.

   c. There are no settings for lefties because there are so few of them in the world.

2. What is a keyboard shortcut?

   a. A set of keystrokes you can press to complete a task you can also perform with a mouse.

   b. You can open a keyboard, rub two wires together, and bypass any computer's security.

   c. There ain't nothin' short about using a keyboard!

3. Which of the following peripherals are best for playing a flight simulation game?

   a. Yoke.

   b. Rudder Pedals.

   c. Flight Stick.

Answers

1. B is correct (my father—a lefty, and proud of it—would shoot me for the third option!).

2. If you answered a, you are correct. As for option b, just call me Bond. Jill Bond...

3. Any or all of these gizmos can enhance your flying experience.

Activity

The next time you find yourself in a computer store, browse through the software and find a game that interests you. (You'll have trouble narrowing it down to one, trust me!)

Next, go over to the peripherals section of the store and test-drive a few of the joy sticks, steering wheels, and other gadgets. Which one feels most comfortable? Which one would work best with the type of game you chose?

Hour 10

Putting It in Writing with a Printer

Because many computers are not sold with printers, it's a purchasing decision you'll most likely need to make on your own. It's also an item you'll need to configure on your own, which means there's a whole lot to learn.

In this lesson, you'll learn everything you need to know in order to choose your printer and get it up and running. But more specifically, you'll learn the answers to the following questions:

- How do I know what kind of printer is best for me?
- Do I need any special software to run a printer?
- What do I have to do in order to tell my computer what kind of printer I have?
- If I share a computer with someone else, is there a way to prioritize print jobs?

Selecting the printer that's best for you is not a simple proposition; a number of factors enter into the equation including the following:

- Sure, we'd all like to have the latest and greatest printer out there, but like it or not, price is often a limiting factor.

- Do you anticipate the majority of your printed output being text for professional looking documents, or is it primarily for family use?

- Are you planning to use multiple printers? For example, I use an old Hewlett-Packard laser printer for work-related documents, while a new Hewlett-Packard color inkjet produces personalized greeting cards made on the PC, photo transfers for making memory quilts and T-shirts, and reasonably good prints of pictures (both photos and kid art) for the grandparents.

- Will you be running multiple copies of most output, or will single copies be the norm?

- How important are a good warranty and/or tech support to you?

After you've got the answers to the above fixed in your mind, you're ready to begin some serious printer shopping. The first narrowing factor is, of course, your printer budget because it's obviously in your best interest to stay within it (you can't spend money you ain't got, right?). But the issue of cost goes far beyond the initial investment. You have to factor in other things like the price of replacement cartridges and whether you need to buy special paper for the printer. (Some lower-end printers might cost less, but you have to buy special inkjet paper for them, which might offset the initial purchase savings in the long run).

> **The brand may make a difference**—Don't assume that all printers using the same technology cost the same to operate. Get to know the cost of supplies for various brands of printers, too. And beware, there are economy cartridges that hold less ink and cost less than their "regular" counterparts. Whatever you do, make sure you're comparing apples to apples.

With the choices narrowed down by total cost of ownership, intended use comes into play. Although it's true that color printer output costs more than monochrome printer output, the price difference might be quickly made up, for example, by creating your own greeting cards instead of shelling out two bucks apiece in the local card shop. If quality printed output is key to a new home business you might have dreams of launching, a laser printer might be well worth the investment. Even if you want to produce spot colored brochures, you can still do so with a laser printer by purchasing special pre-printed paper from an office supply store or mail order specialty paper store. These well-designed papers give you professional quality color output without needing to compromise print quality.

Now that the price and type of printer you need is fixed in your mind, you can focus your attention on the easy part—selecting a brand. Doing this requires you to compare warranties and the availability of technical support between brands. And with the increasing competition among printer manufacturers, purchasing incentives like rebates should also be explored.

Consider also a brand's reliability and length of time manufacturing printers. Hewlett-Packards are pretty hard to beat from a reliability and warranty standpoint, but they might cost more than their Lexmark, Epson, and Canon rivals. Ask your friends what brand they've had good experiences with; consider surfing to newsgroups and Web sites to gather data.

> **Get the latest scoop from the experts**—One place you might want to surf to when considering a new printer is ZDNet at www.zdnet.com. They publish reviews of all kinds of hardware, often pitting one brand against another.

If you've considered all the questions I've posed, your choice should be a whole lot clearer.

Adding a Printer to Your System

With the advent of plug-and-play technology, hooking a printer to your PC is a piece of cake. Of course, because there are potentially two ports (parallel or USB) to which a printer can be connected, you'll want to consult your printer's documentation to discover exactly where you should plug the device. You'll also want to check the printer's box before leaving the store to make sure you have the appropriate printer cable. Few things are worse than getting a new toy home, only to find you can't play with it because you're missing a crucial part!

After the printer is plugged in, you'll need to define the printer within Windows. To do so, simply follow these steps:

1. Click Start on the Windows taskbar, and then choose Settings, Printer.

2. In the Printers window, double-click the Add Printer icon. The Add Printer Wizard shown in Figure 10.1 appears. Click Next to begin working your way through the wizard.

FIGURE 10.1

The Add Printer Wizard is designed to make installing and configuring a printer easier than ever.

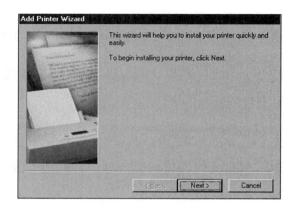

3. Next, you will be prompted to specify whether the printer is a local printer (attached directly to your machine), or a network printer (attached to another machine on your home computer network). Typically, Local Printer will be the appropriate answer. Click Next to continue.

4. Click the name of your printer's manufacturer and model in the respective windows as shown in Figure 10.2. If you don't see your model listed (or you received an installation disk with your printer), click the Have Disk button. If you were able to find your printer, click Next, and then skip ahead to step 6.

FIGURE 10.2

You have literally dozens of manufacturers and models from which to choose.

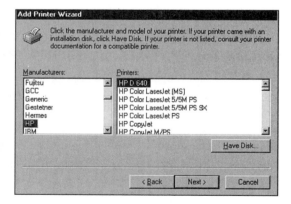

5. If you click the Have Disk button, you'll see a dialog box like the one shown in Figure 10.3. Insert the disk, click your way to the installation files you were provided, and then click OK. Click Next to move on to the next screen in the wizard.

FIGURE 10.3

Select the files you need by clicking the Browse button, and then navigate your way to the files just as you would in Windows Explorer.

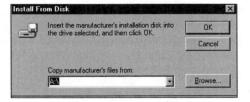

6. You will be presented with a list of available ports on your machine. Windows will more than likely select the right one for you. Click the Next button to continue.

7. The wizard presents the name of the printer model (which you can change to something a bit more friendly), and asks you if you'd like to use this new printer as the default (or always used) printer. Click Yes if this is your first printer, and then click Next.

8. You will then be asked if you'd like to print a test page or not. I suggest you say yes to make sure both the printer and the driver work properly; but make sure the printer's turned on before you wait forever for output! If a page doesn't print properly, contact the tech support people at your printer's manufacturer to see if there are any updated printer drivers for your model and operating system.

9. Click the Finish button to complete and close the Add Printer Wizard.

Setting Printer Properties

Printer properties are basically directions you give the printer to follow each time you print a document unless you tell it otherwise. These properties include paper size and orientation, the number of copies you want each time, the paper tray you want your printer to pull its paper from, and so on.

It just depends... Please note that the appearance of the Printer Properties dialog may vary greatly from the figures you see here. That's because different brands and types of printers can produce radically different dialog boxes since their options and capabilities vary.

To begin setting your Printer Properties, do the following:

1. On the Windows taskbar, click the Start button, and then choose Settings, Printers. The familiar Printers window appears.

2. Click the name of the printer for which you'd like to set properties (typically your default printer), and then click the Properties button near the right end of the Printer window's toolbar. The Printer Properties dialog box shown in Figure 10.4 opens.

FIGURE 10.4

While there are many tabs you can adjust, there's only one you'll want to touch as a beginner.

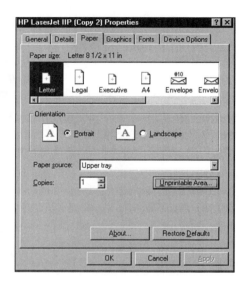

3. The primary tab you'll want to take a look at is the Paper tab shown up in Figure 10.4. In this tab, you'll define the following parameters:

    • Paper size—Use this option to tell your computer what size of paper or envelope you wish to print on.

    • Orientation—Use Portrait for standard "up and down" printing, or Landscape for a panoramic view of your output (great for wide spreadsheets).

    • Paper Source—Since some printers have multiple input trays as well as the ability to hand-feed paper, you'll want to be able to tell the printer where to get its paper.

    • Copies—Use this option to specify how many copies of the document to be printed you want. You'll get a single copy by default.

4. Click OK to save the adjusted settings as your defaults, and close the dialog box. Of course, you can always go back in and change the defaults just as you did here, or you can change them on-the-fly as you submit print jobs.

The Typical Windows Print Dialog Box

Depending on what application you're using, the Print dialog box can vary in appearance. But for the sake of learning, I present the standard Print dialog box. No matter what type of application you use, you'll have similar settings to tweak. This is where the defaults come in handy because they will be translated to the Print dialog box of the application you're using. This can speed up your work dramatically. Take Word 2000 as an example. With the right default options set, all you have to do to print a document is click the Print button on the Standard toolbar. No need to wade through the entire Print dialog box!

To familiarize yourself with printing from within Windows, take a look at the following steps and figures:

1. The best way to learn is to call the Print command from within a standard Windows tool like WordPad. To launch the applet, click the Start button, and then select Accessories, WordPad.

2. Click File, Print to launch the standard Windows Print dialog box shown in Figure 10.5.

10

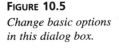

FIGURE 10.5

Change basic options in this dialog box.

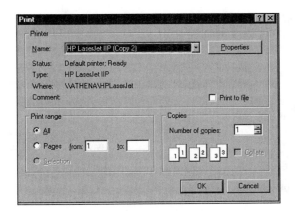

3. Specify which printer to use if you have access to more than one by clicking the corresponding drop-down arrow button, and then clicking the name of the printer you want to use.

4. Next, you'll want to specify which page(s) you want printed by clicking the desired option. Typically, you can choose from any of the options below:

   • All—Prints the entire document when selected.

   • Current Page—Prints the page in which the insertion point is anchored.

While this may seem straightforward, it can get tricky if you've edited a spot, used a wheel mouse to move down the document, and then decided to print. You may then receive a printout of the section you edited, not the one you're viewing. I always click somewhere inside the page I want to print just to be safe.

- Selection—Prints whatever block of the document you have highlighted (or selected).
- Page Range—Here, you can specify which pages you want printed by placing a comma after each number (i.e., 1, 3, 5, etc.), or a page range by using a hyphen, as in 2-5 as an example.

5. Select the number of copies you'd like the job to generate.

6. To make some of the same adjustments you made in the Paper tab shown in Figure 10.4, click the Properties button at the right side of the Print dialog box. Click OK if you changed any of the properties.

> Keep in mind that the options available to you will vary depending on the type of application from which you're printing.

7. In a few moments, the output you selected will roll off the printer.

Canceling or Changing the Order of Your Print Jobs

Let's say you just finished a lengthy report in Word 2000. Just after you send the monster document to the printer, you discover a typo you want to fix. Rather than waste the paper, you can go in and cancel the print job, and then resubmit it when it's fixed.

To cancel a print job, just follow these steps:

1. Click Start, and then point to Settings, Printers. Again, the familiar Printers window appears.

2. Double-click the name of the printer to which the document was sent. You'll see a list of all the documents waiting to be printed. This is known as the print queue.

3. Click the name of the document you want to cancel to select it.

4. Next, click the Document menu, and then choose Cancel Printing. The job will be aborted immediately (though in many cases it will print a little bit of material that may have been stored in its memory buffer).

> **When time is money....** If you've got several items queued to the printer, there might come a time when you need to reprioritize the order in which the items print out. To do this, follow the previous set of steps, only instead of accessing the Document menu, click the document you want to move and drag it to its new position in the print queue.

Now let's say you need to leave home in a hurry and don't want to leave your printer running while you're gone. You can quickly purge everything from your print queue by doing the following:

1. Click the Start button, and then choose Settings, Printers.
2. Double-click the icon of the printer from which you want to purge all documents.
3. In the resulting Print Queue window, click the Print menu, and choose the Purge Print Documents option. The print run will be aborted so you can turn off the printer and leave your home or office safely.

Summary

Between this hour and the brief introduction to printers in Hour 7, "What is a Computer?", you should be armed with everything you need to not only select the best printer for your needs, but to get it set up and generating acceptable output.

Next up, we'll have some fun exploring the multimedia capabilities of your new computer. You'll learn how to play audio CDs, scan a photograph, and much more! It will be one of the most enjoyable lessons in the book; you'll see.

Workshop

Now it's time to see just how much you learned in this lesson. I'll give you a short multiple-choice quiz to test what you learned, followed by a suggested activity designed to enhance the skills you acquired during the hour.

Quiz

Select the best answer to the questions from the choices provided, and then check your answers.

Questions

1. Which printer is the least expensive of the lot?

    a. Laser printer

    b. A generic, unknown brand of color inkjet printer

    c. A Hewlett-Packard color inkjet

2. What is a print queue?

    a. A list of the documents waiting to be printed in the order in which they were sent to the printer.

    b. A line of people standing at the photocopy machine at the office.

    c. A long stick with which you play pool.

3. How do you stop a document from being printed?

    a. Press Ctrl+Alt+Delete.

    b. Enter the print queue, click the document you want to cancel, and then click Document, Cancel Printing.

    c. Turn off the printer.

Answers

1. B is the correct answer. A is the most expensive class of printers, and c is more expensive than b because of HP's name recognition.

2. The best answer is a, at least from the context standpoint.

3. B wins it again! The other two options could have less than desirable results if executed.

Activity

Launch WordPad and type your entire name in a humungous font. Next, access the Print dialog box and tell the printer you want your name printed sideways (or in landscape mode). Send the output to the printer. Did your name come out sideways on the paper? Good; now you'll be ready for the big stuff!

HOUR 11

Getting Sites and Sounds on Your PC

You won't believe the huge number of fun gadgets and gizmos (technically called peripherals) you can attach to your PC! There are scanners that let you turn photographs and original artwork into computer images; there are tools that connect your computer to your camcorder for either still screen captures or video output; there are tiny cameras that mount to your PC, giving you an economical video phone; and there are special digital cameras that virtually eliminate the expense of film and developing.

This hour introduces you to some of these fun toys. You'll learn how they work; how to compare good ones from bad ones; even how to choose the right gadget for you. More specifically, you'll also find out more about the following topics:

- How do I play an audio CD in my personal computer?
- Is there really a Windows tool that lets you record your own voice or sound effects?
- What's the difference between one scanner and another?
- What resolution of digital camera does it take to get 35mm camera quality results?

I love all the ways I can personalize my PC. I can put my son's and daughter's picture on my Windows desktop; I can play my favorite audio CDs in my workspace anytime I want; and I can even scan my son's first math test to email it to his grandparents. It'll amaze you just how many funky things you can do with your PC if you have the right hardware at your disposal!

"The Computers Are Alive, with the Sound of Music..."

PC CD players are a smart lot. Much like super-expensive, high-tech stereo components, you can even program your Windows CD Player to play only the tracks you want; to play the current disk over and over again until you stop it; and to play a CD's chosen tracks at random.

Let's begin with the basics: playing an audio CD. When you insert an audio CD into your computer's CD-ROM drive, the Windows CD Player typically launches on its own. If it doesn't, you can call it into action by clicking the Start button on the Windows taskbar, and then choosing Programs, Accessories, Entertainment, CD Player. You can play the CD by using the buttons on the CD Player panel as shown in Figure 11.1.

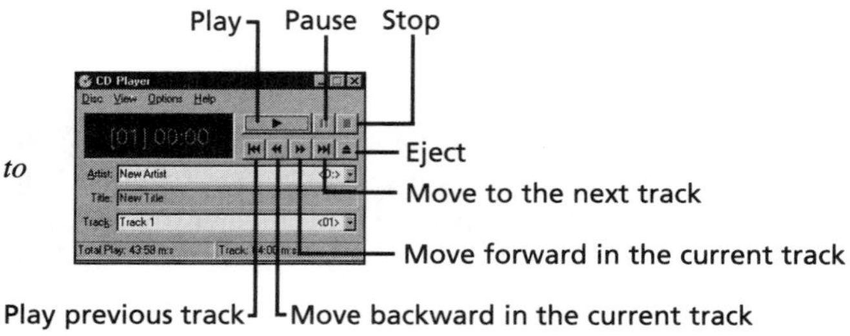

FIGURE 11.1
The Windows CD Player is pretty easy to control.

Setting CD Player Playback Options

By default, the CD Player will play the current disk once through, and then stop. But there are a number of additional playback options available to you as well, all of which can be set with little more than a couple of mouse clicks.

To set them, click the Options menu on the CD Player with the desired CD playing, and click any of the following options to set them. Note that clicking the selected option a second time will remove the checkmark, thus deselecting the chosen option.

- **Random Order**—Instructs the CD Player to play tracks on the selected disk at random. This option is a great way to refresh the predictability of an overplayed CD!

- **Continuous Play**—After the CD Player has played all of the tracks on a given CD, this option tells the player to begin playing the CD all over again. That way when silence strikes, you don't have to jump back to the CD Player to start it again.

- **Intro Play**—Lets you preview the CD's tracks by playing only the first 10 seconds of each song.

Sound Off, Sound On!

I'm lucky; I've got a neato-nifty keyboard with special volume controls across the top. But not all of us are as spoiled; and frankly there are even times when I need to tweak the volume using all of the manual volume control settings.

> **Look twice.** On occasion you might need to adjust the volume on your PC speakers in addition to tweaking the settings on the Volume Control panel. Making changes in both places can not only improve sound quality, but also it can prevent you from beating your head against a wall in frustration, too, when you've worked with the Volume Control and still don't hear anything!

To adjust the volume of your CD Player, double-click the Volume icon in the Windows System Tray to open the Volume Control panel shown in Figure 11.2.

FIGURE 11.2

The Volume Control panel lets you mute some sounds while listening to others.

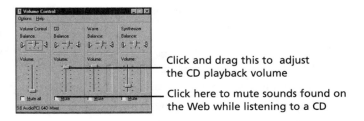

Click and drag this to adjust the CD playback volume

Click here to mute sounds found on the Web while listening to a CD

To turn a specific type of sound up or down, click and drag the respective lever in the desired direction. Or you can shut off a type of sound file completely by clicking its Mute check box. And if you plan on surfing the Web while you're listening to a CD, here's something to consider: Mute every type of sound except for the CD sounds. This prevents you from going into sensory overload as the CD plays, a Web page midi file spews some muzak version of a current hit, and random sound effects all compete for your attention.

Making Your Preferences Known

I'm a self-confessed greatest hits junkie. I oftentimes like only a few songs on any given CD dedicated entirely to a single artist. When possible, I try to buy greatest hits CDs by preferred artists, or those collections you only see advertised on late night TV. One of the things you'll like about the Windows CD Player is you can define all of a CD's track titles, making it a whole lot easier to pick and choose which songs are played on a given CD.

To begin defining and programming in your preferences (or editing the play list as Microsoft calls it) for an audio CD, just follow these steps:

1. With the CD for which you want to define playing, click Disc, Edit Play List on the CD Player's menu bar. A screen like the one shown in Figure 11.3 opens.

FIGURE 11.3

Microsoft makes it easy for you to catalog information for a CD.

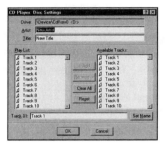

2. Click inside the Artist text box, and then type in the artist's name. Do the same for the title of the CD.

3. Next, click inside the text box near the bottom of the screen that says Track 1, and enter the name of the track.

4. When you're done, click the Set Name button. The text box you just edited will move to the next track, enabling you to enter its information.

5. Keep repeating steps 3 and 4 until all the CD's tracks have been defined.

6. Now it's time to specify which tracks you want to appear in the play list. By default, all the tracks will be played. If you only want to include two or three tracks on your play list, click the Clear All button. This removes all of the tracks, giving you the opportunity to add only the ones you want. If you want the majority of the tracks, leave the play list as is and remove the few you don't want. Your current play list appears in the left pane, while the names of the tracks available to you appear in the right.

7. To add a song to the play list, click its name in the Available Tracks window, and then click the Add button. The selected track will then appear in both windows.

8. To remove a track from the play list, click its name in the Play List pane, and then click the Remove button.

> **Giving in to song obsession.** Have you ever had a song that you just can't seem to get enough of? Well, with the CD Player, you can actually add it to the play list as many times as you want while dotting the list with other tracks of interest.

9. When you're done setting everything up, click OK. The CD Player will then "remember" your defined play list every time you play the respective CD. But redefining that playlist is as simple as clicking the Reset button, and starting all over again.

For the Record...

With a microphone and Windows 98, Second Edition, you can record the voices of friends and family for use in email and on Web pages. The quality isn't professional caliber, but hey, it doesn't cost much, so who can complain?

To begin working with the Windows Sound Recorder, click the Start button on the Windows taskbar, and then select Programs, Accessories, Entertainment, Sound Recorder. The Sound Recorder window shown in Figure 11.4 appears.

FIGURE 11.4

This recorder is even easier to use than the cassette recorders of yesteryear.

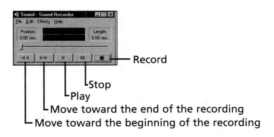

Next, verify that your microphone is properly connected to the back of your PC. If it is, you should be able to click the Record button and begin recording instantly. No more hitting Play *and* Record to set the recorder in motion! Use the other buttons just as you would those on any tape recorder you've used in the past.

To save your recording, click File, Save on the Sound Recorder menu bar, and then give the file a meaningful name and click Save. You'll then be able to access the file from any software application that enables you to insert or embed .wav files.

So big!   Although you can only record 60 seconds worth of audio, you should know that the files are humungous! It'll take what seems like an eternity to mail them, open them, or download them onto a Web page, so use them sparingly.

Selecting a Scanner That Meets Your Needs (and Budget)

Like computers, scanners come in all shapes, sizes, and price points. Choosing the right one for you involves a lot more thought than simply choosing a brand within your budget. Sure, you can get scanners in the under-hundred dollar range, but they might not be capable of doing what you want them to with the level of quality you desire. As is the case with many things, you get what you pay for.

In the following sections, I'll show you just what kinds of things you can do with a scanner. Although the topic might sound like fluff, it's actually critical information when it comes to selecting the best scanner for you. I'll also show you how a scanner works, and give you the scoop on which features are worth paying extra for, as well as which ones might be over-hyped.

What Scanners Can Do for You

Scanners are one of those peripherals that are equally useful for work and play. For work, you can rely on a scanner to convert a paper document into a word processing document; produce high quality images for a corporate Web page; or even scan the merchandise you sell at online auctions. For pleasure, however, you could scan old photographs to preserve them forever (and maybe even touch them up a bit); you could put your children's pictures on special transfer media from which you could produce personalized T-shirts and memory quilt fabric; and you could put current photographs on special themed CDs for long-term storage or sharing.

Whether your needs are professional or entirely for pleasure, it's easy to see how a scanner could come in very handy!

So How Do Scanners Do What They Do?

For people like me who aren't terribly science-savvy, scanners seem to work like magic. In reality, they work by moving a row of silicon cells from the top to the bottom of the scanner's bed. These cells basically bounce light off of and through the object on the scanner bed. The results are then translated into color waves that eventually become the photo-realistic image you see onscreen.

Okay, Which Scanner Is Right for Me?

Because the scanning needs of the average user are fairly basic, I'm going to oversimplify the decision-making process a bit. There are tons of technical details that really only come into play when you're attempting to get super-professional results.

Way back in the fall of 1997, I bought a hundred-dollar scanner, which was incredibly cheap at the time. I have to say that the results have always been more than acceptable for my needs. The same holds true today; why pay hundreds of dollars for a scanner when one for well under a hundred dollars does the trick? If you eventually become a professional graphic artist or Web page designer, then go out and pay the big bucks. But for now, your money would be better spent on a less expensive scanner. That way you can afford to pick up some good photo editing software if you don't receive any with the scanner.

But if you have the money and hope to enlarge and print out photos on your color inkjet printer, here are some things to look for. When it comes to scanner shopping, there are fewer features to consider and compare than you might think. The first one you'll want to take a look at is the number of levels of color a scanner can replicate. Expressed in bits, the general rule of thumb is the bigger the better. In other words, the more bits a scanner operates at, the more authentic the colorization and details of the image. However as you might also expect, there are always exceptions to this rule. Some manufacturers soup up their scanners to deliver better performance than their peers with the same specifications. In any case, the minimum quality you should consider is 24 bits.

Another spec you should factor in is the scanner's optical resolution. Although 600 dpi is best for reproducing fine art, line drawings, and super-detailed photos, 300 dpi is sufficient for the needs of many.

You'll also see mention of parallel and USB scanners. This is where you'll want to have plenty of specs about your computer and software ready. Parallel scanners can work with just about any current PC no matter what version of Windows you're running. Some parallel scanners will even let you pass through to your printer, but you'd better make sure the printer you have will be happy with the scanner you're considering, or neither may work properly.

USB scanners are much faster than parallel scanners, but they require Windows 98 and a special USB port on your machine. Check your system specs carefully before making any final decision, or at least make sure you can exchange the scanner if there's a problem.

I could throw in a ton more technobabble about how a scanner works as well as how the various features can be interpreted, but unless you're doing high quality scanning for a living, just about any scanner will do. Who needs to waste the pages on unnecessary details, right?

11

Introducing the World of Digital Cameras

Do you have dozens of roles of exposed film lying around just waiting to be developed? Are you tired of spending $15 for film and developing of 24 exposures, only to find three or four of them acceptable and even fewer actually good? Have you ever wished you could keep only the good pictures while throwing out the bad? Now you can, thanks to digital cameras!

Choosing a Digital Camera

Unfortunately, choosing a digital camera is a bit more complicated than selecting a scanner. When it comes to selecting a good one, there are tons of things to consider; and in this case, the average user *will* be able to see the difference.

The price of digital cameras varies widely from $50 (for low-resolution kid models) on up to several thousands of dollars for professional models. Let me help you decide which features are worth paying for, and which ones might not be as valuable as the advertising claims.

In the following sections, I examine all the major considerations and advise you on parameters you should look for in making your decision.

Price Does Count

As much as we might wish otherwise, price is still a dominating factor for most of us. Although you can get inexpensive digital cameras (the $50 "toy" variety), be leery of getting pulled in by them. They're a great (not to mention economical) way to teach children basic photography skills, but you can't rely on them for photo-realistic output in all lighting conditions.

Expect to pay $300 or more for a digital camera that truly rivals 35mm quality. Although that might seem like a lot of money, just think of how much you'll save over time on film and film processing! And then there are the intangible benefits of a good digital camera—you can take pictures whenever you want without having to worry about cost or the huge amount of lag time it might take to get the photos developed. Think about it; how many times have you shot up the end of a roll of film on useless stuff just to get to the prized pictures you shot somewhere in the middle of the roll?

Higher Resolution: An Investment Worth Making

No matter what, don't settle for a camera with anything less than 640×480 resolution. Even then, don't expect crystal-clear results.

When you scan an image (or in this case, shoot a digital picture), the result needs to be enlarged in order for it to be of any real use. If it weren't enlarged, you'd have a tiny image about the size of a postage stamp. The downside to this, however, is that when you make a low-resolution image bigger, it can become grainy (or pixelated in nerd-speak). That means the resulting image will not be sharp to the eye.

Given that, take a look at Table 11.1 to see a list of image resolutions and their corresponding results.

TABLE 11.1   Camera Resolutions and Image Production Results

Image Resolution	Product
640×480	Produces a 3×5 printout at best.
Megapixel (1024×768)	Produces an acceptable 5×7 photo-quality image.
1280×1024 (1.3 megapixels)	Produces prints up to 8×10 in size.
1.6 megapixels and up	The higher the resolution, the greater the image detail, and the larger the high quality image you can produce.

Also keep in mind that even if you don't anticipate generating large images, the higher resolution might also enhance the quality of smaller images as well.

CMOS Versus CCD

I won't get too technical on you here, but this is a specification worth knowing a little bit about. CMOS and CCD describe the types of light sensors in the digital camera. Although CMOS sensors generally cost less and have a longer battery life than their CCD counterparts, CCD cameras are more responsive to various lighting conditions. Thus it's possible that a higher resolution CMOS camera might actually generate inferior results when compared to a slightly lower resolution CCD camera. Just some things to keep in mind…

Considerations for Printed Output as Opposed to Online Output

If you plan to use a digitized image on a Web page, you can generally get by with a lower resolution; however, if you're hoping to print your own photographs from digital camera output, you'll want to go with the highest digital camera resolution you can afford, and the best color printer you can get your hands on.

You may not get what you pay for…   Where printers are concerned, paying more doesn't necessarily give you better print quality. Many times the higher price tag can be attributed to increased printing speed or commercial rated durability.

11

Give Me Light!

Digital cameras in any price range will shoot reasonably good pictures in sunlight, but if you hope to make use of the camera inside as well, having flash is a must. Some fancier models even have red-eye reduction, which is a plus when photographing people.

The good news is that although you won't find flash capabilities on the least expensive models, it's becoming more and more standard on other consumer models.

Putting Things Into Focus

Focus features are similar to those found on traditional 35mm cameras—fixed focus (where one size fits all so to speak), auto-focus (where you can focus on a specific object or person although the rest becomes somewhat fuzzy), and manual focus (with f-stops and all the other settings you can tweak on professional 35mm cameras).

In general, the low-end digital cameras use fixed focus because it's the most reasonably priced option. Auto-focus is saved for mid-priced cameras because it offers some artistic freedom without the headaches of knowing about f-stops and such. For the professional photographers among us, you might want to invest in a $1,000-plus camera that gives you the freedom and quality you've grown so used to.

As always, these general rules of thumb are subject to exceptions and change. As more technical features become less expensive to incorporate, you'll start seeing them on lower priced models because all the manufacturers will be competing heavily for your business.

More Power to You!

Digital cameras can eat batteries almost as quickly as I can put away a plate of fresh, hot, and gooey chocolate chip cookies, especially those cameras with LCD displays and flash capabilities.

Although lithium batteries provide the longest life, they can often be so pricey that they offset any savings you might see by switching from a standard camera to a digital camera. I've read that Rayovac's rechargeable alkaline batteries typically last longer than NiCads and will actually save you money in the long run. But your mileage might vary. And to complicate matters further, prices of batteries and other power sources are constantly fluctuating so what might be true as I write this, might not necessarily be true as you read this.

Finally, if you're frequently taking pictures indoors and have access to an electrical outlet, it might be worth it for you to buy the manufacturer's optional A/C adapter.

> **To extend your battery life even further...**   Use the A/C adapter when downloading images to your PC. That way you can shoot the photos unteathered (or without being tied down by the device's power cord and the nearest electrical outlet), and not burn up batteries while performing what could be considered maintenance tasks.

Zooming In on the Subject

Fixed focus cameras might do just fine for shooting scenery or group pictures of your son's swim team, but you'll be much happier with a model that gives you at least a 2x zoom. That way you can tighten the shot to capture a special moment or a silly smile.

But when it comes to zoom lenses, read the fine print. You'll want to be sure you're getting optical zoom instead of digital zoom. The optical zoom resets the resolution of the image you zoom in on to the highest level possible, while digital zoom merely crops the image without considering the resolution. This makes digitally zoomed images appear grainier than their optical counterparts.

Even if you don't read the fine print, the price and zoom factor should be a dead giveaway. Cameras touting noticeably higher zoom factors than the norm are most likely employing digital zooms. Likewise, if the price is obviously lower than the competition for an equivalent camera, that might again be a clue that you're looking at digital rather than optical technology.

11

Getting Connected

At the time of this writing, there are two primary ways a digital camera can be connected to your PC for image download. The oldest (thus the slowest) way is by plugging the digital camera into your computer's serial port. This former standard is quickly being replaced by USB, a method which transfers data tens of times faster than a serial port.

> **Get fired up!**   As you begin researching digital camera specifications, you might see references to FireWire support. Macintosh heavily supports this high-speed connection, but it hasn't really caught on in the world of IBM compatibles. Intel is hard at work developing an even faster successor to USB, known as USB 2.0. You should see more of this in the next couple of years.

But before you buy a digital camera, check your PC's documentation to make sure it can even support USB. While many do, there are still some budget models that might not. As they say, "Better safe than sorry!"

Buying Your Virtual Film

Like traditional cameras need film to store images, digital cameras need smart cards, floppy disks, or other specialized media. The average camera comes with 4 to 8 megabytes of storage, but believe it or not, you can purchase media that will hold as much as 90+ megabytes before you need to dump it onto your computer.

> **On the road again...**   If you plan to take the camera on your family vacation to Disney World, I strongly suggest that you take a laptop computer with you if you have one. This enables you to start each day with clean storage media, and it radically reduces the odds of inadvertently erasing cherished memories. But not all of us have that luxury at our disposal. If this describes you, investing in a high-capacity storage device for your camera should be a priority.

Some storage media can fit right into your computer's floppy drive with a special adapter, while others, like Sony's Mavica, store images on a standard PC floppy disk making it a breeze to use. Although the Mavica has won over tons of fans with it's standardized storage media, it should also be noted that you might fit as few as five high-resolution images on a single floppy. That might be a real pain, especially when all your spare floppies fly out of your pockets while you're on that Disney roller coaster upside down!

Have it All!

The majority of cameras (except for the extreme low end models) come with an LCD display that lets you see what you're getting as you take a picture—a great way to kill those shots that aren't just right on the spot.

Unfortunately, these tiny displays are huge battery hogs. Make sure you get a camera with an optical viewfinder as well and an LCD display, that way you can save your batteries for what really counts—more pictures!

Some argue that LCD displays give you more authentic "what-you-see-is-what-you-get" results when it comes to composing a picture, but although that might be true, remember that we're dealing with computerized images here. With a photo editing program, you can get exactly what you want no matter what actually ended up inside the camera.

You Oughta Be in Pictures!

Although you can email your images to family and friends, post them on a Web site, or print them out on your color printer, how do you share images with non-computer users?

Some digital cameras come with a TV-out outlet that lets you connect the camera to any TV from which you can either give your slide show manually, or program the camera to cycle through the images one-by-one. Of course this implies that the images are still on your camera's storage media which might not be practical.

Speak to Me!

Believe it or not, many digital cameras give you the opportunity to record 30 second sound bytes to go along with each picture. Although this is a wonderful way to preserve that special Mother's Day program your son performed in, or that speech your daughter gave at a school awards ceremony, it does soak up precious space on your storage media. Only you can decide if the sound is important to you or not. However, just because your camera supports sound doesn't mean you have to use it; it can be turned off and on, giving you the opportunity to take advantage of the feature on demand.

Still or Video?

You can also get digital camcorders from which you can create movies and still shots using the software provided. With digital camcorders, the storage media is the tape on which you record the video, so there's no pricey storage media to purchase.

But should you decide to go with a digital camcorder, expect to pay between $800 and $1,000. And if you plan to travel a lot, you'll want to factor in the camcorder's bulkier shell which could be a real pain to lug around.

11

Summary

Wow, who would've thought a PC could do so much with sound and images! Not only did you learn how to play music and record sounds on your new computer, but you were introduced to the technologies of scanners and digital cameras in plain English as well. You should now have enough information to fill your PC with all kinds of fun sights and sounds!

I continue the sights and sounds theme in the next lesson as I take you on a journey through the land of DVDs and TV tuner cards.

Workshop

Now it's time to see just how much you learned in this lesson. I'll give you a short multiple-choice quiz to test what you learned, followed by a suggested activity designed to enhance the skills you acquired during the hour.

Quiz

Select the best answer to the questions from the choices provided, and then check your answers.

Questions

1. What information about an audio CD does the Windows CD Player let you track?

    a. Date the CD was published.

    b. Lyrics for all of the songs on the CD.

    c. Songs included on the CD.

2. What type of scanner is most common?

    a. Flat head.

    b. Compressed bed.

    c. Flat bed.

3. What is a megapixel?

    a. An image resolution of 1024×768.

    b. A fat pixel.

    c. You must be confused; there are only gigapixels!

Answers

1. C; the other non-essential items are not yet included as fields in the CD Players records.

2. I tried to trick you, but I'm sure I didn't succeed. Again, C is the correct answer.

3. A wins; I'd be shocked if you guessed anything else.

Activity

Dig through your CD collection to find your favorite album. After you have it, put it in your computer's CD-ROM drive. Next, fill out the CD information and edit the play list for the CD, including only the tracks you like. Okay, click the Play button and sit back and relax!

What? You don't have an audio CD? Have you been living in the dark ages, or what? Just kidding…. Seriously, now might be a good time to consider purchasing a PC-warming present for yourself. Go ahead, you deserve it for as hard as you've been trying to learn all this stuff! So what's your pleasure? Don Henley? Hall and Oates? John Tesh? ZZ Top? The Boston Pops?

Hour 12

Keeping Your System Healthy Using Windows Tools

Have you ever wished you could catch the season opener of ER while processing your email? Would you like to watch Monday Night Football and browse the Web for player stats at the same time? Or what if you have a report to write, but can't tear yourself away from Star Trek Voyager? Thanks to the availability of such peripherals as DVD drives and TV tuner cards, you can watch while you work (or play).

In this lesson, I'll introduce you to the DVD technology. You'll also find out more about the following topics:

- How do DVD drives work with traditional audio and software CD's?
- Are there many videos out on DVD?
- What do I need to run WebTV for Windows?
- How does my computer learn about the programs offered in my area?

I remember the day DVD came out like it was only yesterday. Popular electronics stores carried only a couple of models of DVD players, and you could count the number of videos available in this format on both hands.

Now it looks as though DVD is here to stay. You can find DVD players in a variety of price ranges, and video discs can be found by the pallet at those wholesale clubs/membership warehouses.

So What Is DVD Anyway?

DVD (or Digital Video Discs) describes the next generation of optical disc storage. Not only can DVDs hold more data and run faster than other optical storage devices, but they can also hold video, sound, and computer data as well. Furthermore, DVD broadcasts at twice the resolution of VHS videos and Dolby sound. Some of the technology's biggest supporters believe DVD might eventually replace audio CDs, video tapes, laserdiscs, CD-ROMS, and perhaps even game cartridges. In fact, the technology has gained the support of major electronics companies, computer software companies, and about half of the movie and music studios. Yep, it looks like DVD is here to stay whether we like it or not!

But there's another subtlety you should understand; that is the difference between DVD and DVD-ROM. DVD refers to the DVD video players you connect to a TV. These players play nothing other than DVD video discs. DVD-ROMs, on the other hand, can be found in newly manufactured computers. DVD-ROMs can read not only DVD video discs, but they can ready audio discs and data CDs as well.

Even if your machine didn't come with a DVD-ROM, you can always upgrade down the road by either swapping the DVD-ROM for the current CD-ROM, or adding the DVD-ROM to your machine as an additional drive.

So You Want DVD but Don't Already Have it?

There are plenty of things you can do to maximize the value of the DVD-ROM you choose. Here are some important considerations:

- **Your current processor speed.** If the computer you wish to upgrade has anything slower than a 133MHz Pentium processor, DVD performance might suffer.
- **The availability of titles you want to view.** Although there aren't many computer software titles that take full advantage of DVD technology yet, remember that a DVD-ROM can play DVD movies as well as any audio CD. And if you're not convinced that there are many DVD videos out yet either, surf over to www.dvdvideogroup.com and take a look around; that should change your mind in a hurry!
- **Durability.** Do you have children who watch the same movie over and over? I know my kids are like that, often wearing out a poor VHS tape within weeks. At least DVDs are more durable, and they don't disintegrate over time like videotapes do.

- **The best in DVD.** To get the most out of DVD video, try to get a set up that includes a hardware decoder board. This essentially maximizes DVD performance while minimizing the strain on your computer's processor. Obviously, it's more technical than that, but that gives you more than enough information to make the best purchasing decision.

> **Don't try this at home!**   If you're new to computing (which you most likely are because you're reading this book), I strongly urge you *not* to try installing a DVD-ROM setup on your own. PC components can be fragile, and the insides of your machine can be confusing at best, and even dangerous if you don't know exactly what you're doing. If you must install such a setup, either do it at the time you purchase your machine, pay to have it done by a professional, or, even better, find a buddy who knows computers to do it in return for beer and a pizza.

- **The speed of DVD.** Get a 4.8x DVD-ROM or faster for optimum performance. Of course, anything slower might not even be available at the time you read this. Technology sure changes quickly.

- **Hardware versus software decoding.** If your computer is slower than a 300MHz Pentium II, it's a good idea to invest the extra money into a hardware decoding board. Faster processors, however, might be able to handle the demands.

- **The rest of the setup.** To get the most pleasure out of DVD videos, you might want a 17" monitor or larger, good multimedia speakers complete with subwoofers, and a high quality sound card. Sure, you can get by with less than this, but this is the optimum setup for DVD video enjoyment.

12

Playing DVDs on Your Computer

When it comes to showing you how to play DVD discs on your computer, there's good news and bad news. Let's get the bad news out of the way first. Given the different software that comes with each DVD-ROM, I can't give you exact step-by-step instructions for playing your favorite videos. I can, however, promise you it won't be at all hard.

After the DVD-ROM and its accompanying software are installed, you'll need to insert the disc you want to view in the DVD-ROM drive. This should automatically fire up the software that came with your chosen DVD system.

Here's where the good news comes in. No matter what the software looks like exactly, you can expect to see at least some of the common Windows application tools with which you've grown accustomed to working. First off, clear, onscreen prompts will guide you through any necessary setup options. After you get into the main player screen, you should see well-known elements like program menus, or Sound Recorder-like buttons that enable you to move through the videos with ease.

Getting to Know WebTV for Windows

Not to be confused with the WebTV set-top boxes that enable you to surf the Net without a computer, or engage in interactive TV, WebTV for Windows gives you powerful television watching capabilities from your PC. All you need is a TV tuner card (like the ATI All-in-Wonder, the Voodoo 3500, WinTV, and so on), a cable connection near your computer, and a good sound system.

The ATI All-in-Wonder was the first TV tuner card supported by WebTV for Windows; therefore the Microsoft developers have presumably had enough time to work out any kinks in software versus TV tuner card compatibility. Support for additional tuners came with Windows 98, Second Edition.

Readying Your System for WebTV for Windows

The first thing you'll need to do is make sure you have a TV tuner card installed in your PC. You can verify this by clicking the Start button on the Windows taskbar, and then selecting Settings, Control Panel. Double-click the Multimedia icon to open the Multimedia window. Here, you can click the relevant plus sign to see whether such a device is installed, and if so, what model it is as well as who manufactured it.

If you didn't purchase one with your machine, you might need to go out and buy one. But again, I urge you to get an experienced computer person to install it for you. I highly recommend the ATI All-in-Wonder cards. Not only will they enhance the graphics performance of your computer games, but the high-end models act as TV tuner cards, virtual VCRs, and movie makers as well. And as I mentioned before, the ATI All-in-Wonder cards were the first to be supported by WebTV for Windows.

Get what you really want (or need).   The high-end ATI All-in-Wonder cards can get up there in price, mostly because of the added features. Some argue that these integrated solutions are a waste because they duplicate the efforts of the graphics card already in your computer. It's important to remember, however, that you get what you pay for, and because many computers come with less-than top-notch video cards, it might be money well-spent. If you don't have many graphics demands and aren't wanting fun features like a virtual VCR or the ability to make family movies that you can email or put on the Web, a separate TV tuner care for well under half the price might more than do the trick.

To install the TV tuner card, make sure you have the instructions that came with the card you purchased; the person who installs it for you will need them because various devices connect to your PC in different ways.

Installing WebTV for Windows

From the Start menu, choose Programs, Accessories, Entertainment, WebTV for Windows (you might also see a WebTV for Windows icon in the Windows Quick Launch bar which you can click to start the application). If you don't see WebTV for Windows on the list, you'll need to grab your Windows disk and install it from there.

The WebTV for Windows wizard guides you step-by-step through setting up the device you have installed on your machine. The steps might vary depending on the TV tuner you have installed. At one point, you'll be asked to visit the Web site that hosts the program guide data. You'll click on its icon, insert your ZIP code, and then close the Internet Explorer window launched for the task.

Getting WebTV for Windows Ready for Action

The first order of business is to download a fresh set of television programs available in your area. To begin doing this, establish a connection to the Internet, launch WebTV for Windows as described previously, and then follow these steps:

1. Click inside the TV Configuration channel listing to select it. In most cases, it's channel 96 TVC, which can be found by scrolling to number 96 (see Figure 12.1).

2. Double-click the TV Configuration channel listing you selected to launch the WebTV for Windows Welcome screen shown in Figure 12.2.

3. Next, click the Go To... button, and then select Get TV Listings. This takes you to a screen that describes how TV listings are obtained. Click the G-Guide link to be taken to the WebTV for Windows Web site via Internet Explorer.

4. A gray Get TV Listings button like the one shown in Figure 12.3 should appear. Click it to start downloading two days' worth of program data.

5. The Web site will take several seconds to download all of the program data. This download is followed by a minute-long set up. When you are told the download is complete, simply close Internet Explorer to return to the Program Guide in WebTV for Windows.

6. Use the scrollbars to move through the listings in search of a program you'd like to see.

12

Scroll up

FIGURE **12.1**

The WebTV for Windows Program Guide Window gives you ample ways to navigate the program listings.

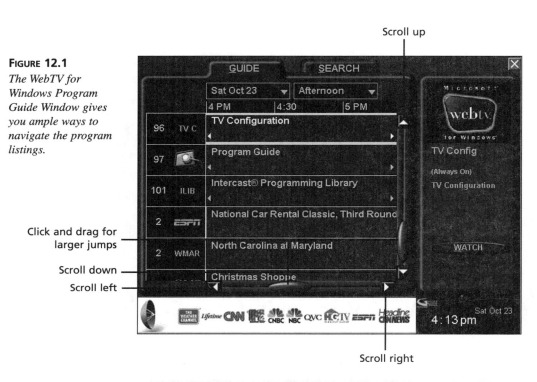

Click and drag for larger jumps

Scroll down

Scroll left

Scroll right

FIGURE **12.2**

The Go To... button is your key to many of the application's routine functions.

Welcome

With Microsoft® WebTV® for Windows® and a TV tuner card, you will be able to watch interactive TV on your computer.

Even without a TV tuner card, you can still see free G-GUIDE' TV listings in the Program Guide.

To get local TV listings, click **Next**.

Go to...

Welcome
Get TV Listings
Program Guide Tour
Configuration Complete

Close   Next   Go To...

FIGURE 12.3

The Gemstar generated Web site already knows your location, so fetching fresh listings takes little more than a mouse click.

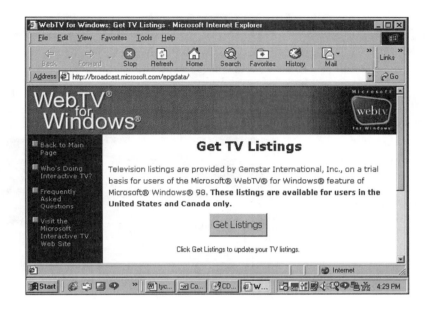

Watching a Program

After you've found a show you want to watch, click the Watch It button.

If you'd like to find additional times at which the selected program is on air, simply click the Other Times button. A Search window displays the results (see Figure 12.4).

FIGURE 12.4

The Search window lists the channel number, network, time, and day the selected program is broadcast.

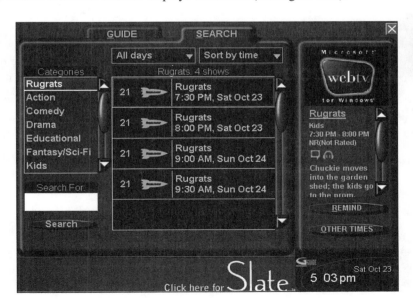

12

Setting Reminders for Favorite Shows

From the Search screen, you can set Reminders so you won't miss the programs you want to see. To do so, follow these steps:

1. Click the Remind button near the bottom right of the screen. The Remind dialog box shown in Figure 12.5 opens.

FIGURE 12.5

By default, no reminder will be set for a program unless you specifically tell WebTV for Windows to remind you.

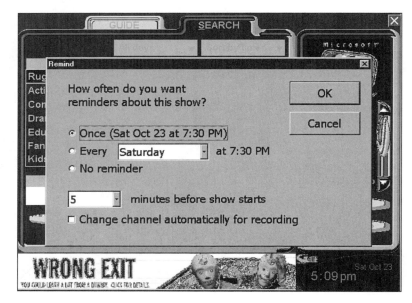

2. Your first decision regarding the reminder is how often you want to be reminded of the selected show—just once, every week or day at the same time (using the drop-down arrow button), or not at all. Just click the radio button for the desired choice.

3. If you requested a Reminder, click the minutes before show starts drop-down arrow button to make a selection anywhere between one minute to a half hour before the program begins.

4. If you have a VCR connected to your computer (or have an ATI All-in-Wonder card that can turn your PC and hard disk into a VCR), you can tell the computer to change to the appropriate channel before starting to record by clicking the Change Channel Automatically for Recording button at the bottom of the dialog box.

5. Click OK to save the Reminder, and close the dialog box.

> **Are you sleeping, are you sleeping...**   If your computer is suspended (or asleep), the computer will not wake up to deliver the reminders.

When the appropriate time comes, a Reminder like the one shown in Figure 12.6 appears. Simply click OK to close the dialog box and tune in.

FIGURE 12.6
Click the channel number and name to move right to the program's channel.

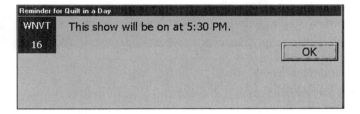

Reminder for Quilt in a Day

WNVT   16   This show will be on at 5:30 PM.

OK

Adding Channels to Your Favorites List

If you have certain channels you watch a lot like your daily soap operas on CBS, or Monday Night Football on NBS, then it might make sense to add these channels to your list of Favorites.

While viewing the Program Guide, press the Alt key to launch the TV Bar shown in Figure 12.7. Use the arrow buttons to display the name of the channel you want to add to your Favorites. After the channel is in view, click the Add button. An icon for the selected channel appears on the TV Bar next to the other buttons.

To remove a channel from this list (say, after the football season ends), launch the TV Bar by pressing the Alt key, click the button representing the channel you want to remove, and then click the Remove button. It's as simple as that!

12

FIGURE 12.7
Nice, big buttons make finding your most-watched channels in a hurry a snap.

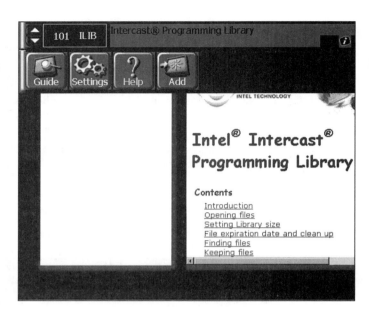

Summary

This lesson only begins to scratch the surface of working with DVD-ROMS and WebTV for Windows, but it gives you more than enough to get you started and to whet your appetite for learning more about your PC. You learned how DVD is different from other "normal" CDs, and you discovered how you can literally watch TV while you work.

Now that you're a hardware expert, it's time to take an in-depth look at some software that can make your life a whole lot easier. We'll start with a general software primer, then work our way to more specific applications like Microsoft Word 2000 and Microsoft Excel 2000.

Workshop

Now it's time to see just how much you learned in this lesson. I'll give you a short multiple-choice quiz to test what you learned, followed by a suggested activity designed to enhance the skills you acquired during the hour.

Quiz

Select the best answer to the questions from the choices provided, and then check your answers.

Questions

1. What does DVD stand for?

    a. Dumb video decoder

    b. Digital video device

    c. Domestic video device

2. Which of the following disk types can be played in a DVD-ROM?

    a. Computer software (CD-ROM)

    b. Music CDs

    c. DVD videos

3. What would be a good device to use to take full advantage of WebTV for Windows?

    a. A tape backup unit

    b. A humungous hard disk

    c. An ATI All-in-Wonder card

Answers

1. B is the answer I was looking for; the other choices were simply meant to trick.

2. All three can be read on a DVD-ROM drive.

3. If you said C, you're right on the money! I know I love my ATI All-in-Wonder!

Activity

The next time you go through a store that carries videotapes, browse through the DVD section. Do you see any discs you'd like to watch? Are there any movies you were surprised to find on DVD? Did you notice some movies are even released on DVD before they're available on videotape?

This little exercise should help you discover whether you could really gain anything by upgrading to DVD if you don't already have it.

12

PART III
Software

Hour

HOUR 13

The Software Primer

Software…the word itself sounds so mundane, yet the very opposite couldn't be farther from the truth. Much like Windows 98, Second Edition acts as the brain for your computer, the other types of software on your PC form what could almost be considered its personality.

Okay, so maybe that sounds a little weird, but think about it for a second. A computer loaded with scads of productivity software suggests someone who gets down to business and stays on task uses the machine. At the other extreme is the system with a screaming video card, sound system complete with subwoofer, nice big monitor, and a sizeable hard drive chock full of the latest and greatest games. If that computer doesn't belong to a kid, it most certainly belongs to a kid at heart!

In this lesson, I'll introduce you to the various types of software. You'll also read more about the following topics:

- What is "edutainment" software anyway?
- How do I get the various types of software?
- Should I register my software?
- When is it time to upgrade my software?

We've already taken an in-depth look at your computer's operating system; now let's shift our focus to other kinds of software you might find tucked away on your machine. I'll also give you some names of popular programs that fit into each category not so much as an endorsement of their quality, but as a way of helping you further distinguish the various types of software from one another.

Software Defined

To perform a certain type of task using your computer—for instance, typing a letter— you need an application or program for that task. When you purchase a new PC, you might receive some applications as part of the purchase. In fact, many of the most reasonably priced systems today are shipped with some flavor of Microsoft Office 2000 (or at the very least, Microsoft Word 2000 which I'll show you in the next couple of lessons.) Likewise, Windows 98, Second Edition is hands-down the operating system of choice for computers sold worldwide. As you saw in the first section of this book, it also includes some mini-applications, for instance a paint program, a calculator, an audio CD player, and the ever-popular solitaire card game among others.

The applications preinstalled on your computer should be more than enough to get you started. In fact, I strongly suggest you hold off buying any new software for your computer until you've spent significant time at the keyboard. (The one exception is, of course, if the only software loaded on your PC is Windows 98, Second Edition. You'll need more than that to get a feel for life at the computer!)

So why wait? Because as time passes, you'll form your own preferences for the types of software you want to use. Software can get expensive, which is why I encourage spending time with an application before you sink loads of money into it. As you'll see later in the hour (and in Hour 24, "Downloading Treasures from the Internet,") demos are a great way to "try before you buy" because they're typically free and give you the opportunity to experience how something works ahead of time.

Can't I just borrow my buddy's disks to try a program out? It might seem simpler to borrow a friend's disks rather than wait for a lengthy download over the Internet, but as long as your buddy has registered the software and is still using it on his computer, doing so is breaking the law. The practice of installing single-licensed software (of which the majority of consumer applications are) on multiple computers at once is referred to as software piracy. It's really no different than stealing a piece of jewelry from your local department store. The same copyright laws that protect books, music, and other works are applicable to software as well.

After you get comfortable using your new system, you'll want to purchase additional applications. Software generally falls into one of the categories described in the following sections.

 What's In a Word? You will hear the terms program, application, or some combination (application program) used interchangeably. They all mean the same thing.

Word Processors

The most common type of application is word processing software. You can use this type of program to create documents such as letters, memos, reports, manuscripts, and so on. If there is something you would have once done on a typewriter, you can now use a word processing program for the task. (Well, maybe not *everything*. Using word processing programs to fill out forms can be a real pain in the neck.)

Word processing programs are much more than just a fancy typewriter, though. They offer many editing and formatting features so that you have a great deal of control over the content and look of your document. Here's a quick list of some of the things you can do with this type of program:

- **Easily edit text.** You can move text from one page to another, even one document to another. You can also copy or delete text with just a few keystrokes or mouse clicks.

- **Format text.** Formatting means changing the appearance of text. You can make text bold, change the font, use a different color, and so on. In Hour 13, "The Software Primer," you'll learn how to make some formatting changes.

- **Format paragraphs and pages.** In addition to simple text changes, you can also format paragraphs (indent, add bullets, add a border) and pages (change the margins, add page numbers, insert a header).

- **Check accuracy.** Most programs include a spell-check tool for checking the spelling. Some programs also include a mini-application (or applet) for checking grammar.

Word processing programs differ in terms of what features they offer. If your needs are simple, you might do okay with the simple word processing program included with Windows. This program, called WordPad, includes basic editing and formatting features.

If you plan to create a lot of documents and want a stunning professional appearance, you might want to purchase a more robust program. One of the most popular programs is Microsoft Word 2000, shown in Figure 13.1. You'll learn a lot about this powerful tool in the next couple of hours. This program includes all the preceding features as well as

13

desktop publishing features for setting up columns, inserting tables, adding graphics, and so on. Word 2000 also includes features for sending faxes, creating Web documents, and much more. Although I can't introduce you to all of these powerful features in this book, you might want to take a look at *Peter Norton's Complete Guide to Microsoft Office 2000* (Sams) by Peter Norton, Jill T. Freeze, and Wayne S. Freeze. This sizeable volume gives you real world advice on using the whole Office 2000 suite of applications.

FIGURE 13.1

Microsoft Word 2000 is the most popular word processing program.

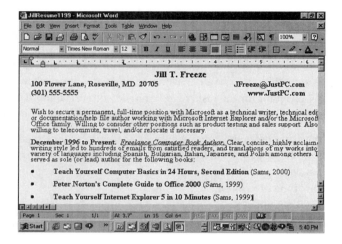

Other word processing programs you'll see on store shelves include WordPerfect and Ami Pro. Of course you should also be aware of a new trend in the industry—free software. For example Sun lets you download StarOffice over the Web or even order a free CD; and Microsoft is hard at work developing its own version of Office to run over the Web. Don't get too excited, though, because some of these solutions may be impractical unless you have a pricey high-speed Internet connection.

To get your free copy of StarOffice, point your Web browser to http://www.sun.com, and click the StarOffice link near the top of the page. Onscreen prompts will guide you through the process.

To produce the highest quality newsletters, brochures, catalogs, and so on, you might want a desktop publishing program. These programs provide even more control of the layout of the page. Microsoft Publisher 2000 (part of many Office 2000 packages) is a fairly simple desktop publishing program, yet it provides oodles of templates to achieve quick, professional-looking results. PageMaker, on the other hand, is a more powerful package; however it might take more time to master the subtleties, not to mention the fist full of cash you'll have to part with to get it on your machine.

Spreadsheets

If numbers are your game, you will most likely work with a spreadsheet application. This type of program enables you to enter and manipulate all kinds of financial information: budgets, sales statistics, income, expenses, and so on. You enter these figures in a worksheet, a grid of columns and rows (see Figure 3.2). The intersection of a row and column is called a cell, and you enter text, numbers, or formulas into the cells to create a worksheet.

FIGURE 13.2

Use a spreadsheet program for any type of numerical data you want to calculate or track.

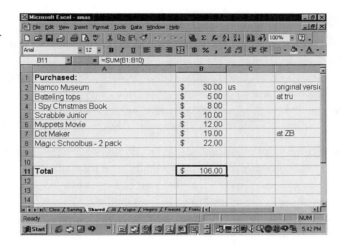

The benefit of a spreadsheet program is that you have so many options for working with the data you enter. You can do any of the following:

- **Perform simple to complex calculations.** You can total a row of numbers, calculate a percentage, figure the amortization of a loan, and more.

- **Format the data.** You can make changes to how text and numbers appear in the worksheet. You can also adjust the column width, add borders, change the alignment of entries, and more.

- **Chart the data.** You can create different types of charts to visually represent the data. For instance, add a line chart to a report to illustrate a sales trend.

- **Manage data lists.** Most spreadsheets also include features for managing simple data lists. You can enter, sort, and query simple data lists using the grid structure of a worksheet.

13

Microsoft Excel 2000, Lotus 1-2-3, and Quattro Pro are all popular spreadsheet programs. I'll tell you more about the most widely distributed, Microsoft Excel 2000, in Hour 16, "Spreadsheet Fundamentals," and Hour 17, "What Your Really Need is a Database."

In addition to spreadsheet programs, you can also use other types of financial programs. For example, you can purchase a program to keep track of your check register. Some of the most popular check management programs are Quicken and Microsoft Money 2000. You can also find programs for calculating your income tax (TurboTax), managing your small business (QuickBooks), handling major accounting tasks (PeachTree Accounting), and so on.

Databases

If word processing and spreadsheets are the first two in application popularity, databases round out the Big Three when it comes to productivity applications. You can use a database program to track and manage any set of data: clients, inventory, orders, events, personal collections, and so on. Database programs vary from simple list managers to complex programs you can use to manage linked systems of information residing on huge mainframe computers at major corporations and educational institutions.

Databases offer a lot of advantages when you are working with large amounts of information. First, you can easily search for and find a particular piece of information. Second, you can sort the data into different orders as needed. Sort a client list alphabetically for a phone list. Sort by zip code for a mailing. Third, you can work with subsets of the data: all clients in South Dakota, all clients that ordered more than $1,000 worth of products, Beanie Babies you paid more than $10 for, and so on.

Some popular database programs include Microsoft Access 2000 (see Figure 13.3), Approach, and Paradox. And as you saw in the spreadsheet section, you can even experiment with lightweight databases by modifying a spreadsheet application. I'll even show you how to do it in Hour 17.

Graphics and Presentation Programs

Even if you aren't artistic, you can use your PC and the right software program to create graphics. Depending on your needs (and skill levels), you can consider any of the three types of programs in this category:

- **Simple drawing programs.** You can use a simple drawing program, such as Paint, which is included with Windows, to create simple illustrations. And larger applications like Microsoft Word 2000 include applets (small applications) like WordArt, and AutoShapes that let you dabble in the visual arts whether you have artistic talent or not.

FIGURE 13.3

Microsoft Access 2000 gives you tons of help in building your own database.

- **Complex drawing programs.** You can also find more sophisticated programs for drawing and working with images. Adobe Illustrator and Adobe Photoshop are two such packages. For more technical renderings, you might consider Visio (see Figure 13.4). A recent acquisition of Microsoft, this product will undoubtedly go through some major revisions and enhanced Microsoft Office integration in the near future. But even older versions of Visio can easily be imported into Word 2000 documents.

FIGURE 13.4

From flow charts to complex computer network diagrams, Visio gives them polish.

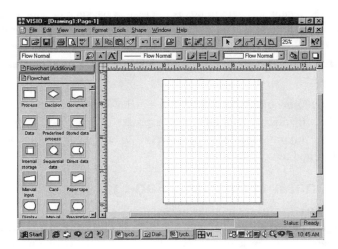

13

- **Presentation programs.** If you ever have to give a presentation, you might want to use a program designed just for creating presentations. You can use this program to create slides, handouts, and notes—a great tool for educators as well as executives or sales people. Microsoft PowerPoint 2000 (see Figure 13.5), Corel Presentations, and Freelance Graphics are popular presentation programs.

FIGURE 13.5

PowerPoint 2000's new TriPane interface makes it simpler to work with than ever before.

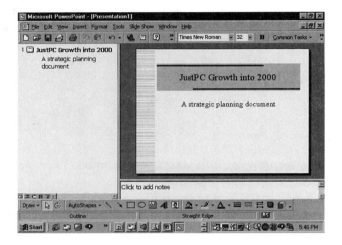

Suites or Bundles

One of the recent software trends is to create a package or suite of the most popular programs and sell them together. For example, Microsoft offers several versions of its Office suite of applications. One is dedicated to small businesses, another contains extra tools for software developers, and a third is designed to be a less expensive collection for home users.

Corel and Lotus offer similar suites that include their most popular word processing, spreadsheet, database, and presentation programs. Microsoft Home Essentials 2000 includes everything from a word processor to an encyclopedia to a greeting card designer, and more.

Personal Information Managers

Most people have several things to keep track of: people, events, appointments, places, and so on. Personal information managers (or PIMs) are just the program for storing names and addresses, keeping track of your schedule, jotting notes, and so on. You can think of this type of program as your "electronic" day planner. Microsoft Outlook 2000 (not to be confused with its little brother, Outlook Express, which comes with the

Internet Explorer suite of applications) acts as a PIM in addition to being an email program.

Games

When you go into a store that sells computer software, you'll see more games than anything else. And within this broad category, there are several classifications of the programs you'll find. Take a look at the following list to see what titles you might find in each category:

- **Puzzle/Arcade**—Just about anything you ever played in an arcade in college can be found on store shelves. Centipede, Pac-Man, and many other favorites along with a slew of pinball machine programs can be found. You'll even find familiar games like Boggle, Chessmaster 5000, and Clue among the selection.

- **Strategy**—Among the list of classic games making up this category include Battleship, Mastermind, Scrabble, the best selling SimCity series, Microsoft's Ages of Empires, and Sid Meier's Civilization. Newer releases include Sid Meier's Alpha Centauri, The Sims, SimThemePark Word, and Railroad Tycoon II.

- **Action**—If you like shoot-em-up games, you might enjoy some of these action titles, too: Duke Nuke'em 3D, Quake, Earthworm Jim, Half-Life, Descent 3, Tom Clancy's Rainbow Six, and Delta Force. But beware that many of these are gory first-person shooter games not suitable for young players.

- **Adventure**—Grim Fandango, Outcast, Riven, Myst, Star Trek: Borg, and the King's Quest series fall into this category. And for those with a sick sense of humor, the womanizing (but admittedly funny) Leisure Suit Larry series can perk things up.

- **Driving**—Whether you want to be behind the wheel of an exotic sports car, a motor cycle, or even a pod racer, you're bound to find something that strikes your fancy amongst these titles: Star Wars Episode I Racer, NASCAR 3, Viper Racing, Lego Racer, Grand Theft Auto 2, Carmageddon and Carmageddon 2 (for those with a strong stomach), Destruction Derby 2, Moto Racer 2, and one of my favorites, Microsoft's Midtown Madness.

- **Simulations**—Simulations are a lot of fun. You can fly an old warbird, drive a tank in a war, pilot a helicopter over a city you built in SimCity, even run a hospital or theme park. Simulations you might want to take a peek at include Microsoft Flight Simulator 2000, SimCopter, X-Wing Vs. Tie Fighter, Theme Hospital, and Independence War.

13

- **Sports**—No matter what your preferred sport is, you stand a chance of finding a game that will put you on the team. Some of the more popular sports titles include Madden NFL 2000, NHL 2000, NBA Inside Drive 2000, Jack Nicklaus Golden Bear Challenge, Deer Avenger 2, Ten Pin Alley, FIFA Soccer 99, Trophy Bass 2, Game Set and Match, and FPS: Ski Racing.

- **Reference/Educational**—Titles found in this category include Compton's Encyclopedia, Microsoft Encarta 2000, Mavis Beacon Typing, home designing software, as well as a wide range of college test preparation software and programs to help you learn a new language.

- **Edutainment**—Geared toward kids, this hybrid of educational and entertainment software is designed to help kids have fun while learning. Popular programs in this category include the JumpStart series, Reader Rabbit titles, Magic School Bus offerings, and similar titles.

- **Miscellaneous**—Now for everything that fits nowhere else…you'll find titles like The Electric Quilt and Quilt Pro (for quilt designing), Microsoft Streets Plus for trip planning, collectibles cataloging software like Beanie Baby Collector and the shareware program called Car Collector (a diecast car cataloging shareware program at www.JustPC.com designed by my husband, Wayne Freeze). You can even find pregnancy and wedding planning software, astronomy programs, and other highly specialized titles.

Internet Programs

If you want to use your computer to hook up to the Internet, you need a Web browser. The two most popular are Netscape Communicator and Microsoft's Internet Explorer (which I'll cover in detail in the final section of this book). These programs also act as email applications. Netscape has Messenger, and Microsoft has Outlook Express. Microsoft's Internet suite also includes an easy-to-use Web authoring tool called FrontPage Express. You'll find out how you can build a Web page quickly in Hour 23, "Design A Web Page in an Hour."

Utility Programs

When you want to fine-tune your computer, you might want to investigate some of the utility programs that are available. These programs might add capabilities to your system such as virus checking, backing up, and so on. Norton Utilities is an example of this type of application. Other utilities include WinZip, which handles file compression; Partition Magic, which helps you subdivide your hard drive; and ScanDisk, a hard-drive repairing tool that comes bundled with Windows.

Purchasing a New Program

Although your computer more than likely came with a number of preinstalled applications, there will come a day where you'll want to make some changes. You might want to upgrade an existing program to the newest version, or you might want to purchase an entirely new program.

You can find software in some retail stores, at online stores and auctions, in computer stores, and through mail order outlets. Scan through any computer magazine to get an idea of what programs are available as well as the cost. You can also use the Internet as a resource for researching and finding programs. For example ZDNet at www.zdnet.com nearly always has reviews posted for software as well as hardware.

Finders Keepers You can find freeware and shareware at many Internet sites. Freeware programs are provided free to you. Shareware programs are provided for you to try without cost. If you like the program, you can pay a small fee to register and continue using the program. www.shareware.com is one of my favorite places to go shopping for shareware online. Some developers even produce postcard ware (where you simply send the developer a postcard from your hometown in turn for registration) or fabric ware (a yard of 100 percent cotton fabric as a form of payment for quilting shareware). I'm sure you'll stumble upon variations of this as time goes on.

When you are looking for new programs to purchase, be sure that you can run that program on your system. Each program has system requirements—the type of microprocessor, amount of memory, hard disk space, video card, and any other required equipment. You can usually find these requirements printed on the side of the software box. Check the requirements before purchasing anything to be sure your PC is capable of running the software. It might even be a good idea to test a demo of the software on your machine when one is available. You can find a whole lot of demos at www.gamespot.com. I'll show you how to deal with them in Hour 24.

13

Often times you'll see a reference to "minimum system requirements" on a program's box. Although technically the application can function with those specs, it might be painfully slow. The reduced performance might not be noticeable in a word processor, but in a driving game, your vehicle might be nearly uncontrollable because of the jerky system performance. Just keep in mind that minimum requirements are just that—minimum. If you want stellar performance, you might want to shop around a bit before purchasing the software, or consider upgrading your system in the near future.

Also, be sure that you get the right program for your system. If you have Windows 98, get Windows 95/98 programs. You can also purchase and run DOS and Windows 3.1 programs on Windows 98, though both probably require a bit more "babying" than most people are willing to give them. Most of the software you find these days is compatible with Windows 98, though most titles should be usable with Windows 95 as well. Many popular programs come in several versions to accommodate various operating systems, so be sure to read the boxes carefully.

As a final precaution, check to see how the software is distributed—on floppy disks or on a CD-ROM. If you have both a floppy drive and CD-ROM drive, you don't have to worry. But if you don't have a CD-ROM drive, be sure to get the version on floppy disks. CD-ROMs have become the most popular (and least expensive for the manufacturer) method for distributing programs, especially large programs, so you might not even be able to find a version on floppy.

So Where's the Best Place to Buy Software?

One of the questions I get asked a lot is "Where's the best place to buy software?" If you're not in a hurry, some of the best prices can be had from online stores where competition is fierce. Sure, you usually have to pay postage, but often the absence of sales tax combined with the lower retail price still makes it worthwhile. Just be sure to research shipping costs and terms before you commit to buy. This information can often be well hidden on a Web site that tries to recoup losses from offering great prices by padding shipping costs.

If you're in a hurry, you can seldom beat Wal-Mart, your local wholesale clubs, or the Sunday sales papers for a good price. If the title you want isn't there, it might be time to visit your local Best Buy, CompUSA, or MicroCenter.

Now that we've dealt with the issues of urgency and price, I'd like to present my personal list of software shopping strategies:

- **Be a scavenger.** Be sure to find out where your local software retailers keep their bargain or clearance bins. You can often stumble on to some good finds there. For example on a recent trip to CompUSA, I picked up copies of SimPark, SimFarm, and Slingo (an addictive cross between Bingo and slot machines) for $1.84 each! SimFarm was originally released for between $30 and $40, although Slingo can still be found in many stores for $19.95. Sure they might not be the newest games out there, but they've given me far more entertainment than the Sunday Washington Post, which costs nearly as much.

- **Good things come to those who wait.** I've discovered something interesting in my area. When a new computer game is released, I typically expect to pay full retail price the first week it's out. I guess it's the price you have to pay to be the first on your block to have it. But I've found if I wait for the Sunday paper advertising circulars that come out after the software has hit the shelves, several stores will have the new release on sale, giving me the ability to secure a better price than I might have otherwise.

- **Pay what you want to for it.** That's right, by cruising eBay, the premiere online auction site at www.ebay.com, you can often buy software for less than half of what you'd find it in stores. For example, my 6-year old son wanted Star Wars: The Phantom Menace game. Somewhat reluctant to shell out $45 or more for it, I turned to eBay and managed to get a factory sealed copy delivered to my home for less than $22! But when dealing with online auctions, there are some precautions you'll want to take. First off, deal only with sellers who have an all-positive feedback rating on eBay. Second, avoid used software like the plague. Sure you can get it cheap, but you can never be certain that the previous owner hasn't registered it in her name, or that he's removed it from his machine. That would potentially make you guilty of software piracy. Also, stay away from software that was bundled with a computer system purchase because it's usually clearly marked "Not for resale." When you go to make an auction purchase, look for things like "in factory sealed box" or "new in box".

Registering Your Software

When you purchase a piece of software, you'll often find a post card in the box asking for your name, address, email address, place and date the software was purchased, and so on. This registration card enables software manufacturers to contact you in the event they make a bug fix available over the Internet, or they simply want to inform you that an updated version of the program you registered is now available.

Occasionally, manufacturers allow you to register their products online. When you install the program, it will ask you if you want to go online now and register the software, or do it later. The choice is yours.

So should you bother registering a piece of software? My answer is a resounding "yes" even though I'm sometimes guilty of forgetting to do it myself. Not only does it keep me up to date on the latest news about my program, but it sometimes produces money saving offers for program upgrades or add-ons. That alone could be worth dealing with the occasional junk mail.

13

When Should I Consider Upgrading My Software?

My answer might surprise you since I make my living as a computer book author, but here goes.

Software is awfully pricey to be continually buying a newer version, especially when you don't really need it. My advice here is the same as it is for contemplating hardware upgrades: If the computer/software does what you want and need it to, don't waste your money; wait until the need or desire is there.

This is especially true for productivity software like Word 2000, Excel 2000, and such. Often times the enhancements are targeted toward corporate or power users, bringing no real value to the average consumer. Of course, an upgrade might be warranted if there are file compatibility issues between your home and work machines.

Games are a different matter, however. Technological advances, the desire to have new levels or playing arenas, and optimized performance might very well make upgrading a game desirable, especially if you really liked the game the first time around. But again, use extreme caution to make sure your machine can drive the latest and greatest offering.

Summary

There you have it—everything you ever wanted to know about the types of software you can get as well as some rules of thumb for purchasing and upgrading your chosen software. You even got a feel for what kinds of titles you'd find in each category of software.

In the next hour, I'll help you get comfortable using Microsoft Word 2000, the most commonly installed word processing program on new computer systems.

Workshop

Now it's time to see just how much you learned in this lesson. I'll give you a short multiple-choice quiz to test what you learned, followed by a suggested activity designed to enhance the skills you acquired during the hour.

Quiz

Select the best answer to the questions from the choices provided, and then check your answers.

Questions

1. Which of the following is *not* a word processing program?

    a. PowerPoint

    b. Ami Pro

    c. Word 2000

2. What's the difference between Outlook 2000 and Outlook Express?

    a. They are the same, it's just that one comes with Office 2000, and the other does not.

    b. Outlook Express sends email quicker than Outlook 2000.

    c. Outlook Express is a smaller, less functional version of Outlook 2000 that's packaged with the Internet Explorer suite of applications.

3. When should you consider upgrading your software?

    a. When your software no longer does what you need or want it to.

    b. Upgrading is only for hardware.

    c. Any time something new comes out, grab it; having the latest and greatest software on your machine is a real status symbol.

Answers

1. A is actually a presentation program designed to create professional looking presentations; it is not by any means a word processing program.

2. The best answer (not to mention the only one that was correct) was C.

3. B is incorrect, and C is a waste of money, therefore; A is again the correct answer.

Activity

Go to your computer and look through the icons on your Windows desktop and the files listed on your Programs menu. Is there anything else you'd like to do with your computer that you don't already have software to handle? List the types of tasks and/or games here:

1.

2.

3.

4.

5.

13

Now pick up a copy of the Sunday paper if you don't get it delivered to your home, and skim the ads for software. Don't forget that places like Target and Wal-Mart sell software, too.

In looking through the ads, try to find at least one application for each task you've listed. So if, for example, you listed letter writing as one of your tasks, you would write down Word 2000 if it appeared in one of the ads. List the application that fits each task in the space below:

   1.

   2.

   3.

   4.

   5.

HOUR 14

Basic Word Processing with Word 2000

Technically, Word 2000 is considered a word processor. Although it does a superior job at that, it's really so much more than a word processor. Word can create Web pages loaded with hyperlinks, and it can produce newsletters that would push the capabilities of many small desktop publishing programs.

Word 2000 brings with it tons of enhancements and improvements over its previous version. And with such busy work schedules and personal lives, few people have time to play with these new features let alone master them. In the next two lessons, I'll provide simple, no-nonsense steps to help guide you through the basics.

Here are some other topics you have to look forward to this hour:

- Find out the various ways you can move through Word 2000 documents.
- Learn how to select blocks of text.
- Make your documents look nice by applying special formatting.
- Discover how to print the parts of a document you want.

To begin this lesson, launch Microsoft Word by clicking the Start button on the Windows taskbar, and then choosing Programs, Microsoft Word. A large screen with toolbars at the top will greet you. For the sake of this lesson, click the New Document button on the Formatting toolbar. It's the button at the far left of the toolbar that looks like a piece of paper with its top right corner folded down.

When you create a new document in this manner, Word 2000 applies a predefined set of attributes to it. Although these settings can be modified as you'll see later in the hour, the defaults are listed in Table 14.1.

TABLE 14.1   Word 2000 Document Defaults

Setting	Value
Font	Times New Roman
Text Size	12 point
Left/Right Margins	1.25 inches
Top/Bottom Margins	1 inch
Tab Stops	Every 1/2 inch
Page Orientation	Portrait

 Hmm, that's not what I thought I was gonna get   If your new blank documents are being created with settings other than these, chances are your normal.dot template was modified at some point. You can use these settings to restore it to its original settings if necessary.

Anatomy of the Word 2000 Work Space

Knowing Word 2000's screen elements will go a long way toward helping you unleash its power. Figure 14.1 points out all the critical elements.

So what do each of these elements do? The quick answer is provided in the following list, but many of these functions will be explored in greater detail throughout this lesson.

- **Title bar.** Contains the name of the program and the name of the document, as well as the Maximize, Minimize, Restore, and Close buttons.
- **Menu bar.** Allows you to select from a variety of pull-down menus needed to execute commands in Word 2000.

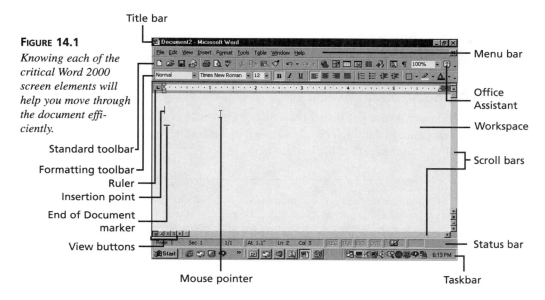

FIGURE 14.1

Knowing each of the critical Word 2000 screen elements will help you move through the document efficiently.

- **Standard toolbar.** Holds shortcut buttons to quickly execute common tasks such as printing, opening a new document, and so forth. This toolbar might be modified to meet your specific needs.

- **Formatting toolbar.** Presents buttons to quickly format text as you work. Selections include font style, font size, text alignment, and text traits (for example, bold, underline).

- **Ruler.** Provides a quick and easy way to guide the setting of tabs and indents in your documents.

- **Insertion point.** Shows you where the text or graphics will be placed. In other programs it is referred to as a cursor.

- **End of Document marker.** Indicates the end of a document with a short, horizontal line. You cannot move past this point.

- **Mouse pointer.** Moves onscreen as you move the mouse to assist you in accessing menus and clicking buttons.

- **Office Assistant.** Serves as your online helper. Ask questions or turn it off as you become more familiar with Word 2000.

- **View buttons.** Enable you to adjust your view of a document. Choose from Normal view, Outline view, Page Layout view, and Outline Layout view.

14

- **Status bar.** Displays information about your document including page count, line number, and so on.
- **Taskbar.** Allows you to toggle back and forth between applications already open, or to launch new applications via the Start button.
- **Workspace.** Consists of a blank page on which you insert text and graphics.
- **Scroll bars.** Move you quickly around a document. Either slide them with your mouse (point to the scroll box, hold down the left button of your mouse, and drag), or click on either side of the box for larger jumps.

> **Remember this!**   Keep these menus and toolbars fixed in your mind because you *will* see them again. Microsoft has worked hard at creating a common interface, making it much easier to learn the various applications in the Office 2000 family.

NEW TERM   **Inter-what?**   The term *interface* refers to the way a program looks, and the way commands are executed within it. Thus, a common Office 2000 interface not only makes applications look very similar, but it helps users overcome the fear and intimidation of learning to use less known members of the popular office productivity suite.

Common Menus and Menu Options

Menus organize a number of commands and options into logical categories for easy reference. Just click the name of the menu to open its pull-down menu. In addition to the names of the options, Word 2000 displays the appropriate icon where available, and lists the keystroke combination needed to execute the same option. Figure 14.2 illustrates a typical pull-down menu in Word.

As you access these menus, you'll discover that for a few seconds, they display the most commonly used options. If you continue to hover your mouse pointer over the menu, it will expand to reveal the entire list of menu commands for the selected menu. These are known as "smart" menus because they "learn" which commands you perform most, and display them first in the list of commands.

FIGURE 14.2

The new Word 2000 "smart" menus make it easier to find the commands you use most.

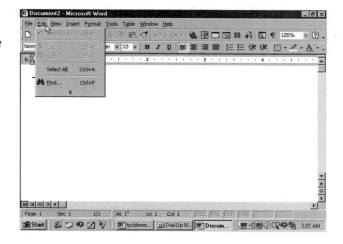

Whoa, what happened?   The thing I dislike most about these smart menus is one second you might be pointing to one command, and, just as you're about to click it, the rest of the menu pops into view. And occasionally this "pop" makes the menu items shift in location, meaning you might not get what you expect when you click. To remedy this, I disable the smart menus. You can do this to by right-clicking over the menu bar and selecting Customize from the shortcut menu. Access the Options tab, and then remove the check mark next to the Menus show recently used commands first check box by clicking the check mark itself.

There are a number of menus shared by the Office 2000 family of applications:

- **File menu.** Gives users access to such commands as opening, saving, and renaming a document; setting print properties as well as launching the printing process; specifying file properties; and exiting the application. This is the first item on Word 2000's menu bar.

- **Edit menu.** Holds commands for cutting, copying, and pasting as well as the search and replace option. Options not available in a given circumstance are grayed out (for example, unless a block of text is selected, Copy will be grayed out). Look here first if you need to make a change in a document.

- **View menu.** Presents options needed to alter the screen's appearance. You can add toolbars, turn them off, create document headers and footers, and view your document in Outline mode to name a few. You can also zoom the page in and out to increase print size or reduce it to fit more onscreen.

14

- **Insert menu.** Allows you to add objects like clip art into a file.

- **Format menu.** This menu allows you to format text or other objects like clip art or tables. If you want to change the way your text looks, add a list to your document, or add a border to your work, look here first.

- **Tools menu.** If there's anything you want to customize, the Tools menu is the place to start. Neat gadgets like the Spell Checker, Word Count, and the AutoCorrect feature reside here.

- **Window menu.** Although the top half of this menu might change from application to application, the bottom half allows you to switch back and forth between open documents within an application (where available). To access a document listed, simply click its filename.

- **Help menu.** Leads you to a variety of Word 2000 help tools.

The Shared Standard Toolbar

Just as there are similarities between Office 2000 menus, there is a Standard toolbar shared by all the applications that has numerous buttons/icons you'll see no matter which application you're working with (see Figure 14.3).

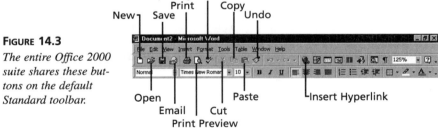

FIGURE 14.3
The entire Office 2000 suite shares these buttons on the default Standard toolbar.

These buttons are more than just shortcuts to the same option within a menu. In fact, in many cases they have radically different results than their menu-driven counterparts even though they essentially accomplish the same thing in the end.

Take the New document command in Word 2000, for example. You can create a new document by choosing File, New to select a document type from Word 2000's library of templates and wizards. You can also create a new document by using a shortcut (clicking the New button on the Standard Toolbar, or by pressing Ctrl+N). Using shortcuts will in this case choose the default Word template—a blank page referred to as the Normal template.

> **Now I'm REALLY confused...** With so many different ways to execute commands, it can be hard to settle on one method. A good rule of thumb is if you want to choose options when executing a command (like base a new document on a resume template, or print only the first page of a 20 page document), follow the menu sequence. If the default (a blank page for a new document, one copy of the entire document to be printed, and so on) is acceptable, use the method most comfortable to you—the menus, the Standard toolbar button, or the applicable keystrokes. There is no right or wrong way; it's all a matter of personal preference.

NEW TERM **Is this a science fiction novel, or what?** With words like *wizard* being thrown around, you might be starting to think you've fallen into a science fiction novel. The fact is, there are wizards in the world of computers, too, but instead of long, flowing hair, beards, and drab-colored gowns, they're disguised as dialog boxes containing questions to guide you through complex tasks. These helpful wizards often take you step-by-step through program installation and configuration, the design of a Web page or newsletter, among other tasks.

Tweaking the Toolbars

Everybody uses Office applications differently. As a result, some of the buttons you use most might be missing on the toolbars. Likewise, other buttons you never use might take up valuable space.

To add a button to a toolbar, follow these steps:

1. Make sure the toolbar you want to modify is in view.
2. Choose Tools, Customize, and select the Commands tab.
3. In the Categories box, click on the category of the button you want to add. The command names and icons (if available) are shown in the Commands box.
4. Click on the desired icon/command, and then drag it into position on the toolbar.
5. Release the mouse button to set the button in place.

To delete a button from a toolbar, do the following:

1. Make sure the toolbar you want to modify is in view.
2. Choose Tools, Customize, and select the Commands tab.
3. If necessary, drag the Customize dialog box to another location (click on the title bar and drag it) until the button you want to delete is visible.

14

4. Click on the button you want to delete, and then drag it off the toolbar.

5. Release the mouse button to complete the deletion.

Keystrokes: Another Way to Get the Job Done

In addition to menus and toolbars, Office 2000 offers a host of shortcuts to access commands using the keyboard. Table 14.2 highlights some of the more common functions.

TABLE 14.2   Office 2000 Keyboard Shortcuts

Function/Command	Shortcut
New	Ctrl+N
Open	Ctrl+O
Save	Ctrl+S
Print	Ctrl+P
Cut	Ctrl+X
Paste	Ctrl+V
Copy	Ctrl+C

Selecting Text

Many commands and operations in Office applications require you to select text first before you can make changes to it. For example, to change the font of text or move a block of text, you first have to select it. Selected text will appear highlighted, so you'll easily be able to see what part of the document you've chosen to manipulate in some way.

Although there are a variety of ways to select items in Office 2000, these steps introduce you to the most commonly used way.

1. Place the mouse pointer at the beginning of the desired text.

2. Click the left mouse button and hold it down while dragging it to highlight a block of text (see Figure 14.4).

3. After the desired area is highlighted, perform your chosen operation on the data as described in the next few sections.

FIGURE 14.4

There's no question which part of the document is about to be modified.

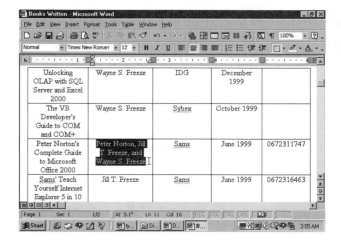

>
>
> **Oops, I didn't get the whole thing!**   If you find you need to adjust the selected text area after you've released the mouse button, there's no need to start from scratch. You can hold down the Shift key and use the arrow keys to highlight the exact area you want, starting from where you click to where you let go of the mouse button.

Selecting Text with the Mouse

As usual, Microsoft gives you a plethora of ways to select text with your mouse. But in this case, you might actually grow to like some of the methods presented in Table 14.3.

TABLE 14.3   Additional Ways to Select Text with Your Mouse

To Select This	Do This
Word	Double-click inside the word.
Sentence	Ctrl+click inside the sentence.
Paragraph	Triple-click inside the paragraph.
Graphic/image	Click the graphic/image.
Entire document	Move mouse pointer to the left of the text until it turns into a left upward pointing arrow (as opposed to the standard right upward pointing arrow) and then triple-click.
Vertical text block	Hold down the Alt key and drag the mouse pointer over the text.
Entire lines of text	Move the mouse pointer to the left of the text until it becomes an arrow; then click the left mouse button and drag the mouse until the desired block of text is highlighted.

14

Selecting Text Blocks with the Keyboard

For some reason, there are people who prefer to work with the keyboard rather than fiddle with the mouse. If you're one of those people, you'll be interested in Table 14.4, the listing of shortcut keys for selecting blocks of text.

TABLE 14.4   Keyboard Shortcuts for Selecting Text

To Select This	Do This
One character at a time to the left of the insertion point	Press Shift+left arrow and repeat until the desired number of characters is highlighted
One character at a time to the right arrow of the insertion point	Press Shift+right arrow and repeat until the desired number of characters is highlighted
The beginning of the word to the left insertion point	Press Shift+Ctrl+left of the arrow, and keep pressing the arrow key to select additional words
The beginning of the word to the right of the insertion point	Press Shift+Ctrl+right arrow, and keep pressing the arrow key to select additional words
The insertion point to the same position in the previous line	Press Shift+up arrow
The insertion point to the same position in the next line	Press Shift+down arrow
The insertion point to the beginning of the current paragraph.	Press Shift+Ctrl+up arrow
The insertion point to the beginning of the next paragraph	Press Shift+Ctrl+down arrow
The insertion point to the beginning of the document	Press Shift+Ctrl+Home
The insertion point to the end of the document	Press Shift+Ctrl+End

Deleting Selected Text and Data

To delete a block of text, select the area and press the Delete button on your keyboard. If you accidentally delete too much, don't panic; press Ctrl+Z, and start over again.

Moving a Selected Block of Text

Back when I was in college, typewriters were the norm. In fact, on more than one occasion, I opted to leave a term paper unorganized rather than go back and retype the thing to get it the way I really wanted it. With computers, life is much simpler.

Moving a block of text from one location to another is an easy process; just follow these steps:

1. Select the text you want to move as described in the previous section "Selecting Text."

2. Cut the text from its current location using one of three ways: click the Cut button on the toolbar, use Ctrl+X, or choose Edit, Cut from the Menu bar. The text will disappear as it is copied to the Clipboard for future use.

3. Move the mouse pointer to the desired location in the document, and single-click to set the insertion point in place.

4. To paste the block of text into the new location, click the Paste button on the toolbar; use Ctrl+V; or choose Edit, Paste from the Menu bar.

Copying Selected Text

Copying a block of text to another location can save vast amounts of time even if you have to make minor edits. Say, for example, you need to write a dozen thank-you letters to companies you recently interviewed with. Rather than type each letter, you might want to consider copying the text of the first letter and pasting it to subsequent pages to construct the rest of the letters. Then all you have to do is re-key the personalized parts like the greeting, company name, and so on. That's *much* quicker than typing each one!

It's not as easy as it sounds　If you were to tell a long-time computer user about the technique you were using to generate multiple thank you letters, they might come back with, "Well why don't you just use mail merge?" Just smile and say, "This way is much easier." Because the fact of the matter is, most new computer users don't have the need to fuss with the complexities of mail merge.

14

To take advantage of this time saving technique, just do the following:

1. Select the text you want to move as described earlier in the hour.

2. Copy the text using one of three ways: click the Copy icon on the toolbar, press Ctrl+C, or choose Edit, Copy from the Menu bar.

3. Guide the mouse pointer to the desired location in the document, and single-click to set the insertion point in place.

4. To paste the block of text into the new location, click the Paste icon on the toolbar; press Ctrl+V; or choose Edit, Paste from the Menu bar.

> **Paste it again, Sam!** If you want to place the copied text in more than one location (as in the example of multiple thank you letters), simply execute steps 3 and 4 as many times as needed. There's no need to reselect the text.

Changing the Text Font

Perhaps the best way to enhance the appearance of your documents is to choose a distinctive font that fits the message. Whether it's script for the body of a formal invitation, or a more playful style for your kids' fundraiser handout, you can find the font for the job.

You can select a font one of two ways: by choosing it before you begin typing the text, or by selecting the text and then applying the change to the selection.

To select a font when there's no existing text to modify, click the arrow next to the Font window of the Formatting toolbar to open the drop-down list box. Choose from the fonts listed.

Notice that by using this drop-down list, you can instantly see what a certain font looks like before you apply it.

Adding Bold, Italic, Color, Underline, and Other Text Attributes

Whether you want to make a word bold for emphasis, or you simply want to italicize the title of a book, you'll want to know how to alter the attributes of your text. The Font tab of the Font dialog box (see Figure 14.5) gives you numerous ways to change the appearance of your text. Start by following these steps:

1. Choose Format, Font from the Menu bar to call up the Font dialog box.
2. Select the Font tab (see Figure 14.5) to choose a style or special effect for your text, and see it in the Preview window before applying it.
3. Click OK to apply the selected type attributes.

FIGURE 14.5
Click the arrow next to each box to see a menu of choices, or place a check mark in the box to apply the effect.

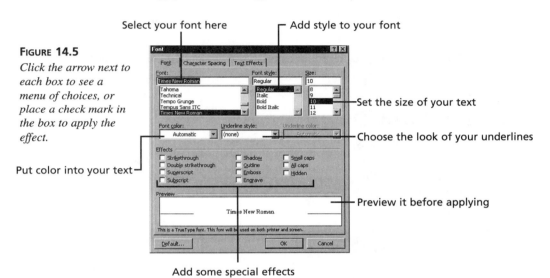

Select your font here

Add style to your font

Set the size of your text

Choose the look of your underlines

Put color into your text

Preview it before applying

Add some special effects

You can incorporate any of these attributes into your text by selecting them from the beginning, or by following the steps for selecting a complex font as described in the preceding steps.

Becoming a Quick Change Artist

The quickest way to change text attributes is to select the block of text you want to change, and then click the applicable button on the Formatting toolbar. See Figure 14.6 for a diagram of which toolbar buttons do what.

FIGURE 14.6
The Formatting toolbar is the fastest way to alter text.

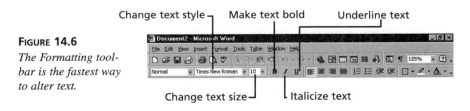

Change text style

Make text bold

Underline text

Change text size

Italicize text

14

Changing the Size of the Text

One way to emphasize certain parts of your document is to change the type size. Again, you can either specify the size before you start typing, or select existing text and change its size. To change type size:

1. Click the arrow next to the Font window of the Formatting toolbar to open the drop-down list box.

2. Choose from the sizes listed, or enter your own number. For those not familiar with point sizes, the larger the number, the bigger the text.

Viewing Your Documents

Word 2000 offers a variety of document views that simplify document editing and formatting, and in some cases even enhance navigation within your document. These views are easily changed by clicking the icons pictured below. To return to Word's normal view at any time, simply click the Normal view button at the left end of the row of View buttons (see Figure 14.7).

FIGURE 14.7

Click any of the four view icons to easily edit or format your document.

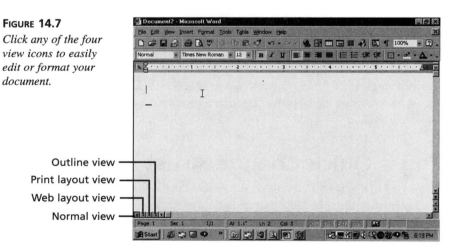

Outline view
Print layout view
Web layout view
Normal view

Available views from left to right include the following:

- **Normal view.** Word's default document view, the Normal view, is the standard view used for document editing and formatting. Although it shows document layout pretty much as it will appear on the printed page, the workspace remains uncluttered for quick and easy editing.

- **Web Layout view.** See exactly what a document would look like if it were turned into a Web page.

- **Print Layout view.** In this view, you can see how a document will look before it is printed. This is a great way to evaluate a document's margins, headers and footers, and so on.

- **Outline view.** The Outline view makes it easy to move or copy entire sections of text because it gives you customizable views of your document. You can see the relative importance of each section title, but only if you apply style codes or build the outline from scratch.

> **Details, details, details...**   If you're anxious to learn more about Word 2000 from a practical standpoint without being overwhelmed or put to sleep, check out *Peter Norton's Complete Guide to Office 2000* by Peter Norton, Jill T. Freeze, and Wayne S. Freeze. This Sams Publishing title can be found in bookstores everywhere.

Keys to Finding Your Way Around a Document

Word 2000 gives you a number of shortcut keys to move swiftly from one location to another in a document. See Table 14.5 for a list of these.

TABLE 14.5   Word Navigation Shortcut Keys

To Move Here...	Press...
One character to the right	Shift+Right Arrow
One character to the left	Shift+Left Arrow
To the end of a word	Ctrl+Shift+Right Arrow
To the beginning of a word	Ctrl+Shift+Left Arrow
To the end of a line	Shift+End
To the beginning of a line	Shift+Home
One line down	Shift+Down Arrow
One line up	Shift+Up Arrow
To the end of a paragraph	Ctrl+Shift+Down Arrow
To the beginning of a paragraph	Ctrl+Shift+Up Arrow
One screen down	Shift+Page Down

14

continues

TABLE 14.5   continued

To Move Here...	Press...
One screen up	Shift+Page Up
To the end of a window	Alt+Ctrl+Page Down
To the beginning of a document	Ctrl+Shift+Home
To include the entire document	Ctrl+A

Inserting Text

To insert text in an existing Word document, move the pointer to the desired location, click once to set the insertion point, and then simply begin typing.

Deleting Text

We're all human; therefore, we're bound to make mistakes. As much as we might hate to admit it, there are times when the words just don't flow. Maybe sentences go on for an eternity. Or perhaps you fail to retrieve the right word at the right time. Whatever the case, you'll be relieved to know there's a method to delete text to suit just about any work preference.

You might delete text in Word 2000 in any of these ways:

- Use the Delete key to delete characters to the right of the insertion point.
- Use the Backspace key to delete characters to the left of the insertion point.
- Select a block of text, and then press Delete.

Are you sure you want to get rid of it altogether?   If you're about to delete a large block of text you might want to use later, consider using the Cut function instead of delete to temporarily copy the information to the Clipboard. This way the deletion isn't permanent until you exit Word. And with Office 2000's multiple Clipboard feature, subsequent "cuts" will be added to the Clipboard entries until they are specifically added to a document.

Undoing Changes

If there's one set of keystrokes to memorize in Word, it's Ctrl+Z. Knowing how to undo something in a flash can save hours of reformatting, typing, and so on. Undo can also be accessed by clicking the Undo button on the toolbar.

Word has a multiple level Undo feature, you can click the arrow next to the Undo button to see a list of operations you can undo. If you undo an item way down on the list, all the items above it will be undone as well. In this case, re-keying or reapplying the formatting might save you more time than using Undo. If you change your mind after undoing a change, you can always redo it by clicking the Redo button on the Formatting toolbar.

Aligning Text

After you get the words down on paper (or electrons as the case is with computers), you might want to spruce them up a bit. One way to do this is to modify the alignment of the text.

Text in Word 2000 can be aligned in four different ways—flush left (as this book is), centered, flush right, and justified (stretched out to make both margins even). To align your text any of these ways, select the block of text, and click the appropriate button on the toolbar, as shown in Figure 14.8.

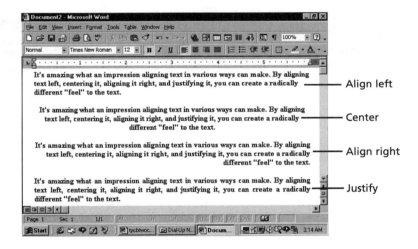

You can also choose the alignment beforehand, and then enter the text to achieve the desired look if you know the look you want to achieve before you even start typing.

Creating Bulleted and Numbered Lists

There are two kinds of lists you can use to draw the attention of the reader: bulleted and numbered lists. Bulleted lists use small icons, or bullets, to indicate each item in the list. Word 2000 even gives you the opportunity to use graphics bullets where the bullets are

14

tiny pictures instead of the usual dots. Numbered lists use a numbering system for the items. Both types of lists can be modified to use different bullet and numbering styles.

Entering New Text Formatted as a List

To create either kind of list before you start typing, follow these steps:

1. Type the text leading up to the list.
2. When you're ready to enter items on the list, place the insertion point at the location you'd like the list to appear.
3. Click the Numbering or Bullets button on the Formatting toolbar.
4. Type each section of text followed by the Enter key to set up subsequent bullets or numbered sections.
5. When the list is complete, press Enter, and then click the Numbering or Bullets button again to turn off the formatting. (Samples of the resulting lists are illustrated in Figure 14.9.)

FIGURE 14.9

This figure shows simple numbered and bulleted lists.

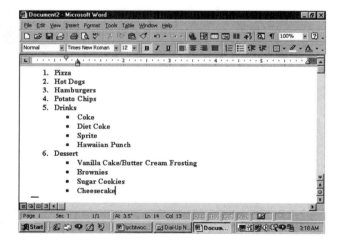

Generating a List from Existing Text

Select the text to be turned into a list and then click the desired list button on the Formatting toolbar. Keep in mind that each list entry must be followed by a hard return (pressing the Enter key); otherwise, the items will all be placed on a single list entry. This might require you to insert returns after you have formatted the list.

Changing the Bullet or Numbering Style

If standard bullets or numbers don't catch your fancy, you can apply something a bit more distinctive. Choose Format, Bullets and Numbering, and then select either the Bulleted or Numbered tab as appropriate. The Bulleted tab gives you access to little black boxes, check marks, and other bullet styles. The Numbered tab can turn standard numbers into letters or even Roman numerals. Simply choose the style you want, then click OK to apply it.

Setting Spell Checking Options

Nothing's more embarrassing than sending out an important letter with a typo that could have easily been avoided. Save yourself the headaches by accepting the help of Word 2000's spelling and grammar checker.

Word's spell check feature can go crazy when it encounters acronyms, Internet addresses, and other unfamiliar text. The good news is you can save time dealing with these elements by telling Word to ignore them.

Choose Tools, Options, and then select the Spelling & Grammar tab. From here, you can enable or disable the spell checker by clicking the check box next to the Check Spelling as You Type option near the top of the tab. You can also tell Word to ignore words in uppercase, words with numbers in them, or filenames and Internet addresses. This will save you time when running through your document to correct potential errors.

Get It Right the First Time with Grammar Checking

I ain't got no problem with proper grammar, but if I did, this tool would sure help! It's great for helping you rewrite passive voice into active voice, but it's not infallible. There are definitely times (like the first sentence of this paragraph) when you'll need a second opinion, but the benefits make it worth trying anyway.

To set grammar checking options in Word 2000, follow these steps:

1. From within any Word document, choose Tools, Options, then select the Spelling & Grammar tab (see Figure 14.10).

2. In the Grammar section of the tab, you can specify whether Word should check grammar as you type, or whether you want any grammatical errors to be hidden. You might also check grammar the same time you check spelling by placing a check mark next to that option.

14

FIGURE **14.10**

The grammar options selected in this figure tell Word to keep grammatical errors in view in the current document, and to check grammar the same time spelling is checked.

3. To have Word check for more specific errors, click the Settings button to bring up the Grammar Settings dialog box (see Figure 14.11).

FIGURE **14.11**

Select the elements you want Word to check in the Grammar and style options box, or request Word to double-check up to three usage requirements in the Require section of the Grammar setting dialog box.

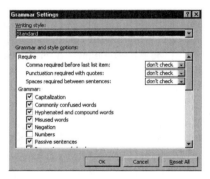

4. Scroll down the Grammar and Style Options list box to select the elements you want Word to check for. Options include checking for improper capitalization, use of double negatives, and passive voice.

5. In the Require section, choose any of the three usage requirements—comma placement, use of quotation marks, and the number of spaces between sentences—and define their usage in the drop-down lists next to each one. For example, you can specify that sentences must have one space between them, and Word will tell you if it finds one that doesn't follow this rule.

6. Click OK to return to the Spelling & Grammar tab, and then press OK to apply your newly defined options.

Performing the Spelling and Grammar Checks

Word 2000 gives you the ability to correct grammar and spelling as you work, or you can perform a single pass of spelling and grammar checking when your document is finished.

I prefer to address issues as they're detected because my mind is still in the proper context to know what I really intended to say. If I take care of it at the end, I might have forgotten the point I was trying to make.

To address problems as you work, simply right-click over a word or phrase with a green (spelling) or red (grammar) squiggly underline. For spelling errors, the resulting shortcut menu will often present you with a number of possible choices for the word you had intended to type. To select a suggested word, simply double-click it. The menu also gives you the opportunity to ignore words, or add them to your personal spell-checking dictionary. For grammatical errors, Word will tell you what type of problem it found, and will occasionally even rewrite the sentence for you. Again, you can double-click the suggested fix to apply it.

If remember the day like it was yesterday. It was 4 a.m., and I was finishing up the last of an Excel chapter for my *Using Office 97* book. Then for some bizarre reason, my laptop froze. When I booted my system again, they were gone—14 precious pages of manuscript! Sure I had saved them, but I made the mistake of relying on Word's AutoSave feature alone.

I don't want the same thing to happen to you, so I strongly urge you to click the Save button on the Standard toolbar every few minutes for insurance.

The first time you click Save in a new document, you'll see the Save As dialog box shown in Figure 14.12. Just click inside the File Name text box, and type in the desired filename. Of course before you enter a filename, it would be even smarter to click your way to a descriptive folder that will enable you to find the document again in a snap. If you don't, every document you ever create will be stored in the nondescript My Documents folder. After you've entered a name for the file, click the Save button in the lower-right corner to close the dialog box.

14

Figure 14.12

Navigating the Save As dialog box is similar to finding your way around in Windows Explorer—just double-click a folder to see the files and folders within it.

Opening an Existing Word Document

Many longer documents require more than one work session to complete them. As such, it won't be long before you'll need to go back and open documents. To do so, just launch Word 2000 as usual, and then use one of these methods to locate and open the document you're looking for:

- If you recently worked with the document you want to open, try clicking the File menu, and then look at the bottom of the drop-down menu. There you'll see a list of the last four documents you worked with in Word 2000.

- If the document's not on that list, click File, Open to access the Open dialog box. You'll notice that it's nearly identical to the Save As dialog box pictured back in Figure 14.12. Double-click your way to the appropriate folder, and then double-click the name of the document you want to open.

But I can't see the right folder! If the necessary folder does not appear on screen, you might need to click the Up One Level button (the yellow folder button with the upward pointing arrow) until you get to a location you recognize.

Printing a Word Document

What good is the most eloquently written document if nobody ever sees it? That's right, no good at all; that's why you'll want to understand the subtleties of printing documents in Word 2000.

Although you can crank out a single copy of your whole document by simply clicking the Print button, I suggest you take the time to get to know the Print dialog box so you know just how much you can do with a document before you send it to the printer. For an in-depth review, flip back to Hour 10, "Put it in Writing with a Printer".

To begin working with the Print dialog box, follow these steps:

1. Open the document to be printed (that is, or course, if it isn't open already), and then choose File, Print, or press Ctrl+P. This opens the Print dialog box (see Figure 14.13).

FIGURE 14.13

The Print dialog box gives you full control of your output.

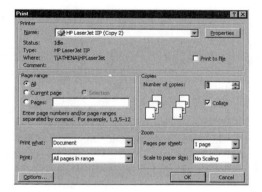

2. Once in the dialog box, confirm that the correct printer is defined. If it isn't, click the drop-down arrow next to the Name box to see the list of available choices. Click on the desired printer. Most typical users will have only one printer, so most likely you won't need to make any adjustments.

3. Specify the pages to be printed in the Print Range window (use 1–5 to print pages one through five, and 1,5 for pages one and five) followed by the number of copies to be printed in the Copies window.

4. Select the Collate check box if you want multiple copies of a document to be printed in order, or leave it unchecked if you want all of the page ones printed first, then all of the page twos, and so on. Of course you need only bother with this option if you're printing more than one copy of the document.

5. After you have all of the correct options selected, click OK to print.

14

Summary

In this lesson, I gave you enough information to create a simple document. You were shown the parts of the Word 2000 workspace, how to select blocks of text, and even how to generate a printed copy of your document. But this only scratches the surface of what you can do in Word 2000.

Hour 15, "Reducing Your Workload and Enhancing Your Image Using Word 2000," whets your appetite for the more advanced functions available in Word such as inserting tables and clip art, building a complex document with the help of a wizard, and so on.

Workshop

Now it's time to see just how much you learned in this lesson. I'll give you a short multiple-choice quiz to test what you learned, followed by a suggested activity designed to enhance the skills you acquired during the hour.

Quiz

Select the best answer to the questions from the choices provided, and then check your answers.

Questions

1. Which of the following is a part of the Word 2000 workspace?

    a. Scroll bar

    b. Status bar

    c. Cocktail bar

2. What is the keystroke sequence to perform the Cut command?

    a. Ctrl+CUT

    b. Alt+X

    c. Ctrl+X

3. Which of the following options cannot be set in the Print dialog box?

    a. The color in which the text should be printed

    b. The specific pages of the document you want printed

    c. How many copies you want printed

Answers

1. I'm sorry to say there is no cocktail bar in Word 2000 (A is the answer).

2. This one was a bit tricky, but C was the proper choice.

3. A is the answer I was looking for. The text color is specified in the document itself, not in the Print dialog box. And of course selecting colors for your document is only useful if you have a color printer, or plan to convert the document to a Web page.

Activity

Here's a simple but fun exercise that will help you try out the many neat basic features in Word 2000:

1. Launch Word and create a new blank document.

2. On the first line, type your full name; on the second line, enter your street address; finally, on the third line, insert your city, state, and ZIP code.

3. Press Enter to place the End of Document marker beneath your text.

4. Now select your name only, using one of the techniques you learned in this lesson.

5. Using the drop-down arrows on the Formatting toolbar, select a font that matches your personality. And while you're at it, make your name 16 points in size, and make it bold to give it the proper emphasis.

6. Just for fun, click Format, Font and select a funky text color from the resulting dialog box. Remember to click OK to exit the dialog box.

7. Finally, select all three lines of text, and center them using the Center button on the Formatting toolbar.

I'll bet you never thought word processing could be so much fun! (Okay, maybe calling it "fun" is stretching it a bit.)

14

Hour 15

Reducing Your Workload and Enhancing Your Image with Word 2000

This might shock you, but using the more advanced features of Word 2000 might cut your work time in half, and improve the appearance of your documents a hundred times over. And the amazing part is I'm not exaggerating a bit when I say that.

In this lesson, I show you how to give your documents that final professional polish. Here are some additional topics I'll cover this hour:

- Discover how to create great looking documents in a flash with the help of templates and wizards.
- Find out how to add headers and footers to your documents.
- Learn how to program Word to do some typing for you—really!
- Eliminate documents where a couple of lines spill over onto a second page using the handy Shrink to Fit feature.

Templates and Wizards: An Overview

Templates and wizards can go a long way toward helping you create professional looking documents whether you're a manager for a major corporation, a high school student wanting to submit high quality college application materials, or a grassroots nonprofit organization seeking funding.

So what are these things, and how do they work?

NEW TERM *Templates* are documents or worksheets that contain the text, graphics, macros, customized toolbars, and formulas needed to create standardized documents.

NEW TERM *Wizards* are interactive help utilities that guide you step-by-step through an operation, offering explanations and tips along the way. Wizards will also ask you questions to help customize the output.

Achieving Professional Results Using Word 2000 Templates

Word 2000 gives you a variety of templates from which you can generate professional-looking letters, memos, and resumes. And in this case, by "professional" I mean with preselected formatting, fonts, and occasionally even suggested text. That way you'll know the document will make the proper statement because experts essentially designed it.

To access this library of templates from within Word 2000, click File, New to look through your choices. You'll notice categorized tabs make finding what you're looking for a whole lot easier. And if your system was upgraded from a previous version of Word like mine was, you'll even have access to the old templates as well. As you browse the tabs in the New dialog box, watch for the special Word template icons shown in Figure 15.1.

FIGURE 15.1

Distinctive icons make it easy to tell which items are templates, and which items are wizards.

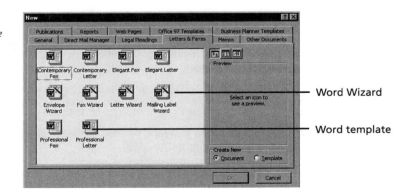

To begin working with a template, simply double-click the appropriate icon, and a new document based on the selected template will appear.

More, more, more!   If you can't find an appropriate template or just want to have more choices at your disposal, establish a connection to the Internet, and then click Help, Office on the Web. This will take you to Microsoft's Web site from which you can often download new templates and wizards. And don't let downloading them intimidate you; Microsoft will guide you every step of the way.

Working with a Template

If you know the basic Word 2000 editing techniques (which you should if you paid attention during the previous lesson), you're in luck. Take the Professional Resume Template as an example. Creating a nice-looking resume is as easy as entering and deleting text. No need to worry about formatting or font selection—it's all done for you! Just click in the area in which you'd like to work, and then begin typing.

Templates can save you infinite amounts of time, enabling you to focus on content instead of formatting issues.

Switching Templates On-the-Fly

Suppose you spent hours inserting text into a template only to find at the end you're not as happy with it as you could have been? You might want to consider switching templates to see if the results are any better. I call this "switching templates on-the-fly" because you already have a document to which you can apply the template.

Great templates think alike!   If you want to experiment with the look of a template-based document, be sure to apply a similar type of template, or you might get some pretty unusual results. That means if you're working with a resume, use another resume template, not a legal briefing template. If you don't, that resume you worked so hard to create could turn into a garbled mess of text.

To apply a new template to a document using a similar template, do this:

1. Open the document in which you want to change the template.

2. Click Tools, Templates and Add-Ins to open the Templates and Add Ins dialog box shown in Figure 15.2.

FIGURE 15.2

The Templates and Add-Ins dialog box allows you to dramatically alter the appearance of a document in a few short steps.

3. Click the Add button to open the Add Template dialog box.

4. Browse through the folders to find the desired template, and then click it to select it.

5. Click OK to return to the Templates and Add-Ins dialog box.

6. Confirm that the file you selected is currently loaded. It will appear in the Global Templates and Add-Ins box.

7. Click the Attach button to open the Attach Template dialog box.

8. Select the desired template again, and then click Open to return to the Templates and Add-Ins dialog box.

9. The path to the template you just selected should appear in the Document Template text box.

10. Check the Automatically update document styles check box to change the styles displayed by the current template.

11. Click OK to attach the new template to the active document.

By performing these steps, you can turn a professional resume (see Figure 15.3) into something noticeably different (see Figure 15.4).

FIGURE 15.3

A resume draft using Word's Professional Resume.dot template…

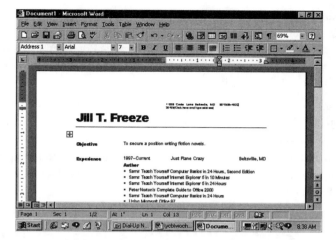

FIGURE 15.4

…can quickly be changed to this by following the steps provided.

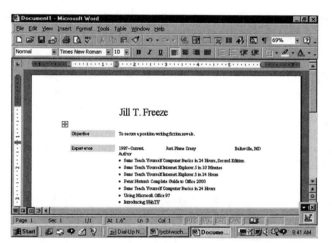

For a More Customized Document…Use a Wizard

Like templates, wizards result in high quality professional-looking output. The main difference between wizards and templates is that wizards help you create a customized document whereas templates create standardized documents.

For example, you can use the Letter Wizard to create a letter. The wizard will ask you questions about how many letters you want to write, what date you want to have appear on the document, whether the letter will be printed on plain paper or preprinted letter-head, and so on. A template, on the other hand, will simply produce a boilerplate form letter into which you can insert text.

To locate these wizards, click File, New from within Word 2000. You'll see the same New dialog box shown back in Figure 15.1. Just double-click the icon corresponding to the wizard you want to work with, and you're on your way! The wizard will launch, ask-ing you all kinds of relevant questions. Follow the onscreen prompts to help the wizard build the desired documents, and then begin editing the document just as you would have done with a template.

Adding Page Numbers, Titles, and Other Important Information Using Headers and Footers

Headers and footers allow you to print page numbers, document titles, and other repeat-ing information at the top or bottom of the page. Using headers and footers can add an air of professionalism to documents, and applying page numbers can help keep unbound documents in order.

To begin working with headers and footers, choose View, Header and Footer to open the Header and Footer toolbar shown in Figure 15.5.

FIGURE 15.5

Header and Footer toolbar items make creating headers and footers a breeze.

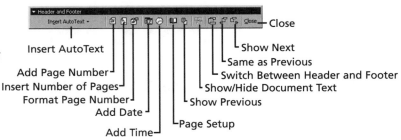

The following list describes what each of the buttons on the Header and Footer toolbar does:

- **Insert AutoText.** Click this button to select a predefined header or footer from the AutoText list. For instance, you can select the Author, Page #, Date option to have Word automatically insert your name flush left, a centered page number, and the date flush right.

> **Hey, that's not my name!** If you want to edit the name that appears in the Author field, choose Tools, Options, and then select the User Information tab. Enter the name as desired in the Name text box, and then click OK.

- **Add Page Number.** Set the insertion point in the desired location in the header (press Tab once to center the element, or twice to place it flush right), and then click this button to add the page number to your document header or footer.
- **Insert Number of Pages.** Use this button to create a "Page ? of ?" format in the desired location.
- **Format Page Number.** With this button, you can select the format of the page numbers, and you can even tell Word what page number to begin numbering with—an invaluable tool when you want to omit page numbering on the first page of a document.
- **Add Date.** Set the insertion point using the Tab key if desired, and then click this button to add the current date to the document's header or footer.
- **Add Time.** Works the same way as adding a date, of course it adds the time instead of the date.
- **Page Setup.** This button enables you to define page margins and instruct Word to use a different header/footer for the document's first page.
- **Show/Hide Document Text.** Use this button to show/hide the document's text as you work on the header or footer.
- **Same as Previous.** Make the current header/footer the same as the previous one.
- **Switch Between Header and Footer.** Move between the header and footer on a given page by clicking this button.
- **Show Previous.** Show the previous page's header/footer.
- **Show Next.** Show the next page's header/footer.
- **Close.** Click this button to exit the header/footer view.

After you've defined a header and/or footer for your document, you can go in and edit it by clicking the Print Layout View button near the bottom left of the Word workspace, and then click the element you want to modify.

Creating Tables in Word

Tables are an exceptional way to summarize large amounts of data in relatively little space. But even if you don't work with numbers a lot, you can put tables to good use for aligning columns of text.

There are essentially two ways to incorporate tables into your Word document:

- By formatting the table in Word itself
- By using an Excel worksheet

Obviously, if the data is already formatted in Excel and requires the use of defined formulas, that might be easiest. (We'll discuss this option in more detail in the next lesson.) However, if it's a simple table you need to create, Word might very well be up to the task.

Building a Simple Word Table

Simple tables are defined as tables having a maximum of five columns. The number of rows can easily be expanded, as you'll see. For more complex needs, try clicking Table, Insert Table to define a larger number of columns. To build a simple table in Word, follow these steps:

1. Place the insertion point in the location you want to begin the table.

2. Click the Insert Table button on the Standard toolbar to open a drop-down box of rows and columns that looks like a miniature table, as shown in Figure 15.6.

3. Select the range of cells that equal the number of rows and columns you want to include in your table. To do this, simply move your mouse pointer down to the drop-down box and highlight the desired number of cells. To select more rows or columns than are shown in the drop-down box, hold down the left mouse button (after clicking the Insert Table button of course) and keep dragging the mouse pointer down and to the right, releasing it when the right number of rows and columns is displayed.

I need more space!   Need more than four rows in your table? It's easy to add more. While in the last cell of a table (the bottom-right cell), press Tab to add another row.

FIGURE 15.6

Click the Insert Table button to begin creating your table in Word.

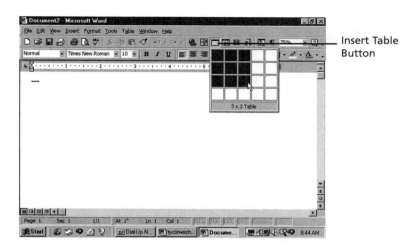

Insert Table
Button

4. Enter data in the desired cell by clicking on it, and then typing text as usual. If the text you enter is wider than the cell allows, a second line will be created within the cell to accommodate the excess.

5. To move to the next cell, press Tab. To return to the previous cell, use Shift+Tab.

Using AutoFormat to Improve Your Table's Appearance

If you really want to make an impressive table, consider using the AutoFormat tool to perk it up with a few quick mouse-clicks. To begin working with AutoFormat for tables, you'll want to do the following:

1. Place the insertion point inside the table.

2. Choose Table, Table AutoFormat to open the Table AutoFormat dialog box shown in Figure 15.7.

FIGURE 15.7

From the Table AutoFormat dialog box, you can select from dozens of table formats including multicolor tables that are perfect for publishing on the Web.

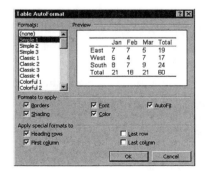

3. Choose the format you want to use in the Formats list box. You can preview it in the Preview box before applying it.

4. Click OK to confirm your choice and return to the main document.

> **Trying to achieve a different look?** If you don't see a format you like in the Table AutoFormat dialog box, or would simply like to change the appearance of your table text, you can do so manually by selecting the cells to be changed, and then proceeding as you would normally in Word.

Building More Complex Tables in Word

By selecting Table, Insert Table, you can build a table with up to 63 columns and an infinite number of rows. What's more, this larger table can be formatted with Table AutoFormat exactly like its smaller counterpart to give it a professional appearance.

To build this bigger table, follow these simple steps:

1. Position the insertion point in the desired location.

2. Choose Table, Insert Table from the Standard toolbar to open the Insert Table dialog box pictured in Figure 15.8.

FIGURE 15.8

Use the Insert Table dialog box to create tables up to 63 columns wide.

3. In the Number of Columns spin box and the Number of Rows spin box, select the desired number of columns and rows either by typing the number directly, or by using the arrow buttons next to each box.

4. In the Fixed Column Width spin box, select the desired cell size using the arrow buttons, or by selecting AutoFit to have Word determine the size of the columns. AutoFit to contents means the columns will be adjusted to accommodate the columns data, but the resulting table will not span the entire width of the page. It will be aligned just as you've defined neighboring text alignment. AutoFit to window means the columns will be stretched to span the whole width of the page.

5. You can apply AutoFormat at this point by clicking the AutoFormat button, or you can make your decision after you see the table's contents in its final form by following the steps in the AutoFormat section.

6. Click OK to create the table and close the Insert Table dialog box.

Emphasizing Content with Borders and Shading

When used judiciously, borders and shading can be extremely effective at drawing attention to selected text. You can use borders to add class to your animal rescue league's fundraising handouts; or use the shading option to draw attention to a quote from the principal in your school PTA newsletter.

Don't leave me out here all alone!   Shading is seldom used alone, which is why I've included shading and borders in a single sequence of steps. Typically, a shaded box is outlined in a thin border at the very least.

Making use of these features is easier than you might think. To take advantage of them, perform the following steps:

1. Right-click on any visible toolbar to open a shortcut menu. Select Tables and Borders to display the Tables and Borders toolbar (see Figure 15.9).

FIGURE 15.9
Use the Tables and Borders toolbar to create dynamic borders and shading effects.

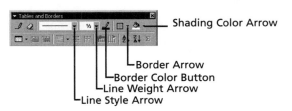

Shading Color Arrow

Border Arrow
Border Color Button
Line Weight Arrow
Line Style Arrow

2. Select the text around which you'd like to place a border (or the section of text you want to shade) by using the text selection techniques described in the previous hour.

Just so you know...   If no text has been selected, Word will find the insertion point and apply the formatting to that paragraph.

3. Click the arrow next to the Line Style box to choose a line style for the border.

4. Click the Line Weight arrow to choose the thickness of your border.

5. Click the Border Color button to add color to online documents or color printer output.

6. Click the arrow next to the Border icon to open a palette of available border styles. While the desired option is most frequently Outside Border, you have a number of options to choose from.

7. Click the Shading Color arrow to see a pop-up shading palette from which you can make your selection.

8. To close the toolbar to maximize your workspace, click on the Close (X) button at the top-right corner of the box.

A girl/guy's gotta have options   Want more border and shading options than the toolbar gives you? Select the text you want to add shading or a border to, and then click Format, Borders and Shading to display the Borders and Shading dialog box. From there you can access a large number of choices.

Working with Columns in Word

If you need to produce a newsletter for your son's nursery school, a brochure for your new business, or a magazine mock-up, you'll want to know how to work with columns in Word. To set up columns:

1. Set the insertion point where you'd like the columns to begin, or select the text you'd like to format in columns.

Stylistically speaking...   If you want a large headline to span the width of multiple columns, put the headline in place before formatting the columns.

2. Click Format, Columns to open the Columns dialog box pictured in Figure 15.10.

3. Choose the desired format of your columns in the Presets area. You can also specify a number of columns in the Number of Columns spin box or select the Equal Column Widths box.

4. To place lines in between columns, check the Line Between check box.

5. You can preview the options you chose in the Preview area.

6. Column layouts can be applied to selected text, the entire document, or from a designated point within a document. You can set this option in the Apply To drop-down list box.

7. Click OK to confirm your selections.

FIGURE 15.10
The Columns dialog box gives you incredible flexibility when it comes to formatting multicolumn documents.

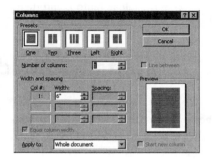

Using Shrink to Fit

Nothing's more frustrating than typing a letter only to find two lines of it spill over on to the second page. Word has a feature to save paper (and your sanity) called Shrink to Fit. To access this feature, follow these steps:

1. Click the Print Preview button on the Standard toolbar. This will display your document as it would appear on paper (see Figure 15.11).

Multiple Pages   Shrink to Fit

FIGURE 15.11
Click the Print Preview button on the Standard toolbar to see just how much of your text falls over to the next page.

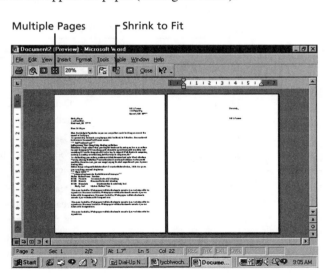

2. Click the Multiple Pages button so you can see just how much text hangs over onto the second or final page.

3. To squeeze stray lines onto a single page, click the Shrink to Fit button. The results will be shown on the same Print Preview screen.

4. Close Print Preview by clicking the Close button, and then proceed as usual with printing the document.

Organizing Your Thoughts by Building an Outline

Remember in high school when your English teacher used to make you turn in an outline for your term papers? It was always such a hassle to type it because I'd inevitably find something I'd want to change, but I'd be too lazy to retype it. Well, thanks to computers, not only is creating an outline easy, but it's a snap to reorganize, too!

To start building your outline, create a new blank document and enter Word's Outline view by clicking the Outline View button (fourth one from the left) on the horizontal scroll bar. From this view, you can assign varying levels of importance to your topics or heading titles.

Rather than go into great detail about how to use the Outline toolbar, Table 15.1 gives you everything you need at a glance.

TABLE 15.1 Outline Toolbar Buttons and Functions

Button	Button Name	Function
←	Promote	Increases the level of a heading
→	Demote	Decreases the level of a heading
⇒	Demote to Body Text	Use this button to enter body text while in Outline view
↑	Move Up	Pushes the selected heading(s) up one level in the outline
↓	Move Down	Moves the selected heading(s) down one level in the outline

Button	Button Name	Function
✚	Expand	Shows all subheadings and body text under the selected heading
▬	Collapse	Hides subheadings and body text under the selected heading
1 2	Show Headings	Expands or collapses the outline to show the specified heading level. For example clicking 2 shows only levels 1 and 2.
All	All	Toggles to expand or collapse the entire outline or hides all body text
▤	Show First Line Only	Toggles to show all body text, or only the first line of the body of text
ᴬ𝘈	Show For	Toggles to show or hide character formatting
▣	Master	Toggles between Master Document and Document view Outline view. If Master Document is selected, the Master Document toolbar will appear

To continue creating your outline, simply enter text as you would normally do in Word. Then use the arrow buttons illustrated in Table 15.1 to assign the appropriate level of importance to your headings. The resulting outline format is illustrated in Figure 15.12.

An outline quick trick   You can also use the Tab key to decrease the header's level of importance, or Shift+Tab to increase its level of importance.

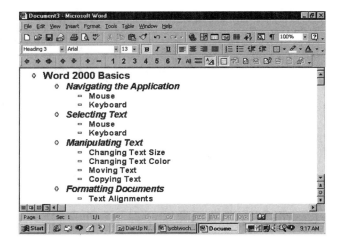

Editing an Outline

Don't like the placement of a particular topic? Moving it in Word's Outline view is a
snap. To do so:

1. Place the document in Outline view by clicking the Outline View button on the
   horizontal scroll bar.

2. Collapse the outline so that only its headers are showing.

The case of the missing text   Failing to collapse the outline before moving
headers could result in inadvertently leaving text fragments behind. Because
body text moves with its parent header, selecting it while fully collapsed is
the best way to ensure that everything gets moved safely.

3. Set the insertion point in the location to which you'd like to move text.

4. To select outline text to be moved, click on the + or – at the beginning of the heading you want to move. Note that clicking + takes with it all subheaders and body
   text up to the next + at the same level as the header to be moved.

5. Confirm that the highlighted text is the text you want to move.

6. Click on the highlighted text, hold down the left mouse button (you'll see a box
   appear at the base of the mouse pointer's arrow), and drag the text to its new
   location.

7. Release the button to place the text in its new position.

Oops.   Text show up in the wrong location? Never fear—just press Ctrl+Z and start the process again from the beginning.

Viewing the Outline While You Write

Sure you can switch into Outline view within seconds, but Word has another option for letting you see the outline of your document as you write: Document Map. This feature displays a map of your document's headers on the left side of your screen. Look at Figure 15.13 to see how this feature works.

FIGURE 15.13

Word's Document Map feature allows you to see your outline as you write.

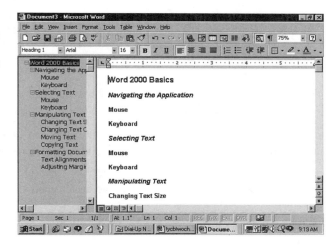

To enable the Document Map option, click the Document Map button on the Standard toolbar, or, if it does not appear on your toolbar, click View, Document Map. Now you can see the outline on the left side of your screen as you write.

Using AutoText to Lighten Your Workload

We've all spent hours crafting paragraphs that pack a punch, so why not recycle our ingenuity? Word 2000's AutoText feature allows you to store frequently used phrases, sentences, even paragraphs so that they can be retrieved effortlessly without the hassles of trying to find the phrase amidst hundreds of files. No copying and pasting, either.

Before you can have Word type for you, you'll need to do a little bit of programming. Follow these steps to program your own AutoText entry:

1. Select the text or graphic you want to store as an AutoText entry.

2. Choose Insert, AutoText, New.

3. Word proposes a name for the AutoText entry that you can accept, or you can type a new one.

4. Click OK to save your entry and exit the dialog.

> **Getting ready for action!** If you plan to create, insert, or modify lots of AutoText entries, you might want to use the AutoText toolbar instead of following the steps above. To display the AutoText toolbar, right-click on any visible toolbar, and then place a check mark next to AutoText.

So how do you tell Word when and what to type? You have multiple options when it comes to inserting an AutoText entry in your document, including the following:

- Enable AutoComplete by clicking Tools, AutoCorrect, and then clicking the Show AutoComplete Tip for AutoText and Dates check box on the AutoText tab. When the AutoComplete tip box appears, press Enter to accept the AutoText entry.

- Choose Insert, AutoText, and then select the desired entry from one of the categories listed.

- From the AutoText toolbar (see Figure 15.14), click the All Entries button, and make your selection.

FIGURE 15.14
The AutoText toolbar simplifies creating and inserting multiple AutoText entries.

Editing an AutoText Entry

Should the contents of an AutoText entry change, you can edit the entry by doing the following:

1. Insert the AutoText entry into the document as described in the previous steps.

2. Edit the entry as desired.

15

3. Select the revised AutoText entry text.

4. Choose Insert, AutoText, New, and then type the original name of the AutoText entry.

See? I told you Word could literally do your typing for you!

Summary

In this lesson, you were introduced to a number of Word 2000 features designed to enhance both your image and productivity. You learned the ins and outs of creating headers, footers, and tables, and you became comfortable working with shading, borders, and outlines. And finally, I proved my claim that Word 2000 can literally do your typing for you. To learn more about the powerful features in Word 2000, check out *Peter Norton's Complete Guide to Office 2000* by Peter Norton, Jill T. Freeze, and Wayne S. Freeze.

Next up, Hour 16, "Spreadsheet Fundamentals," will help you grow comfortable with the world of spreadsheets.

Workshop

Now it's time to see just how much you learned in this lesson. I'll give you a short multiple-choice quiz to test what you learned, followed by a suggested activity designed to enhance the skills you acquired during the hour.

Quiz

Select the best answer to the questions from the choices provided, and then check your answers.

Questions

1. Which tool/feature asks you a series of questions to help you create a custom document?

    a. Wizard

    b. Template

    c. AutoComplete

2. Can you format a Word document into columns?

    a. No way; you need a desktop publishing program for that!

    b. Yes

    c. Only documents that exceed one full page of text

3. What do you call the feature that helps you squeeze overflow text onto the last page of a document?

   a. The Amazing Ginzu Letter Formatter

   b. Honey, I Shrunk the Letter!

   c. Shrink to Fit

Answers

1. The answer is Wizard (a). Templates are essentially document boilerplates, and AutoComplete has nothing to do with document creation.

2. B wins this one.

3. Okay, so I'm being a little silly here, but you gotta have fun, right? Obviously the correct answer was C, Shrink to Fit.

Activity

The best way to discover some of the hidden gems in a program is to take the time to explore its menus. To encourage you to do this, I'm going to give you a list of Auto features in Word 2000. It's up to you to scour the menus to tell me which are real features, and which are not.

Place a circle around Auto features you find in your travels, and place an X through the "fake" features.

AutoFormat	AutoSummarize	AutoFit
AutoComplete	AutoIndex	AutoText
AutoCorrect	AutoTab	AutoSave
AutoCaption	AutoReturn	AutoControl

Four of the features listed here are not legitimate. Some are probably more obvious than others. To check your work, type any of the features you see here into Word 2000. If the feature does not exist, a red squiggly line will appear underneath it.

HOUR **16**

Spreadsheet Fundamentals Using Excel 2000

Have you ever wished you could track personal holiday spending, or play around with various tax scenarios before filling out the papers? If so, you'll gain a whole lot from this introductory spreadsheet chapter.

For some reason, many people are intimidated by spreadsheets. Maybe it's because of all the spreadsheet-specific terms, or perhaps those who fear spreadsheets are math phobic like me. Whether you're terrified to start working with numbers, or you can't wait to jump right in, I promise to do my best to make this lesson easy to follow.

This hour introduces you to Excel 2000 and spreadsheet terms and functions in general. Following are some other topics I'll cover in the course of this lesson:

- Learn the proper names for spreadsheet elements.
- Discover how to navigate your way around Excel worksheets.
- Find out how to add a group of numbers in an instant using AutoSum.
- Apply descriptive headers and footers to your worksheet before you print it.

Learning the Spreadsheet Lingo

Knowing the proper terms for what you want to accomplish in Excel makes learning to use the program that much easier. The general Excel definitions you want to know include those in the following bulleted list. Obviously, dozens more are sprinkled throughout the lesson as you explore each function.

- **Spreadsheet**—A matrix of data cells arranged in columns and rows.
- **Worksheet**—Excel's term for an electronic spreadsheet.
- **Cell Address**—As you'll see in Figure 16.1, Excel cells are "containers," capable of holding data. They are arranged in a series of lettered and numbered columns and rows. For example, the active cell in Figure 16.1 is A1 because the cell in the first column, A, and first row, 1, is highlighted. The cell address also is displayed in the Name box at the left end of the Formula bar.
- **Workbook**—Because you may want to create multiple related worksheets, Excel enables you to store them all together in a workbook.
- **Range**—In Excel, you're often asked to select or perform an operation on a range. A range is simply Excel's counterpart to Word's block of text—it's a group of cells chosen at one time that you can manipulate any number of ways, as you'll see throughout the next couple of lessons.

Anatomy of the Excel 2000 Workspace

To get the most out of Excel, you want to be familiar with its critical screen elements because these elements often hold the key to time-saving shortcuts. Figure 16.1 presents all these elements, which are explained in detail later in the hour.

FIGURE 16.1

Getting to know Excel's screen elements.

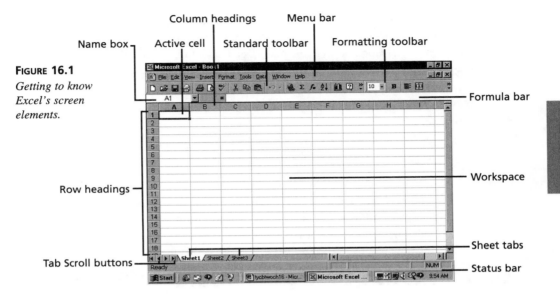

Column headings · Menu bar · Name box · Active cell · Standard toolbar · Formatting toolbar · Formula bar · Workspace · Row headings · Sheet tabs · Tab Scroll buttons · Status bar

Although many of these elements are the same as those found in Word, following are some new ones.

- **Active Cell**—A cell with a dark border (called a *cell selector*) around it. The active cell is the one you've selected to enter or edit data.

- **Column Heading**—The lettered boxes across the top of Excel's workspace. Clicking one selects an entire column of cells, which you can format or move as a whole.

- **Row Heading**—The numbered boxes down the side of Excel's workspace. Clicking one selects an entire row of cells, which you can format or move as a whole.

- **Sheet tabs**—Click these to move from one worksheet in a workbook to another.

- **Tab Scroll buttons**—If you can't see all the sheet tabs in your workbook, use these buttons to scroll to the ones that are hidden offscreen.

- **Formula bar**—This bar has two parts: a name box that displays the name given to the selected cell (or the cell's address if no name has been given) and a box displaying the selected cell's contents.

- **Formatting toolbar**—Excel's Formatting toolbar is nearly identical to Word's, except that it includes five useful buttons for formatting numbers—Currency Style, Percent Style, Comma Style, Increase Decimal, and Decrease Decimal.
- **Standard toolbar**—Excel's Standard toolbar replaces a few Word-specific buttons with AutoSum, Paste Formula, Sort Ascending, and Sort Descending buttons. This toolbar also gives you instant access to Excel's powerful ChartWizard and mapping function.
- **Name box**—This box at the far left end of the Formula bar holds the address of the cell or cell range currently selected in Excel.
- **Menu bar**—In Excel, a Data pull-down menu replaces Word's Table menu.
- **Status bar**—The left side of Excel's status bar tells you which mode Excel is in (Ready, Enter, or Edit). The other parts contain information about commands being executed, whether Caps Lock is on, and so on.

Using a Mouse to Move Around in Excel

To make a cell active, place the mouse pointer in the desired location and click. The cell selector (a thick dark border) appears around the cell you choose. If the cell is offscreen, you may need to use the vertical and horizontal scroll bars to find it. These scroll bars look—and work—just like those found in Word. Click the arrow buttons for small moves, or drag the scroll box in the appropriate direction for larger moves.

Using a Keyboard to Move Around in Excel

You will find a number of shortcut keys invaluable for working with larger worksheets and workbooks. Table 16.1 lists the most common ones.

TABLE 16.1   Keystrokes for Navigating Through Excel

Press This/These	To Move Like This
The Name box, enter the cell address, then press Enter	Jumps to the cell specified.
F5	Displays the Go To box. Simply enter the desired cell address and click OK to move directly to that cell.
Arrow keys	One cell in the direction of the arrow.
Tab	One cell to the right.
Shift+Tab	One cell to the left.
Enter	One row down.

Press This/These	To Move Like This
Page Up/Down	One full screen up or down.
Ctrl+Home	To the beginning of the worksheet (usually cell A1).
Ctrl+End	To the last cell of the worksheet.

Moving Between Sheets

The fastest way to get to another sheet in the active workbook is to click the appropriate sheet tab at the bottom of Excel's workspace. If the tab you want is out of view, use the tab scroll buttons next to the sheet tabs to find it. From left to right, these buttons perform the following actions:

- Moves to the first sheet in the workbook
- Moves to the previous sheet (using the current sheet as a guide)
- Moves to the next sheet (also using the current sheet as a guide)
- Moves to the last sheet in the workbook

Entering Worksheet Labels

One of the first things you want to do when creating a worksheet is to enter labels for the various columns and rows. These title labels show you (or anyone else entering data into your worksheet) where the various data types and calculations go. To enter these labels, perform the following steps:

1. To begin labeling the columns across the top of the screen, select the first cell in which you want to enter a label.
2. Enter the title you want to give to the first column of your worksheet. To do this, simply begin typing the text as you would in Word.
3. Press Tab to label the next column to the right, or press Enter to move to the next line and begin labeling the rows.
4. Press Enter after you type each row title.

Trying to fit in. If some of your labels extend beyond the edge of a cell, see the section "Resizing Cells with AutoFit" in the next lesson.

Entering Numbers into Excel

The next step when creating a worksheet is to fill in your labeled columns and rows with appropriate numbers. Simply activate the cell into which you want to place data by clicking it, and then enter the appropriate number. You can use the keystrokes presented in Table 16.1 to move from one cell to another.

Selecting Cells

You select a cell by clicking it. To select a range of Excel cells, however, choose from the following options:

- To select a large range of onscreen cells, click the first cell, hold down the mouse button, and drag it until all the desired cells are highlighted (see Figure 16.2). This is perhaps the fastest way to select a large range of onscreen cells.

FIGURE 16.2

Click the first cell you want to select, and then drag it until the entire range you want to select is highlighted.

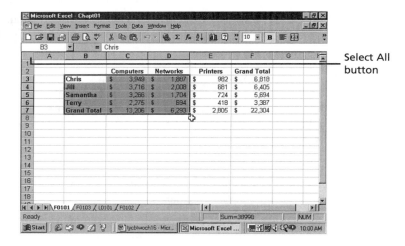

Select All button

- To select a large range of cells that extends off the screen, click the first cell, use the scroll bars to find the last cell in the range, and press and hold the Shift key while you click the last cell.

- You also may use the keyboard to select cell ranges. Click the first cell to activate it, press and hold the Shift key, and use the arrow keys to highlight the area you want to select.

- Selecting nonadjacent cells involves clicking the first cell, holding down the Ctrl key, and then clicking additional cells.

- Select all the cells in a worksheet by clicking the Select All button, which is a blank button located above the row numbers and to the left of the column letter headers (refer to Figure 16.2).

- To select an entire row or column of cells, click the heading for the row or column you want. In other words, click the A to highlight that entire column, or 1 to select that entire row.

16

Editing Cell Contents

As they say, the only thing constant is change, so you'll undoubtedly find yourself making changes to your spreadsheets as well.

As you look through the following steps, you'll notice how closely they parallel steps executed in Word. That was Microsoft's whole point with Office 2000—to make everything similar. Given that, you already know how to change font size and color in Excel. You'll find other commands similar as well.

To edit the contents of an Excel cell, follow these simple steps:

1. Select the cell you want to edit.
2. Enter Edit mode by double-clicking the cell, pressing F2, or clicking the formula box.
3. If you use one of the first two methods, the insertion point appears at the beginning of the cell. If you use the formula bar, the insertion point appears up there instead.
4. The keys on your keyboard work differently in Edit mode. The left and right arrow keys move through the cell one character at a time, for example, rather than shifting you over an entire cell. Likewise, Home and End take you to the beginning and end of the cell respectively.
5. Insert or delete characters as you would in Word 2000.
6. After you complete your edit, click the Enter button (check mark) next to the formula bar, or press the Enter key.
7. To abort the edit, press Esc or click the Cancel button next to the formula bar.
8. Finally, Excel returns to Ready mode, enabling you to continue with data entry or formatting.

Copying, Cutting, and Pasting Excel Data

Excel's Copy, Cut, and Paste functions are very similar to those found in Word. To copy or move a range of cells, perform the following steps:

1. Select the cell or range of cells you want to copy or move.

> **Not so fast, buddy!** For now, you should use these techniques only to move data, not formulas. Of course, because you don't know how to enter formulas yet, this shouldn't be a big deal. Although you can use these methods with formulas, you might encounter significant consequences. Read the section "Moving and Copying Cells Containing Formulas" later in the hour before trying these steps on formulas.

2. To copy the data, choose Edit, Copy. To move the cell(s), choose Edit, Cut. A moving dashed line, called a *marquee*, appears around the selected range.

4. Click the destination cell.

5. Press Enter to copy or paste the cell(s) in the new location. This returns Excel to the Ready mode.

6. If you want to copy the range of cells repeatedly, simply click the destination cell and choose Edit, Paste rather than press Enter. This keeps you in Move Data mode until you press Esc after the last copy or move.

Moving or Copying Cells Using Drag-and-Drop

Drag-and-drop is perhaps the fastest and easiest method to manipulate data within a screen view. You can drag and drop data to a new location in Excel by performing the following steps:

1. Select the cell or cell range you want to move or copy.

2. Place the mouse pointer on the thick border of the selected data. This turns the pointer's cross into an arrow.

3. To move the highlighted cells, click the border and drag the cell or selection to the new destination.

4. To copy the selected cell(s), press and hold the Ctrl key while dragging the selection to its new destination.

Moving and Copying Cells Containing Formulas

I haven't shown you how to make use of formulas yet, but this should come first anyway. If you attempt to copy or move a block of cells containing a formula, the results could be quite unpredictable, or just plain wrong. That's why I wanted to take you through these important steps before addressing formulas in detail.

You need to keep in mind some special considerations when copying or moving cells with formulas. Following are two of the most important:

- When you copy a formula cell, Excel has a feature that enables a formula to change relative to the location to which the formula is copied. If you copy the cell containing the formula for adding the numbers in your first column to the bottom of the second column, for example, it totals the new numbers in the second column, not the original numbers in the first column.

- If you move a cell containing a formula, however, the cell references do not change. Therefore, if you move the formula cell for adding the numbers in your first column to the second column, the cell still displays the sum of the first column, no matter what changes you make to the numbers above it.

Inserting and Deleting Rows and Columns

As time goes on, you'll need to modify the size of your worksheet. You do this by inserting or deleting rows or columns in your spreadsheet.

To insert or delete a row or column in your worksheet, perform the following steps:

1. Select an entire row by clicking 1, 2, 3, or whichever number corresponds to the row above where you want to add a new row (Excel will add the new row above the selected row); or column by clicking A, B, C, and so on (the new column will be inserted to the left of the one you selected). You also can select multiple rows or columns to add the same number of rows or columns to your worksheet. If you select three rows, for example, three rows will be inserted on top of the first row in the selected range, and so on.

2. Right-click the selection to open the shortcut menu shown in Figure 16.3.

3. Choose Insert or Delete.

FIGURE 16.3

*Use Excel's shortcut
menu to insert or
delete elements of your
worksheet.*

Inserting a Single Cell

You might find that you need to add a single cell to a worksheet, without adding an
entire row or column. Excel will add the new cell or cells above or to the left of the cell
you selected for the insert function.

I suggest you use this technique sparingly, however, because it can get pretty confusing,
especially when formulas are involved. If you do decide to perform this task, all you
have to do is follow these steps:

1. Select the cell location where you want to insert the new blank cell(s). You can
   insert multiple blank cells by selecting the same number of cells as you want to
   insert.
2. Choose Insert, Cells from the Menu bar.
3. Click Shift cells right or Shift cells down, as appropriate.

Adding and Deleting Worksheets

You can add a single worksheet to the open workbook by choosing Insert, Worksheet
from the Menu bar. The new worksheet will be inserted after the current worksheet. If
you want to add multiple worksheets, hold down the Shift key, and then click the number
of worksheet tabs you want to add in the open workbook. After you make your selection,
choose Insert, Worksheet. The new worksheets are added to the end of the workbook.

Deleting a worksheet from your workbook also is a simple task. To select the worksheets
you want to delete, see Table 16.2.

TABLE 16.2   Selecting a Worksheet in Excel

To Select This...	Do This...
A single sheet	Click the sheet tab
Two or more adjacent sheets	Click the tab for the first sheet, and then hold down the Shift key, and click the tab for the last sheet.

To Select This...	Do This...
Two or more nonadjacent sheets	Click the tab for the first sheet, and then hold down the Ctrl key and click the tabs for the other sheets.
All sheets in a workbook	Right-click a sheet tab, and then click Select All Sheets on the resulting shortcut menu.

After you select the sheets, you can delete them by choosing Edit, Delete Sheet from the Menu bar.

Copying and Moving Worksheets

As your workbook begins to take shape, you might want to do some rearranging. You might even decide to put some worksheets into a separate workbook. To move or copy worksheets between workbooks, perform the following steps:

1. To move or copy sheets to another existing workbook, open the workbook that will receive the sheets.

2. Move to the workbook that contains the sheets you want to move or copy, and then select the sheets as shown in Table 16.2.

3. Choose Edit, Move or Copy Sheet.

4. In the To book box, choose the workbook into which you want to move or copy the sheets. You can move or copy the selected sheets to a new workbook by clicking New book.

5. In the Before sheet box, choose the sheet before which you want to insert the moved or copied sheets.

6. To copy the sheets rather than move them, choose the Create a copy check box.

I hope you know what you're getting into.... Use extreme caution when you move or copy sheets. Calculations or charts based on data on a worksheet might become inaccurate if you move the worksheet.

To rearrange the order of the worksheets in your current workbook, you can drag the selected sheets along the row of sheet tabs. To copy the sheets, hold down the Ctrl key, and then drag the sheets; releasing the mouse button before you release the Ctrl key.

16

Adding Your Data with AutoSum

Adding numbers is one of the most common things people want to do with their spread-sheet data. Although more advanced formulas and functions are presented in the next hour, this section shows you how to get quick results with Excel's AutoSum feature.

To apply AutoSum to a range of cells, follow these steps:

1. Activate the cell in which you want to place the sum of the information added together.

2. Click the AutoSum button on the Standard toolbar. Excel tries to guess which data you want to add (see Figure 16.4).

FIGURE 16.4

Excel has "guessed" here that the cells above the AutoSum entry are what you want to add.

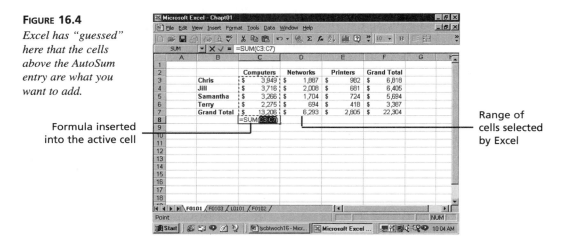

Formula inserted into the active cell

Range of cells selected by Excel

3. If Excel has selected the correct range of data, press Enter to apply the formula to the active cell. The total of the cells will appear in the active cell.

4. To select a different range to which you want to apply AutoSum, simply select the first cell in the row or column of the desired numbers, and drag the mouse to select the rest of the cells you want to add.

5. When the hash marks (sort of like the dashed lines that appear around the edges of a coupon) appear around the desired data range, click the AutoSum button to apply the formula. The total of the numbers you selected appears in the active cell.

Give the cell a name. You might want to label your sum by inserting a title in an adjacent cell. This clarifies the number to people seeing your work-sheet for the first time.

Make Your Worksheets Look Good Using AutoFormat

If you're in a hurry but still need to make a good impression, consider using AutoFormat to make your worksheets look their best.

To apply AutoFormat to your worksheet, perform the following steps:

1. Select the range of cells you want to format.
2. Choose Format, AutoFormat to display the AutoFormat dialog box (see Figure 16.5).

FIGURE 16.5

Use the AutoFormat dialog box to choose a format for your table, and then preview it in the Sample box.

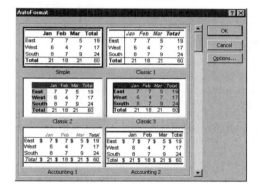

3. Click the Options button to display a list of formatting elements. Insert and delete the check mark next to each element to toggle on and off the various formatting options. You can preview these in the Sample window before applying them to the actual data in your worksheet.
4. When you see a result you like, click OK to accept it.

Be on the safe side... Before applying AutoFormat to a range of cells containing formulas and cell references, be sure to save your worksheet so that you can verify AutoFormatting has maintained the integrity of your data.

Supplying Headers or Footers for Your Worksheets

Much like headers and footers add a professional touch and sense of organization to Word documents, so, too, do they enhance Excel documents.

16

Excel 2000 comes with a number of preset headers and footers, which should serve the purpose well. To apply one of these, perform the following steps:

1. Click the worksheet to which you want to apply the headers or footers.

2. Choose View, Header and Footer from the Menu bar.

3. Choose the Header/Footer tab.

4. In the Header or Footer box, click the drop-down arrow and select the header or footer you want (see Figure 16.6).

FIGURE 16.6

Click the drop-down arrow next to the header or footer box to choose a header or footer that most adequately meets your needs.

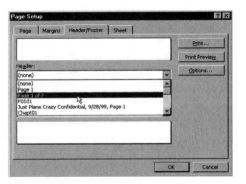

5. Click OK to apply the header and/or footer.

Saving Your Worksheets

Flip back through the Word lesson (Hour 14) that discusses how to save a document. The steps you can take there will work here as well. It really is that simple!

Printing Excel Worksheets

If you're anything like me, you find it easier to review a paper document than a screen full of electrons. This especially is true for spreadsheets. I'm much more at ease marking up a printout of the spreadsheet, which I later can go back and edit as necessary.

To print your own Excel worksheet, perform the following steps:

1. Select the range of cells you want to print.

2. Choose File, Print to display the Print dialog box shown in Figure 16.7.

FIGURE 16.7

The Print dialog box enables you to specify which parts of the worksheet you want to print—the selected text, the entire workbook, or the active sheet.

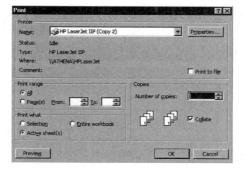

16

3. Select the printer to which you want to send the output. In the vast majority of cases where only one printer is installed, Excel will "know" the name of the printer to use.

4. Select the part of the workbook you want to print. The active worksheet means that only the tab currently displayed will print, whereas the entire workbook means everything on each tab of the file.

5. Select the number of copies to be printed.

6. Click OK to send the output to the printer.

Setting and Clearing the Print Area

Printing only part of a worksheet used to be a major hassle. Not so with Excel 2000. To print a specific section of a worksheet, follow these steps for the best results:

1. Select the area of the worksheet you want to print.

2. Choose File, Print Area, Set Print Area from the Menu bar to save the selected range.

3. Choose File, Print, and then click OK; press the Print button, or press Ctrl+P. Any of these methods will produce a printed copy of the selected cells.

Excel will remember the specified print area until you manually clear it by choosing File, Print Area, Clear Print Area. To confirm that Excel will print what you expect it to, enter Print Preview mode.

Getting What You Want the First Time by Setting Page Setup Options

Because printing worksheets that actually look good can be a daunting task, you might want to use the Page Setup and Print Preview options in cases where making a good impression is of primary importance.

To work with Excel's Page Setup options, perform the following steps:

1. Choose File, Page Setup to display the Page Setup dialog box shown in Figure 16.8.

FIGURE 16.8

Use the Sheet tab of the Page Setup dialog box to select the print quality of your output and, if needed, gridlines and row and column headers as well.

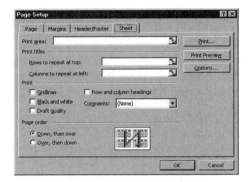

2. Select the Page tab to begin setting the options and work your way through all the other tabs (see Figure 16.9).

FIGURE 16.9

Be sure to set the page orientation of your document in the Orientation section because many worksheets look better in landscape than in portrait orientation.

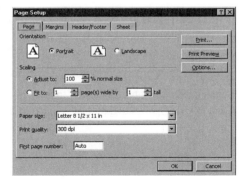

3. Some of the options you want to be sure to address are described in the following list:

- On the Page tab, select Portrait or Landscape for your document's orientation. Many worksheets look best in landscape mode.

- Select Fit to on the Page tab to squeeze your worksheet into as little space as possible. It's similar in concept to Word's Shrink to Fit feature, which tries to fit a few lines of stray text onto one less page of paper.

- Use the Margins tab to place your worksheet in an appealing position. The easiest way to do this is to specify that the worksheet be centered both Horizontally and Vertically.

- Use the Header/Footer tab to apply a header and/or footer to your output. You can select from a variety of predefined headers and footers, or create your own.

- To print the column headings on each page of a worksheet, go to the Sheet tab and specify that columns be repeated on each page. This is a must-have feature for long worksheets.

4. After you set all the desired options, click OK to close the dialog box.

Using Print Preview to Get the Best Results

To see what a document will look like printed, use Excel's Print Preview feature. This also gives you an opportunity to tweak your document if you see something that isn't quite right. To use Print Preview, perform the following steps:

1. Choose File, Print Preview, or click the Print Preview button on the Standard toolbar. The Print Preview window appears (see Figure 16.10).

2. Click the Zoom button to take a closer look, or click Setup to go back and tweak some of the options.

3. Click Close to return to Normal view, or click Print to begin printing the document as you see it.

16

FIGURE **16.10**

Enter the Print Preview screen to make sure the output meets your needs before sending it to the printer.

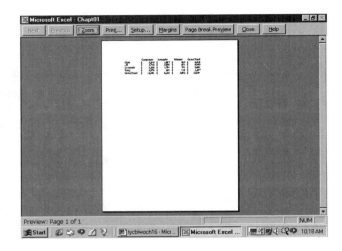

Setting Margins in Print Preview Mode

One of the most common adjustments people want to make to their worksheets before sending them to the printer is to reposition the margins. You can save time by doing this in Print Preview mode, as explained in the following steps:

1. Click the Print Preview screen.

2. Click the Margins button to see indicators that show where your margins fall (see Figure 16.11).

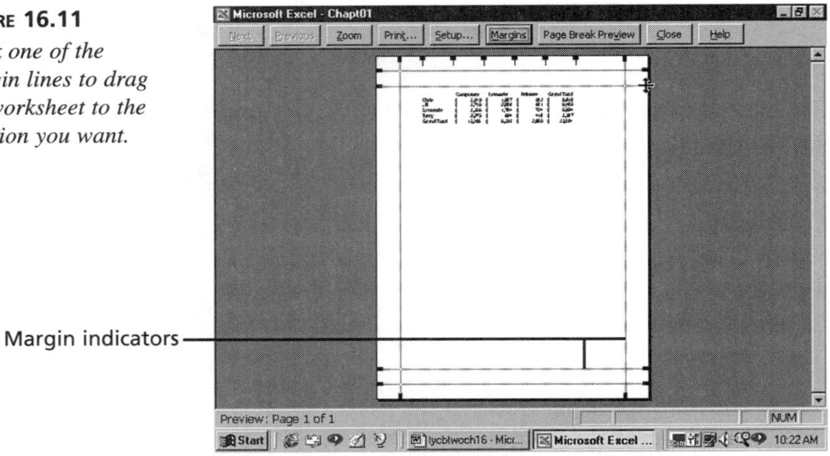

FIGURE **16.11**

Click one of the margin lines to drag the worksheet to the position you want.

Margin indicators——

3. Click the margin and column indicators, and drag them to reposition the worksheet on the page.

4. Click Print to send your creation to the printer.

Summary

After working your way through this lesson, you should be pretty comfortable building a basic spreadsheet. Hopefully, any intimidation you might have felt also is gone. With a firm grounding in spreadsheet lingo and the anatomy of the Excel workspace, you're ready to tackle an even bigger challenge.

This bigger challenge comes in the next lesson, Hour 17, where I show you how to create an Excel database. I also introduce you to building charts from your personal database.

Workshop

Now it's time to see just how much you learned in this lesson. I'll give you a short multiple-choice quiz to test what you learned, followed by a suggested activity designed to enhance the skills you acquired during the hour.

Quiz

Select the best answer to the questions from the choices provided, and then check your answers in the following section.

Questions

1. When it comes to software, which term is not unique to spreadsheets?

    a. Cell

    b. Tab

    c. Worksheet

2. Can you move a worksheet from one workbook to another?

    a. Of course; piece of cake!

    b. Workbooks and worksheets are the same thing.

    c. Only if their file names begin with the same letter.

3. What do you call the feature that helps you squeeze a worksheet into as little space as possible?

    a. The Amazing Ginsu Worksheet Formatter

    b. Honey, I Shrunk the Worksheet!

    c. Fit To

Answers

1. The answer is b. You can find tabs in every Office 2000 application, as well as in Windows itself. Of course, they don't all look the same, but the question addressed the term, not the behavior of the element.

2. The only possible answer is a. The other options couldn't be further from the truth.

3. You chose c? You win! If you chose anything else, you obviously didn't learn anything from the last silly question like this!

Activity

Launch Excel, and down the first column, type in the types of monthly household bills you pay, such as gas, electricity, phone, mortgage, and so on.

In the second column, insert some ballpark figures for each type of bill. It doesn't matter whether they are exact. This is just an exercise designed to help you get used to using Excel.

Click the first empty cell underneath the column of numbers, and click the AutoSum button. The total of your monthly bills should appear in the selected cell.

Next, give AutoFormat a whirl to make your budget look nice.

Hour 17

What You Really Need Is a Database...

Do you have a baseball card collection or some other type of collection you want to be able to sort or search? Perhaps you are in charge of maintaining the membership list for your daughter's gymnastics team. Then again, you might have a purely business need in mind—the capability to track where the customers of your small start-up company are from. Whatever the case, you could benefit by creating a database.

A *database* essentially is a collection of information organized in such a way that you can sort, filter, and analyze it. Many people think they have to use a "real" database program such as Microsoft Access. Not so. In a number of cases, you can successfully create an Excel database.

In this lesson, I show you how to do just that. In addition, following are some other topics I cover this hour:

- Learn how to create your own special data entry form.
- Discover how to use AutoFit to adjust the size of your columns to fit the largest entry.
- View the data you want by performing searches and filters.
- Analyze your data visually by creating charts.

Creating an Excel Database

Before creating a database, the first thing you'll need to do is to decide what types of information (or fields) you want to maintain for each record or entry. Take an audio CD collection as an example. You might want to keep track of the CD's artist, recording label, title, date released, and perhaps even a list of tracks on the CD.

Going through this process is vitally important to the success and usefulness of your database. After all, you can have megabytes of information stored in a database, but what good is it if you can't learn anything from it? Consider taking the time to plan your database in writing. In addition to listing the types of fields you want to include, approach the task from a second angle—listing what types of information you want to be able to deduce from the database. Following up with the audio CD example, some questions you might jot down include, "Can I find out how many Billy Joel CDs I have?" "Will I be able to tell on which CD I can find a certain song?"

At first, it may appear that the questions return the exact same results as listing fields you want to track; however, take the time to do the exercise anyway on the off chance it may uncover something you hadn't thought of.

After you adequately plan your database, you can begin creating it as follows:

1. Launch Excel with a blank workspace.
2. Enter the field names in row 1, one per cell. These columns and rows of information make up what database programmers refer to as a table.
3. If you want these field headers to be visible no matter where you are in the worksheet, select the row below the field header row and choose Window, Freeze Panes. Now the field headers will always be visible to simplify accurate data entry.
4. Begin filling the table with data, using one row for each CD (or whatever bit of information constitutes a record for your database).
5. Periodically save your database by clicking the Save button on the Standard toolbar.

Using a Data Form to Enter Excel Database Records

Excel's Data Form feature helps you enter, edit, and find Excel database data. The Data Form is a dialog box that holds text boxes for up to 33 database fields (see Figure 17.1).

FIGURE 17.1

Use the vertical scroll bar to the right of the text boxes to move from one record to another.

17

To begin using a Data Form, follow these steps:

1. Select any cell within the database. If it does not yet contain data, enter the column headers from which Excel can build the data form.

2. Click Data, Form from the Menu bar to display the data form shown in Figure 17.2.

FIGURE 17.2

A data form like this one can make data entry more comfortable by removing table clutter from your sight.

3. To add records, click the New button, and then enter the data in the appropriate field. Press Tab to move to the next field, or simply click inside the desired text box and begin typing.

4. Choose one of two ways to save the new record:

   - Click the New button to automatically save the current record and enter a new one.

   - Click Close to save your work and close the data form.

Editing Data with the Data Form

Suppose that you've created a database filled with contact information for your son's Boy Scout troop and one of the families moves, requiring you to change the address. Make your life easier by performing the following steps to use the Data Form to find and edit records.

1. Select a cell inside the database table.

2. Choose Data, Form on the Menu bar to open the Data Form.

3. Click the Criteria button to display an empty Data Form (notice that the word Criteria appears above the column of buttons).

4. In one or more of the text boxes, type in the criteria for which you want to search.

5. Click the Find Prev or Find Next buttons, as necessary, until you locate the record you want.

6. Edit the record by changing the desired text box.

7. If you decide to return to the original record after changing some of the fields, simply choose Remove before saving the record. This restores the entry to its previous state, which is immensely helpful should you accidentally edit the wrong record.

8. To delete the record permanently, click Delete on the Data Form.

9. After you finish, click Close.

10. Save your workbook as usual.

Resizing Cells with AutoFit

Although you have a variety of formatting options available to you in Excel, AutoFit is great for quick cell resizing. AutoFit makes the column width fit perfectly to the contents of the selected cell. In addition, if you select the whole column, it adjusts to fit the longest text entry in the column.

Using AutoFit One Column at a Time

Because rows automatically resize themselves as needed, you'll find that you use AutoFit most frequently to resize columns. To resize a column, perform the following steps:

1. Move the mouse pointer to the border between the column header you want to resize and the next column header to the right. The mouse pointer turns into a vertical line with a double arrow running crossways through it.

2. Double-click this location to resize the column on the left to fit the longest entry.

If using a keyboard is more comfortable to you, try clicking the letter head of the column you want to adjust, and then choose Format, Column, AutoFit Selection from the Menu bar. Excel adjusts the column width of the selected text to fit the longest line exactly.

Resizing a Range of Cells with AutoFit

Using AutoFit on a group of columns is almost as easy as applying it to a single column. Just perform the following steps:

1. Click the first column header and drag the mouse pointer through the last column you want to resize.
2. Confirm that the range of columns you want to select is highlighted. This might involve scrolling through the table to verify the fact.
3. Double-click the border between any two of the selected column headers to resize the entire selected area.

Sorting Excel Database Records

17

Knowing how to sort your database can help you take advantage of even more advanced Excel functions, such as subtotaling a group of records or counting entries that meet specific criteria. To sort your database, perform the following steps:

1. Select any cell in the table of the database you want to sort.
2. Choose Data, Sort from the Menu bar to display the Sort dialog box (see Figure 17.3).

FIGURE 17.3

The Sort dialog box enables you to sort up to three database fields in ascending or descending order.

3. Click the Sort By drop-down list box to choose the field by which you want to sort.
4. Select Ascending or Descending to specify the sort order for the selected field.
5. Repeat the process if necessary for sorts within sorts by using the Then By boxes.
6. Click OK to sort the database as specified.

You also can perform a simpler sort if your database meets any of the following criteria:

- The database contains only two column headers/fields.
- The column by which you want to sort comes either first or last in order.

To perform one of the preceding sorts, perform the following steps:

1. Select the column header by which you want to sort your data.
2. Highlight the remainder of the database table.

> **Help; I can't reach it!** If you can't highlight the entire data table after selecting the desired sort column, you should abort the simple sort and perform it using a Sort box, as described in the previous section. Continuing at this point would jumble your records—some of the fields would be sorted, while others would remain in their original positions.

3. Click the Sort Ascending or Sort Descending button on the Standard toolbar.
4. Be sure to save your newly sorted table before closing or exiting to avoid having to perform the sort again in the future. This especially is useful if you want to maintain an alphabetized table in your database.

Using AutoFilter to Find Specific Data

You sometimes might want to extract records that meet specific criteria. If you run a small veterinarian clinic, for example, you might want to send checkup notices to families whose pet is due for vaccinations during a specified month. Perhaps you want to print a list of your Beach Boys CDs only. To do this, you need to filter your database. To begin filtering records in an Excel database, perform the following steps:

1. Select a cell within the database.
2. Choose Data, Filter, AutoFilter from the Menu bar. A drop-down arrow appears to the right of each column header (see Figure 17.4).
3. Click on the drop-down arrow next to the column you want to filter, and then select the desired filter option. You can choose from the following options:

- You can select only records containing one of the field's listings. For example, you can extract all the records of people who live in South Dakota from the State field.
- You also can choose only records left blank in the chosen field.

- By selecting Top 10, you can filter the most common values in the selected field—a quick way to see of which artist you have the most CDs.

- Choose All to remove any filters from the selected field.

- By choosing Custom, you can use the Custom AutoFilter dialog box shown in Figure 17.5 to specify multiple criteria for advanced filtering. You could view customers from a particular ZIP code, for example, or search for people expressing an interest in your products from a particular state.

FIGURE 17.4

To the right of each cell is a drop-down arrow to a list box that contains an entry for each different element in that column. Select the filter option you want to use from this list.

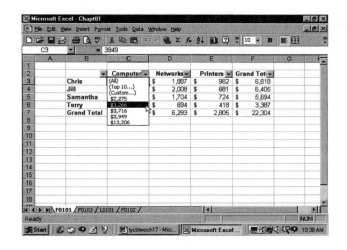

17

FIGURE 17.5

Use the Custom AutoFilter dialog box to select multiple filtering criteria.

3. You will see only the records in the database that meet the criteria you defined, which you then can edit or print.

4. To remove the filter, choose Data, Filter, AutoFilter to remove the check mark next to AutoFilter.

Grouping and Subtotaling Your Database

Excel also groups and counts data in your database. This enables you, for example, to count the number of people from each state.

To group and then count selected data in your database, perform the following steps:

1. Select a cell within the database.

2. Sort the database as directed earlier in the hour so that all the records are grouped according to the field you want to group and subtotal. You can group your CDs by artist, and then later count the number of CDs you have for each artist, for example.

3. Choose Data, Subtotals from the Menu bar to display the Subtotals dialog box (see Figure 17.6).

FIGURE 17.6

Use the Subtotals dialog box to count or average like data (among other functions).

4. In the At Each Change In drop-down list, choose the field by which you want Excel to group your records.

5. In the Use Function drop-down list, specify which function you want to perform on the data.

6. In the Add Subtotal To list, select the same field by which you chose to group your data.

7. Choose OK to subtotal your database.

8. To remove the grouping, choose Data, Subtotals, Remove All. Your database will return to normal.

Calculating Simple Statistics on a Cell Range

Excel makes it easy to perform a simple analysis on a selection of cells. You can apply any of the following functions to a group of selected cells:

- **SUM(range)**—Gives you the total of the selected range.
- **AVERAGE(range)**—Calculates the numerical average for the selected range.
- **MAX(range) or MIN(range)**—Returns the maximum or minimum value in a range.
- **COUNT(range)**—Indicates how many non-zero cells are in the range.

To apply these functions to a range of cells, perform the following steps:

1. Select the cell in which you want to place the result of the calculation.
2. In the Formula Bar, enter an equal sign, =, followed by one of the function names in the preceding bulleted list, and then an open parenthesis, (. The result should look like Figure 17.7.

17

FIGURE 17.7

In addition to the format of the function being shown in the active cell, you'll notice that the formula box now carries the function name.

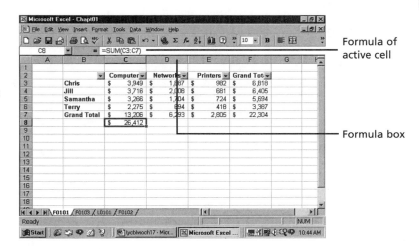

Formula of active cell

Formula box

3. Click on the first cell in the desired range. A moving dashed line appears around the cell.
4. While holding the mouse button down, drag it along to cover the desired range of cells, and then release the button. The cell range now should appear in the active cell and on the formula bar.

Um, I have a problem here... If you're placing the result of the calculation right below the selected range, be certain you haven't accidentally selected the formula destination cell as well. Doing so will give you a circular reference error, which will result in you having to reselect the cell range.

5. Place a closing parenthesis,), at the end of the range to complete the formula.

6. Press Enter to see the result in the active cell.

Applying More Complex Functions

In addition to enabling you to perform basic calculations on a selected range of data, Excel guides you through a number of complex functions using the Formula Palette. To apply a complex formula, perform the followings steps:

1. Select the formula's destination cell.

2. Choose Insert, Function from the Menu bar, or click the Function button on the Standard toolbar to display the Paste Function dialog box (see Figure 17.8).

FIGURE 17.8

The Paste Function dialog box gives you quick access to the numerous function categories and function names available in Excel.

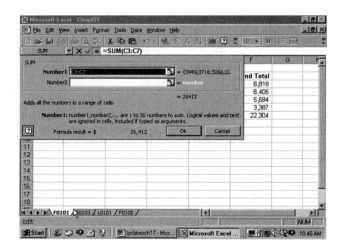

Alternate access. You can access the Function Palette by clicking the Edit Function button on the Formula bar and then clicking the Formula box's drop-down list arrow to see a list of functions. If the function you're looking for doesn't appear on that initial drop-down list, however, you'll need to choose More Functions to get to the Paste Function box shown in the preceding figure. The steps presented in the preceding numbered list are merely a shortcut. The alternate method for accessing the Formula Palette described here is best used to quickly access the palette for the most recently used function. This eliminates the need to look through the various categories and function names in the Paste Function box.

3. Select a category from the Function Category list.

4. In the Function Name box, choose the function you want. If you're not sure which one you really want, click one and view its description in the gray area below the windows.

5. After you make your selection, click OK.

6. The Formula Palette displays the arguments you need to enter for the function and an explanation of the active argument box (see Figure 17.9).

FIGURE 17.9

The PMT Formula Palette helps you calculate loan payments even if you can't remember all the formula elements needed to do so.

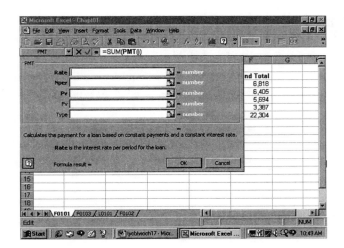

7. Enter the appropriate number or cell address for each argument.

> **Less is better.** Do not use formatted numbers as part of your arguments; instead, use arithmetic expressions. To select 8% as the Rate in the PMT Formula Palette, for example, enter **.08**. If 8% is the annual percentage rate, enter **.08/12**. Likewise, you should omit commas in large numbers because commas are used as separators in a formula.

8. After you enter all the arguments, click OK to see the result appear in the selected cell.

Using ChartWizard to Visualize Your Data

Creating a dynamic, professional-looking chart can speak volumes for your data because it shows, not tells, the reader what's going on. To create a chart in Excel, perform the following steps:

1. Open the worksheet or database table from which you want to build a chart.

2. Select the range of data you want to chart.

3. Click the ChartWizard button on the Standard toolbar to guide you through the process.

4. The first step in using the Chart wizard is to select a chart type. Start with the Standard Types tab. Select a chart type and sub-type of interest; preview the result by clicking the Press and Hold to View Sample button.

5. If you don't see anything you like there, try the Custom Types tab shown in Figure 17.10. Based on your data, the selected chart type automatically appears.

FIGURE 17.10

The Custom Types tab in Chart wizard enables you to preview your data in the selected chart's format on-the-fly.

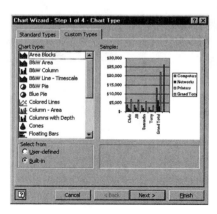

6. Accept the data range you want to use by clicking Next.

7. Step 3 of the Chart wizard enables you to set the following options:

   - **Titles Tab**—Enables you to assign to your chart and various parts of it a title, where applicable.

   - **Legend Tab**—Enables you to place a legend by your chart. You can even select the legend's position based on your page's layout.

   - **Data Labels Tab**—Enables you to choose how your data is labeled—by value, by percent, by name, or a combination thereof.

8. Step 4 asks where you want to place your chart—in its own sheet or embedded in the current sheet.

9. Click Finish to place the chart.

Moving and Sizing the Chart or Map

To move or resize your chart, follow these simple steps:

1. Select the chart you want to move and/or resize by clicking on it. Small black selection handles appear around the object's parameter (see Figure 17.11).

FIGURE 17.11

The chart with which you intend to work clearly is identified.

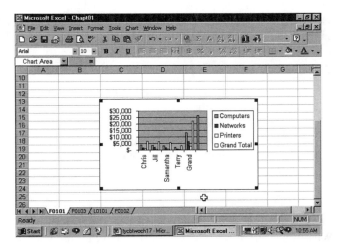

2. Position the mouse pointer over a handle, at which point it will turn into a double-headed arrow.

3. Click and drag the handle in the desired direction to make the object larger or smaller.

4. To move the object, click inside its boundaries, drag it to a new location, and then drop it into place.

Summary

I've always found it easier to design a simple database in Excel rather than resort to using overly complicated database software. Now you can do it, too. What's more, you learned how to sort, filter, and perform calculations on your data in addition to charting it.

These two lessons barely scratch the surface of what you can do with Excel 2000. To learn more about the powerful features in Excel 2000, check out Peter Norton's *Complete Guide to Office 2000* by Peter Norton, Jill T. Freeze, and Wayne S. Freeze.

In the next hour, Lesson 18 shifts focus to the Internet and what it can do for you.

Workshop

Now it's time to see just how much you learned in this lesson. I'll give you a short multiple-choice quiz to test what you learned, followed by a suggested activity designed to enhance the skills you acquired during the hour.

Quiz

Select the best answer to the questions from the choices provided, and then check your answers in the following section.

Questions

1. Which of the following is not a database term?

    a. Table

    b. Record

    c. Chart

2. What is the difference between sorting and filtering your database?

    a. A sort puts items in a specified order, while a filter extracts only records that meet a certain criteria.

    b. The two concepts are virtually identical.

    c. Sorts and filters were not covered in this book.

3. How do you resize a chart?

   a. Click inside the chart's area, and drag it to size.

   b. Click the chart to select it, and then click and drag one of the black handles in the direction you want.

   c. You can't resize them; what you see is what you get.

Answers

1. While you can create charts from a database, it is not a database term per se; therefore, c was the appropriate answer.

2. a is the only acceptable answer to this question.

3. The correct answer is b. The procedure in answer A simply moves the chart, and c is a false statement.

Activity

Remember that simple budget worksheet you created at the end of the last lesson? Well, now I'd like you to open that file, and then create a simple pie chart from it. Doing this illustrates how much of your monthly budget is dedicated to each type of bill.

17

PART IV
The Internet

Hour

HOUR 18

What Is the Internet, and What Can It Do for You?

The Internet is big, and I mean really big. Try this little game some night while watching the tube. Watch each of the commercials carefully and keep a mental tally of how many companies have Web sites listed in addition to, or even in place of, a 1-800 number. You'll be surprised just how many companies have made their presence known in cyberspace. What's more, *Internet, Information Superhighway*, and *email* have become household words, and some sources estimate that as many as 40 million of us in the United States alone surf the net! Amazingly, that number grows daily by leaps and bounds.

In this lesson, I'll take you on a brief tour of the Internet's 30-year history (yes, it really is that old!), and, for those who are still a bit skeptical about all the Internet hype, I'll give you dozens of good reasons why you might want to venture online. You'll discover the answers to the following questions as well:

- Is it true that I can actually save money by surfing the net?
- What other neat things can you do online?
- What are newsgroups, and why would I want to get involved with one?
- Is there anything I should know before I participate in an online chat?

Imagine, for a moment, that the world was totally oblivious to a person's gender, race, disability, religion, or size. What if big bucks, a fancy wardrobe, and a castle of a house no longer matters when it comes to how you are perceived by others?

Sound too good to be true? Well, in a way it is, but life in cyberspace is as close as you'll ever get to the existence described here. Online, your capability to communicate your intelligence, personality, and generosity shine through while the things that don't really count as much in the bigger scheme of things—like physical beauty and a fascinating career to match—virtually go unnoticed.

Sure, the media gives the Internet a bad name (after all, it seems like every convicted criminal hung out in a chat room at one time or another, according to the papers), but the fact is that far less crime occurs on the Internet than in the offline world; you just hear about Internet-linked crimes more often because, face it, the Internet is big news these days. Of course, you need to exercise sound judgment while you're online, just as you would when visiting a big city for the first time. You've got to stay alert and know what you're doing.

In the following sections, I try to counteract all the bad stuff you hear about the Internet by giving you oodles of good reasons to go online. After a bit of reading and exploring, I'm sure you'll agree a cruise on the information superhighway is well worth the trip!

Save Time and Money Surfing the Net

Believe it or not, investing in a connection to the Internet can actually save you money in the long run. My husband probably disagrees because of all the late-night auction surfing I do, but you can save money there, too, as you'll learn later on.

There are monthly fees associated with such a connection, but you easily can offset them, as you'll see in the following sections.

Hang Up the Phone and Grab the Mouse!

How much did you spend on long distance calls last month? I'm not trying to pry, but it really is relevant to the point I'm trying to make. Did you know that for the cost of your monthly Internet access, you'd be lucky if you could get three hours per month of talk time for the same amount of money? That's if you could secure a dime-a-minute rate any time of day for an extended period of time. Seriously, that's a measly 45 minutes a week you could spend chatting with your grandchild about his school science project; or you could spend getting caught up on the events in your daughter's pregnancy; or you could spend cultivating a new friendship…

I don't know about you, but I think this is one of those instances where quantity counts. I like being able to log on any time of day to share a funny story with a friend. There's something comforting about knowing you can ask someone a question without having to bug him or her on the telephone. Those people can go about their business and give you their undivided attention when it's convenient, which is nice for both parties.

If you decide to hook up a microphone or one of those fun WebCams discussed in Hour 11, you can end up with a video phone that beats ol' Ma Bell, hands down.

Suppose that none of the people you call regularly have Internet access. You can point out to them that if they spend as much money calling you as you do them, it might be worth getting them to link up, too. Personal computers are decreasing in price at an amazing rate. They no longer are a pricey luxury, but a reasonably priced necessity. If the people you make that suggestion to are intimidated by computers, they might want to consider a WebTV that works a lot like your VCR and remote control. WebTV Classic units can be had for $50 or less, putting them in the impulse-buying price point.

18

SOS (Save Our Stamps)

Some of us just aren't phone people. We'd rather write a 20-page letter than spend five minutes on the phone. Besides, long distance phone rates are expensive.

Well, if you thought sending a letter was cheap compared to using the telephone, just think of all the postage you can save by logging on instead of licking a stamp. Email can be an extremely cost-effective alternative for staying in touch, and compared to the time delay of letter writing, the quick turnaround of email really is significant. If you live in Maryland and send a letter to your parents in rural South Dakota via the United States Postal Service, for example, the letter will take four or five days to get there. Assume that your parents answer the letter and then place their reply in the mail the same day.

Another four to five days must pass for the letter to get back to you, and that's not factoring in weekends. Suddenly, close to two weeks have passed before you receive the answer to a question, or a reaction to your big news. If you're anything like me, by the time you finally get a response, you've forgotten what you wrote to them in the first place!

End the waiting and use email. You'll love the quick response time, and you'll really be blown away the first time you're logged on at the same time as your recipient. You'll find yourselves firing email back and forth quicker than fourth graders pass notes in the classroom!

Magazine Mania

I have a confession to make. As I stand in long grocery store lines, I've been known to grab my favorite magazine, flip through it, skim the articles of interest, and then put it back. In fact, I rarely buy the magazines displayed at the counter because I usually have ample time to read the parts I would have read had I bought the magazine in the first place. So why throw my hard-earned money away, right?

Now before you accuse me of stealing, I must say I've given up my old habit in favor of an even better approach—browsing online versions of magazines. Sure, I don't get everything I'd get in the printed edition, but they're still an invaluable entertainment and research resource. Check out the magazine list at `www.newslink.org/mag.html`, sponsored by the American Journalism Review, to see whether your favorite magazine is online, and then simply follow the corresponding links to see what it has to offer.

How can magazine publishers afford to do this if it allows people to avoid buying the paper versions? Simple—the publishers sell online advertising as well, so the more people that visit their Web site, the more they can charge for online advertising, which helps offset any lost revenue from magazine sales. And, in many cases, the pared down online version doesn't dissuade their regular subscribers from renewing anyway.

If you're frugal like me, or just want to sample a magazine before buying a copy or subscribing to it, this link will definitely save you money in the long run by helping you make informed magazine purchases.

No News Is Good News (or Is It?)

Think of all the things you could do if you eliminated that hour (or more) you spend watching the news every day on television. You could finally get yourself on a good exercise regimen; you could plant a colorful bed of flowers and tend to them each day; you could read that new Stephen King novel you've been dying to get your hands on; you could prepare a healthy meal rather than settling for fast food again.

Chances are you have something you would rather spend that extra hour doing. You can't live in a vacuum, however; you need to know what's going on in the world. So how do you find the news you need, and leave all the useless fluff behind?

Well, if you haven't already guessed where I'm going with this, it's time to recaffeinate yourself. Seriously, you'd be surprised just how much time a good Internet news site can save. You all have different needs when it comes to the kind of news you like to track, and which locales you want to know more about. Only you can determine which site will ultimately become your favorite. You've got to start somewhere, however, so here are a few places you'll want to check out:

- *USA Today*, the popular national newspaper, at www.usatoday.com gives you access to a host of national and local news.

- Another valuable tool is Reuters Online at www.reuters.com. This searchable newswire service gives you up-to-the-minute news on specified subjects, or you can scan its headlines for the biggest news.

- Another site I love visiting to catch up on news, newsgroups, and new information on the Web is DogPile at www.dogpile.com. With a single mouse click, you can tailor your search for the news wires, newsgroups, the Web, and more, and it will return results from multiple search engines at once.

- Last but not least, you can never go wrong with CNN (www.cnn.com) as a reliable, frequently updated news source.

Finally, for concentrated local coverage, visit www.newslink.org/news.html (the *American Journalism Review's* list of newspapers online) or check your favorite television network's home page for links to a local affiliate. Most networks' news centers maintain home pages dedicated to hometown issues, or at the very least provide storm tracking for hurricanes and blizzards.

So what are you going to do with your saved hour?

Avoid Club Confusion

If you've ever belonged to a video or music club, you know what a pain it can be to remember to return those dated postcards. How many videos have you ended up keeping even though you didn't like them because returning them was such a hassle?

Now with a connection to the Internet, you can join the clubs knowing that you can quickly and conveniently say no to the merchandise you don't want. So, if you've hesitated joining thus far, take another look. It can be a convenient, economical way to get the newest releases first. Browse the Columbia House Record, Video, and CD Club at www.columbiahouse.com to locate videos, computer games, and audio CDs and cassettes.

Finance Your Dream Home

Remember those decadent homes you've seen on your Sunday drive, or in local real estate magazines? Well, if you really want to live like that, the money to pay for it is going to have to come from somewhere. Surf over to the Homes and Land Electronic Magazine at `www.homes.com` to check out their nifty mortgage calculator. You can figure out how much your mortgage payment would be based on how big your down payment is, and the interest rate you secure. You also can discover whether it's more economical for you to buy or rent, along with other interesting calculations.

By running some sample analyses, you can see just how much house you can afford, given your income. All you have to do is enter some basic numbers, and let the mortgage calculator do the rest. Just be sure to read carefully what it's asking to avoid getting unpredictable results. The way you express the interest rate can be confusing, for example, so be sure to read all the details.

Get Carded

Is anyone else in shock over the price of greeting cards nowadays? I mean, what used to be a relatively minor expense in relation to a gift has now turned into a big deal. The average greeting card now costs well over $1.50. I used to send Christmas cards to more than 70 people until I saw I was spending in excess of $125 on mailing these cards alone. That's a considerable chunk of anyone's holiday gift-giving budget.

Last year, I started slicing people from my Christmas card list right and left just to bring the cost down, but I felt like such a Scrooge…

This year, I plan to try something a little different. Rather than cross people off the list altogether, I may opt to send a virtual greeting card—it's free, and it tells people I'm thinking of them. While I wouldn't advise doing this for your spouse's birthday, it's a great no-cost way to bring a smile to someone's face on a rough day. Some of the sites even let you program in the date on which the card should be sent, so you'll never be accused of missing a special occasion again. On top of that, many sites let you choose a song or sound bite from a popular show or movie to add to your card.

Watch for special banner ads from sites offering this service around holidays such as Valentine's Day, Mother's Day, and so on. Consider visiting any of the following sites for a "just because" occasion:

- At the E-Cards Web site at `e-cards.com`, you can send a free electronic postcard to anyone with an email account and Web access. During the times the site has an advertising sponsor, money will be contributed to the World Wildlife Fund for each card sent. Best of all, none of this costs you a penny.

- 123Greetings at `www.123greetings.com` gives you a ton of flexibility when it comes to sending electronic greeting cards, including the capability to schedule the mailing date, select music, and even to introduce you to some unusual holidays of which you may not even have heard!

- One of the earliest arrivals on the e-card scene was Blue Mountain Arts at `www.bluemountain.com`. You'll still find an enormous selection of choices at this old favorite.

- If you want a banquet of choices, consider this list of the best 100 virtual greeting card sites: `www.cyberpanda.com/postcard/best.shtml`. If you look carefully, you'll notice that you also can send virtual flower bouquets. I wouldn't recommend doing that for a significant other, however, unless they're frugal and have a good sense of humor!

Listen Up!

Are you tired of trying to figure out who in the world sings that song you've been hearing on the radio 20 times a day? Try Billboard Magazine Online at `www.billboard.com`. Here, you'll find the weekly ratings of songs in various genres, along with audio tracks of many of the top-rated artists and songs. While it will take some time to download the soundtrack (don't worry, we're talking a few minutes, not hours), your mind will rest finally knowing who sings the song.

Now for the obligatory tie-in to this section's theme—Billboard Online's site gives you the opportunity to sample snippets of today's hottest music which, in turn, helps you choose the CDs you want to buy before shelling out the money. Because each album has three or more tracks available for your listening pleasure, you stand an even better chance of spending your music bucks wisely. And, no more fighting over those headphones in music stores!

Get There Inexpensively

You'd be surprised at how much you can save by being your own travel agent. You can shop for airfares or select an economical hotel or romantic hideaway from the comfort of your own home. Travel resources are an interesting lot, however. Because some of them are sponsored or underwritten by specific companies, you may not see as broad a selection as you might expect, so read your results carefully.

To locate the best airfare, try the following sites:

- Travelocity at `www.travelocity.com` gives you the opportunity to search for airfares based on price or time of departure. You also can take advantage of last-minute travel bargains or select a hotel. Some services do require you to sign up for an account, but no cost is incurred.

18

- One of my favorite airfare sites is Flifo at www.flifo.com. From here, you can search for a flight based on a variety of criteria, and you can even check the arrival times of incoming guests.

> **Seeing is believing.** If you have young children who are anxiously waiting for Grandpa and Grandma to fly into town, you might want to take them to www.thetrip.com, where they can watch the plane fly over the United States in realtime; I know my Christopher and Samantha love watching it!

- Don't like flying? Try Amtrak at www.amtrak.com to learn about the schedule and fares for each stop on the Amtrak line. You can even get the scoop on the company's current travel incentives and promotions.

Having saved hundreds of dollars on airfare, it's only natural that you would want to search for a place to stay, too. Try some of the following resort and hotel sites:

- TravelWeb at www.travelweb.com enables you to search for hotels based on a number of criteria, and then links you to online reservations systems, where available. This site also provides photos of the properties and information about their amenities. The big problem here is that the hotel selection is limited to certain chains.
- Browse the Hotel and Travel Index Online at www.traveler.net/htio to see information, including reviews, on thousands of hotels throughout the world.
- Perhaps the best deals are made by locating the desired hotel's site directly. Take the Holiday Inn Sunspree in Orlando, for example. By going to www.kidsuites.com, you can search the hotel's reservation system to check for availability of a room during specified dates.

Taxing Times

It's April 14th, and you're panicking because you don't have your taxes done. Just as you're about to fill out the last page, you discover you need some obscure tax form from the IRS. It also is 9:00 p.m., so the library is closed and you have to be at work early in the morning for a meeting. What's worse is you went to the library last weekend and spent hours tracking down and photocopying all the forms you thought you needed. Grrr!

If you have a printer, you might be in luck. By visiting the IRS's Web site at www.irs.gov, you might be able to print the forms and the instructions you need in a snap. Have the form numbers handy, fire up your printer, and you're ready to go!

Read 'Em and Weep (or Buy Them)

I've lost track of how many books I've purchased only to find that after reading the first chapter, I just couldn't get into it. Sometimes the style is too dry; other times the book has no personality. No matter the case, however, books are too expensive to just toss your hard-earned money at them. Sure, you scarf up the latest Tom Clancy, Mary Higgins Clark, or Danielle Steel novel because you know it'll be good, but when you try a new author for the first time, it's nice to know what you're getting into without loitering for hours in bookstore aisles.

The Washington Post's Chapter One feature at `www.washingtonpost.com/wp-srv/style/longterm/books/books.htm` gives you the opportunity to read the first chapters of books before you buy them. You also can browse bestseller lists and read a host of book reviews, which—in theory—should help reduce the likelihood of disappointment in a book.

You also can find chapter excerpts of a book at the Web sites of authors, publishers, and some smaller, more specialized bookstores.

Comparison Shop Without Wearing Out Your Shoes

18

Believe it or not, many of your favorite stores also are online, so it's possible to comparison shop without getting blisters. Just as grocery stores in proximity to one another compete for your business, online merchants do the same.

Take two of the biggest book merchants on the Web, for example: Amazon Books at `www.amazon.com` and Barnes and Noble at `www.barnesandnoble.com`. Amazon had a huge following among netizens because it was one of the first and the largest bookstores on the Web. With Barnes and Noble and a large number of competitors now on the scene, the companies are vying for your business by offering deep discounts on books on the bestseller lists, and other price reductions. This high level of competition will continue to appear on the Internet as e-commerce sites continue to sprout up. It pays to shop around, and you're the one who stands to benefit.

Thanks to the technology of the Internet, however, you don't need to hop from Web site to Web site to comparison shop. You can visit a few key comparison-shopping sites that literally will do all the work for you!

To find some of the best prices around, check out the following:

- Bottom Dollar at `www.bottomdollar.com`, you can search some of the largest online merchants, such as Amazon.com, QVC, and KBKids to find the best price on your selected product.

- ComparisonShopping.net at www.comparisonshopping.net links you to the premiere comparison shopping search tools for buying books, digital cameras, even for finding the best long distance and credit card rates.
- PricePulse at www.pricepulse.com is where you'll want to go to seek the best prices on computer equipment, stereo gear, and other random electronics.
- Finally, it may be worth your while to pay a visit to SelectSurf at www.selectsurf.com/shopping/compare/. You'll be directed to a batch of helpful comparison shopping tools.

Lose Your Package?

Aunt Millie didn't receive that package you sent her for her birthday? Next time, use package tracking to protect your goodies. While that terrycloth robe is replaceable, those special photos of the baby may not be. So, the next time you mail a package, write down the tracking number, and surf to one of the following sites to monitor its progress:

- UPS at www.ups.com
- US Postal Service at www.usps.gov
- Federal Express at www.fedex.com
- Airborne Express at www.airborne.com
- DHL Worldwide Express at www.dhl.com

Be Your Own Operator

How many times have you had to dial directory assistance to get the phone number of the florist in your grandmother's town, or the number of your old college roommate that you accidentally threw out? Save yourself the pricey fees by looking up your own phone numbers at one of the following Web sites:

- Big Book at www.bigbook.com gives you access to a searchable yellow pages complete with maps, driving directions, and the capability to maintain your own address book based on listings you select. Figure 21.3 shows an example.
- With the AT&T Toll-Free Internet Directory at www.tollfree.att.net/dir800, you can obtain the toll-free number to many of your favorite businesses. Let them pick up the tab for your call!
- Switchboard at www.switchboard.com will help you find a variety of businesses in a selected category within the area you specify. You also can obtain personal white page listings from this site.

- InfoSpace is another Web site you may find useful. In addition to doing standard people and business searches, you can perform reverse lookups of phone numbers and addresses—an invaluable tool if you find an unlabeled bit of information scrawled on the back of an envelope.

Over a Dozen Creative Uses for Your Internet Connection

I challenge you to walk into a bookstore some day and count the number of "cool sites on the Internet" books. They're everywhere, but what's really worth noting is that in a majority of cases, they do little more than present a list of sites, one-paragraph description, and a URL for the sites—information you can get from any old search engine. Granted, these books presumably have weeded out some of the useless sites, but still, not a whole lot of value has been added there.

This section, however, takes a look at how you can actually use some of the many resources on the Internet to enhance your lifestyle and productivity.

Make a New Friend

It's easy to make new friends on the Internet (although you should first be intimately familiar with the contents of Hour 22, "Before You Spend Significant Time Online..." which I'll cover in a few lessons). You can make friends by reading your favorite newsgroup and then contacting someone with similar values or interests; you could meet them in a chat room; or you could discover them while participating in a mailing list. No matter where you meet them, however, you now have email at your disposal, so getting to know one another and keeping in touch will be easy and affordable.

Choose the Best College

Whether you're a junior in high school or a senior citizen wanting to pursue a longtime passion, you might want to find a college offering classes in a specific area of interest. It's a big decision, so why not use the Internet to narrow down your choices?

Perhaps the best place to start is ".edu: U.S. News Colleges and Career Center" at www.usnews.com/usnews/edu/home.htm. From this comprehensive Web site, you can find colleges based on your intended major, the college's location and size, and the selectivity of the school's admissions criteria. You can even apply online. You also can explore graduate schools, financial aid requirements, admissions test preparation, and *U.S. News and World Report's* ranking of the colleges.

18

One of the neatest features of this site is that after you search on your college criteria, you get a list of colleges that meet exactly that criterion. From the list, you can click your way to various resources of the selected institutions, including door-to-door driving directions from your home to the colleges of your choice.

Have fun searching for the perfect college, and revel in how much money you saved not buying all those select-a-college books!

Put Those Leftovers to Good Use

It's the Sunday after Thanksgiving, and you're fresh out of creative ideas for turkey leftovers. In fact, your family may start taking hostages if you produce another turkey sandwich! What do you do?

Hop on to the Internet and surf over to the Epicurious Eating Recipe File at www.epicurious.com/e_eating/e02_recipes/recipes.html. You can search well over 6,000 recipes from the likes of *Bon Appetit, Gourmet,* and *House and Garden,* or even recipes from new cookbooks. Your search is based on key ingredients or the type of dish you specify. (In case you're curious, I found over 125 recipes for turkey, ranging from turkey lasagna to turkey quesadillas.) Or, if you prefer, you can just browse through the database for inspiration.

This site may very well be responsible for restoring family peace at the end of November!

Pick the Perfect Pooch

Say that quickly three times in a row! Seriously, have you contemplated getting a dog, but weren't sure which breed would be best for your family and the size of your home or property? The Waltham Pet Foods Company has created "Select-a-Dog" on their home page at www.waltham.com to help you make the best decision possible. Just surf on over to the URL above, click the link to the Dogs section, and then click the Select-a-Dog link.

The questionnaire asks you a series of questions ranging from how much money you want to spend feeding the dog each week, to the ages of children that would be living with the dog. The site analyzes your responses, and then returns the best breed of dog based on the answers you provided. You see a color picture of the dog and a description of the breed's traits. In most cases, "Select-a-Dog" provides you with more than one breed that closely matches your criterion. Simply select the breed's name, and then click Go to see similar information on the other breeds you chose.

Chart a Path

Have a baby shower coming up? Need to host a silver wedding anniversary party? Wouldn't it be nice to include a professional-looking map with step-by-step directions in the invitations so that your guests know how to get there? We've all received those illegible scrawlings that do more harm than good, but now you can be the envy of all your friends by including a map that actually helps your guests get to their destination. You can even call on these sites to help you plan the quickest way to get from work, to home, to your son's soccer practice, to your daughter's ballet lesson in record time.

All you need is a printer, and Internet connection, and your mouse pointing to one of the following addresses:

- MapQuest at `www.mapquest.com`
- Zip2 at `www.zip2.com`
- CyberRouter at `http://route30.delorme.com`

Become a Virtual Volunteer

More than a million nonprofit organizations in the United States alone rely on the support of volunteers to fulfill their mission. Whether you're a retired corporate executive who would like to act as an advisor to such an organization, or a homemaker who wants to help further the work of a favorite cause, distance need not exclude you. A lot of advice can be exchanged via email, and in many cases, an organization can use people in different locales to spearhead regional fundraising efforts.

You can link up with organizations needing your help by browsing their Web site, or by sending them email expressing an interest in their efforts. More recently, however, a number of online volunteer clearinghouses have emerged. As nonprofits rely increasingly on the Internet to recruit volunteers, you'll see even more of these sites crop up.

The best way to find organizations needing help in your area is to press the Search button on your remote control or wireless keyboard, and then type the word **volunteer**, followed by the name of your city, state, or preferred cause. A sample entry might be `volunteer maryland animals` or `volunteer orlando`. The search engine will return a list of Web sites that will point you in the direction of a host of opportunities unique to your location and special interest. Simply highlight the site you want to visit, and then press Go to see whether there's a good match between what you can offer and what the organization needs most.

18

Expand Your Collection, or Learn More About It

Maybe you've collected Barbie dolls for years and finally have more time (and let's be honest, more money as well) to devote to building your collection. The Internet is a great place to learn more about your collection, whether it's miniature die-cast cars, postage stamps, or Christmas ornaments. You can get the lowdown on the value of some of your pieces, learn interesting tidbits about factory errors that resulted in extremely limited (and valuable) runs, or even get a sneak peek at what's coming down the road so that you can plan and budget your purchases.

Many manufacturers of collectibles have set up Web sites. Some of the more prominent ones include the following:

- Matchbox Toys at www.matchboxtoys.com
- Hot Wheels at www.hotwheels.com
- Barbie Collectibles at www.barbie.com
- Enesco, Inc. (Precious Moments, Cherished Teddies, and other products) at www.enesco.com
- Coin Universe at www.coin-universe.com
- Hallmark Cards, Inc. (for their collection of holiday ornaments) at www.hallmark.com
- Lladro figurines at www.lladro.es
- LGB trains at www.lgb.com
- Fleer or Skybox trading cards www.skybox.com
- Beanie Babies, Beanie Buddies, Pillow Pals, and Attic Treasures at www.ty.com.

While manufacturers provide a reliable source of information about upcoming products, keep in mind they're going to be biased. The more objective and critical reactions of diehard collectors and the related gossip may be more your cup of tea. To find sites like these, use Internet Explorer's Search Assistant feature as described in the lesson dedicated to Web Surfing 101 (Hour 20: "Web Browsing with Internet Explorer 5"). You'll have to be patient though, since I don't cover this until the lesson after next. It may take some time to weed out the good from the bad, but after you do, you'll be amazed by the way these sites and the people who frequent them enrich your collecting experience.

NEW TERM   **Ring around the Web sites!** Many sites dedicated to collectibles have formed *rings* to link similar sites. By clicking the Barbie ring icon on a selected Web page, for example, you are automatically transported to the next Barbie site in the ring. This is a terrific way to immerse yourself in data about your favorite collectable.

You can also purchase items for your collection from a variety of online storefronts or from a fellow collector in a newsgroup. Just make sure to read Hour 22, "Before You Spend Significant Amounts of Time Online…" before doing so.

Choose Your Junk Mail

It might seem like you have no control over the junk mail that gets stuffed in your mailbox, but now you can at least control the catalogs you receive. Visit any of the following sites to add your name to or remove it from a mailing list; however, be sure to read their policies carefully about whether they will share or withhold your name from other interested parties. You don't want to be surprised at receiving catalogs you never intended to order.

- Catalog Site at www.catalogsite.com
- Catalog World at www.catalogworld.com
- CatalogLink at www.cataloglink.com
- Catalog Request Center at www.catalog.netcart.com

These should be more than enough to get you started. If you don't see a way to order a catalog from the company of your choice on one of these sites, consider using Internet Explorer's Search Assistant to take you directly to the company's site.

18

Learn More About a Medical Condition

The world of medicine can really baffle a person. What's worse is that medical professionals will sometimes dump a diagnosis on you, and then rush you out of the office before you can even catch your breath to ask a simple question. While no printed fact sheet can (or should) replace the wisdom of a professional, it can answer a few of your questions and make you a more educated patient. That way, you can ask focused and informed questions the next time you visit your doctor. Browse these Web sites for an overview of hundreds of medical conditions.

- HealthGate Free Medline at www.healthgate.com is a potentially bountiful resource if you know how to spell the condition you want to research.
- Healthfinder at www.healthfinder.gov is a great resource if you're looking up one of the conditions they have listed. This site has a large number to choose from, but neither of the conditions I wanted more information about were available. Of course, that may change as the site grows in popularity.
- Mental Help Net at www.cmhc.com is a tremendous resource and reading area on mental health issues ranging from depression to anxiety.
- Prevention's Healthy Ideas at www.healthyideas.com/index.html offers ideas for a more natural approach to healthcare.

Web sites dedicated to educating consumers about the medications they take also are available. Because not all physicians thoroughly explain potential side effects of these medications, it may often be up to you to learn more details. Check some of the following sites for more information:

- To get the latest information on drugs recently approved by the FDA, visit `www.fda.gov/cder/da/da.htm`. You may even be more up to date than your doctor by browsing this site.

- Visit HealthTouch at `www.healthtouch.com/level1/p_dri.htm` to search on the name of your medication, but be sure to have the correct spelling. You can learn all about the medicine you're taking from this site, including what it does, the potential side effects, and so on.

- RxList at `www.rxlist.com` gives you more information (it even includes some clinical studies) than HealthTouch, but there is a downside—RxList is a little harder to navigate and it has a smaller number of medications listed. They do list the 200 most commonly used drugs, however, which means the odds of finding what you need are still pretty good.

Hundreds, if not thousands, of Web sites are dedicated to specific medical conditions, which you can find using Internet Explorer's Search Assistant as described in Hour 20, "Web Browsing with Internet Explorer 5." You also might find a number of special support groups (either a newsgroup or mailing list, sometimes both) on the Internet. Read the lesson on emailing and newsreading with Outlook Express for more information on how to find a specific newsgroup, or visit `www.liszt.com` to search for a mailing list.

Have a Good Laugh

As you've read this book, you've probably noticed my love of humor. It creeps in at some of the strangest times, I know, but I admit it's my favorite coping strategy. If you want a good laugh or need to come up with a funny ice breaker for a speech you have to give, consider tapping into the vast resources of the Internet. Humor sites range from politically incorrect jokes to Microsoft jokes to profession-specific jokes.

Visit a few of these sites, but don't do it in the middle of the night—you might wake the kids by laughing!

- Updated daily, The Funny Firm at `http://users.aol.com/funnyfirm/funny.htm` contains loads of original and current jokes, humor bits, and one-liners. While the site is geared toward comedians and radio professionals, it still makes for fun browsing.

- Want to make fun of your own name or the name of others? Check out the Internet Anagram Server at www.wordsmith.org/anagram/index.html. I'm sorry to say that my name is so boring, no anagrams were found. But I take great comfort in knowing I'm married to "a sneeze we fry" (Wayne S. Freeze to the anagram-impaired). At least his name is interesting!

Plan Your Day Trip or Vacation

Grandkids out of school for the day and clamoring for someplace fun to go? Have a week's vacation you need to use before the end of the year or you'll lose it? Surf the Web for great ideas, whether you're planning your trip a year ahead of time or an hour ahead of time.

Consult the following Web sites to locate special events of interest:

- Festivals.com at www.festivals.com enables you to search a database of over 20,000 festivals, fairs, and special events worldwide. You can conduct your search based on the location, the dates, or the type of event, so finding something fun to do just got a whole lot easier.
- For family-centered entertainment, surf over to Disney's Family.Com at www.family.go.com. From there, you can hop to a variety of local sources.
- If you're craving cotton candy and carnival rides, surf over to FairsNet at www.fairsnet.org for the most complete listing of fairs out there. This site even includes links to fair home pages (where available) so that you can get the latest information about your special event.
- If music is your passion, visit Festival Finder at www.festivalfinder.com to locate information on over 1,300 music festivals in North America.

The following sites can help you choose a travel destination:

- The Directory of Travel at www.travel.org is your one-stop shop containing destination links worldwide.
- Another terrific resource is CityNet at www.excite.com/travel/, which includes not only destination links, but links to movie theater information, local newspapers, and so on.

For information on a specific destination, consult the Internet Explorer Search Assistant.

18

Extend Your TV Viewing Experience

We all have a favorite TV show that we just can't seem to get enough of, whether it's a daily soap opera or a weekly science fiction thriller. Luckily, the television networks and some very dedicated fans have produced a phenomenal number of Web pages and newsgroups, enabling us to get our fix of the show between airings.

If you want more information about a TV show, perhaps the place to start is the Web site for the network that broadcasts the show. Typically, the network's home page can be reached at www., followed by the network name (NBC, CBS, or FOX), and then .com. (PBS is an exception and can be found at www.PBS.org as is ABC which can be found at www.abc.go.com.) Because these sites are so large and well traveled, navigating through them to find your favorite show should be pretty easy.

Some of the best stuff, in my opinion, is the information gathered by the fans. Some of the better fan sites provide you with obscure facts about your favorite actors, color photos, biographies, even links to online interviews and question-and-answer sessions. You also can learn how to join a fan club or how to write to your favorite star.

To start finding information about your favorite show, check out the following sites:

- TV Net at www.ultimatetv.com for a searchable mega-directory of resources (including Web pages, newsgroups, and episode lists) dedicated to TV shows.
- Sony Online at www.sony.com for information on a whole host of popular contemporary shows.

Here again, you can take that Search Assistant for a test drive to see how well it finds sites dedicated to your favorite shows.

The History of the Internet

Now that I've gotten your attention by showing you all the neat things you can do with the Internet, it's time to get down to business. All this cool technology didn't just pop up over night. (Be honest, you wouldn't still be reading this lesson if it started with the history part, would you?)

When people think of the Internet, the World Wide Web and email often come to mind. In actuality, the Internet is not these things at all. The Internet is really a group of computers hooked together that are capable of speaking to one another in a common language. (See Figure 18.1 for a graphic on how the Internet is formed.) The World Wide Web and email are simply modes of communication. Much like humans rely on letters and telephones to communicate, computers use things like Usenet, the Web, and email. (You'll learn much more about each of these in remaining lessons in this book.)

FIGURE 18.1
Machines attached to the Internet are so tightly interconnected, it almost resembles a cloud.

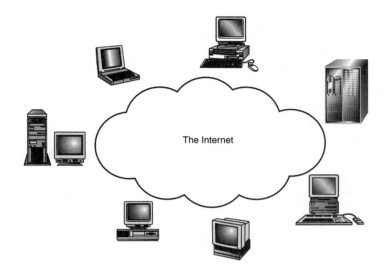

The Internet

To say that the Internet has experienced explosive growth over the past decade could be considered a gross understatement. Take a look at Table 18.1.

18

TABLE 18.1 Increasing Number of Host Machines Connected to the Internet.

Year	Number of Hosts
1969	4
1971	23
1981	213
1984	1,024
1986	5,089
1987	28,174
1988	56,000
1989	159,000
1990	313,000
1991	617,000
1992	1,136,000
1993	2,056,000
1994	3,864,000
1995	6,642,000
1996	12,881,000

From Winding Dirt Road...

This staggering growth was no accident—many key events and technological breakthroughs led to the Internet becoming what it is today.

Back in 1969, when man first walked on the moon and people were bopping along to *Sugar, Sugar* by the Archies, the Department of Defense (DoD) commissioned the Advanced Research Projects Agency (ARPA) to research computer networking. What better way for researchers to share their knowledge than to exchange data via computer, right? What resulted was a network of four computers that became known as *ARPANET*.

NEW TERM   **Networks aren't just for TVs anymore!** A network results when a group of entities are connected together, whether they're a group of legal professionals, a bunch of local TV stations, or, in our case, a group of computers.

A mere two years later, email was invented and ARPANET nearly quadrupled in size. Just to give you an idea of how long ago that was in the scheme of things, sending a letter first class in the United States cost only eight cents back then. (Luckily for us, postal rates didn't increase as quickly as the size of ARPANET; it only seems like it!)

Over the following decade, ARPANET grew at a steady clip, adding its first international connection in 1973. Colleges and universities gradually tapped in to the network as well. In fact two of these universities, Duke and the University of North Carolina, established Usenet in 1979. Usenet gave researchers and scholars a forum to discuss information on very specific topics. Rather than emailing all interested parties about a finding or hypothesis, researchers could post their thoughts for all to see and respond to.

Something was still missing, however. Not every computer could speak the "language" of ARPANET. It was sort of like having a bunch of brilliant scientists gathered from around the world with no translator in sight. For this reason, ARPA declared the Transmission Control Protocol/Internet Protocol (TCP/IP) as the protocol suite for ARPANET in 1982.

Now before you put down this book in frustration (or boredom), let me explain why this development is so important. TCP/IP gave computers of all kinds a common way to exchange information. In other words, those brilliant scientists from around the world finally found a translator! This development planted the seeds for growth of the Internet as we know it today.

To Paved Two-Lane Highway...

As the number of computers linked to the network passed 10,000 in 1987, there was no question that the Internet had reached adolescence. It grew ten times its size between 1987 and 1989, but it was still considered far from mainstream technology. You had to know the right people in the right places to check out the Internet because access was still pretty much limited to researchers and scientists.

And let's be brutally honest here—the Internet wasn't terribly exciting back then anyway. Not only was stuff next to impossible to find, but what you did find was in bland fixed font text or, worse yet, a bunch of jumbled characters that computer scientists refer to as *UUencoding*. But again, the Internet existed for the exchange of information, not for drooling over pictures of [insert your favorite object of browsing here]. That came later!

To Information Superhighway!

By the time 1991 rolled around, there were a whopping half million computers linked to the Internet, but that was just the beginning. 1991 can easily be considered the birth of the information superhighway. The University of Minnesota gave us Gopher, which enabled users to click through menus of information made available to the public. (See Figure 18.2 for a sample Gopher screen.) Finally, people could surf for the good stuff without necessarily knowing what was where! Gopher may seem a little old-fashioned and unproductive when you compare it to the Web-based search engines we know today, but it was a major breakthrough for its time.

FIGURE 18.2
Gopher: It ain't pretty, but it was useful for its time.

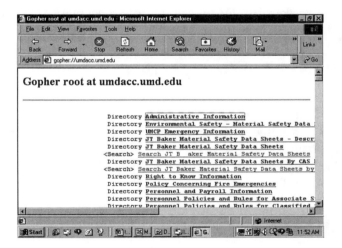

While the World-Wide Web also made its debut in 1991, it wasn't until 1993—when Mosaic (the first graphics-based Web browser) took the Internet by storm—that the Web stepped into the limelight. Not only had the number of computers on the Internet passed two million, but the White House came online, bringing a Web page and email addresses for the First Couple. The Internet was indeed starting to make its presence known.

The plot thickened in 1994 as electronic shopping malls appeared, and Pizza Hut began accepting orders online. Some ingenuous college students even found a way to program Coke machines to respond to commands given over the Internet! The Internet was here to stay, and more and more people were taking an interest in it each day.

In mid-1996, there were nearly thirteen million computers making up the Internet, and some sources estimate that the Internet doubles in size each week! Although Internet access had become easy to obtain, some limitations still existed. Computers capable of accessing the Internet were expensive, and you really needed to know what you were doing to get online successfully. Then there was the gruesome and confusing hunt for an Internet Service Provider....

Things got even more interesting with the introduction of WebTV, a low-cost, user-friendly set top box that enables you to access the Internet using your television set. Combine that with plummeting PC prices, and it's easy to see how the Internet became a household word. What's more, leading PC manufacturers knew that the Internet was a driving force in the increase of personal computer sales, so many offered sizeable rebates on computer purchases in exchange for a long-term commitment to the affiliated Internet service provider.

Now that you know the life story of the Internet, let's take a closer look at the services offered on the Internet.

The Web of Information

Ah, the Web...millions of pages of information on every topic imaginable—some factual, some fictional—some informational, others just plain fun. The Web is undoubtedly the most high profile service available on the Internet. Nearly everyone—corporation and individual alike—has a piece of the Web to call their own. In Hour 20, " Web Browsing with Internet Explorer 5," and Hour 23, "Build a Web Page in an Hour," you'll learn the details of how this popular service works.

Elementary Email

After you start sending email to a friend or a family member, you're not going to want to stop. The convenience, simplicity, and affordability of it all will spoil you forever! But how does email work specifically? Here's an oversimplification because the grungy details don't really concern us anyway.

Email isn't much different than snail mail (mail delivered by the U.S. Postal Service). You put an address on the correspondence, and then rely on someone else to get it to its destination. With snail mail, you rely on a bunch of machines and a handful of people to do the work. With email, you have dozens of computers that act as virtual mailmen (or mailpersons to be politically correct). Each method has its place, but with email, there are no yucky tasting envelopes or stamps to lick!

As for which is quicker, no contest. You'll have to trust me on this one for now, but I'll prove it when we take a closer look at emailing with Outlook Express. When it comes to the economy of sending email, every letter is free as opposed to costing 32 cents or more, regardless of how many pages you've written. Furthermore, sending an email to Australia from Maryland costs no more than sending email across the street. Finally, the addresses are a whole lot shorter, too. Rather than needing the person's name, street address, city, state, and postal code, all you need is one line of text (in my case, simply JFreeze@JustPC.com).

A Nose for News (or Gossip)?

Most of us have a healthy dose of normal human curiosity, whether we care to admit it or not. Likewise, many of us like to flaunt our knowledge, and we feel good when we can inform others or set the record straight on rampant, inaccurate rumors. Newsgroups are the perfect place to get the most up-to-date information available. News of upcoming products leak out for the world to see before companies are ready to tip their hands; trade show attendees share what they saw with others who couldn't attend; people trade advice about products not worth buying, or steer you to reputable dealers and coach you on fair pricing…it's a neat experience.

18

Of course, the medium also lends itself well to misinformation and the work of all kinds of characters. (Wait until you experience your first April Fool's Day on the Internet! You'll see all kinds of crazy rumors and announcements generated for the sole purpose of a good laugh. One year, someone started the rumor that a popular *Star Trek* series was being cancelled. You should have seen the ruckus!)

The key to it all is to use your judgment before jumping to any conclusions. Remember that you have the World Wide Web at your disposal now, so you can easily verify much of what you hear by poking around a bit.

You may be wondering how, if people all over the world can post articles to a newsgroup, this all works. When each person originates a message (be it a new article or a posted response to an existing article), that message is given a unique message ID, usually some kind of control number. All the servers linked to the Internet use that identifying number to make sure the message is sent to all the other computers that need to view it. This number also keeps the message from appearing on one computer multiple times because the servers are smart enough to turn away duplicates.

Because you can choose from literally thousands of newsgroups, they are organized in a hierarchical fashion. For example, there are newsgroups with a `rec` (recreation) prefix, `misc` (miscellaneous) prefix, a `comp` (computer) prefix, and so on. Take a sample newsgroup by the name of `misc.kids.pregnancy`. Because of the hierarchical structure of newsgroups, you'll find a large number of groups carrying the `misc` prefix, and a smaller number sharing the `misc.kids` prefix, until you reach a standalone group such as `misc.kids.pregnancy`. It forms a tree of sorts that can always grow (see Figure 18.3). In this case, `misc.kids.pregnancy` could eventually house groups by such names as `misc.kids.pregnancy.multiples` or `misc.kids.pregnancy.highrisk`.

FIGURE 18.3

A sample newsgroup hierarchy.

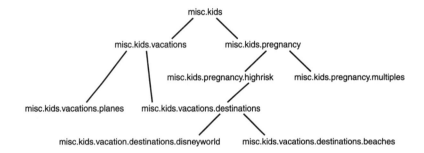

This logical organization of newsgroups makes the techniques for finding groups of interest presented in Hour 21, Emailing and Newsreading with Outlook Express, even more beneficial.

Virtual Chats

If you wanted to meet someone these days, how would you go about doing it? Whether you're looking for the love of your life, or trying to find a buddy to trade collectibles with, chat rooms and cyber communities are terrific options. Because participating in a chat is relatively straightforward, I'll cover everything you need to know right here.

Chat rooms are places you can go to "converse" with people who share your interests in realtime. Many corporations host online chats about their products, while professional sports associations often invite celebrities to interact with their fans. Likewise, there are countless free chat rooms dedicated to various interests. It's a fabulous medium because it brings a larger number of fans closer to celebrities than any other. For the first time ever, fans can ask famous NASCAR drivers how they got their starts, or a 70-year old woman can tell her favorite soap opera star how much she appreciates her work.

So how do chat rooms work? Most commonly, chat rooms display screens of text in which each person's screen name is followed by their contributions (or words). At first, you may find it almost impossible to locate the answers to questions asked, or to match up comments and the reactions they elicit. Your screen may look like a random mish-mash of unrelated gibberish. Never fear, a little time and experience will change all that. You'll be a pro before you know it!

When you decide to take part in a chat, you'll typically be asked to register at the site hosting the chat. This is where you'll get the opportunity to choose a screen name, which is the information other chatters see about you. Anything you want the others to know is up to you to tell.

While registering for a chat generally carries no fees, it gives hosts a way to control the content of their rooms. If someone at a certain screen name's email address violates the chat room code of conduct (such as uses profanity, harasses another member, and so on), the chat room host can block the user from future use of the site; thus, registration protects you at two levels—by keeping your real name secret, and by giving the host the power to ban misuse of the chat room.

Knowing What to Look for in a Chat Room

18

Before you jump feet-first into an online chat, you may want to sit a spell and scope out the scene. See what types of topics the group leans towards, or get a feel for how well humor will or won't be received.

It's also important to get adjusted to the rhythm of the group. Does the group have many participants, or just a few regulars? Do people use any special headers to make finding related comments easier? Obviously, if a chat room has many participants, it'll take longer for people to respond to questions or comments because there's a higher volume of input to which to react. In addition, the use of headers, even if it's simply putting the screen name of the person who's comment you're responding to at the beginning of your message, can greatly simplify the lives of chat room participants.

So you're ready to get involved, huh? Finding a chat room that fits your personality and interests is the first step. So where do you start? Try a few of the following suggestions:

- Watch your favorite news groups for pointers to chat rooms dedicated to related topics.
- While visiting Web sites of interest, watch for notices of celebrity chats, chat rooms supporting the site's mission, and so on. The Home and Garden Network at HGTV.com, for example, routinely conducts chats with the stars of its shows.

- Use Internet Explorer's Search Assistant to zoom in on possible chat rooms of interest.

- Check out some of these general chat sites: `www.talkcity.com` or `www.chathouse.com`, or search on your favorite topic, show, followed by the word `chat`.

Cyber Sense: Things to Keep in Mind While Chatting

Participating in a chat is pretty simple because you often find explicit onscreen prompts telling you what to do when. Following, however, a few chat-specific things to keep in mind to help ensure the safety and privacy of your experience:

- Be sure to use people's screen names, even if you know their real names. It's an issue of privacy. If people elect to use screen names for their online activities, then it's up to you to respect their wishes.

- Use caution when telling others about yourself. Much like you look around before using an ATM machine to withdraw cash, you should think twice before revealing a large amount of information about yourself, especially in chat and newsgroup forums where hundreds, if not thousands, of people have access to the information.

- If a dialogue turns into a two-way debate, "take it outside," as they used to say in old western movies. There's no need to take up everyone else's time and system resources if the conversation has turned into a two-person shouting match. You can accomplish the same thing using email.

- Remember that what is written is not always what is meant. A fair chunk of a sentence's interpretation relies on voice inflection and body language. It's best to clarify the person's intentions before jumping to conclusions or getting defensive.

Summary

This lesson is unlike most others found in this book in that it focuses on information as opposed to teaching you how to do something, step-by-step. You were presented with some unique ways to use the Internet to save time and money, you discovered how the Internet evolved over time, and you got to take a peek at each of the services supported by the Internet.

In the next hour, I'll arm you with the information you need to find the best Internet service provider in your area. You'll also learn what information you'll need to get from them in order to set up the connection in Windows.

Workshop

Now it's time to see just how much you learned in this lesson. I'll give you a short multiple-choice quiz to test what you learned, followed by a suggested activity designed to enhance the skills you acquired during the hour.

Quiz

Select the best answer to the questions from the choices provided, and then check your answers in the following section.

Questions

1. Which of the following cannot currently be done over the Internet?

   a. Online vision screening where the results are emailed to a lab, and then glasses or contacts are built to spec.

   b. Order pizza from Pizza Hut.

   c. Email a letter to the President of the United States.

2. How old is the Internet?

   a. 50 years old

   b. 30 years old

   c. 5 years old

3. What is the most high-profile service offered on the Internet?

   a. Chat rooms

   b. Email

   c. The Web

Answers

1. a. If only we could do it that way instead of going to the doctor and getting our eyes dilated…

2. The correct answer is b, 30 years old, although the Internet has only been a household word for far less time.

3. The Web is everywhere; just take a look at TV commercials some time. c is the answer to this one.

18

Activity

As you get ready to embark on your journey through the information superhighway, jot down five ways the services described here could enhance your life. Examples might include the following:

- I could stay in better touch with my sister
- I could do research for my projects from home

1.

2.

3.

4.

5.

Hour 19

Setting Up a Connection to the Internet

As they say, you have to crawl before you can walk. Before you can even get started with Internet Explorer 5.0, there's a lot you'll need to know no matter what your situation. Even if you have yet to buy your computer, I've got you covered. This hour focuses on the basics like the hardware you need and how to establish an Internet connection. The next hour shows you how to get and install Internet Explorer 5.0.

In this hour, you'll learn the answers to the following questions among others:

- I'm not even linked to the Internet; how do I find an Internet Service Provider (ISP)?
- Is there anything I should ask a prospective ISP before signing on the dotted line?
- How do I configure Windows 98, Second Edition to establish an Internet connection?

Hardware Requirements

Because you're reading a lesson about getting connected to the Internet, it seems only logical that I start with Internet Explorer's minimum system requirements because that's the Internet suite of applications most commonly installed on new computers.

According to Microsoft, you need the following hardware to run Internet Explorer 5.0:

- A 486DX with a 66 MHz processor (though a Pentium is strongly recommended).
- 16MB of RAM for Windows 98 users.
- Mouse.
- Modem at a speed of 28.8bps or faster like 33.6 or 56bps. The bps stands for "bits per second" of data transferred, so the higher the number, the more data that can be transferred in the same amount of time. For the best performance possible, you might eventually want to check with your telephone and cable companies as well as your Internet Service Provider to explore high-speed connection options like cable modems, ISDN, or DSL.

Whatever you do, please remember that the CPU speed and RAM are Microsoft's suggested minimum to run the suite under Windows 98, Second Edition. If you purchased your system new, you have nothing to worry about. If, however, you got the system as a hand-me-down, you might want to investigate the hardware further to avoid frustration and disappointment later on.

Finding an Internet Service Provider

Having all that great new computer gear and software with no Internet connection is like being all dressed up with no place to go. You're going to want—and need—a connection to the Internet to make it all work.

Now that you know your computer is up to the task of taking on the Internet with Internet Explorer 5.0, it's time to go looking for an Internet Service Provider (ISP).

When you booted your computer for the first time, odds are your desktop contained a solitary folder that was littered with icons for AOL, MSN, Prodigy, and CompuServe among others, each of them vying for your Internet service dollars. So how do you cut through the confusion? Read on!

ISP's and Online Services Explained

Because you've selected Internet Explorer 5.0 as your Internet tool of choice, online services such as CompuServe might not be a viable option. These highly visible, content-enriched services typically use proprietary Web browsers, newsreaders, and such, though there is a new trend for these services (specifically America Online) to accept standards-based Web browsers. Before signing up for service, be sure to verify their support of Internet Explorer 5.0.

What exactly does added content mean? In America Online's case, it means they publish special articles and information for their subscribers that no one else has access to. It might be a favorite print magazine that's agreed to make its content available to America Online subscribers only, or it might be an investment article written by a noted expert especially for America Online. You never know what kind of goodies you'll find. An Internet Service Provider, on the other hand, just gives you the access, leaving you on your own to find worthwhile content.

Because online services are often plagued by incessant busy signals (see what happens when you get too popular?) and their fees can be somewhat pricey (hey, that added content costs money!), many people turn to Internet Service Providers for their Internet access.

When it comes to ISPs, there are a few different "flavors" so to speak. You can choose a national provider like Netcom, Gateway, MCI, or AT&T; a regional provider like EROLS; or a local provider (like SmartNet, the one I use in Laurel, Maryland).

There are pros and cons to each of them. If you live in a remote area where calling just about anywhere is long distance, you might need to go with one of the services offered by a telephone company just to get a local dial-up number. Or if you want dedicated and personal technical support as you get acquainted with your computer and the Internet, you might want to choose a local provider where every single customer's satisfaction is vitally important.

19

See the section titled "So Where Do I Find a Good One?" later in this lesson for some ideas on how to find the ISP that's right for you.

Assessing Your Needs

Providing Internet service has become such a lucrative and highly competitive business that you're almost pelted with opportunities to sign up without even looking for one. You might find an AOL disk in a recent computer magazine. Or CompuServe might mail you a disk with a free offer to try them for a month. If you bought a new computer, tons of trial software for Internet services is preinstalled. Your phone bill might even include an offer to jump online with them! You'll have no trouble finding a provider, but finding the *right* one, well, that's another story.

Read the fine print.   Offers promising free Internet service for a given amount of time might be tempting, but there could be a catch. Many of them request credit card information which makes me incredibly nervous. Supposedly having a credit card number protects the online service should you attempt to use services that levy a fee. That's all fine and dandy, but I've heard far too many stories of people's accounts not getting properly canceled after the free trial is up and they opted not to subscribe. Of course that means additional charges are applied to your credit card. Please read all the restrictions and requirements of the offer before supplying payment information. It can save you lots of aggravation in the end.

Before you even begin the big hunt, however, you'll need to ask yourself a few questions:

- **How much time will you/your family spend linked to the Internet each month?** Although flat-rate Internet service is common, there are still a few ISPs that limit the amount of access. If you doubt you'll spend much time online, you might actually save money by finding an ISP that offers limited access for less money.

- **How much technical support will you need?** If you are comfortable around computers, technical support might not be important, but if you just got your computer, you might welcome all the help you can get. The mere availability of tech support is not enough, however. Even the most lauded technical support isn't worth squat if it ends at 5:00 p.m., just before you get home from work!

- **Do you need Internet software?** Many ISPs offer complimentary copies of some of the more popular programs to their customers. If you need it, this might factor into your decision of which ISP to choose because there won't be any software to buy or download.

- **Where do you live, in a large city, or in the middle of nowhere?** If you live in a larger city, you'll have no shortage of ISP choices. If, on the other hand, it takes a long distance phone call to call the nearest large city, you might have to spend a little more time searching for an ISP with a local dial-up number.

- **Do you travel often?** Whether you're an executive frequent flyer or a retired senior with wanderlust, you might find the hundreds of local dial-up numbers offered by the national ISPs valuable if you're always on the go. That way you can check your email from just about anywhere.

- **Are you planning to publish your own Web page?** Although many ISPs give you disk space on which to store your Web page with a basic account, you might be able to cut a deal for an account without this benefit if you have no desire to dabble with Web page publishing. But before you reach such a drastic conclusion, you might want to browse Hour 23, "Design a Web Page in an Hour" to see just how easy publishing your own Web page can be!

Your answers to the these questions should give you a good feel for which features are important to you in an Internet Service Provider. Jot down the things that are important, and keep the list with you as you do your research.

Now on with the search....

So Where Do I Find a Good One?

For starters, you can check out the providers who have included access software on your new computer. It doesn't cost anything to take a peek, but before you sign up, just be sure you're clear about cancellation procedures, required method of cancellation notification, how much notice you need to give, and so on.

Beyond that, the best place to start is to ask friends with Internet service how they feel about their provider. Would they recommend them, or would they switch if they could? Are they plagued with busy signals and system downtime? Do they get help when they need it? Is the ISP responsive when problems do arise?

Simply asking around should give you some strong leads. If it doesn't (or if you're the first of your circle of friends to get online), you might want to consult the business section of your local paper (ISPs will often advertise there), or go back to the old standby—the Yellow Pages.

When You Interview an ISP...

After you have a couple of positive recommendations in hand, get your list of desired features in an ISP, and start making calls. In the majority of cases, you'll find a provider you want to work with from the list of those recommended by your friends, but that doesn't mean you should go into it blindly. After all, your needs might very well be different from theirs.

19

When you interview an ISP (and yes, I did mean interview), you'll want to ask the following questions. Not only will they help clarify whether an ISP offers what you want it to, but they'll give you some insight into the stability of the provider.

- **Do you have a local dial-up number for my area?** Why pay for toll calls if you don't have to? Besides, you could go broke in a heartbeat...

- **How long have you been in business?** Although it might not seem like a relevant question, it can provide some clues of what the service might be like. A newly established ISP might support the latest and greatest modem speeds and Internet protocols, but there could be some glitches. For instance, user-to-modem ratios might not have stabilized. As a result, you might experience busy signals while the company is growing. Older companies, however, might have had enough time to build up a contingency plan should something go wrong (that is, have replacement modems on site, have a backup server, and so on). Newer companies might offer more attractive "get to know us" rates that could make the potential risk worth taking. And these newer, smaller companies might be more willing to please their customers in order to keep them.

- **What kinds of service plans do you offer?** Look for the one that most adequately meets your needs, not some plan with all the bells and whistles that you'll never use. Just because one ISP offers more than another for the same price doesn't mean it's the best choice for you, especially if that "more" is something you're not likely to play with.

> **Getting more for less**   Some Internet Service Providers offer phenomenal rates for long-term contracts. Although these incentives can be a great way to save money with an established provider, use caution when considering them with a new provider. Competition in the ISP industry is fierce; ISP's come and go. I'd recommend giving a new ISP a trial period before committing to a long-term contract, especially if you have to pay a lot of money up front.

- **What is your user-to-modem ratio?** The answer to this question is perhaps the best predictor of whether you'll experience nonstop busy signals when you want to surf. Optimally, an ISP will have one modem for every five accounts (meaning a 5-to-1 user to modem ratio), but many seem to settle on one modem for every eight accounts. Being a subscriber to an 8-to-1 ISP, I can tell you that you'll experience some busy signals even at that level. The key here is the smaller the ratio, the better. Be extremely leery of anything higher than one modem for every eight subscribers.

- **Do you have multiple dial-up access numbers?** If so, that reduces the likelihood of getting a busy signal even further.
- **What are your technical support hours?** The answer given here is most critical for those who would like the extra help. As I mentioned earlier, even technical support from Bill Gate's hand-picked team of experts is no use if they've gone home by the time you get a chance to log on.

When you combine the answers to the questions above with your list of desired ISP features, the choice that's best for you should stand out.

So what are you waiting for? Let's get signed up!

Information to Gather from Your New ISP

When you go to sign up for your Internet service, you'll want to have a pen and paper handy to take notes. The ISP will give you more information than you ever wanted to know about the Internet, including the items in Table 19.1.

TABLE 19.1   Information to Gather from Your ISP/Online Service

Information	Notes
IP Address	A set of four numbers between the numbers of 0 and 256, separated by periods.
Type of IP Address	Static or Dynamic
Subnet Mask	A 12-digit number formatted the same way as the IP Address.
Gateway Address	Another similarly formatted 12-digit number.
Host Name and Domain Name	Not all ISPs use them, but if they do, they will provide them.
Mail Server Name	Your email server's domain name, often in the format of `mail.provider.com`.
Domain Names Server (DNS)	Takes the format of a 12-digit IP Address.
News Server Name	The news server's domain name.
Email Address	Your email address in the form of `yourname@mail.provider.com` or `yourname@provider.com`.
Type of Incoming Mail Server	POP3 or IMAP4
Logon Instructions	What the ISP will ask you before a connection is established.

continues

TABLE 19.1   continued

Information	Notes
Dial-Up Phone Number	This is the number your computer will dial to get Internet access. Get a second number if you can in case you encounter a busy signal on the first number.

NEW TERM **Static versus Dynamic IP Addresses**   A *static IP address* means you are assigned the same number each time you dial in to your provider. A *dynamic IP address* means that one is assigned to you at random when you dial in. In the case of the dynamic IP address, the number is passed on to your computer by the provider's server.

NEW TERM *POP3 and IMAP4*   *POP3 (Post Office Protocol)* is a method of receiving incoming mail that requires you to download mail onto your local machine for viewing unless you explicitly select an option in your mail program to keep it online. It's the most widely used and supported incoming mail protocol in use today. Conversely, IMAP4 keeps the mail on the server so you can check it from anywhere without having to download it to your machine. This protocol is less common, but is a fabulous tool for traveling executives and other business people on the go.

They didn't give me an IP Address!   If your provider gives you a dynamic IP address (one created on-the-fly), you will not receive this bit of information at sign up time. Your computer will retrieve this information each time you log on.

My addresses don't have the .com after them; what's wrong?   The .com was for demonstration purposes only. It's possible that your ISP will issue .net addresses instead. These suffixes or extensions are technically known as domains—top-level domains, more specifically. They signify what kind of entity is providing the information on the given site (that is, .com for commercial entities, .gov for government entities, .edu for educational institutions, and so on).

Got all that written down? Good; Windows will ask for it when you go to set up your Internet connection. And don't worry about what all of that gobbledygook means. All that matters is that you're able to provide it for the Windows Internet Setup Wizard, which is discussed next.

Setting Up Your Internet Connection

Get ready, I'm about to put you to work. In the remaining few minutes of the hour, you're going to learn how to set up your Internet connection using Windows 98's Dial-Up Networking Wizard.

I don't see the steps you've listed here; help!   Microsoft loves to tweak the look of its wizards. It seems every new release of Windows or Internet Explorer comes with a slightly modified Internet connection wizard, making it almost impossible to guarantee what I write about will be the exact same thing the reader actually sees. And if you've poked around Windows at all, you're probably aware that there are multiple ways to configure an Internet connection to begin with.

To make life simpler, I'm outlining the steps to follow using the Windows 98 Dial-Up Networking tool. If you have Windows 95 or choose to use a different dial-up connection tool, never fear, you'll be asked for similar information, the screens might just look a little different.

Are you ready? Grab the list of information you received from your Internet Service Provider, and take this book over to your computer.

Setting up Your Connection Using the Windows 98 Dial-Up Networking Wizard

To begin working your way through the Windows 98 Dial-Up Networking Wizard, follow these steps:

1. Double-click the My Computer icon on your Windows desktop. This opens a My Computer window that holds several icons, one of which is called Dial-Up Networking.

2. Double-click the Dial-Up Networking icon to produce a Dial-Up Networking window. Note that this window looks a whole lot like the My Computer window, except there's a lot less clutter!

3. Double-click the Make New Connection icon to launch the Dial-Up Networking Wizard.

4. The Wizard asks you to name the computer you are dialing and select the desired modem from the drop-down list (see Figure 19.1). With regard to naming, try to make it meaningful to you, like "Work 1" or "Work Emergency". Just click inside

the text box and begin typing. As for the modem, the Dial-Up Networking Wizard will attempt to detect the type/brand of device you have installed. If you have just one modem installed, as most people do, you might not have to do a thing. Click Next to continue.

FIGURE 19.1

Give your connection a descriptive name that will mean something should you eventually configure more connections.

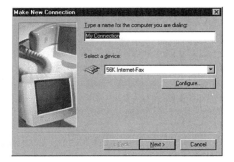

Take a number. If your ISP has given you more than one dial-up number to use, you might want to somehow incorporate the phone number into the connection's name. That way, you can tell one ISP dial-up number from another at a glance without having to dig around. I use the last four digits of the dial-up number as part of the connection name.

5. In the Telephone Number text box, type a phone number for your computer to dial. Type the area code in the Area Code box and select a country code if applicable (see Figure 19.2). Click Next to continue.

FIGURE 19.2

Type in the phone number your Internet Service Provider gave you.

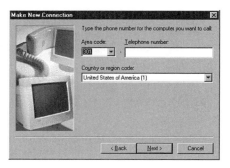

> **Need an area code to call across the street?**   In Maryland (and I'm sure in other locales as well), you are required to use the area code minus the prefixing 1 for local calls. Because Windows automatically puts a 1 in front of area codes entered in the Area Code field, you need to enter all 10 digits in the Telephone Number box and leave the Area Code field blank.

6. A dialog box appears telling you that you successfully created the connection (see Figure 19.3). Click Finish to exit the wizard.

FIGURE 19.3

You made it; you've successfully set up your computer to go online!

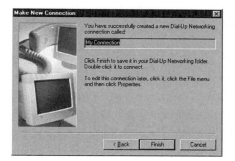

If done correctly, the Wizard will create an icon to the Internet connection in the Dial-Up Networking folder of the My Computer window. The newly created icon will carry the connection name you gave it in the first step of the Dial-Up Networking Wizard. If your ISP gave you a backup number to use, repeat the process to configure that as well.

So what about all the other information you had to get from your ISP? You'll use it later on to configure your email program and news newsreader.

19

Connecting to the Internet

Now it's time to see if that connection actually works. Follow these simple steps to link up to the Internet:

1. From the Windows desktop, double-click the My Computer icon.

2. In the My Computer window, double-click the Dial-Up Networking icon. The Dial-Up Networking window appears.

3. Double-click the name of the connection you want to dial. The Connect To dialog box shown in Figure 19.4 appears. Verify that the information is correct, enter your username and password, and then click the Connect button. Windows will begin establishing the connection.

FIGURE **19.4**
*The Connect To dialog
box will become an old
friend before you
know it.*

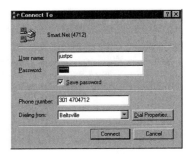

Wanna save some time? Who doesn't! Be sure to check the Save Password
check box if you want Windows to remember your password for you.

Summary

We covered a fair amount of ground in this hour. Not only did you learn what kind of
hardware is needed to run Internet Explorer 5.0, but you also learned tons about finding
the right Internet Service Provider given your specific situation. And on the practical
side—well, maybe nuts and bolts side is more accurate—you set up your first connection
to the Internet and confirmed that it worked.

In Hour 20, "Web Browsing with Internet Explorer 5," you'll put that new Internet connection to good use as I teach you the basics of Web surfing with Internet Explorer 5.0.

Workshop

The following workshop helps you solidify the skills you learned in this lesson.

Quiz

Select the best answer to the questions from the choices provided, and then check your
answers.

Questions

1. How much RAM should a computer have in order to run Internet Explorer 5.0?

    a. 8MB

    b. 12MB

    c. The more the better!

2. Which of the following pieces of information will you need from your Internet Service Provider in order to make a viable connection to the Internet?

    a. The name of your mail server.

    b. Your password.

    c. The dial-up phone number.

    d. All of the above

3. What's so great about the Dial-Up Networking Wizard?

    a. It leads you step-by-step through the process of creating a connection to the Internet, making the process simpler than ever before.

    b. It can understand voice commands.

    c. There's no such thing as a Dial-Up Networking Wizard!

Answers

1. Although b is also technically correct for Windows 95 users, c is the best answer. The thought of running Windows on 8, much less 12, megabytes of RAM is enough to make grown men (and women) cry!

2. D is the correct answer. You'll need all of this information and more to configure your connection to the Internet.

3. B hasn't happened yet. (Notice the word yet; I think the capability might come sooner than you think.) As for c, well, you obviously didn't follow along with the lesson. Shame on you! That leaves a as the best answer.

19

Activity

Grab a pencil and paper and prioritize the following ISP requirements from most important to least important:

- Tech support available during the hours I'm likely to need it most.

- Reasonable monthly rates for connections.

- Disk space included on which to store a personal Web page.

- Unlimited access so I can surf as much as I want.

- Local dial-up number from my calling area.

- A company that I know is going to be there years from now.

- Different pricing schemes so I can save money if I only plan to access the Net a little.

- Various modes of payment because not everyone has credit cards and such.
- I'm willing to commit to a multiyear contract in exchange for better rates.

With this list of priorities in hand, start calling any friends and associates who are on the Internet to see who they use. Be sure to ask for the good and the bad so you can match the pros and cons with your own priorities and needs.

After you've chosen a few candidates, it's time to give them a call and ask some questions. When you're satisfied you've found a good match, you can proceed with signing up for service.

HOUR 20

Web Browsing with Internet Explorer 5

The vast majority of first-time computer owners finally decide to take the plunge because they want to get on the Internet. How do I know? Because rebates from Internet service providers have popped up everywhere, making PCs more affordable than ever. Combine that with the fact that the Internet is just plain fun, you get new computers flying out the door at an astonishing rate.

In this hour, I'll bring you up to speed on using Internet Explorer, the premiere Web browser created by Microsoft. After this lesson, you'll be cruising the Information Superhighway like you've been there all your life!

Here are some other topics you have to look forward to this hour:

- Familiarize yourself with the many ways you can visit a Web site.
- Discover how to save a Web page to your Favorites list.
- Learn how to search the Web using Internet Explorer 5's new Search Assistant.
- Find out how the AutoComplete feature can save you time.

The Web Surfing Primer

Before I jump into the nitty-gritty of using the Web browser itself, I'd like to introduce you to some of the basic Web concepts.

When you're sitting in front of your TV watching Monday night football or your afternoon soap, take special note of the commercials. Even more than 1-800 numbers, you'll hear things like, "Come visit us on the Web at www.DietCoke.com." It's proof positive that the Web is not only mainstream, but it's here to stay.

The www stuff is called a *Web address*, or *URL*. To continue on with the Diet Coke example, if you enter www.DietCoke.com into Internet Explorer, you'll soon be visiting the official Web site of Diet Coke. The first page you see typically is referred to as the *home page*. On this page, you usually will see text, some of which may appear in a different color, or at the very least underlined. This unique text is referred to as a *link*, a fundamental concept of the Web.

> **Hidden links.** In an attempt to make sites more aesthetically appealing, Web page designers often will make "invisible" links. In other words, the plain text and link text look identical. So how can you tell where the links are that will take you elsewhere? Simply run your mouse pointer over the page. An arrow-shaped pointer indicates basic text. A pointing finger means your mouse is on a link you can click to be taken to another Web page.

When you click a link, you are transported to another page on the current Web site, or even to a different site entirely. This interconnection of links is how the Web gets its name.

So there you have it—an oversimplification of Web concepts. But hey, we all know you'd rather be surfing than reading technobabble anyway, right?

Seeing the Sites

With Internet Explorer 5, there are more ways to jump to a Web site than you can possibly imagine (see Figure 20.1). The methods include any of the following:

- Type the URL into the Address Bar and then press Enter (or click the Go button at the right end of the Address Bar).
- Click the Favorites menu item and select a site from the pull-down menu of previously saved favorites (of course you won't find much here if you haven't saved any pages yet).

- Use the Favorites button to open a Favorites window on the left side of the browsing area. That way you can hop from Favorite to Favorite without having to reopen menus.

- The drop-down arrow button to the right of the Address Bar opens a list of recently visited URLs. Just double-click one to pay a visit.

- The History button takes you back in time to sites you've visited over the past three weeks. More on how to work with this later in the hour.

- After you browse several pages in the current Internet Explorer 5 session, you can click the drop-down arrow next to the Back button to jump to up to nine of the most recently visited sites.

- Click the Back button to browse back through recently visited Web pages one at a time.

- If you've used the Back button to return to other pages, you can use the drop-down arrow next to the Forward button to skip ahead to any of the up to nine pages you visited in the current session.

FIGURE 20.1

Move to a Web page in any of these ways.

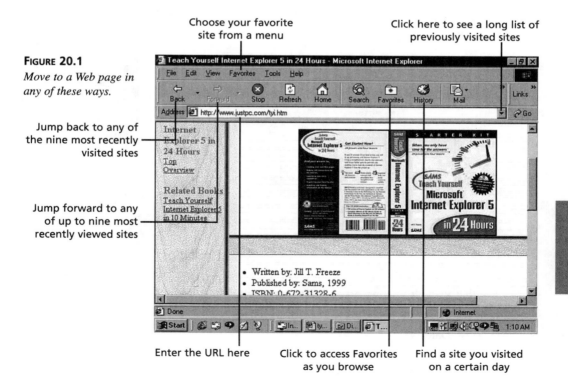

Choose your favorite site from a menu

Click here to see a long list of previously visited sites

Jump back to any of the nine most recently visited sites

Jump forward to any of up to nine most recently viewed sites

Enter the URL here

Click to access Favorites as you browse

Find a site you visited on a certain day

20

Revisiting History with the History Button

Have you ever read something that you wanted to go back and find at a later date only to discover you can't remember where you read it? It happens more frequently than you might think. Maybe you're searching for a new gymnastics club for your daughter. You see one you kind of like, but you decide to keep looking for something better. A couple of days later, you decide to get more information from that first club you sort of liked, but you didn't save the Web page as a Favorite. What do you do now?

Thanks to the History button, you're not out of luck. If you can remember the approximate date on which you visited the site, you stand a fair shot of finding it again. Just click the History button, click the link that best corresponds to the suspected date, and then glance through the list of sites until you locate a URL that looks familiar (see Figure 20.2). It may take a couple of tries, but you'll find it eventually.

FIGURE 20.2

By default, you can isolate any day over the past week, or any week for the past three.

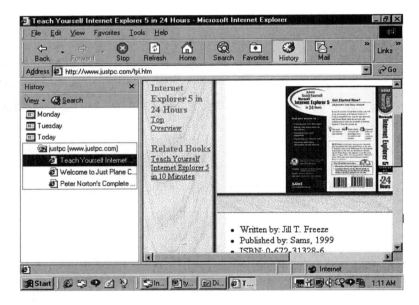

If you haven't got time for a leisurely stroll down memory lane, however, then you'll love that View drop-down arrow in the upper left corner of the History pane. Just click it and point to any of the following special views to help find that mystery page:

- By Date
- By Site
- By Most Visited
- By Order Visited Today

You also can search the History links by clicking the History pane's Search button, or by selecting Search from the bottom of the View drop-down menu. Just type in a word or words, and Internet Explorer 5 will go back in time and attempt to retrieve that lost gymnastics club.

Getting out of History mode is a snap—just click the History button on the Standard toolbar a second time, or click the "X" in the upper right corner of the History frame. Your Internet Explorer 5 viewing area returns to its full size.

An Improved Way of Working with Favorite Web Sites

After you find a Web page worth revisiting, you'll want to file it in an easy-to-find location by right-clicking the page while it's onscreen, and selecting Save As Favorite from the shortcut menu.

The latest version of Internet Explorer gives you wonderful Favorites management capabilities, as you'll see in the next few sections. They've even made it possible for you to exchange your Favorites lists with others and browse Web sites offline!

> **We can't do it all in an hour!** I'll try to cram as much in this hour as possible, but I certainly won't hit on everything. If you want to know more about Internet Explorer 5, I suggest you pick up a copy of my book *Sams Teach Yourself Internet Explorer 5 in 24 Hours*, ISBN: 0672313286, available through just about any online book store, or through your local book store.

Organizing Your Favorites

There are multiple steps involved in organizing your Favorites, as you'll see:

1. With Internet Explorer up and running, click the Favorites menu item, and then choose Organize Favorites. The Organize Favorites dialog box pictured in Figure 20.3 opens.

2. The first thing you'll need to do is create some folders in which to store your favorite Web sites. Try to place your Favorites into specific categories such as Cats, Quilting, Places To Go, Dreamcast Games, Job Hunting, and so on. Also keep in mind that you can nest folders as well. So, underneath the Places To Go folder, you might have subfolders for Museums, Fairs, and Vacation Spots, for example. When you have some good folder names in mind, click the Create Folder button. To create a nested subfolder, just click the folder under which you want to place the new folder, and then click Create Folder.

20

FIGURE 20.3

The Organize Favorites dialog box makes it quick and easy to keep your favorite Web sites in order.

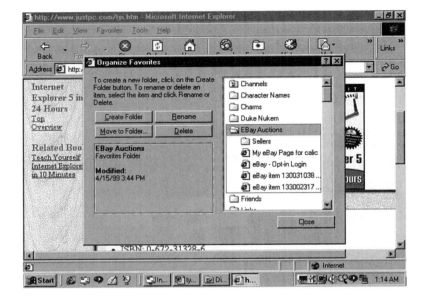

3. A new folder appears at the bottom of the screen (or in the location you specified if it's a nested folder). Its blue highlights prompt you to enter a name for it. Type in the chosen name, and then press Enter. The folder has been created.

4. Repeat the process until all of your favorite Web pages have a logical home.

5. Now comes the fun part—moving the pages to their new homes. Click on the first link in your list of Favorites.

6. Click the Move to Folder button to display the Browse for Folder dialog box shown in Figure 20.4.

7. Click on the folder to which you want to move the selected page, and then click OK.

8. The selected item now will appear in its new folder. Repeat the process of selecting a link and moving it until all of the links have a home.

9. To see which pages are located within a folder, click on the folder once. The page titles will appear underneath their specified folder. Click the folder again to "hide" the pages.

10. When everything's in its place, click the Close button to leave the dialog box.

Now you have a neat and tidy list of Favorites that's easy to navigate and easy to share with others, as you'll see a little later in the following sections.

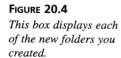

FIGURE 20.4

This box displays each of the new folders you created.

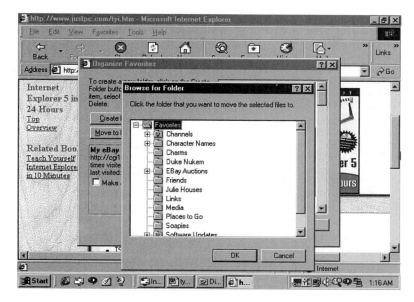

Sharing Your Favorite Sites with Others

The capability to share Web sites and Favorites lists with others in a variety of ways is one of the most useful enhancements to Internet Explorer 5. For the first time, you can effortlessly swap links with users of that other Web browser (Netscape), and email Favorites folders of links to others sharing your interests. It even makes toting favorite links from work to home or vice versa a breeze.

With Internet Explorer, there are several ways to share your favorite Web sites with family, friends, and associates. They include the following:

- Emailing a link to the Web page
- Sending the entire Web page
- Exporting your entire Favorites list
- Exporting a single folder full of goodies
- Sending the page as an HTML file attachment
- Importing Favorites sent to you by others (or transferring your Favorites from work to your home machine or vice versa)

We cover many of these operations in detail in the sections that follow.

20

Emailing a Link to a Web Page

Follow these steps to send someone a link to one of your favorite sites:

1. While you're browsing the page you want to share, click the File menu item, and then point to Send, Link by Email. Internet Explorer will launch Outlook Express to assist with the task. The subject line will be filled in with the title of the page, and the link will already be printed as part of the message.

> **Say what you're thinking.** Go ahead and add any text you want to the message (you'll learn how to do this in the next lesson). That way, the recipient knows why you thought the link might be of interest to him or her.

2. Type in the email address (or use the Address Book as described in the next hour) you want, and then click Send. The recipient will receive a message similar to the one shown in Figure 20.5 (assuming that he or she is using Outlook Express).

FIGURE 20.5

Here is what the person receiving the link will see in his or her electronic inbox.

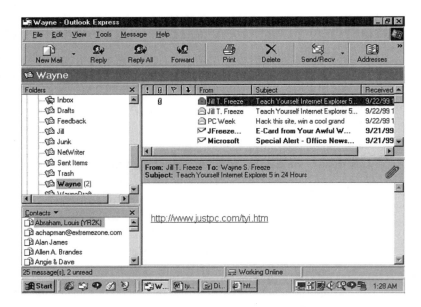

Emailing the Entire Web Page

Use these steps to send the entire Web page to a recipient. Before going to all the trouble, of course, you'll want to make sure the recipient has the capability to read HTML-formatted mail.

NEW TERM   **HTM what?** HTML stands for *hypertext markup language*, the special programming language that makes a Web page look similar to any visitor whether they're using a PC, a WebTV, or a Mac.

To send the page to someone else, follow these steps:

1. Browse to the Web page you want to send.

2. Click the File menu item, and then choose Send, Page by Email.

3. Internet Explorer will launch Outlook Express and give you an opportunity to fill in the recipient's email address and any additional text.

4. When everything's ready to go, click Send. Output similar to Figure 20.6 will be sent to the recipient's email account. Note that the recipient might need to maximize his or her email screen to see the page in its full glory.

FIGURE 20.6

Sending the entire Web page is one way to be sure the recipient checks out the page.

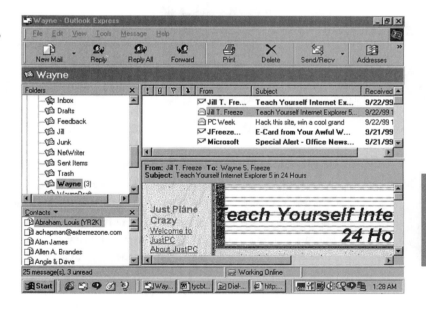

20

Exporting Your Favorites List

What if you change jobs and want to take your list of favorite professional-related Web sites with you? Or, suppose that you're getting a new computer and are handing your old one down to the kids. Wouldn't it be great if you could take your Favorites list with you? Follow these quick steps to get the job done:

1. From within Internet Explorer, click File, and then point to Import and Export. The Import/Export Wizard in Figure 20.7 appears. Click Next to begin.

FIGURE 20.7

The Import/Export Wizard is your starting point for exchanging Favorites.

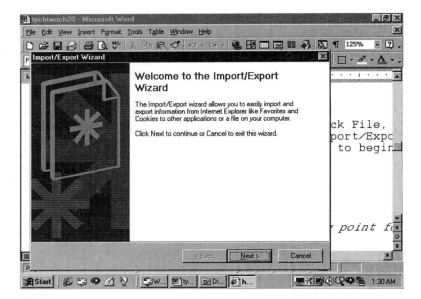

2. Choose Export Favorites from the list of possible actions, and then click Next.

3. Next, you'll need to choose the folder you want to export. Just click it, and then click Next. Please note that you can only export one folder at a time.

3. The Export Favorites Destination screen gives you two options: 1) to export your Internet Explorer 5 Favorites to another Web browser on your system (like Netscape), or 2) to save it to a file location by clicking the Browse button. After you locate the spot, give the file a descriptive, easy to remember name such as Shopping or Cat Favs. Internet Explorer automatically will save it as an HTML file with an .htm file extension. After you make your selection, click Next.

Where should I put it? If you plan to take the file to work, you may want to cut a disk containing the file, which will mean using the A: drive. If you're connected to a LAN or similar network, consider saving the file to one of the shared directories for easy retrieval. If you plan to email the file to yourself or somebody else, just tuck it away in an easy-to-remember spot on your C: drive so that you can easily attach it to an email note.

4. The wizard displays a message saying that you've successfully completed the Import/Export Wizard. All you need to do is click Finish to complete the process. A small dialog box appears saying that the export was successful. Click OK to close the wizard.

Importing Those Favorite Links

Now it's time to get those imported Favorites where they belong—back on a computer! Follow these steps to import Favorites into another copy of Internet Explorer:

1. On Internet Explorer's File menu, select Import and Export. The Import/Export Wizard launches. Click Next to begin the process.

2. Next, you will need to select Import Favorites from the list of actions provided, and then click Next.

3. Browse to the location in which the Favorites list was saved. It may be your A: drive if you transported the list via disk, or a saved email attachment if you mailed it to yourself. Note that an email attachment must be saved to your hard drive before you'll be able to import it.

4. When you find the file, double-click it, and then click the Next button.

5. At this point, you may specify a folder under which to nest the imported favorites by clicking on it; otherwise, its own folder will be created. Click Next to proceed.

6. A message appears that tells you that you are about to complete the wizard. Click Finish to make it official. A small dialog box appears that tells you the import was executed. Click OK to acknowledge the dialog box and dismiss the wizard.

20

But what about Netscape? As mentioned, these HTML files can be imported into Netscape as well, but you'll need to consult the procedures in the help files of the target version of Netscape for the most up to date, step-by-step directions.

Dealing Specifically with Emailed Sharing

To perform the export/import via email, there are some things you'll need to know. First, the export is performed exactly as previously described. To send it via email, you'll need to launch Outlook Express, begin composing a new message, and then click the Paperclip icon and browse to the desired HTML file to attach it to the message.

If you're on the receiving end of a Favorites list passed on by email, you'll have to save the file attachment somewhere on your computer before you can perform the import as described previously.

Searching the Web Using Internet Explorer 5's New Search Assistant

Searching for material on the Internet can be a real frustrating experience, especially when your boss needs to know the answer to a question quickly, and you have no idea where to begin your search for the answer. If you've spent any time at all working with search engines, you've undoubtedly noticed how different they are. The same search string entered into multiple engines can produce wildly unpredictable results.

While Microsoft can't decide which search engine is best, given the types of searches you tend to run, they can make it easier to call your preferred search engine into action. Follow these steps to try working with the new Search Assistant:

1. With Internet Explorer and an active connection to the Internet running, click the Search button on the Standard button bar. The Search Assistant pane on the left side of the screen, as shown in Figure 20.8, appears.

2. Click one of the five radio buttons shown to specify the type of search you want to perform.

3. Don't like the search engine you see listed underneath the Search text box? Click the Customize button second in from the right edge at the top of the Search Assistant pane. The page shown in Figure 20.9 appears, giving you a large selection from which to choose.

4. Place a checkmark next to the search providers you want to use, and then click the Update button at the bottom of the screen.

Did you choose more than one provider? If you chose more than one provider in a given category, you can rank them by clicking a provider's name, and then using the up and down arrows underneath the list. That way, you can determine which provider is used first.

FIGURE 20.8

The Search Assistant pane enables you to search while you surf.

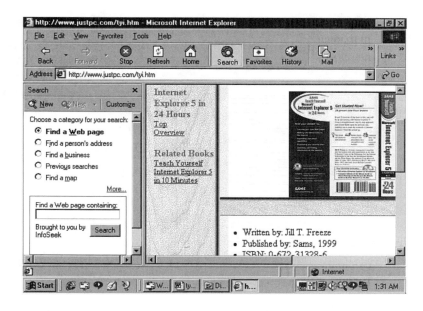

FIGURE 20.9

Place a checkmark next to the provider(s) you want to use. Don't forget to scroll down the page; you have a lot of choices to make for each category!

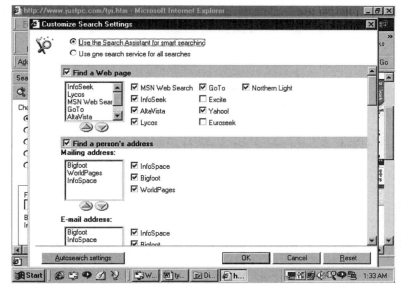

20

5. Enter your word or phrase in the text box and click the Search button to perform the search as normal. The results appear in the Search Assistant pane, as shown in Figure 20.10.

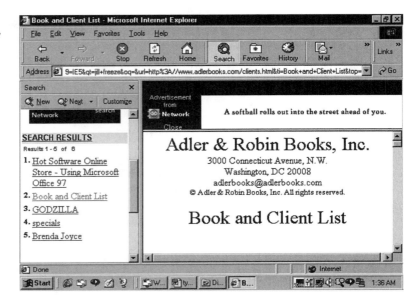

6. To view a link, simply click it. The page will appear in the main viewing window, as you saw in Figure 20.10.

7. When you want to switch to a new link, just click it—no more clicking the Back button twenty times in a single search to return to the search results page!

8. To try the next search provider in the order you have defined them, click the Next button at the top center of the Search Assistant pane. Or, if you want to try the search in any of the other providers on your list, use the drop-down arrow from which you can select a search engine by name.

9. After you complete the search, simply click the Search button on the Standard button bar again, or click the "X" in the upper-right corner of the Search Assistant pane. The Search Assistant pane will disappear, and your Internet Explorer screen will return to normal.

Finding Things on a Web Page

Some Web documents can ramble on forever, which is why you'll want to know how to perform a search within a specified Web page. That way, you can cut to the chase, so to speak. Just follow these steps to perform a search on the current Web page:

1. With the page you want to search displayed in Internet Explorer, click the Edit menu item, and then point to Find (on this page). The dialog box shown in Figure 20.11 appears.

> **A shortcut.** Rather than using the menu commands, you can press Ctrl+F to display the Find dialog box.

FIGURE 20.11

Internet Explorer's Find dialog box helps you get where you want to go on a Web page quickly.

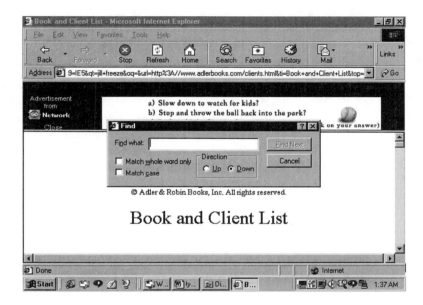

2. Type in the word or phrase you want to find on the current page.

3. Tell Internet Explorer whether you want it to look for a whole word match, and whether you want it to match the case of the text you entered. Just place a check mark in the appropriate box(es).

4. Click the Find Next button to send Internet Explorer after the next occurrence of the word or phrase. You can even click the Up or Down button to tell Internet Explorer which way to search. (By the way, Down is the default search direction.)

5. After you complete the search, click the Close button at the top right side of the Find dialog box, or click Cancel. Either will remove the box from the screen.

20

Introducing AutoComplete for Forms

If you've ever used the Internet Explorer Address Bar to work with Web sites, then you've already encountered a form-like element—a text box complete with drop-down arrows ready for you to insert the text of your choice.

You'll routinely come across forms on Web pages you visit, whether it's a search form at your favorite online bookseller, or a basic search engine form. The first time your enter text into a form, Internet Explorer 5 will ask you whether you want the Web browser to "remember" your entry. Known as *AutoComplete for Forms*, this feature, when enabled, will recall entries typed into a given form by displaying a drop-down box of selections much like you see with the new Auto Complete for Web Addresses. To accept a sugges-tion on a future visit to the same form, merely double-click it, and then click the neces-sary button to start the search.

While the feature is tremendously helpful for repeated searches at the same location on the same topic, it also can be a potential invasion of privacy. Suppose that you're trying to research your company's competition, look into a personal medical condition, or track down an elusive Pokemon for your son's birthday. Someone who uses the computer after you could see what you've been searching for. Of course, they'd have to be visiting the exact same sites as you did, but if you work with common search engines, it's a distinct possibility.

In response to this potential concern, Microsoft gives you the opportunity to enable, disable, and clear this Auto Complete feature.

Modifying AutoComplete Forms Settings

To change the way AutoComplete works on your computer, follow these steps:

1. On the Internet Explorer Tools menu, choose Internet Options.
2. Click the Content tab to open it. In the Personal Information section of the screen, you'll need to click the AutoComplete button. The AutoComplete Settings dialog box appears (see Figure 20.12).
3. Check or uncheck the Forms item as desired to turn the AutoComplete Forms fea-ture on or off.
4. If you want to leave AutoComplete for Forms enabled but want to clear your entries, click Clear Forms.

Hold it right there! Clicking Clear Forms will delete everyone who uses the computer's AutoComplete for Forms entries. A better strategy for protecting your privacy might be to turn off the feature when you begin using Internet Explorer, and then turn it back on before leaving the application.

FIGURE 20.12

The AutoComplete Settings dialog box is where you can really take control over this powerful feature.

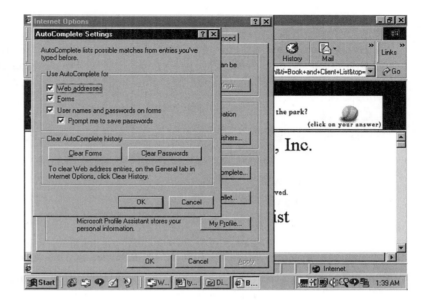

5. After you finish adjusting the settings, click OK. You then will need to click Apply and then OK to close the Options dialog box and continue working in Internet Explorer.

> **This works for Web sites, too.** You can use the preceding strategies for protecting your privacy with regard to the Web sites you've visited by disabling AutoComplete for Web Addresses while you're working. Remember, turning off AutoComplete for Forms protects your privacy on one level, but other users of your machine could accidentally stumble on to the sites you visited by accessing the History entries, or by seeing them in the Address Bar drop-down list.

20

Summary

In this hour, you were taken on a whirlwind tour of Internet Explorer. While it wasn't even close to scratching the surface of all of the neat things it can do, it gives you more than enough to get started. You know the basic terminology, how to get from one Web page to another, how to work with Favorites, even how to search the Web for a site of interest.

The next lesson will be another jam-packed hour as you explore emailing and news reading with Outlook Express.

Workshop

Now it's time to see just how much you learned in this lesson. I'll give you a short multiple-choice quiz to test what you learned, followed by a suggested activity designed to enhance the skills you acquired during the hour.

Quiz

Select the best answer to the questions from the choices provided, and then check your answers in the following section.

Questions

1. What does the History button do?

    a. Enables you to search or browse through an assortment of Web sites you visited during the past three weeks.

    b. It launches a special Web page dedicated to American History.

    c. It's a special search engine that will fetch historical information on any date you give it. It's a joint project between Microsoft and the Associated Press.

2. What do you call the Web sites you save and put on a special Internet Explorer list so that you can revisit them with ease?

    a. My Sites

    b. The Best of the Net

    c. Favorites

3. Can the AutoComplete feature "remember" Web addresses and information you type in to forms?

    a. Yes, as long as the feature is enabled.

    b. No. AutoComplete only remembers your name.

    c. There's no such thing as AutoComplete; this was a trick question!

Answers

1. If you chose a, you are correct. While the other choices might have been fun, that's not what the History button does in this application.

2. Okay, those who did *not* say c, go back and reread the lesson!

3. Again, a is the proper choice. AutoComplete can be a tremendously helpful feature after you get comfortable working with it.

Activity

Here's another listing exercise for you. Take a moment to think about all your interests, be they professional or hobby related. Now make a list of ten possible Favorites folder names. Ten may sound like a lot, but it's not when you factor in all aspects of your life, including things you've always wanted to learn about/do, but never had the time.

Feel free to list your answers here, or on a piece of notebook paper.

1.

2.

3.

4.

5.

6.

7.

8.

9.

10.

20

Hour 21

Emailing and News Reading with Outlook Express

As we enter the new millennium, one thing is certain—more and more people are going to be using email as a form of communication. What was once an activity engaged in by college-aged nerds has become as commonplace as reading the daily paper. In addition, the concept of communicating by email is only going to grow in popularity as computer prices continue to fall, and user-friendly surfing machines such as the WebTV keep emerging.

Get ready for another fast-paced lesson, because in this hour, I'll be teaching you about emailing and news reading with Outlook Express.

Here are some other topics you have to look forward to this hour:

- Tell Outlook Express where to pick up your email.
- Understand the different ways Outlook Express behaves, depending on whether you have a POP3 or IMAP email account.
- Familiarize yourself with the various parts of the Outlook Express workspace.
- Learn tips that will help you find good newsgroups to subscribe to.

Adding an Email Server to Outlook Express

Before you can do much of anything with Outlook Express, you'll need to set it up to recognize the mail server you'll be using.

To begin the process, launch Outlook Express by clicking the Outlook Express icon on your Quick Launch Bar (or by selecting Programs, Outlook Express from the Start menu), and then follow these directions:

1. Click the Outlook Express Tools menu and select Accounts. Verify that the Mail tab is the one that's active. The Internet Accounts window appears as shown in Figure 21.1.

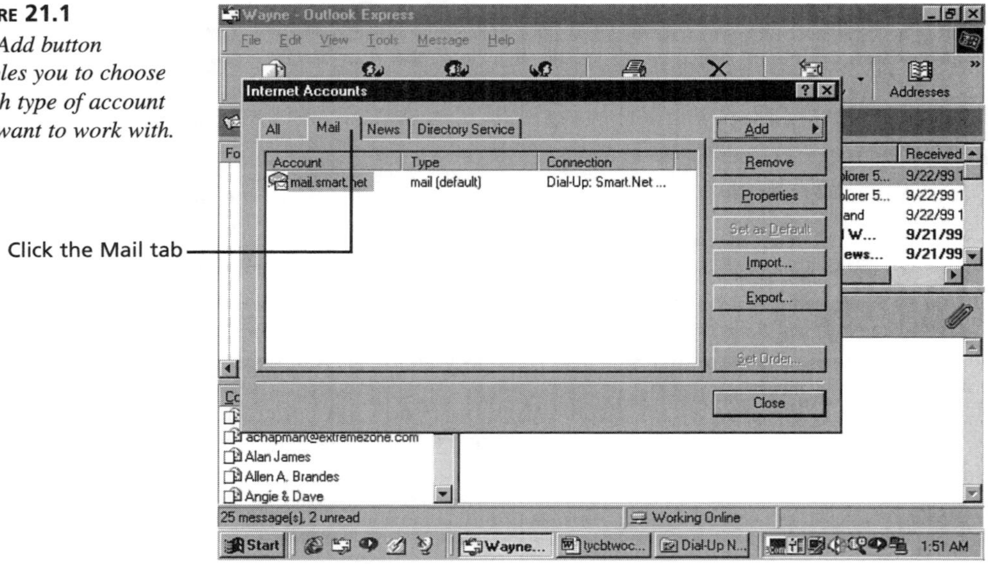

FIGURE 21.1

The Add button enables you to choose which type of account you want to work with.

Click the Mail tab

2. Click the Add button and select Mail from the list. The Internet Connection Wizard launches.

3. The first screen asks you to enter your name as you want it to appear in the From field of your outgoing email messages. Type it in, and then click Next.

4. Next, you are asked to provide the email address assigned to you by your Internet service provider. At this point, you also can opt to set up your own Hotmail account that will enable you to check your email from remote locations. Click Next when you're finished.

5. The next screen asks you to define which type of incoming mail server you have—POP3 or IMAP. Use the drop-down arrow to make your selection. (If you're not sure of your selection here, don't be afraid to ask your Internet service provider (ISP).) You then must type in the names of both the incoming and outgoing mail servers before clicking Next.

6. Your Internet logon information is requested in this screen, namely your account name/userid and password. After you enter them, click Next to continue.

7. You now are asked to tell the wizard which type of connection you want to establish. Connect Using My Phone Line is the most common option. Click Next to proceed.

8. Select which modem you'll use to connect to the account, and then click Next.

9. This screen asks which dial-up connection you want to use to access the mail server. Most likely, you'll choose from an existing one. Click Next.

10. It's time to celebrate; you've entered all the information needed! All you have to do is close the Accounts dialog box, and then click Finish.

Now Outlook Express will know where to look for incoming mail, as well as where to route outgoing messages. Take a deep breath; you made it!

The Anatomy of the Outlook Express Workspace

You've got to send email to receive email, that's just sort of the way it works. (Well except for that pesky virtual junk mail, but that's another story…).

Before you can do anything else with Outlook Express, of course, you'll need to learn your way around the workspace. What are the various screen elements called? What kinds of things will you see there? These are all critical bits of information you'll need to make the most of this lesson as well as Microsoft's help files. Figure 21.2 illustrates a sample Outlook Express screen.

21

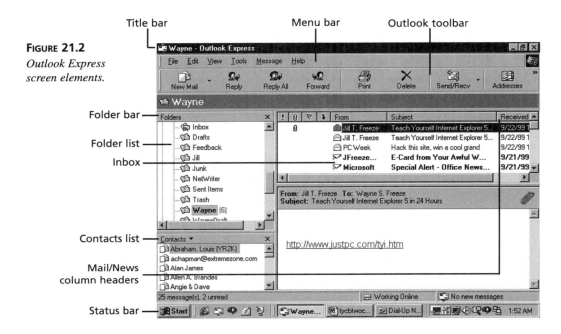

FIGURE 21.2
*Outlook Express
screen elements.*

Title bar ┐   Menu bar ┐   Outlook toolbar ┐

Folder bar
Folder list
Inbox
Contacts list
Mail/News
column headers
Status bar

The title bar, menu bar, and Outlook toolbar (or button bar) are nearly identical to ones you'll find in other Windows applications. The title bar presents the name of the application along with the name of currently selected element, and the menu and button bars are tweaked slightly to include functions needed for Outlook Express's messaging capabilities. Table 21.1 describes elements unique to Outlook Express and how they function.

TABLE 21.1 Outlook Express-Specific Elements and Their Corresponding Functions

Element	Function
Folder bar	Displays the name of the currently selected folder.
Folder list	Holds the folders you've defined in Outlook Express, including ones for your mail and news server.
Inbox	Lists all messages contained in the currently selected folder.
Contacts list	If you have a meager-sized contacts list like I do, you can see nearly every entry in the contacts list pane.
Status bar	Tells you how much of the selected message or file has been downloaded.
Mail/News column headers	Label each of the displayed elements in the currently selected folder.

Now that you've got your bearings, zoom in on the toolbar buttons you'll use in Outlook Express (see Figure 21.3).

FIGURE 21.3

Use the Outlook Express toolbar to get the job done quickly.

They are, from left to right, as follows:

- **New Mail**—Click this button to start composing a new email message.
- **New Mail Drop-down Arrow**—Click this button to compose a new message with one of the pieces of stationery supplied with Outlook Express.
- **Reply**—By clicking this button with a message selected and/or displayed, you send a reply to that message to the author only, not anyone else who may have received the message.
- **Reply All**—Use this button with the desired message displayed or selected to respond to everyone to whom the message was originally sent.
- **Forward**—Want to share an email message with someone else? Select it, and then select the Forward button.
- **Print**—If you need a hard copy of a piece of email, this is the button to click.
- **Delete**—Use this button to delete the currently selected message. Note that the message will just be crossed out and tagged until you deliberately purge it.
- **Send/Recv**—This button, which sends and checks your mail while connected to the mail server, opens a window that reports the status of tasks currently being handled by Outlook Express. It also reports on any errors it encounters.
- **Send/Recv drop-down arrow**—Use this button to send everything in your outbox, receive all the messages on your mail server, or both.
- **Addresses**—Click Addresses if you want to look up, add, or edit a contact in your Address Book.

Composing an Email Message

For your email message to reach its destination, you'll need to have the recipient's email address. This address is commonly expressed in the format *personsname@adomain.com*. Any address not conforming to the proper format will result in the message being returned to the sender.

21

NEW TERM **Domain**—The name given to a computer that is an officially registered provider of information on the Internet. Domain names usually are made up of two or more elements separated by periods. Some examples are `msn.com`, `webtv.net`, `umass.edu`, or `justpc.com`.

Sending a Message to One Recipient

To send a message to another person on the Internet, follow these simple steps:

1. With Outlook Express up and running, click the New Mail button. A New Message window appears (see Figure 21.4).

FIGURE 21.4

The New Message screen is where your outgoing correspondence begins, whether you're sending a note to one person or many people.

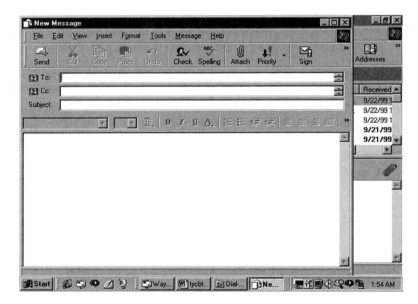

2. The insertion point blinks in the To: field, prompting you to enter the desired email address. Type in the address, verifying that it conforms to the standard email address format. You also can select an address from your address book by clicking the To: button, and then double-clicking the names of the desired recipient(s).

3. Next, click the Subject: line area and enter a descriptive title for the message.

4. Now click inside the main pane of the New Message window, which is where you'll write the body of your message.

5. After you finish typing your message, click the Send button on the far left of the message toolbar to send it on its way.

Sending a Message to Multiple Recipients

You can send a message to multiple people using a variety of ways, and each method means something slightly different.

You can include multiple email addresses in the To: line; just separate them with a comma (,) or semicolon (;). This method is best used in instances where every addressee is a targeted recipient of the message. If you manage a group of people, for example, you might want to notify all of them when you'll be out of the office on vacation. In this case, each person is the intended recipient of the message.

You also can use the CC: (carbon copy) line for multiple recipients. This differs from the method previously described in that addressees defined on the CC: line are not expected to take action on the message. If, for example, you need to send an important note to a client, you may want to send your boss a copy of the note for his or her information. This is the perfect time to use the CC: line. And, if you need to, you can include multiple addresses on the CC: line simply by separating them with a comma or semicolon.

Finally, you can use the BCC: (blind carbon copy) line. Placing addresses in this line makes them invisible to the primary recipient of the message. You may want to use BCC: when emailing a staff member about potential disciplinary action so that your boss has a copy for his or her information. This may help you down the road should the situation turn ugly. To use this item, click View, All Headers.

Creating the Message Body

You may think there's little more to composing a message than just plain typing. Well, you're only half right. Yes, it can be that simple, but you can do so much more with formatting messages in Outlook Express. You can generate a bulleted list; use flashy stationery; add a unique signature, and so on.

There's only so much we can do... If you want to learn how to do all kinds of fancy stuff in Outlook Express, you'll want to pick up *Sams Teach Yourself Internet Explorer 5 in 24 Hours*, which goes into all kinds of detail about the program's more advanced features.

It all begins with Outlook Express's counterpart to the Standard toolbar—the Message toolbar (see Figure 21.5). If you'll recall the lessons located in the software section of this book, you'll undoubtedly recognize some of the buttons and their functions. They are as follows from left to right:

21

FIGURE 21.5

*These buttons handle
your basic text manip-
ulation.*

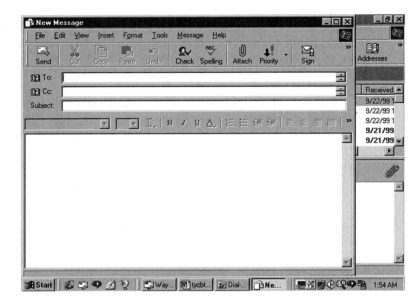

- **Send**—Click this button to send your message on its way after you finish writing.
- **Cut**—Want to move a block of text somewhere else in your message? Just select it using your mouse, and then click the Cut button. The text will disappear and be held on a virtual clipboard until you paste it in the location you want.
- **Copy**—Select text you want to have repeated elsewhere in the message (or in another message for that matter), and then click the Copy button. The text will remain in its original location as well as on the clipboard for later use.
- **Paste**—Use this button to place text stored on your clipboard in the position you want.
- **Undo**—If you need to undo the last formatting change you made, use this button. It works for deleting text, too, but is slower than using other methods such as the Backspace button, the Delete button, or highlighting the desired text and pressing Delete.
- **Check**—Can you only remember part of an email address? After you type in the portion you know, click the Check Names button. Outlook Express will search your Address Book for a match. If it finds more than one, it will list them all so that you can choose the one you want.

- **Spelling**—Use this tool to check your email message for spelling errors prior to sending it.

- **Attach**—Click this button to attach a file, such as a Word document or scanned photo, to the current email message. That way, if the recipient has the proper software, he or she can view the attachment and work with it as well.

- **Priority**—If you need to draw attention to a message, this is the way to do it. Choose this button to cycle through your options. These are Normal (default), High, and Low priority.

- **Priority Drop-down Arrow**—You also can set a message's priority by clicking the Set Priority arrow and dragging the mouse pointer to the desired priority level.

- **Sign**—An advanced safety feature that lets you digitally sign your messages. That way, others can tell that a message is really from you.

- **Encrypt**—Another advanced security feature that scrambles the content of your message so only the recipient can read it.

- **Offline**—This button lets you work with Outlook Express without needing to be connected to the Internet.

The toolbar immediately above the New Message window—the Formatting toolbar—gives you all kinds of tools to help you format your message and make it look nice. It's identical to Word's Formatting toolbar, so you should have no difficulty creating the text effects you desire.

Assessing What You've Got Before Reading Your Mail

Before going any further, you need to establish which type of email server you're running on—POP3 or IMAP. While it may not seem like a big deal in the scheme of things, you should know that Outlook Express behaves differently depending on the type of mail server you're using.

When you log on to your Internet service provider and launch Outlook Express, the mail you've received appears in the Message List box, often called the *Inbox*. Several items are displayed by default for each piece of mail (see Figure 21.6); they include the following:

21

FIGURE 21.6

Use this information to determine what a message is about before you open it.

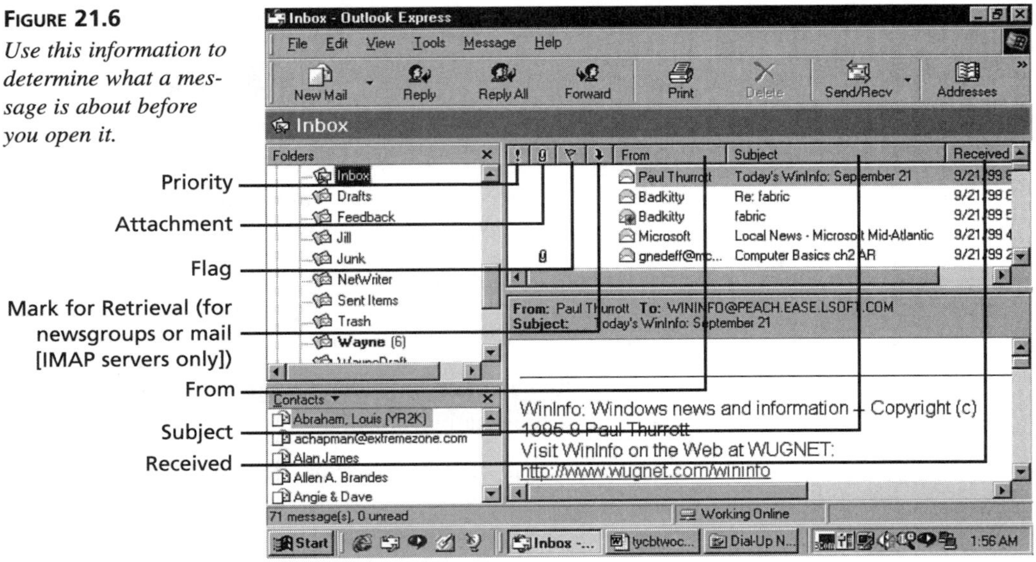

Priority —

Attachment —

Flag —

Mark for Retrieval (for newsgroups or mail [IMAP servers only]) —

From —

Subject —

Received —

- **Priority**—The first column is the Priority column. Look here to see which messages are high and low-level priorities. If a message carries a high priority level, a red exclamation point appears. If it's low level, a blue down-arrow will appear. Finally, if this column is blank, it means the message carries the normal default priority level.

- **Attachment**—Presents a paper clip icon to indicate whether a file attachment is present in a given message.

- **Flag**—Click inside this column to flag a message for later action/attention. A little red flag icon appears to remind you that you need to revisit the message.

- **Mark for Retrieval**—People accessing an IMAP mail server can leave all their messages on the server and check the ones they want to download by clicking this column.

- **From**—This column displays the name or email address of the person or company sending the email message.

Who? Can't see the full name of a message's sender? Just run your mouse over the line in question. A screen tip-like box displaying the full content of the line appears. This trick works for long subject lines as well.

- **Subject**—Hopefully this column provides a vivid description of the message's content so that you know where to place it in your personal priority list. Of course, the subject title's accuracy relies entirely on the sender, so you'll need to judge it accordingly.

- **Received**—This bit of information tells you when the given message appeared in your mailbox.

Hey, who took my mail? If you configured your Internet connection to take advantage of IMAP support, you'll see two inboxes: one under Outlook Express that will remain empty, and one under the name of your IMAP server that will hold all your messages. Sound confusing? It can be, but I'll attempt to clarify all that in a few moments.

Reading a Message

When you click a message, its contents will appear in the Preview pane (see Figure 21.7).

FIGURE 21.7

Click a message to see it in the Preview pane.

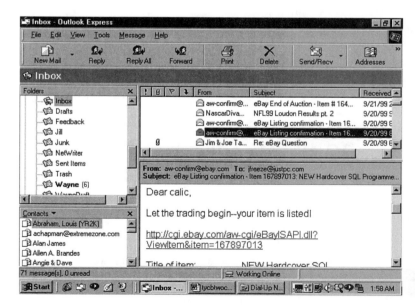

If you want to work with a copy of the message in its own message window, double-click it. When you're finished reading, click the Close button to shut the message window.

New messages will appear in boldface type with a closed envelope icon. After you read a message, the envelope icon will appear to be opened (see Figure 21.8). If you use an IMAP server, you'll see a partial envelope icon that means the message is on the server, but hasn't yet been downloaded to your machine.

FIGURE 21.8

Outlook Express makes it easy to see which messages you have and haven't read.

Unread messages

Read messages

Messages on your server, but not on your machine (IMAP only)

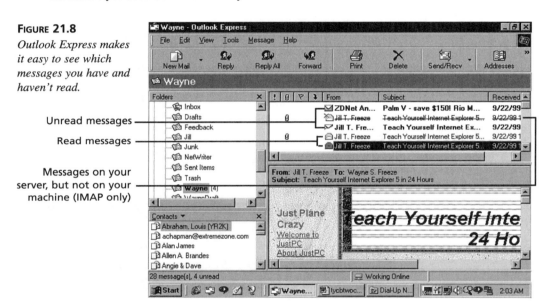

Taking Action on a Message

After you receive a message, there are a variety of actions you can take on it ranging from deleting it, to replying to it, to saving it. In the following sections, you'll see just how simple it is to perform each action.

Deleting a Message

As time goes on, you'll get more junk mail than you know what to do with. That's why you'll want—and need—to know every possible way to delete a message.

When you glance at your message list, you can tell some items are junk mail at the get-go because you won't recognize the From address, or the subject line will read some-thing outrageous like "Make $10,000 in a week!" To delete these, all you have to do is click the message to mark it, and then press the Delete key.

The message will be moved to the Deleted Items folder where it will remain until you empty your electronic trash on POP3 accounts. To empty the trash, so to speak, click the Deleted Items folder, and then choose Empty Deleted Items Folder.

IMAP users will have messages marked for deletion after which they'll have to click the Purge button to clean house. (See Figure 21.9 to learn what deleted messages will look like.)

FIGURE 21.9
Messages marked for deletion will have a line drawn through their entries in the message list.

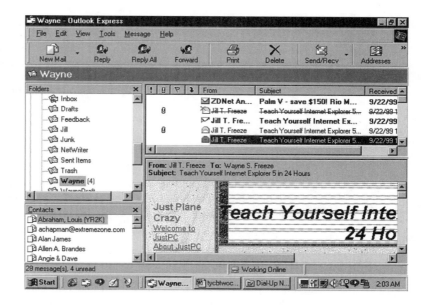

Hey, it won't let me delete! This is one of those bizarre things that can make new IMAP users crazy. Because the messages in your inbox are stored on your mail server, you'll need to be connected to the server to process the deletions. If the connection dies unexpectedly, guess what? You'll keep hitting dead ends until you reconnect

Mastering multiple deletions. You can save tremendous amounts of time and keystrokes by deleting multiple messages at once. To delete messages scattered throughout the message list, click each message while holding down the Ctrl key, and then click Delete. To delete a group of contiguous messages, click the top one, press and hold down the Shift key, and then click the bottom one. All messages in between the two points should be highlighted. Click Delete to delete them all (or at least mark them for deletion).

21

Then there are the messages that need further examination before you can delete them. Maybe the subject line seems intriguing, but turns out not to interest you, or maybe a Web site sends a weekly electronic newsletter that you read and then promptly delete.

In these cases, you'll most likely double-click the message to read it, and then click the Delete button on the message's toolbar when you're finished.

Uh-oh, I made a mistake! You may not be able to bring a message back once it's been deleted or purged from your system, but you can undo a deletion prior to exiting Outlook Express. Just right-click the message you marked by accident, and select Undelete from the shortcut menu. If the message has already been moved to the Deleted Items folder, you'll need to go there, right-click the mistakenly deleted message, and select Undelete from the shortcut menu. It's that easy.

Going, going, almost gone! Just because you delete an email message does not guarantee it's gone for good. Most corporations and government agencies perform routine backups of their networks, meaning a potentially damaging email message could come back later to haunt you.

Forwarding a Message

Suppose that one of your friends sends you a great joke and you want to share it with another buddy. This is the perfect time to forward a message. The procedure is so easy. In fact, it doesn't even require a lengthy step-by-step walk-through.

Double-click on the message to open it if it isn't open already. Next, click the Forward button. A window similar to the New Message window will appear, only this window will include the entire text of the forwarded message as well.

All you need to do to send the message on its way is fill in the To: line, and then click the Send button. Before clicking Send, however, feel free to enter a personal message above the forwarded message.

Replying to a Message

Replying to a message works similar to forwarding a message described earlier. You click either Reply or Reply All, add your message, and then click Send. Because you're responding to a message you've received, there's no need to fill in the To: line—Outlook Express does it for you.

Saving a Message

No matter how much you try to avoid it, there will always be some messages you won't have the heart to part with, like that cute joke your nephew sent you. In the workplace, you'll find keeping a log of messages almost mandatory. If the messages remain in your inbox until you delete them, your inbox will become unmanageable sooner or later as a result of the sheer volume of messages. Furthermore, if you leave large numbers of messages on your IMAP mail server, you may "max out" your allocated disk space on your ISP's machine before you even realize it, which can lead to additional fees and/or problems. POP3 users escape that worry altogether, because the messages are stored on the local machine after they are downloaded.

With Outlook Express, you can save a message to your machine simply by leaving it in your Inbox, although it's probably a better idea to click its icon in the Inbox and drag it to a local folder to keep your Inbox down to a manageable size.

Checking for New Messages

By default, Outlook Express will automatically check for new email messages every half hour. You can ask it to refresh on demand by pressing the F5 key or clicking the button.

Adding a News Server to Outlook Express

Remember how you had to set up Outlook Express to recognize your mail server? Well, the same holds true for news servers. Just follow these simple steps to make your news server available to Outlook Express:

1. Click the Outlook Express Tools menu and select Accounts. The Internet Accounts window appears.

2. Click the Add button, and select News from the list. The Internet Connection wizard launches.

3. The first screen prompts you to enter your name as you want it to appear in the From field of your outgoing newsgroup posts. Type it in, and then click Next.

4. In the next screen, you are prompted to provide your email address, which will be used in the Reply To line of any news articles you post. Click Next.

5. Next, you are asked to supply the name of your news server. You also will be asked whether you need to log on to the news server with a special userid and password. If you check this box, you'll be prompted to supply the necessary userid and password.

21

6. See? This was even easier than setting up the mail server—at least there were fewer steps! Go ahead, click Finish to complete the final step. You then will be asked whether you want to download a listing of all the newsgroups available on the news server you defined. Because this is the only way you'll know for sure which groups are available to you, say Yes. Be prepared to wait a little while, however, because it takes more than a few seconds to download information on tens of thousands of newsgroups.

So How Do I Find the Good Stuff?

Because each person has a unique set of interests, it goes without saying that our definitions of "the good stuff" will vary widely. Given that, I'll have to show you how to find groups matching your interests rather than pointing you to specific newsgroups.

You can find a good newsgroup numerous ways, but here are a few of the more reliable methods:

- **Word of mouth**—You seldom go wrong with newsgroups recommended to you by friends and associates. People like me, who've been cruising the information superhighway since it was a dirt footpath, tend to know which groups generate great dialog as opposed to spam-infested groups containing endless flame wars on off-topic subjects. (How's that for a nice image?)

- **Found it on the Web**—While researching a certain subject, you may wander across a Web site that's proven to be a wealth of information. Sites specializing in a topic often will point you to useful newsgroups. These usually are excellent leads to follow.

- **Search me**—Surf over to Deja News at `http://www.dejanews.com` and perform a search on a topic of interest. The search results will reveal which groups discuss your favorite topics. Why is this potentially more useful than Outlook Express's newsgroup search function? Because newsgroup discussion topics aren't always covered in the name of the newsgroup. If you ask Outlook Express to find newsgroups with Beanie Babies in their name, for example, you won't get any hits (at least at the time this book was written). A newsgroup search on Deja News, however, reveals that Beanie Babies are discussed in the newsgroup `rec.toys.dolls`.

- **Browse the list**—If you have eyes with great stamina, you may want to simply browse through the list of newsgroups available on your news server. To access this, launch Outlook Express and then click the name of your news server. A screen like the one shown in Figure 21.10 appears, listing each newsgroup to which your Internet service provider subscribes. (If you've already subscribed to some newsgroups, you'll need to click the Newsgroup button on the right end of the toolbar to access this window.) Simply use the scrollbar to move your way through the list. And don't say I didn't warn you that it would be a lengthy proposition!

FIGURE 21.10

If you have multiple news servers set up, as seen here, you can manage any of them from this window by clicking their names.

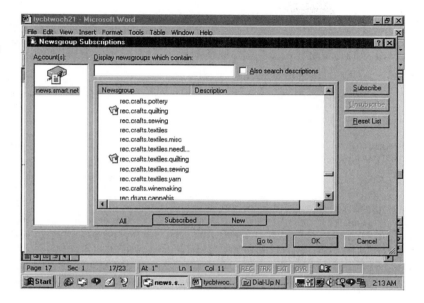

- **Search the list**—Outlook Express enables you to perform a search on the list of available newsgroups. To perform one, enter the desired word in the Display Newsgroups Which Contain: text box, and then press Enter. A list of newsgroups like the one shown in Figure 21.11 will be returned.

It's not what it seems. Searching newsgroups isn't as straightforward as you might think. The reason? Think about how newsgroups are named—usually a string of words separated by periods as in misc.kids.vacation. As such, you can't easily search a word in the traditional sense; you need to search for strings of characters instead. Take the search "cat." A newsgroup search will return everything from category to Catholic to cat to even education. So how do you hone in on what you want?

Checking the Also Search Descriptions box can help, but the search engine will still search a string of characters. This means that you'll still have many to sift through. One trick I've found that helps considerably is to include the period in the search, as in .cat. While you'll still find some irrelevant content, the number of items is reduced immensely.

21

FIGURE 21.11

A newsgroup search should narrow the field of possibilities considerably.

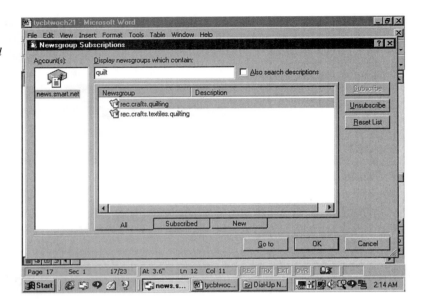

Subscribing to a Newsgroup

Before you can subscribe to newsgroups, you'll need to make sure you have a list of those available on your computer. If the list doesn't appear when you access a news server, click the Reset List button.

While viewing the names of the newsgroups in the Newsgroup Subscriptions window, you can subscribe to a group using one of two methods. You can either double-click its name, or click it to select it and click the Subscribe button. From that moment on, the groups to which you subscribed will have a special icon next to their names, and they will all appear in a separate pane when you click the Subscribed tab at the bottom of the window (see Figure 21.12). They also will appear on the File List in alphabetical order under the name of the news server.

Unsubscribing to a Newsgroup

When you no longer want to read the group on a regular basis, you may want to unsubscribe to it. To do this, simply right-click the newsgroup's name, and then click Unsubscribe on the shortcut menu. That's all there is to it!

FIGURE 21.12

A special icon appears next to newsgroups to which you've subscribed.

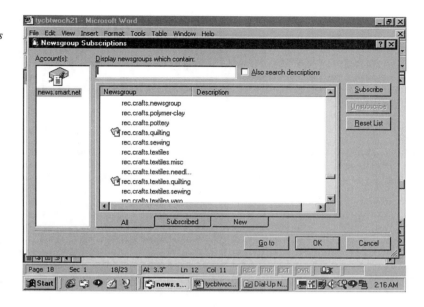

Reading a Newsgroup

You needn't be subscribed to a newsgroup to read it; however, you typically will be subscribed to a newsgroup when you go to read it.

You never know what you may find out there. All types of people frequent newsgroups these days. Given that, you should be prepared to potentially encounter offensive content while browsing. That's not to say you'll find racist or sexually explicit content everywhere you go, but you should know that it does exist so that you can protect your kids (and even yourself) from opening offensive messages you might encounter.

Follow these steps to begin reading your favorite newsgroups:

1. Launch Outlook Express with a live connection to the Internet.
2. Scroll down your File List until you see the name of the newsgroup you want to read. If you cannot see the group on the list and a plus sign appears next to the name of the news server, you'll need to click the plus sign to expand the folders underneath the news server.

21

3. Double-click the newsgroup's name to begin reading. By default, messages are pre-sented in the order they were posted, with the freshest being shown first. A plus sign next to the message means the message is part of a thread (ongoing topic of discussion) and that there are responses to it that you can see by clicking the plus sign (see Figure 21.13 for an example of an expanded thread).

FIGURE 21.13

An example of just how involved a thread can get.

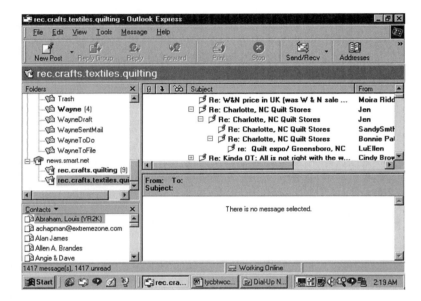

4. To begin reading a message, all you have to do is double-click it. The article appears in a window similar to the one you use to read email.

5. From within a post, there are multiple actions you can take on it:

   • **Save this Message**—Takes you to a traditional Save As dialog box. Note that you can save the message with a special newsgroup file extension (.nws) that must be viewed using Outlook Express, or you can choose a Text file (.txt) that can easily be viewed in Microsoft Word, Word Pad, and so on.

   • **Print**—Click this button to send the message to your default printer. Outlook Express will use its default settings, which should be fine in the majority of cases. If you want to have more control over your output, you'll want to click File and choose Print to access the Print dialog box. You have the same options available here as you do in other Microsoft applications.

- **Reply to Group**—This button launches a Reply message window. Note that messages composed in this manner will be posted to the newsgroup for the entire world to see, as evidenced by the presence of the Newsgroup line item as opposed to the To: line. You compose the message just as you would a regular email message.

- **Reply to Author**—Clicking this button routes your message directly to the author of the post to which you're responding. In fact, Outlook Express even inserts the author's email address and the subject line he or she used in the original post prefixed with an RE: for you. This is the best way to share a rel evant personal experience, show your support, or share an off-the-wall fact that may not be of general interest to the entire group.

- **Forward**—If you want to send a newsgroup article to a friend or colleague via email, click this button, type in the person's email address (or double-click the To: icon to use an entry from your Address Book), add any notes you want to include, and then click Send.

- **Previous**—Click this button to view the message that came before the one currently displayed.

- **Next**—To move to the next message in the list, click this button.

Posting Your Own Message to a Newsgroup

If, after much observation and research, you've decided to go ahead and post your question or comments to a newsgroup, follow these simple steps:

1. Click the folder of the newsgroup to which you want to post your message.

2. Click the New Message button on the Outlook Express toolbar. A standard New Message box opens, with the name of the selected newsgroup already filled in.

3. Type in the text of your message as you do with an email message. Don't forget to check your spelling.

4. When the message meets with your approval, click the Post button. Outlook Express displays a message saying your post is about to be sent to the news server and that it may not show up immediately in your display.

5. Click OK to close the message box and continue working in Outlook Express.

21

Canceling an Article You Posted

Suppose that you put a collectible up for sale in one of the newsgroups that allows such posts, and you sell the item within a day. Canceling the post not only reduces the load on news servers throughout the Internet, but it gives people one less article to browse, and it keeps you from having to send a million, "I'm sorry, but I've already sold it" emails.

Before you begin, there's something else I should clarify. You can only cancel articles you submitted, not articles from others that may be offensive or off-topic.

To recall or cancel an article you posted to a newsgroup, perform the following steps:

1. Connect to the Internet and then open the newsgroup in which you posted the article by clicking its name on your File list.

2. Find your article, and then right-click over it. Select Cancel from the resulting shortcut menu. A message box then appears to let you know that the cancellation is in progress.

> **It takes time.** Please note that this will not instantly remove your article from news servers across the world; this will take some time. You also should be aware that canceling a post will not remove it from the computers that may have already downloaded it with other messages from the same newsgroup. This means that someone who has read the newsgroup containing your post may have the article cached on his or her system, thus making it available even after you retracted it.

3. Click OK to let Outlook Express know that you agree to the terms of the cancellation.

Summary

Wow! So ends another exhausting hour. Not only did you learn how to configure Outlook Express to process mail and newsgroup posts, but you were exposed to the many actions you can take on a select message. In addition, you discovered how to find newsgroups of interest and subscribe to them so that you can skim through them any time you want.

The next lesson is one of the most important ones you'll find in this book. It's dedicated to Internet etiquette (or Netiquette) and ways to conduct safe online business transactions. Definitely read it carefully before you spend a large chunk of time online.

Workshop

Now it's time to see just how much you learned in this lesson. I'll give you a short multiple-choice quiz to test what you learned, followed by a suggested activity designed to enhance the skills you acquired during the hour.

Quiz

Select the best answer to the questions from the choices provided, and then check your answers in the following section.

Questions

1. In the context of Outlook Express, what does BCC mean?
    a. Big Comfy Couch
    b. British Communication Channel
    c. Blind Carbon Copy

2. When it comes to expressing your opinion in a newsgroup, which is the best policy?
    a. Be judicious in what you say, because the post could come back to haunt you, even after you think it's long gone.
    b. Say whatever you want; nobody can find anything on the Internet anyway.
    c. Don't express an opinion at all because Uncle Sam is watching every word that's said.

3. Can you cancel an article you posted to a newsgroup?
    a. Nope, what's done is done.
    b. Yes, but you can only cancel your own posts.
    c. You can cancel any post you find offensive or even mildly annoying.

Answers

1. Another "gimme" question—c was the appropriate answer.

2. a is the best rule of thumb when it comes to letting your opinions be known.

3. If everyone had the power to cancel anyone else's posts, there'd be nothing left on the newsgroups. One person's innocent remark can make another person livid because no two people are exactly alike. Accidents do happen, however, so Microsoft gives us tools with which to cancel our posts. The answer b was the best of the three choices.

21

Activity

If you don't believe email is a fast method of communication, try this neat little experiment. Compose a new message and place the following address in the To: line: `Netwriter@JustPC.com`. Type **Basics Test** in the Subject line, and then click the Send button. Wait a few seconds, and then press the F5 key to refresh your inbox. You should see an almost immediate response from the Netwriter autoreply I've set up, barring a major Internet traffic jam that is.

Can you believe it? A message traveled to my mail server in Maryland and back to you that quickly. I don't care if you live across the street or halfway around the globe, that's pretty amazing!

Hour **22**

Before You Spend Significant Time Online...

Now that you're an expert on how your computer and the Internet work, it's time to examine the subtleties of life online. Venturing out on the information superhighway without being acquainted with the tips in this hour is like driving a Porsche on the crowded streets of New York City without knowing the meaning of street signs, traffic signals, and other common rules of the road—somebody could get hurt!

But seriously, I'm not trying to scare anyone; it's pretty hard to get into trouble simply surfing the Web. It's not like an Internet policeman will pop out of your monitor and handcuff you should you inadvertently violate one of these rules, but if you plan to become involved with some of the newsgroups or intend to make a few new e-pals, knowing these rules of the road will give you everything you need to establish a peaceful, online presence. (It'll also keep you from looking like a bumbling newbie, which could be useful, too!)

In this lesson, I'll introduce you to some valuable "rules of the road." But wait, there's more; you'll also learn about the following in this hour:

- Discover the accepted forms of "netiquette" (or Internet Etiquette).
- Learn about the cryptic emoticons and abbreviations you'll find in your email.
- Find out why using a screen name is so important.
- Become a safe online shopper.

So What Is Netiquette Anyway?

Well, I've already given you a hint, but here's a better explanation. Back when the Internet was in its infancy, all its users had a common frame of reference. They had to be expert computer scientists or researchers to gain access to the Internet. As the Internet grew, a common language and culture evolved. *Netiquette*, short for *network etiquette*, is the result of that growth.

Think of netiquette as the Internet equivalent to a regional culture/language. Take the United States as an example. My mainstay, Diet Coke, is referred to as "pop" in South Dakota, where I grew up. In Massachusetts where I went to college, "tonic" (pronounced tahw-nic) was often used. Here in Maryland, "soda" is the preferred term. This Internet language, along with all the emoticons and abbreviations you'll learn about later in the hour, make up a part of the Internet's culture, as do the guidelines found in these pages. Together, they make up what has become known as netiquette—the regional dialect for the Internet, if you will.

Trust me, I didn't come up with this lengthy lesson full of guidelines all by myself. In 1995, the Responsible Use of the Network (RUN) Working Group of the Internet Engineering Task Force (IETF) drafted a document (known as RFC 1855) highlighting netiquette guidelines for a variety of users and environments. This document was written as a way to integrate the exploding number of inexperienced new users on the Net as quickly as possible.

I pulled the items most relevant to the average user, translated them to plain English, and added easy-to-understand examples, so what you read here should be both useful and entertaining—I hope! For easy reference, I have created top 10 lists of no-no's for each of three categories—email, newsgroups, and mailing lists.

22

> **If you're a real glutton for punishment...** I mean a person who always wants to learn more and more about a subject—you can find the whole collection of RFCs on the Web at http://www.iepg.org/docset/. You'll learn more than you ever wanted to know about how the Internet works and why things are done the way they are. Be forewarned, however; the reading isn't as entertaining as it is here. In fact, it could be argued that the RFCs make a wonderful drug-free alternative to sleeping pills!

Top 10 Email Rules of the Road

Email is great for its immediacy, but like writing a letter, it can have its disadvantages. For example, unless you specifically describe your emotions, there's a lot of room for misinterpretation. In addition to pointing out some of these subtleties, the following items illustrate some of the most common mistakes made by people new to the Internet.

> **If I've said it once, I've said it a thousand times...** Please note that many of these common mistakes also apply to newsgroups and mailing lists, but I chose not to repeat them to save space and to keep you from getting bored.

1. No Peeking!

Be careful what you write; it may come back to haunt you! The Internet is not a perfect place. As is the case in the real world, it's possible someone may try to sneak a peek at your correspondence. While the likelihood of that happening is pretty small, this is one of those instances where it's better to be safe than sorry. Use the following rule of thumb: If you'd feel uncomfortable putting a message's contents on a postcard and dropping it into a mailbox, then you probably shouldn't email it either.

2. Knock, Knock

Be sure to verify email addresses before sending a long or personal message for the first time. Maybe you're trying to track down an old classmate by the name of Elise Sudbeck. You find an ESudbeck@webtv.net which you're pretty sure is her, but you can't be certain. Drop ESudbeck a note mentioning your alma mater and desire to get back in touch, and then wait for a response before getting personal. It's sort of the Internet equivalent to asking, "Who's there?" before answering your door late at night. Double-check who's at the other end before making yourself vulnerable.

3. I'm Sorry, I Thought...

Many email addresses are made up of a person's first initial followed by their surname (or as much of it that will fit into the allotted space). Take my email address, for example. I use `JFreeze@JustPC.com` for personal email. Given my current Internet service provider's eight-character userid limit, I'm still okay because my name is short. If my name were Donna Stephenson, however, I might have a little trouble. DStephen might cause some confusion for people trying to find me since it could just as easily stand for Dwight Stephens. This might force me to consider other alternatives like DonnaS or even my job title (such as `adviser@umass.edu`).

New Term   **Show me your userid, please!** Pronounced "user-I-D," this is the technical term for the part of your email address that comes before the @ sign.

The job title alternative brings us to the next precaution: Know exactly who you're emailing. For all you know, `adviser@umass.edu` could be an intake address for students' questions that is accessed by the entire advising staff, not a personal account. It makes perfect sense to confirm the situation before sending anything of a personal nature.

4. SHOUT!

One of the most common mistakes people new to the net make is to type their entire message in capital letters. My friend, Tracy, ventured out to a newsgroup to start a dialogue on TV violence. Her toddler managed to reprogram her keyboard so her message appeared in all uppercase. For nearly a week, her inbox was flooded with reprimands from self-appointed net police. I don't think she's resurfaced since! Because emotion and voice inflection are not always identifiable by words alone, capitalization emerged as the notation of choice for shouting. Likewise, the asterisk (*) is used on each side of a word or phrase to denote emphasis just as bold or underlining would do in word processing. Sheesh, I can't *believe* anyone would write an entire message in capital letters. WHAT ARE THESE PEOPLE THINKING?!

5. :-)

If you don't know what this symbol means, don't worry. You'll hear much more about smileys and all the other emoticons later on. For now, it serves as a gentle reminder to use emoticons to clarify potentially confusing statements. Use them sparingly, however, to avoid diluting their effect. Smileys are like exclamation points; if you overuse them, you'll find yourself soon resorting to double smileys to communicate a higher level of emotion!

6. Read Before You Reply

This rule of thumb probably is more relevant in the workplace than for leisure use of the Internet, but it's a good one to practice just the same. Before responding to any email, check the other messages in your inbox. You may find a person who has asked for help or advice in one note has solved his problem before you even got online, and he may have sent a second note to that regard. Checking multiple messages from the same person before responding to any of them could save you both a lot of time.

It's also a good idea to scan the header of the message before responding to make sure you were the primary recipient of the email. You may have been copied on a note directed to someone else. Figure 22.1 illustrates a sample email header.

FIGURE 22.1

This figure shows a message about to be forwarded to someone.

In the case of the headers shown in Figure 22.1, `BuckyHeyer@WebTV.net` is the primary recipient and `WFreeze@JustPC.com` is copied for his information. You'll also note the FW: in the Subject line.

7. Sign on the Dotted Line

Remember those mail headers I told you to check so diligently before responding to a message? Well, some email programs and newsreaders strip them, leaving no return address. While most modern applications keep this information intact and visible, you'll want to sign your name just in case. This further identifies you as the author of the message or post should the information be unavailable in the header.

8. Around the World in 80 Milliseconds

Well, maybe not that fast, but pretty darn quick just the same. Sometimes it's hard to grasp the true scope of the Internet. It's easy to forget that the person you may be emailing is just as likely to be across the world as she is across town. Given the multicultural nature of the net, there are a few things you can do to make everyone feel at home, no matter where they live.

- Be patient when waiting for a response to a note sent internationally. The message you sent this morning may get to its destination within minutes, but its recipient in a far away land may just be crawling into bed given the time difference. Give it time (24 to 48 hours, depending on the urgency of the message) before resending it or, worse yet, responding in anger.

- Use caution when including colorful expressions or slang in your email—they might be taken literally by someone who does not speak English as a primary language. He might interpret someone's statement about a redneck as being someone with short hair who's been out in the sun too long!

- Humor is another of those things that may not translate well, especially sarcasm. Save the humor until you know the recipient well. If you can't resist cracking a funny, however, consider using emoticons or other tell-tale notation like <grin>, <g>, or ROTFL (if you're one to laugh at your own jokes).

9. I Don't Get It...

My husband will be the first to tell you I get worked up over the stupidest things sometimes, but this is one of my pet peeves—email messages without subject lines. You see, when I scan my incoming mail while I'm writing, I want to see subject lines that have meaning. I want to know whether I should drop everything and attend to the matter, or if I can deal with it at a more convenient time. Odds are if it's blank, I'll ignore it for a while.

I've even been known to get a little devious with my own subject lines. When I was trying to get in touch with one of my over-committed business contacts, I knew I had to be creative to catch her attention amidst the fray. Because she's a fellow chocoholic, I simply put "Chocolate!" in the subject line. It worked, too, as I heard from her just a few minutes later.

Let's get this straight—I'm not recommending that you use misleading subject lines. After all, that would defeat the purpose. I'm merely pointing out that, as is the case with many things, there's more than one way to deal with them.

10. Don't Believe Everything You Read

You may not realize this, but in many email programs, a user can configure his email address to read anything he wants it to. Want proof? Look at Figure 22.2.

FIGURE 22.2

Deceptive addresses like this are commonly found in junk mail.

Oftentimes, a spoof or forgery is blatantly detectable as in `seeu@home.soon`. Obviously, someone's attempting to be cute. But there's a darker side to this, too. Businesses mass-mailing unsolicited garbage (usually something utterly distasteful like "Babes Here: Get 'em While They're Hot") will frequently alter their return email address to avoid an onslaught of angry return messages. Luckily, some mail servers (like mine) will reject bogus email addresses, which cuts down the number of deceptions (at least a little bit).

Obviously, if you can pull that off, impersonating another user (at least on the surface) should be a breeze. I'm surprised soap opera writers haven't latched on to this. Imagine what trouble the odd man out of a steamy love triangle could cause for his competition by merely impersonating him in email notes!

The moral of the story is if you ever get a piece of email that seems highly out of character for the sender, consider doing the following before responding emotionally:

- Click Reply to see whether the address matches the one you see displayed in your inbox
- Send an email note back asking for confirmation of the message
- Phone the individual to talk it over

Top 10 Newsgroup Rules of the Road

Newsgroups are wonderful forums. You can exchange thoughts and information with countless people from around the world; you can pool the wisdom of experts in a variety of fields; and you can gain the respect of others based on your thoughts and intellect as opposed to your appearance, race, sex, and so on. To make the most of the forums, however, involves some giving as well. The following ten pointers look at issues of concern to people new to Usenet.

A friendly reminder... Remember to keep the following pointers in mind as you work with newsgroups.

1. Know the Territory

Before posting to a newsgroup or mailing list, read the group for a few weeks to get a feel for its climate. This is perhaps the best way to learn the preferred format of subject lines, which topics actually are discussed in the group, and how participants react to humor. Another thing you should do before posting is track down the FAQs (frequently asked questions) for the group to make sure your question isn't already answered there. Some newsgroups periodically post the FAQs while others maintain them on a Web site. The larger, more organized groups do both.

Getting the FAQs (pronounced "fax"). To find an index of FAQ Web sites, fire up Internet Explorer, then visit the Internet FAQ Consortium at http://www.faqs.org/.

2. Turn the Other Cheek

If you plan to get involved in some of the newsgroups, be prepared to get flamed. There are millions of people in this world, many of whom may disagree with your opinions or comments, no matter what they may be. A few people may act on this disagreement by sending you volumes of statistics on why you're wrong. An even smaller group may send you notes that read something like, "Look you dweeb, you're way off-base, here. What a lunatic! Your email account should be revoked!" These are known as *flames*. It's wise to ignore these crackpots since letting them know you're riled up could be just the positive reinforcement they need to continue being obnoxious. If someone has made a valid point, by all means feel free to thank that person if you feel it is appropriate. And, of course, it goes without saying that you all will never flame anyone, right?

22

3. It's a Small World

Remember that a vast majority of the newsgroups are read by thousands of people worldwide, and one of those people might be your boss or a future boss. If you aspire to be the manager of the Barbie doll section of your local FAO Schwarz, for example, you probably don't want to post a note on `rec.collecting.dolls`, griping about the store's high prices. Many newsgroups are archived for future reference, so although your words may have disappeared from the news server you use to access Usenet, they may still be accessible by other methods.

Be your own detective. Use the DejaNews search engine to see what your friends are saying online or to search for all newsgroup articles mentioning a particular subject. You can access DejaNews by launching Internet Explorer and typing the following in the Address Bar: `www.dejanews.com`.

4. KISS

The acronym for *Keep It Simple, Stupid* applies to the Internet as well. Unlike TV, snail mail, or radio, where the cost of sending the message falls exclusively with the sender, the cost of email or a newsgroup post is absorbed by both the sender and the recipient(s). This cost takes the form of increased time online to download and read the message/post, and the extra disk space required to store the note. In some ways, sending email or posting to a newsgroup is like mailing a letter with postage due—the contents better be worth it! While the cost may not seem like much in the scheme of things, it's hard to swallow in principle when that message is unsolicited junk mail.

You may not be able to do much about the people who litter your inbox or post off-topic ads to your favorite newsgroup (although I have been known to press Reply and bounce the message back to the sender just to be annoying), but there are ways you can cut costs and conserve resources when emailing friends and associates or making use of the newsgroups:

- When responding to a message or post, delete any unnecessary text. Keep only enough to give the reader proper context for your comments. Look at Figures 22.3 (an original message) and 22.4 (response with comments) to see how a typical response may be cut to conserve resources.

- Should you eventually decide to go into business on the Internet, don't send large amounts of unsolicited information to people via email or Usenet. If you must employ direct email and Usenet as sales tools, send/post a brief message describing your offerings, and then ask interested parties to click Reply to request further details.

FIGURE 22.3
A long message or post...

FIGURE 22.4
...can be shortened without losing its meaning.

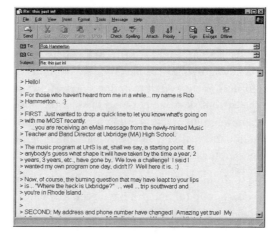

Know what you're doing. Before posting any kind of advertising to a newsgroup, make sure it's allowed. One advertising post to a group strictly forbidding advertising could hurt far more than it could help your business.

- Avoid posting simple "me, too" follow-ups. It takes up valuable bandwidth and frankly, unless you're a recognized expert on the topic at hand, people couldn't care less whether or not you agree. If you have additional information to pass along, then naturally it's okay to do so.

22

New Term **Strike up the band(width)!** *Bandwidth* is a measurement of how much data can move through a channel (such as your modem and computer) at once. Obviously, the shorter the post, the quicker it will download onto your screen. That's why keeping messages short is referred to as "saving bandwidth."

5. Get to the Point

When posting an article or comment, cut to the chase. Don't ramble, get on your soap box, or wander off-topic. And for heaven's sake, whatever you do, don't waste precious time and resources simply to point out people's typo's or spelling errors! This, more than anything else, will mark you as an immature newbie, which can in turn ruin your reputation and credibility in the group. People mellow pretty quickly, however, with an apology and a few intellectual insights. After all, we all get carried away from time to time. If we didn't, we wouldn't be human!

6. The Line Dance

Okay, I admit it; I watch a couple of soap operas on occasion. One newsgroup, `rec.arts.tv.soaps.cbs`, discusses my favorite soaps, *As the World Turns* and *The Bold and the Beautiful*, among others. Because the number of shows covered and the volume of posts is so high, a few subject line conventions emerged. Posts concerning my favorite show begin with ATWT, followed by a colon, a space, and then the specific subject matter. A sample subject line might read "ATWT: Lily's New Haircut." Each show has its own subject line prefix, and in cases where all the shows are involved (such as posts about Daytime Emmy Award nominees), the word `ALL` becomes the prefix. Other groups use a `Q:` to denote a question, `FS:` to mark items for sale, and so on. Reading the group and FAQ before jumping in will help you look like an experienced netizen (Internet citizen).

7. Don't be a Spoil Sport!

While technically this could have been discussed in the preceding section, it's important enough to give it its own space. When posting a message to a newsgroup that discusses television shows, sporting events, and so on, be careful not to spoil the outcome of the show or event for others. Nothing's worse than scanning the NASCAR newsgroup before watching your video tape of the race only to see some bozo post in huge letters: "TERRY LABONTE CLINCHES THE CHAMPIONSHIP TODAY!!!" The race is ruined for you, and you can be sure the poster of the message will get a fair amount of angry email. If you want to talk about the end of the most recent blockbuster movie or discuss a controversial call by a referee, place the word "SPOILER" in uppercase in the subject line. Even insert a few blank lines at the beginning of your post for good measure; that way no one can blame you for spoiling their fun, and you can still talk about anything you want.

8. Before Clicking Reply...

Newsgroups can pose some interesting challenges when it comes to getting information to the right person. If you want to share your wisdom with the original poster by email, there are some things you need to check before sending the note, as in the following:

- If the full header is intact, read the article carefully to confirm that the reply-to address matches that of the original author. I can't tell you how many times I've gotten email intended for the originator of a post and because I no longer had access to the original post without a lot of work, I was forced to send the note back to the kind soul offering help/advice. Odds are that advice never reached its destination. Do yourself (and others) a favor: If originating a post, include a signature with your name/screen name and email address to simplify responding.

- If you're posting a follow-up to the newsgroup, make sure the original author's email address is easy to find so others may respond directly via email if they wish.

- Follow-ups to follow-ups complicate matters even worse. In the interest of saving bandwidth, vital header information often is inadvertently edited out. In this case, it's usually best to simply post your contribution rather than risk it not getting to the source. In addition, if you're contributing to a thread that's been around for awhile, do your best to keep header information intact.

9. Use the Groups to Your Ad-vantage

Everything has its place on the Internet, ads included. If you even think about posting ads on some newsgroups, you'll practically get run off the Internet with email messages and flames. Other newsgroups, such as `rec.toys.marketplace`, not only welcome ads, but they make up a fundamental part of those groups' charters. Interestingly, it doesn't seem to matter whether you're launching a full-scale business or merely parting with an old collectible gathering dust, the outcome is the same.

To locate groups welcoming ads, search the various newsgroup hierarchies for words such as "marketplace" or "for-sale". Just because a group doesn't carry one of these extensions in its name doesn't mean it snubs ads, however. Take `rec.toys.cars`, for example. Collectors from around the world discuss everything from the paint quality of the latest Matchbox car releases to the newest Hot Wheels variations to hit the pegs. Ads from fellow collectors, however, also make up a key part of this group's culture. The best way to determine whether ads are accepted in a group is to read the FAQs. If they prove to be elusive, hang around for a while; in a week or two your answer will be obvious.

22

> **Beware of scalpers!** Scalpers are people who frequent toy stores, snatch up all the good stuff (such as limited edition Hot Wheels, *Star Wars* figures, Beanie Babies, and so on), and try to sell it on the Internet for outrageous prices. If you participate in a newsgroup regularly, you'll most likely make some new friends who can eventually help you build your collection at cost or for trade.

10. Giving Thanks

If, after reading the FAQs and monitoring a newsgroup for awhile, you'd still like to post a question to get reactions/input from the rest of the participants, consider doing the following:

- Thank everyone in advance for their help/comments.
- Offer to post a summary of all the recommendations if there's sufficient interest in the subject.
- If there isn't enough interest to justify posting a formal summary, at least offer to email a summary to those expressing an interest in your findings.

Generally, the Internet is a very cooperative, helpful place, and showing appreciation for the time people give to help you can only help in the long run.

Mysteries of the Net

Earlier, I talked a lot about conserving resources and what you can do to lighten the load; however, there's more to it than making liberal edits and avoiding unnecessary posts. Bandwidth-saving techniques often involve abbreviating words and phrases to save space. In the following sections, I'll cover the most common abbreviations as well as some of the emoticons and expressions used to convey emotion on the Internet. To give you an idea of just how much you'll learn, try to decipher the message in Figure 22.5.

Okay, are you ready for the translation? Here it is:

"Hi! I'm writing about the car you have for sale. I have a Corvette I might be willing to trade for your Porsche 944 Turbo S; want to deal? My 'Vette's really cool <big grin>! By the way, how long have you had your car? I've had mine for three fun years :-)(happy about what he just wrote)! My mother-in-law keeps wanting me to get rid of it :-((sad about what he wrote). Maybe she'll give in if I give her a rose, Rolling on the floor, laughing!"

FIGURE 22.5

Messages passed along via the Internet can sometimes look like they're written in an exotic language.

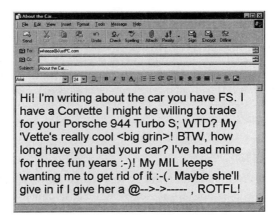

> Hi! I'm writing about the car you have FS. I have a Corvette I might be willing to trade for your Porsche 944 Turbo S; WTD? My 'Vette's really cool <big grin>! BTW, how long have you had your car? I've had mine for three fun years :-)! My MIL keeps wanting me to get rid of it :-(. Maybe she'll give in if I give her a @-->->----- , ROTFL!

Alphabet Soup

Stumped by the title of this section? You won't be for long. As you saw in Figure 22.5, translating email and newsgroup posts can get a little tricky to the untrained eye. Odds are that if you watch your favorite newsgroup for a few days, you'll see a post from a frustrated newbie pleading, "Can somebody please tell me what ROTFL means?" Well here it is, your definitive guide to all the quirky abbreviations you'll find lurking in your email or news articles. Maybe not *all* (things change so quickly on the Internet, you know), but certainly more than enough to get you rolling.

About now you may be thinking, "Hey, this stuff should be in an appendix, not in the middle of a book." I disagree, and here's why. When's the last time you read the glossary in the back of a book verbatim? I thought so! These goodies are too fun and important to be missed. By the time you work your way through the alphabet soup in Table 22.1, Figure 22.5 won't even phase you.

TABLE 22.1 Common Abbreviations Found on the Net

Acronym	Definition
AND	Any Day Now
AFAIK	As Far As I Know
B4N	Bye For Now
BTA	But Then Again
BTW	By The Way
CU	See You

22

Acronym	Definition
CUL	See You Later
EOT	End Of Thread
FWIW	For What It's Worth
FYI	For Your Information
G	Grin
GMTA	Great Minds Think Alike
IAC	In Any Case
IAE	In Any Event
IC	I See
IMHO	In My Humble Opinion
IMO	In My Opinion
IMNSHO	In My Not So Humble Opinion
INPO	In No Particular Order
IOW	In Other Words
JIC	Just In Case
LOL	Laughing Out Loud
OTOH	On The Other Hand
POV	Point Of View
PTB	Powers That Be
RE	Regarding
ROTFL	Rolling On The Floor Laughing
TAFN	That's All For Now
TIA	Thanks In Advance
TPTB	The Powers That Be
YMMV	Your Mileage May Vary

As you can see, most of these abbreviations are derived from common figures of speech. Few need further definition; however, one in particular, YMMV, always seems to baffle newbies when they first hear it. YMMV, which stands for "Your Mileage May Vary" simply means, "This was my experience, but yours may be different." I guess you could say it's one way to cover your rearend online.

These aren't all the abbreviations you'll see, however. If you frequent any of the collectibles/for sale groups, you may see some of the abbreviations shown in Table 22.2.

TABLE 22.2   Abbreviations Found in For Sale/Marketplace Groups

Acronym	Definition
FS	For Sale
FT	For Trade
MIB	Mint In Box
MIP	Mint in Package
NRFB	Never Removed from the Box
WTB	Want To Buy
WTD	Want To Deal
WTT	Want To Trade

Furthermore, many narrowly focused groups will abbreviate names of commonly discussed people or topics, such as a show's key characters (DD for Daisy Duke from *The Dukes of Hazzard*), star race car drivers (DE for Dale Earnhardt), or members of the family (MIL for mother-in-law) to create their own shorthand. Rarely does this evolving shorthand need to be explained because the group's readership normally will catch on quickly given the context of its use. Unfortunately, the only way to learn these secrets is to watch a given group for a period of time. It's a given that each group will have its own abbreviations—that's simply part of the culture.

I Second That Emotion!

If you thought punctuation was great at capturing emotion in writing (exclamation points to convey excitement; an elipsis to express a voice trailing off in an unfinished sentence), then you'll really be impressed by the use of punctuation on the Internet. Take the following for example: BTW, :-). BTW is short for "by the way," as you saw in the previous section. The "smile" part of the title, however, is made up of a colon (:), followed by a dash (-), and then a close parenthesis mark ()). If you hold this book in front of you and rotate it clockwise (or merely tilt your head to the left) and read the example again, you'll notice that the three punctuation marks actually form a smiley. Punctuation used online in this manner make up a number of emoticons (a word derived from emotion and icon), as you will see in Table 22.3.

TABLE 22.3   Common Emoticons

Put Together...	To Mean...
:-) or :)	I'm smiling or happy about the preceding thought/comment
:-(or :(	I'm frowning or unhappy about the preceding thought/comment

Put Together...	To Mean...
;-) or ;)	I'm winking at you
<:-)	Dumb question
:-*	A kiss

Those are just some of the emoticons. The net is literally flooded with creative variations of the smiley. While I'd like to give credit where credit is due, it's next to impossible to trace how some of these evolved. Take a look at Table 22.4 to see a few of the more unique ones I've found over time.

TABLE 22.4   Some More Unusual Emoticons

This...	Means This...
&:-)	From a person with curly hair
:-(=)	From a person with big teeth
C=:-)	From a chef
:-)}</////>	From a guy in a suit and tie (tie design may vary)
@->->—	A rose

These emoticons are most frequently placed at the end of the sentence or phrase to which it refers to clarify the emotion or intention behind the message.

> **Sticks and stones...** Obviously emoticons are not a substitute for judicious word choice. A scathing or snide remark could still hurt, regardless of how many smileys follow it.

If you'd like to learn more about emoticons and their meanings, read the `alt.culture.emoticons` newsgroup.

Express Yourself

As if abbreviations and emoticons aren't enough, there's yet another way to express yourself on the net. Expressions are words or phrases embedded between open and close chevrons (< and a >, such as <grin>, for example). Used the same way as emoticons, these expressions are capable of communicating subtle differences in emotion that is hard to capture with an emoticon. Take a basic smiley emoticon that communicates contentment. Changing that :-) to a <grin> adds a playful dimension to the message, and so on. Table 22.5 contains some of the more frequently used expressions.

TABLE 22.5 Popular Expressions You'll Find Online

This...	Means This...
<grin> or <g>	Grin
<big grin> or <G>	Big grin
<blush>	I'm embarrassed by the comment
<snicker>	Playfully making fun of someone
<giggle>	Being silly
<getting on/off my soapbox>	About to begin/end a speech about a subject you feel very strongly about
<raising eyebrows>	Disbelief over a matter

It's easy to see how all these elements have come together to form a rich culture that, for the most part, doesn't discriminate mainly because it is so diverse. The Internet is a great place to be yourself because you'll always find someone else who shares your beliefs and values, and you won't be judged by your wardrobe or waistline.

Some people believe the anonymity of the Internet makes it a cold place; it's just the opposite in my opinion. For all you know, `simba@justpc.com` (not a real email address) could be a 10-year old fan of Disney's *The Lion King*, or it could be a famous novel writer hiding behind a screen name. You never know until that person decides to reveal a clue to his or her identity. Until then (and most likely even then), "simba" will be treated with the same respect (or disrespect) other netizens are treated.

Protecting Your Privacy by Using a Screen Name

In some ways, venturing on to the information superhighway is like visiting a big city for the first time—you'll want to conduct yourself in such a way as to have a safe and enjoyable time. That's not to say that the Internet is a hotbed of crime because it isn't. Like anywhere else, however, you'll want to take some basic precautions to ensure your safety and privacy.

When you set up your email account, you are asked to select a name to use as your email address. In corporate America, email addresses often take the form of a person's first initial followed by their surname. Take me for an example. I use `JFreeze@JustPC.com` for my business account. It gives clients the sense of dealing with a real, legitimate person as opposed to some faceless person at the other end of a modem.

There are times, however, that you would just as soon be a faceless person at the other end of the modem. Using JFreeze, for example, gives advanced computer users plenty of information to begin tracking my physical location. While the capability to find you gives potential customers or clients a sense of legitimacy and stability, it's not necessarily a desirable thing if you plan on frequenting chatrooms or even newsgroups.

Experienced Internet users wanting to track you down could go to a Web site based on your domain name (JustPC in my example) to see whether such a Web site exists and use it to search for clues to your location; they could plug your name into any number of search engines to draw clues from news articles you may have posted; they could search a host of online phone books and pair the entries up with clues found elsewhere, and so on. The list goes on and on. When it comes right down to it, however, there are no more clues available to potential "bad guys" on the Internet than there are in the "real" world. Someone could follow you around, paw through your mail, dig through the contents of your trash can…you get the idea.

The media alone could scare you away by painting the Internet as the equivalent of wandering into the streets of Washington, D.C. alone in the middle of the night. Before you unplug your computer and put it up for sale at a church flea market, however, rest assured that there is plenty you can do to have a positive and safe experience on the Internet. The options are a heck of a lot more effective than anything you could do to protect yourself in the real world, too.

I'm not a pessimist by any means. In fact, it is my belief that crime resulting from using the Internet is far more uncommon than the media makes it out to be. It's a truly rare incident that couldn't have been avoided by using a little common sense and a few tips from someone who's been surfing the information superhighway since it was a dirt road.

Be Anyone You Want to Be!

Perhaps the best place to start is by selecting a screen name for yourself. Choose something fun that expresses your personality or a passion of yours. If you're a basketball fan, for example, choose something such as `celticfan`. Other options might include `UMassalum`, `catlover`, `fluteplayer`, or `NTRPRZ` for a *Star Trek* fan. Use some creativity to come up with alternatives in case your selection is already taken.

Even if you've already selected your email address, think of a good screen name to use for online chats, auction sites, and so on.

Respecting the Rights of Others

If you've chosen a screen name to maintain your privacy, chances are others have done the same. As you make more friends online, you'll start to correspond with one another using your real names in email notes.

When encountering these friends in online chatrooms, newsgroups, and other public forums, be careful not to reveal their real names. Including their names in a posted news article or in the context of a multiperson chat is a direct violation of their privacy. If it should happen by accident, simply apologize and try to be more careful in the future.

Shopping on the Information Superhighway

Imagine shopping for the holidays without having to do battle over a parking space, or without having to jump out of the path of runaway baby strollers loaded with packages (Where *are* the babies, anyway?)... it's a dream come true, right?

With your new-found link to the Internet, you can be enjoying the holidays this winter without all the blood pressure-raising agony. Bake a batch of fresh sugar cookies while your friends brave the preholiday shopping crowds at the local mall.

Buying from a Buddy... Is It Safe?

After you've spent some time in your hobby newsgroup of choice, you may be tempted to fill out your collection (or that of a loved one) with purchases from some of the other newsgroup participants. Unfortunately, this can have mixed results. As you saw earlier in the hour, scalpers often feed off these newsgroups, making it seemingly impossible to acquire that limited edition Christmas ornament without paying hefty secondary market prices.

There are a number of kind souls, however, who will help a fellow collector out without price-gouging. I met quite a few of these while frequenting rec.toys.cars. So if you decide to make a purchase from someone you met on a newsgroup, follow these tips to improve the odds of having a positive Internet purchasing experience:

- Read the newsgroup for awhile and watch for any "bad dealer" posts. If you don't see anything on the person you plan to buy from and the amount of the purchase is fairly significant, you may want to consider posting a message asking for anyone else's experience with that person. Be sure to request that responses be emailed to you so as not to inadvertently start a flame war if experiences are mixed.

22

- Read the newsgroup's FAQs to see whether anyone maintains a safe dealer list on a Web page. Many newsgroup veterans will maintain such a page for their fellow collectors. If the FAQs and a few weeks of browsing the newsgroup don't direct you to such a site, post a message asking whether there is such a place you can go for your answers.

- Does the person you're dealing with have a Web page dedicated to her business? If so, she may be more legitimate than her counterpart merely posting a few things for sale here and there.

- Does the person or business accept credit cards? If they do, that also can be interpreted as a sign of permanence and legitimacy.

- Has the person participated in any other group discussions, or has he surfaced only to sell things? A person appearing only to post for sale ads may not necessarily share your love of the hobby; he may just be a scalper in disguise.

> **Get to the bottom of the matter quickly.** Save some time by going to www.dejanews.com and searching for the person's email address to see the newsgroup articles he or she has posted over the last month. These should give you valuable clues.

- Know what you're buying. If you aren't buying something MIB (mint in box) or MIP (mint in package), get to know your hobby's grading standards. Diecast cars, for example, are graded C10 for a perfect piece, and the number goes down in specific increments, depending on the type of blemish, its location, and so on. Many hobbies have specific books collectors have come to accept as the standard for grading. Consult the FAQs for further details.

Is My Credit Card Number Safe on the Net?

Is your credit card number safe on the Internet? Unfortunately, the answer is "it depends."

Many e-commerce sites use something called *SSL* (*Secure Socket Layers*) to encrypt your entire business transaction including, most importantly, your credit card number. This protects your personal information from being viewed by unauthorized parties.

NEW TERM **Encryption**—(pronounced "en-crip-shun") means information is scrambled using a code or password so that others can't read it.

While SSL is supported by a number of large Internet storefronts, many still do not have the resources to implement such technology. In these instances, you'll want to find alternative methods for shopping with them, such as sending an order through the mail or calling in your credit card number.

How can you tell if a site supports SSL? Most commercial Web sites make a big thing out of it by mentioning that fact in key data entry locations. Internet Explorer also displays a small icon showing you whether you're in a secure environment, and some even flash up a message saying you're about to enter a secure server (see Figure 22.6).

FIGURE 22.6

Internet Explorer displays a padlock when logged on to secure sites. It also displays an S (for secure) behind the `http:`.

Just because a Web site doesn't support SSL, however, doesn't mean that you have to shop elsewhere. Consider any of the following options:

- Make notes on the products you want to purchase, jot down the company's phone number, and then call and place the order the old fashioned way. Not only do you still avoid the Christmas crowds, but you save paper and a stamp as well. If they have a 1-800 number, even better!

- If you're not a phone person and aren't in a hurry, you can send the order via snail mail. This can save you money in the long run if the company's number is a toll call for you.

- Some merchants are equipped to take your order online, and then hold it until you phone in your credit card number.

- Finally, other merchants enable you to set up an account with them so that all you have to do when visiting their site is enter a userid and password, make your selections, and then process your order as normal. Your credit card information and shipping address remain on file with the merchant so that you don't have to rekey and submit it again.

Shopping online offers other benefits, as well. In many instances, you don't have to pay sales tax on the items ordered. While postage and handling is charged, you often don't have to spend much to save money overall. If your state sales tax is 5 percent and you spend a hundred dollars, for example, that's $5 saved. Even with the flat rate $4.95 shipping charges used by some, you still come out ahead, and you don't have to break your back lugging the stuff through a mall full of full-contact shoppers!

When It Comes to the Web, All That Glitters Is Not Gold

Remember the days when students had to schlep off to the library to research their term papers? I was one of those students. I pawed through dusty card catalogs; I scanned library shelves for hours trying desperately to find a book that had obviously been improperly shelved; and I spent hours taking copious notes from reference books unable to be checked out. (But no, I didn't have to walk to school in six feet of snow, never missing a day!)

In all seriousness, gathering data from the Internet has simplified the lives of many students. Rather than running out to the library at odd times of the day, students can now use the family's PC to research their papers from the safety and comfort of their own homes.

Using computers as a research tool, however, is not for students only. In fact, there are times in our lives when we're all students, regardless of our age or how many years we've spent in the classroom. Consider the following situations:

- You want to invest in a camcorder, but the salespeople at the local electronics stores don't have a clue as to the specifications of each unit and how they differ. Where do you get the information you need? The Internet, of course. Use manufacturers' Web sites to research the product specifications and suggested retail price, and then venture out to the newsgroups to get the reaction of people who've been using the equipment you're most interested in.

- Have you been transferred to a new area, but have no clue how to begin house hunting or searching for the best school for your children? The Internet can give you some solid facts to work with before you travel to the new location and investigate first hand.

- We don't like to dwell on unpleasant things, but they can happen. Again, the Internet can help you along the way. Whether you or a loved one has been diagnosed with a condition you'd like to learn more about, or whether you'd like to become involved in an online support group to help you cope with the situation, it's all available from the privacy of your home with your computer. It's no substitute for sound medical advice, but it can help you ask the right questions, make an informed decision, and get the emotional support you need.

- Did your granddaughter find a box turtle in the woods out back, but you don't know what to feed it? Or maybe she wants to keep it, but you have no idea what kind of home little Tessie turtle needs. You can find all the answers online, and even find forums in which to ask your questions.

These are just a few situations for which the Internet and your new PC can help you research the information you need. The possibilities are virtually endless. We've all heard the old cliché, "Free advice is worth what you pay for it." If that were truly still the case, however, no one would believe a thing seen on the Internet. So what makes the Internet different? How can we be sure the information we're seeing and basing our decisions on is accurate?

The issue of determining information integrity has grabbed the attention of many prominent scholars since online content is being sited more and more as a source in written papers. In the following section, I'll give you some ways to evaluate the information you find online for its validity, whether you're researching your dissertation or trying to make an informed decision regarding the purchase of a major appliance.

The Importance of Evaluating Online Information

Many people view the Internet as one big encyclopedia full of knowledge, but they lose sight of the fact that real encyclopedias have entries written by noted experts on the subject. Furthermore, these entries pass through the hands of droves of editors before publication. While you have experts on the Internet as well, you also have a high proportion of people who think they're experts. This requires the information-gatherer to work even harder to sort the diamonds from the rocks.

Luckily, researchers and librarians have come up with some criteria to help us evaluate the information we find on the Web. These criteria include a Web site's scope of information; the authority and bias of the data maintained on the site; the accuracy of the information; the timeliness of a site's content; the permanence of the Web site; any value added features included on the site; and the presentation of the information.

You'll explore each of these criteria in detail, and then take a look at how to evaluate different types of Web sites (such as sales and marketing Web sites, advocacy Web sites, and personal Web pages) using these criteria.

Scoping Out the Information

22

The depth and breadth of the information found on a given site depends on the intended purpose and audience of that Web site. Many government sites, for example, archive their data for future use, whereas a personal Web page might report on the latest *Star Wars* action figures found in the stores, and then delete that information as time goes on since it's no longer of value.

To evaluate the scope of a site, look for the following:

- **Stated purpose of the site.** Many Web pages have a stated purpose for their existence. For advocacy or nonprofit organizations, the Web site's purpose may mirror its organizational mission statement, or at a minimum act as an extension of part of its mission. Even personal Web pages may have a stated purpose. Use these statements of purpose for clues to the site's comprehensiveness and potential biases.

- **What they say is covered.** Oftentimes, a Web master will sacrifice overall subject comprehensiveness in order to specialize in a specific area. A gardening club, for example, may strive to produce the most comprehensive site out there on roses rather than publishing dribs and drabs on a variety of plants and flowers. If a site chooses to specialize, it's likely that the site will not only attempt to cover the topic in depth, but it will provide links to a number of additional reliable sources specializing in the same topic. These focused sites often are some of the best places to glean a ton of information about a given topic.

NEW TERM **Take me to your (Web) Master!** A *web master* is the person who is responsible for coordinating a Web site's content, design, and functionality.

- **Site comprehensiveness.** You can tell a site's breadth and depth of information by scanning its list of topics, site map, or internal links. The volume of information also can provide some clues.

It's easy to see how the items in the preceding list work together to give you a good feel for the scope of a Web site's content. You need to know a lot more than the scope of a site's content in order to evaluate it effectively, however.

Determining the Authority and Bias of a Site

One of the best ways to assess the biases of a Web site's content is to look at what's presented and ask, "What does the Web site's owner have to gain from presenting the material as he does?"

Obviously, if a company's Web site says its Zoom910 model of camcorder is the best thing around, you'll weigh the statement a lot differently than if a noted and trusted consumer advocacy group's Web site states the same thing. The company has something to gain by touting its product, whereas the consumer advocacy group merely wants to do right by the consumer with no biases.

Here are some things you should look for when attempting to evaluate the authority and bias of a Web site:

- **Who provided the information and why?** If a commercial entity (usually sporting a URL ending in .com) produces or even sponsors the Web site, the information is almost guaranteed to be biased in some respect. No profitable company is likely to highlight its shortcomings or product weaknesses online for all to see unless they're legally obligated to do so (as in the case of tobacco products and the mandatory Surgeon General's warning). Web sites maintained by advocacy groups or nonprofit organizations (often with .org extensions) also can be biased, however, since they exist to right a perceived wrong. As such, they're likely to exaggerate the facts to make a case for their existence. For these reasons, it's important to weigh what is said and put the content into perspective given the potential biases.

- **Is a specific point of view being pushed?** Objective sites will merely communicate the facts without inflicting a point of view on the reader. When evaluating a site for the integrity of its information, you also should be wary of over dramatic use of language, which could signal an exaggeration of the facts.

- **Seeing a stamp of approval.** Web sites that are truly exceptional in content tend to draw a lot of attention. A statement of support from noted experts and organizations in the given field increase the odds of the information being at least reasonably accurate. These stamps of approval can show up in the form of reciprocal links, awards given to the site, and posted quotes or comments from field experts.

 Reciprocal link—Two Web sites give links to one another, thus forming a reciprocal link.

After you know where the site's information comes from and have any potential biases fixed in your mind, you're ready to start examining the accuracy of the information itself.

The Pursuit of Accuracy

Unless you know the names of all of the field's experts, you may have a tough time evaluating whether what you're looking at is legitimate, or is merely a product of a wannabe expert.

To assist you in this quest for accurate information, look for the following in the Web sites you visit:

22

- **Cited sources.** If a Web site cites the sources of its information and the sources appear to be legitimate, chances are the information is accurate. You could double-check them to be certain, but that would defeat the purpose of providing easily accessible information on the Web.

- **Who came up with this stuff, anyway?** A Web page's author or compiler sometimes will include a link to his or her credentials. At that point, you can decide for yourself whether the person is an expert or even a reliable source.

- **A recognized source of value.** If you're visiting the American Association of Retired Persons (AARP) home page, for example, chances are you'll respect any sources it links you to, with the assumption that surely the AARP would be judicious in granting links. Seeing the site in question referenced by a variety of prominent and reliable sources gives the site, and the information contained therein, more credibility.

Day-Old Data?

One of the things that's plagued print media since the beginning is its long turnaround time. The content of printed materials (with the exception of newspapers of course) often becomes stale before it ever reaches the hands of its desired audience. It's a sad fact of life, yet it's one of the things that makes the Internet so intriguing. Information can be updated within minutes to reflect pivotal news events, changes in the law, or other pertinent information that can change at a moment's notice.

Just because you can quickly update Web content doesn't mean that it is updated frequently in reality. When a leading toy manufacturer finally made its online presence known, I sent them an email note pleading that they keep their site updated so that it would maintain its value. But, like many other large corporations, the information quickly became stale and worthless, and was seldom updated. Web pages created by the collectors of this manufacturer's products soon became the freshest, most reliable source of information. It kind of makes you wonder why they even bothered expending the effort (not to mention the money) to get online in the first place!

So, how do you avoid the pitfalls of day-old data? Here are some things to look for when assessing the freshness of a site's information:

- **Check the "expiration" date.** Many Web pages have a "revised on" date reference somewhere on the page. Depending on the type of content the page provides, the information could be considered old after as little as an hour. Many news sites update themselves as frequently as every 15 minutes, whereas some sites undergo a scheduled weekly update, which is more than enough. This is one of those instances where your judgment comes into play.

- **Revision policy.** In addition to a revised or modified-on date, many Web sites also display a policy for updates. Statements such as "This page is updated every 15 minutes," are common. Unfortunately, in many cases, you must simply just wait and see when the information will be updated.

- **Hibernating hyperlinks.** Stumbling onto countless error codes when trying to follow a Web page's links also may be an indicator of a poorly maintained, thus potentially out-of-date, Web page.

Using out-of-date information can have undesirable results in many circumstances. If the data appears to be old, you might want to consider looking elsewhere before relying too heavily on such questionable information.

Here Today, Gone Tomorrow!

Whether a site is permanent can tell you a great deal about the information it provides. Finely crafted Web sites produced by college students can disappear after they graduate; or sites that move from server-to-server like cheap antique reproductions at a flea market can be cover-ups for shady activity. It's wise to know what you're dealing with, so consider checking for the following:

- **Now you see it, now you don't.** Whether it's a system upgrade or a new organizational affiliation, Web pages occasionally need to be moved. Look for notices about impending change of location for the Web page. Most reputable Web pages will plan a change of location and will prepare users well in advance by placing a notice prominently on the home page. With careful planning, they might have registered their own domain name, thus making relocation virtually seamless to the user. Sites that suddenly change location without notice should raise a red flag in your mind.

- **The Web page owner's relationship to the host site.** If the Web page belongs to the government or a major corporation, chances are it's relatively stable. If, however, the page is maintained by a student using her university Internet account, count on it moving or even disappearing altogether within a few years, or maybe even months. That doesn't make them bad sources; it just means you'd better grab the information you want while you still can.

22

- **Transitory information.** There are some cases where the site's information may be of temporary value. Consider a politician's election page, or a page dedicated to the aftermath of a tragedy like an earthquake or plane crash. After these sites have served their purpose, they most likely will not continue to be updated, and may even disappear after a certain amount of time. If you need information from a site like this, it's best to get it when you see it, just in case it disappears.

Time is of the essence anywhere, especially on the Internet where the number of Web sites grows by some staggering number each month. Unless you see signs that a Web site archives its data for future access, it's best to get the information while you can.

Value-Added Site Features

Some Web sites include value-added features such as sections moderated by an expert, search engines, navigational help, and so on. Because of the time and effort that went into designing and creating them, these sites are likely to be around much longer than their typical counterparts.

Beauty's in the Eye of the Beholder

We've all seen flashy Web pages with little content to back up the special effects, but there are some presentation and design elements that contribute to the professionalism and legitimacy of a Web site. These include intuitive site organization targeted to the specific audience; appropriate use of graphics and other multimedia features; and navigational links back to the home page or site map of the site. Use of these elements implies a planned, stable Web site that you can return to with confidence.

Questioning Your Sources

Given all these factors, how can you possibly evaluate a site's worthiness as a resource? Just use the following questions as a guide. The more questions to which you answer "yes," the higher the quality of the source.

1. Is it clear who is sponsoring the Web site?

2. Is there a way to verify the legitimacy of the company/organization/individual (a phone number or street address, not just an email address)?

Check it out! Because it can be hard to verify the legitimacy of an individual, it's wise to use extreme caution when relying on a personal home page as a source of information. For best results, try to find the source of the claim or statistic to verify the information.

3. Is the page relatively free of typos and grammatical errors? While these may not seem like important considerations, they communicate a lack of quality control, which means other information may go unverified.

4. Are the sources of factual information cited so that you can double-check the page's claim with the original source?

5. Is any advertising on the page clearly set apart from informational content?

6. Is there a date posted on the page indicating when the content was last updated?

7. Has the page been completed as opposed to being under constant construction?

8. Is the information advertising-free?

9. Are the biases of the company/organization/individual clear?

10. Can you tell when the Web page first appeared on the Internet?

Web sites are not substitutes for good, sound research, but they can be a vital source of timely information and leads to more obscure resources. By using the preceding questions as a guide, you should have a better feel for which Web sites are potential gold mines for information.

Summary

Whew, that was some hour! I know it was long, but since it was mostly reading instead of steps you had to follow, I figured it was still doable in an hour. In this hour, you learned all about the culture of the Internet, how to make safe transactions, and how to evaluate the integrity of the information you see online.

The next hour's going to be crammed full of goodies, too, because I'm going to show you how to make your own Web page in an hour using FrontPage Express.

Workshop

Now it's time to see just how much you learned in this lesson. I'll give you a short multiple-choice quiz to test what you learned, followed by a suggested activity designed to enhance the skills you acquired during the hour.

Quiz

Select the best answer to the questions from the choices provided, and then check your answers in the following section.

Questions

1. Which of the following is *not* acceptable Internet etiquette?

    a. If your response to a post is of interest only to the original poster, email it to them directly rather than posting it on the group.

    b. Before contributing to a newsgroup, read the FAQs to be sure your question isn't addressed there.

    c. When starting a new business, gather as many email addresses as you can from relevant newsgroups and email them all with your offerings.

2. What do :-) and :-(mean?

    a. I'm happy about what I wrote/I'm sad about what I wrote.

    b. These marks mean nothing on the Internet or anywhere else.

    c. Hey, you don't put punctuation marks together in that order!

3. When it comes to information found on the Internet...

    a. You can't believe a word you read.

    b. You should evaluate what you read to help determine the integrity of the information.

    c. Accept everything you see as the gospel truth; no lies or tall tales are allowed on the Net.

Answers

1. If you engage in the behavior described in c you may get run off the Internet faster than you can bat an eye!

2. ais the appropriate answer here. If you chose anything else, you've obviously been snoozing through the lesson!

3. Neither a nor c true, so bis the correct answer. You can find information ranging from heavily researched facts to bold faced lies.

Activity

Now that you're familiar with many of the abbreviations, emoticons, and expressions found on the Internet, you're ready for this little exercise.

Try composing a note using as many of the items you learned about during the hour as you can. You can produce the message in Word 2000, Outlook Express, or even on paper. It doesn't matter. The object is to use as many of them as you can while keeping the message understandable.

HOUR 23

Design a Web Page in an Hour

Nearly everyone on the Internet dreams of creating their own Web page. Some hope to launch businesses via their Web site, whereas others simply want to build a virtual shrine of sorts to their favorite actor or musical group.

In this lesson, I'll introduce you to FrontPage Express, Microsoft's light-weight, user-friendly Web site design application. By the time you reach the end of this hour, you'll have greater insight into the following:

- What are the parts of the FrontPage Express workspace called?
- How do I format the text for my Web page?
- What's the easiest way to link to another page on my site?
- Can I use this program to put images on my Web pages?

Learning the Lay of the FrontPage Express Land

As I've done throughout this section of the book, I'd like to present the application's workspace using a screen shot with callouts (see Figure 23.1). This will help you quickly learn just which buttons are located where. You'll almost instantly notice that you've encountered a bunch of the buttons before in Outlook Express (or in Word if you use Microsoft Office).

FIGURE 23.1

The FrontPage Express workspace is your blank canvas on which you'll begin designing your work of art.

Title bar
Menu bar
Standard toolbar
Format toolbar
Forms toolbar
Primary workspace
Status bar

The Title bar and Menu bar serve the same function here as they've done in other applications covered throughout this book. Even the Formatting toolbar is nearly identical.

Formatting Web Page Text

One main feature of a Web page is its computer platform independence. A Web page built on a Windows 98 machine like yours can be viewed by a Windows 95, Windows 3.1, Macintosh, UNIX, or any other system with a basic Web browser. To reach this degree of universal accessibility, text in Web pages use formatting styles rather than specific font sizes—point size—as in a word processing program. In FrontPage Express, headings used for titles and subtitles can range in size from the largest (Heading 1) to the smallest (Heading 6).

Follow these steps to enter and format some text on your Web page:

1. Start FrontPage Express. Depending on how your machine is configured, you might have to dig for it a little. Most commonly, the application can be found by clicking Start, and then choosing Programs, Accessories, Internet Tools. If you don't see it there, you may need to install it from the CDs that came with your system, or download the latest version free of charge from Microsoft at www.Microsoft.com.

2. In the FrontPage Express window, type your first heading.

3. Select the text you just entered by clicking in front of it and dragging the mouse across the rest while holding down the left mouse button.

Make up your mind ahead of time. If you know what style you want to use for the text before you type it, you can set the style parameters and then begin typing. That way you don't have to go through and select the text you want to format.

4. From the Change Styles box in the toolbar, click the arrow to reveal the drop-down options list (see Figure 23.2).

Click here to view your
Style options

FIGURE 23.2
The Change Styles box helps you select your text style and size.

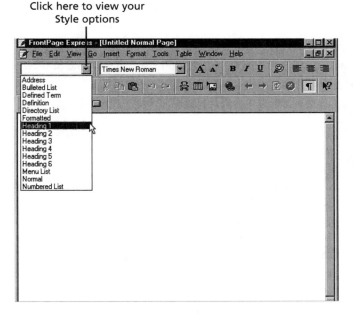

23

5. From the Options list, click a text style choice. Heading 1 or Heading 2 is suitable for a Web page title. The text changes to reflect the selected size.

6. Keeping the text highlighted, click one of the Alignment buttons to make the text align to the Left, Centered, or Right. By default, the text will be aligned left.

7. If desired, click the standard Bold, Italic, or Underline style buttons.

8. Click anywhere on the blank page to clear the highlight and continue working in FrontPage Express.

Save me! Save your work often. This is a good habit to follow in just about any computer program you work with. When you save your newly-created Web page, you'll notice that it will carry an htm or html file extension, the Web counterpart to Word 2000's doc extension.

Repeat these steps to continue adding text to your Web page, varying the text styles between Headings and Normal.

Adding Color to Your Web Page

The color scheme used on a Web page can go a long way toward creating a certain "feel" or mood. For example, warm shades of reds, yellows, and oranges would fit right in on a Web page for a chimney sweep, whereas cooler shades of green would work well for a lawn service.

With FrontPage Express, you can add color in a couple of ways: by defining text colors, and selecting a background color or image.

To begin painting your Web page with color, follow these steps:

1. With the Web page you want to modify open, click Format on the Menu bar, and then choose Background. The Background tab of the Page Properties dialog box opens (see Figure 23.3).

2. On the left side of the tab, you'll see two drop-down boxes—one for the background color, and one for the main text of the Web page. Click the corresponding arrow button to see a list of available colors from which you can choose. Simply click a color's name or swatch to apply it.

3. The right side of the tab enables you to define colors for text hyperlinks, visited hyperlinks, and active hyperlinks. Unless you're really careful, it's easy for some text colors to blend in with the background making the content illegible, so choose your colors wisely.

4. When you've finished selecting your text and background colors, click OK to apply them.

FIGURE 23.3

The Background tab lets you apply all sorts of color to your page.

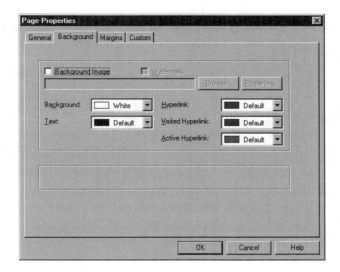

To use an image for the background, start by opening the Background tab as described above, and then click the Background Image check box. From there, you'll need to click the Browse button, choose the Other Locations tab, verify that the From File option is selected, and then click the Browse button again to surf your way to the desired image file.

The first few times you attempt to design a Web page, you might find yourself doing a lot of things over again in order to make them look good. Don't let this frustrate you; like anything else, designing Web pages takes practice.

Sounds Good to Me!

If you want to get fancy and aren't terribly concerned with how long it takes visitors to download your Web page, you might want to consider embedding a sound file in your page. Although this file can be anything from a voice recording stored on your computer to a funny sound effect, it's most commonly music.

To place a sound file on your Web page, choose Insert, Background Sound. An Other Location tab similar to the one used to apply an image to your page appears. Verify that the From File option is selected, then click the Browse button to begin clicking your way to the desired sound file. After you've found it, double-click it to select it, and then click OK to apply it to the page.

23

> **The sound of silence.**   You won't hear anything (or see animated files move) unless you launch Internet Explorer and preview the Web page there. To do this, launch Internet Explorer, and then click File, Open. Click your way to the Web page's file, and then open it as usual. From within Internet Explorer, you should see all the sights and sounds you worked so hard to create.

Linking: What the Web's All About

Whether you created links between multiple pages or links to your favorite Web sites, links are a fundamental part of Web site development. In the sections that follow, you'll learn how to connect pages within your Web site, and you'll discover how to connect your page/site to others around the world.

Linking as You Go

The simplest way to create links within your own Web site is to create them as you build them. Say one of your interests is NASCAR racing. Maybe you'd like to build your own page of NASCAR-related links. It's simplest to highlight the NASCAR racing bullet on your home page, and then create the new page. Skim through the following steps to see why this way is easiest:

1. Launch FrontPage Express and open the page from which you want to create additional pages/links.

2. Highlight the word or phrase you'd like to turn into a link. This is where the reader will click to be taken to the new page.

3. From the FrontPage Express Insert menu, select Hyperlink.

4. Click the New Page tab of the Create Hyperlink dialog box to see the dialog box shown in Figure 23.4.

5. FrontPage Express will automatically enter a title for the new page and create a URL based on the text you highlighted. If you don't like the name FrontPage Express has created, feel free to change it by clicking inside the Page Title or Page URL text boxes and typing in new information.

6. When you're satisfied with the page title and URL name, click the OK button.

7. In the New Page dialog box shown in Figure 23.5, select Normal Page.

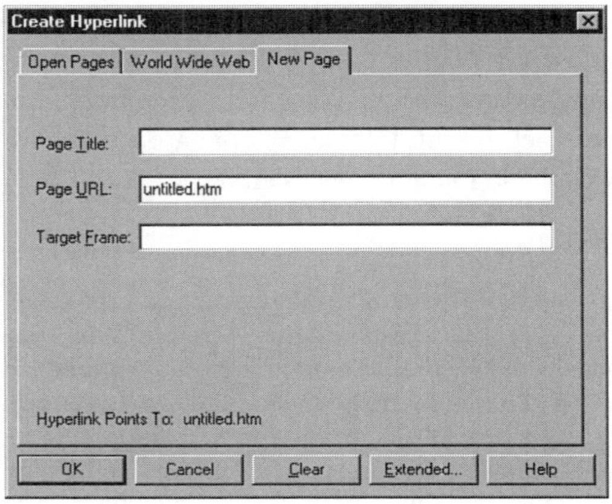

FIGURE 23.4

FrontPage Express will attempt to create a new page title and URL (Web address) for the page you're about to create.

FIGURE 23.5

Notice that you can create all kinds of Web pages using FrontPage Express.

8. Click the OK button, and FrontPage Express will display a brand new blank page that you can begin designing to your heart's content.

Linking to Other Web Sites

There are oodles of valuable resources on the Internet (and oodles more that are just plain fun to visit). In light of that fact, you'll want to be sure you know how to create links from your Web page to other Web pages.

Before I jump into the steps, there are a couple of things you can do to make the process run more smoothly. As you execute the steps to link to another Web site, you'll discover you need to enter the URL of the Web site to which you'd like to link.

23

Well it's a little more complicated than that. If the Web site's address is short and you can remember it off the top of your head, typing it in is no problem. If, on the other hand, it's a long, cumbersome one, or you can't remember it, you'll need to establish a connection to the Internet, fire up Internet Explorer, open the Web site, and copy and paste its URL into the dialog box as described next.

Copy and paste? In case you need a quick refresher course on some Windows program editing basics, here it is. When you have the Web page you want to link to displayed in Internet Explorer, click inside the Address bar. The whole URL should be highlighted. (If for some reason it's not, you can always click at the far left end and drag the mouse to the opposite end to select the entire address.) After the URL is highlighted, right-click it and select Copy from the shortcut menu. You'll paste it in as directed later by right-clicking the text box described next (see step 6) and choosing Paste from the shortcut menu.

Follow these steps to connect your Web page to another Web site:

1. If needed, connect to the Internet to pull up the necessary URL.
2. Launch FrontPage Express, load the page in which you'd like to place the link, and highlight the text you want to turn into a hyperlink.
3. From the Insert menu, choose Hyperlink.
4. Select the World Wide Web tab in the Create Hyperlink dialog box. (This is the tab that should open by default.)
5. Use the drop-down arrow if needed to make sure the Hyperlink Type is defined as http: (see Figure 23.6). You'll notice that the appropriate http:// prefix appears in the URL box.
6. Next, enter the desired URL into the URL box by either typing it or copying and pasting it as described in the previous Note.
7. Click OK when you're finished to complete the link.

Believe it or not, you can also use these same steps to link to email addresses, such as "Please email Jill Freeze for additional information," where Jill Freeze is a link to my email address. That way, when a visitor clicks the link, his or her email program will launch with the defined address already in the To: line of the message.

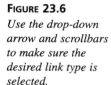

FIGURE 23.6

Use the drop-down arrow and scrollbars to make sure the desired link type is selected.

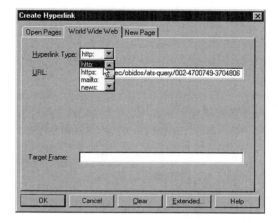

To link to an email address, follow the steps for linking to another Web page. This time, in step 5, select mailto: as the link type. Then all you have to do is enter the appropriate email address in the URL box. Linking to a special newsgroup is just as easy—choose news: as the link type, and then enter the group's name in the URL box.

Including Images on Your Web Page

A Web page without graphics would be pretty bland. With a wide range of clip art available for download over the Internet plus FrontPage Express's ability to use images you might have scanned or taken with your digital camera, perking up your Web page will take little effort.

The steps you'll need to follow to include an image on your Web page are fairly straightforward. Just do the following:

1. Open the Web page to which you want to add an image.
2. Click in the location you want to place the image.
3. From the Insert menu, select Images to open the Image dialog box shown in Figure 23.7.
4. With the Other Location tab open, click the Browse button to click your way to the file you want to add.
5. When you find the file you want, double-click its name to return to the Other Location tab. Click OK to exit the dialog box and put the image in its place.

23

FIGURE 23.7

The Browse button lets you access any image on your computer.

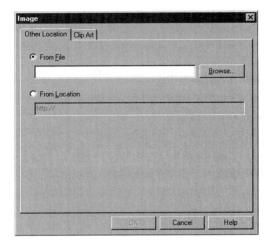

The Need for Speed.   If you plan to use an image repeatedly throughout your Web site (as might be the case with a graphical logo), consider clicking the From Location option on the Other Location tab and entering the URL of the image. That way, you can store the image in one location as opposed to each page (which saves you space on the Web server for other goodies), and it dramatically reduces the image download time for your visitors.

Publishing Your Web Page

Most Internet service providers prefer that you save your Web page/site to their FTP server. To do this, take the following steps:

1. Open the page you want to place on the Web in FrontPage Express.

2. Open the File menu and select Save As. The Save As dialog box appears, displaying the name and location of your Web page file.

3. Click OK. If you used any images or other files in your Web page, a dialog box appears asking if you want to save these files to the Web server (see Figure 23.8).

FIGURE 23.8

FrontPage Express will prompt you to add any extra files you used to the current Web folder.

4. Click Yes to All. The Web Publishing Wizard launches and then overlays an Enter Network Password dialog box.

5. Type your username in the Username text box, tab to the Password text box and type your password. Click OK.

The memory of an elephant.   FrontPage Express is set up to save your password, so you won't need to enter it the next time you publish a Web page. Hey, anything to make life a little easier, right?

6. The Web Publishing Wizard reappears, displaying an explanation of what you are about to do. Click Next.

7. You are first asked to select your connection method. By default, FTP should be selected. Click Next.

8. Type the name of your FTP server (and the name of the Subfolder containing your Web pages if applicable). Click Next.

9. The Wizard tells you it's ready to publish your page(s). Click Finish to proceed.

Technical difficulties, please stand by...   If you should encounter a problem while trying to publish your Web page, you might need to verify that you entered the necessary information correctly on the Web Publishing Wizard. If you still run into problems, consult your ISP for assistance.

Summary

This lesson gave you everything you need to know to design your own Web site. You learned the fundamentals of linking pages together, and discovered how to polish your pages with colors and sounds.

In the next hour, I'll show you where to find goodies you can use on your pages. You'll also learn how to download the items and unzip them so they can be installed (in the case of computer programs) or used within FrontPage Express for Web design.

Workshop

Now it's time to see just how much you learned in this lesson. I'll give you a short multiple-choice quiz to test what you learned, followed by a suggested activity designed to enhance the skills you acquired during the hour.

23

Quiz

Select the best answer to the questions from the choices provided, and then check your answers.

Questions

1. What do you call it when two Web pages are connected?

    a. A chain.

    b. A link.

    c. Siamese twins.

2. Which of the following cannot be done in a FrontPage Express background?

    a. An image can be used.

    b. The color can be changed.

    c. The selected image can be turned upside down as the perfect April Fool's joke.

3. Why can't you hear the sound file you inserted into your Web page?

    a. Because you have to open the page's file in Internet Explorer in order to hear it.

    b. Because you can't embed a sound in a Web page.

    c. Because you haven't set the right FrontPage Express sound playback options.

Answers

1. B of course! I could understand it if you chose A by accident, but C? No way!

2. C was the answer we were looking for here.

3. If you chose A, you are correct! B is false; as for C, there is no such thing as a FrontPage Express sound playback option!

Activity

Maybe you should take a break to fortify yourself with food and drink; this exercise could take awhile!

I'd like you to launch FrontPage Express and begin working on your own Web page. For the sake of the exercise, you might want to use the following format:

Welcome to [Your Name]'s Home Page!

I've created this site to share some of my favorite subjects with you. They include the following:

- Interest 1
- Interest 2
- Interest 3
- Interest 4
- Interest 5

Now go in and change the colors of the text and background to match your personality or mood. Save this Web site, because you may want to use it as the basis for future experiments in Web page design.

23

HOUR 24

Downloading Treasures from the Internet

Wouldn't it be great if you could test drive that much talked about computer game before you buy it? After all, few stores allow the return of software after it's been opened. And wouldn't it be nice to have a cat background and special cat icons for that Web page you're designing for your local animal rescue league? I'll show you how to do this and more in this final lesson.

The following questions will also be answered along the way:

- Can I recover from a botched download if my link dies, or do I have to start all over again?
- What in the world is a Zip file, and what do I do with it?
- Do I have to pay for clip art and Web art I download from the Internet?
- Where can I find all this neat stuff?

Before you begin downloading all the nuggets you'll find online, there are some things you'll want to do to prepare yourself. For starters, you'll want to make sure you have a current version of an antivirus program (such as, Norton, McAfee, and so on) installed on your computer. Many PC manufacturers have started pre-installing virus protection software on their new systems, so do a bit of poking around your computer files to see if you have one already. If not, then definitely go out and buy one if you plan on download-ing a lot of files from the Internet.

Then after you've located or purchased an antivirus program, take a few moments to play around with it. Pore through its menus and dialog boxes to make certain you know how to set it up, or at least be able to run a virus scan on demand.

When—and only when—you feel confident working with your antivirus program, you can start downloading to your heart's content.

Must-Have Tools of the Downloading Trade

Over the years, I've downloaded thousands of files from the Internet—gymnastics Web art for my daughter's home page, new Duke Nuke'em levels for my son, demos of games I'm thinking about buying as gifts, clip art I used for my kids' nursery school newsletter I edited, and especially utilities that have not only made my life easier, but have saved my sanity as well.

In the sections that follow, I'll introduce you to some of the most useful utilities I've found that you'll want to consider installing on your computer too. I'll also explain why you'll want them so you won't think this is all a commercial plug for the respective com-panies!

Chasing Away the Download Demons

Nothing's worse than being in the middle of a huge download when your link to the Internet dies. In the past, the only option was to start the download over again.

When I beta tested Internet Explorer 5.0 for Microsoft, I noticed they had included a neat SmartRecovery utility in their setup program. No matter where the link died, SmartRecovery was able to go in and pick up where it left off. No starting over again, which is especially nice when downloading a 20MB Web browser!

Unfortunately, you couldn't make use of SmartRecovery on anything but Internet Explorer-related downloads. For months and months I wished I could find such a utility for other downloads. Finally, between book projects, I found the time to go searching the Web to see if anyone had undertaken such a project. Surely they had; it seemed like such an obvious need for someone to fulfill...

My travels landed me at the home page for a company called Netzip. A little digging uncovered a gem called the Download Demon. Download Demon is a slick utility that enables you to pause a download at any time (great when a nasty electric storm blows in), and then resume it when you're ready. And should your link peter out midstream, Download Demon will automatically pause itself so you can re-establish the connection and continue with the download as if nothing had happened. Oh what a life-saver this little beauty has been!

To get your own copy and install it, all you need to do is follow these simple steps:

1. Connect to the Internet and then launch Internet Explorer by clicking its icon on the Windows Quick Launch bar.

2. In the Internet Explorer Address Bar, type **www.netzip.com**.

3. On the home page, you'll see a section devoted to their incredibly popular Download Demon. Click the Download Free link.

24

The only thing constant is change. As you'll discover after you get a few months of surfing time under your belt, Web sites are often given a facelift to freshen them up. This may mean the placement of links on a given Web site may change. Don't panic; just click around, and you'll find it in no time. This is especially true for the tools I suggest you install in this lesson.

4. A Web form appears, asking you to enter your name, email address, postal code, and to check whether you want to be notified of new Netzip news. Fill in the requested information, and then click the Download button.

5. You are redirected to ZDNet, where a final Web page appears, complete with product information, installation instructions, and system requirements. once you've read the information of interest, click the Download Now button to download Netzip Download Demon 3.0.

6. The File Download dialog box shown in Figure 24.1 appears. Check the Save to Disk option, and then click OK.

7. A Save As dialog appears. By default, you should find yourself in the Desktop directory. If you don't, you'll need to double-click your way to the appropriate folder.

8. Once inside the Desktop folder, click the Save button. The Download Demon file will be downloaded in a matter of seconds. Internet Explorer tells you the download is complete by displaying the window shown in Figure 24.2.

FIGURE 24.1

After the Download Demon is installed, this screen will be a distant memory.

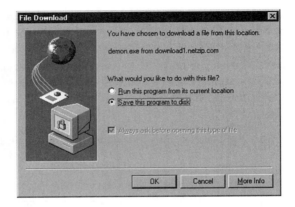

FIGURE 24.2

Internet Explorer keeps you informed of your progress.

9. Click OK to close the dialog box. If you click the Show Desktop button on your Windows Quick Launch Bar, you'll see that an icon for the Download Demon now resides on your desktop.

10. Double-click the Demon icon on your Desktop to start the installation process. At that time you will also be asked to close any Web browsers you might have open. It is essential to shut the browsers down because the Download Demon is hooked into your Web browser, which can't be done while the application is active.

11. You will be asked if you want to install Download Demon on your machine. Click Yes. A status bar will keep you posted on the state of the installation.

12. After the installation is complete, you'll need to click OK to close the dialog box. In some cases, you may even be asked to reboot your system in order to complete the installation.

This process doesn't take as long as you might think because Download Demon is actually a very small, compact file. Downloading the program should take a minute at the most; the time it takes to execute all the other steps depends on the speed with which you work more than anything else.

Downloading Files with the Help of Download Demon

Now that you've gone to all the trouble to download and install the Download Demon, it's finally time to reap the rewards of your efforts.

When you find something you want to download, all you have to do is follow these steps to get the file on your machine:

1. Click the link leading to the file you want to download. This fires off the Download Demon as pictured in Figure 24.3.

To keep you entertained while the download is running, the Download Demon fires off a second window underneath the first that provides links to a number of potentially interesting bits of information. Of course, you can always do your own surfing by clicking the Close button on the second window, and continuing to browse the Web with Internet Explorer.

All the while, the Download Demon keeps you apprised of the time remaining in the download as well as the percentage of the file that has already been retrieved.

2. (Optional) Should you wish to suspend the download for any reason, you may do so by clicking the Pause button. When an Internet link is lost, Download Demon will automatically pause itself (see Figure 24.4).

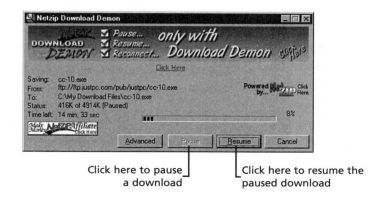

Click here to pause a download

Click here to resume the paused download

24

3. If you paused the download or lost your Internet link, continue retrieving the suspended download by re-establishing your connection to the Internet (if necessary), and then click Resume. The Download Demon picks up right where it left off!

4. When the program has finished downloading, a screen like the one shown in Figure 24.5 appears. If you're ready to install the program on the spot, click the Install button. A variety of onscreen prompts will guide you from there. If you want to deal with the program later (or if no Install button is displayed), simply click Close.

FIGURE 24.5

Take it or leave it; you can work with your completed downloads now or later.

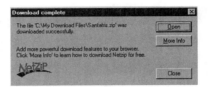

WinZip: Another Useful Tool in Your Downloading Arsenal

When you're cruising the Internet for program files, there are three types of files you'll most typically encounter: .exe files (which are applications you can install using the Download Demon), .cab files (Microsoft's proprietary file compression tool, which can also be installed via the Download Demon), and .zip files (compressed files that will need to be processed through the WinZip tool discussed here).

NEW TERM **Suck it all in!** A game demo can be a hundred megabytes or more, making downloading a formidable task for anyone but those with super high-speed Internet connections. Zipping the files makes them smaller, using a process known as file compression. Compressed files usually carry the .zip file extension, which requires a tool like WinZip to unsquish them before installing them.

Getting Your Own Copy of WinZip

As they say in scouts, "Always be prepared." Now you can be prepared to handle any Zip files you encounter on the Web. Just follow these steps to retrieve the WinZip tool and install it on your computer:

1. Connect to the Internet, and then launch Internet Explorer.

2. In the Address Bar, type `www.winzip.com`.

3. When the WinZip page is fully loaded, you'll see a link that says "Download Evaluation Version." Click the link.

4. You will be taken to a second Web page that lists the downloads the company has available. Look for the WinZip for Windows 98 link, and click it. (The link won't be worded exactly like this. Because updates and new versions are frequent, the link name is subject to change.)

5. For some reason (probably because Netzip has a product that competes with WinZip), the Download Demon does not launch on attempts to download WinZip; you'll have to tough it out with Internet Explorer's dialog boxes this time around. Choose the Save to Disk option, and then click OK.

6. You'll be prompted to save the file. The Desktop folder of the Save As dialog box should appear by default. If it doesn't, you'll need to click your way to it so the Web browser will be able to find it when it needs it. And since the file has already been named, you're spared the hassle of giving it one yourself. Just use the name they gave you, and save as usual. The Save As dialog disappears as soon as the file is safely saved.

24

> **When is a default really a default?**   When you launch a new session of Internet Explorer, the Desktop folder will be the default. If you've downloaded something into another folder during the current session, that folder will appear as the current folder in the Save As dialog box.

7. To begin installing WinZip, click the Start button on the Windows taskbar and choose Run.

8. When the Run dialog box shown in Figure 24.6 opens, click the Browse button and double-click your way to the Zip file you downloaded (it should be easy to spot because the filename will most likely contain the letters z-i-p).

FIGURE 24.6

The Run dialog box helps you install WinZip.

9. Double-click the WinZip file, which closes the Browse dialog box and returns you to the Run dialog box with the file's address (or path, to be technically correct) in the Open text box.

10. Click the OK button to begin installing WinZip on your system. The WinZip Setup dialog box is displayed.

11. Press the Setup button to run the setup program. Another dialog box called WinZip Setup is displayed, prompting for the name of the folder where you want to install WinZip.

12. Press OK to use the default folder location. The WinZip files will then be copied to the appropriate folder and the WinZip Setup wizard starts.

13. Just follow the directions in the wizard to complete the setup process.

> You will be asked to choose between the WinZip classic user interface and a wizard driven interface. The instructions in the rest of this chapter assume that you chose the classic user interface.

Unzipping Files You Download from the Internet

Now that you've used the Download Demon to fetch a huge Zip file successfully, you'll need to unzip that file in order to install and eventually run it.

In the steps that follow, I'll show you how to unpack and install zip files using WinZip:

1. Launch WinZip by double-clicking its icon on your Windows desktop, or by launching it from the Start menu. The screen in Figure 24.7 appears.

FIGURE 24.7

The colorful WinZip workspace will eventually hold the list of files packed in the zip file.

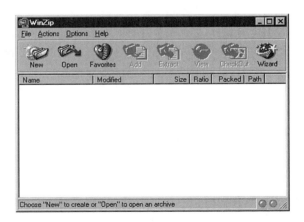

2. Click the Open button on the WinZip toolbar to launch the Open Archive dialog box. You'll immediately notice how similar it is to the Open and Save As dialog boxes you worked with earlier in the book.

3. Double-click your way to the zip file you want to unpack/install just as you would navigate to files in Windows Explorer.

4. When you find the zip file, double-click it to display the individual files in the chosen archives.

5. To begin the installation, take a look at the WinZip toolbar. If you see an Install button near the right end of the toolbar, click it to get started with the installation. Because programs use various installation wizards, you'll need to follow the onscreen prompts to complete the process.

6. If the Install button is not visible, you'll need to skim through the list of files packed into the zip file to find a setup program or an .exe file. After you find one, just double-click it to begin installing the contents of your zip file. Again, there will be onscreen dialog boxes to guide you through the necessary steps, so you'll never be left hanging.

Packing Up Your Own Files

The more time you spend on your new computer, the more complex your documents will become. That's mostly because your increased comfort with the machine and its software eventually encourages experimentation with more advanced features like Web pages with animated graphics, and documents with clip art.

If you ever need to send documents created in Word or Excel to a colleague via email or even to yourself at work, you may appreciate the increased speed of download if you "zip" the file(s). I use WinZip all the time to package chapters and screenshot images for my editors; it makes a huge difference. In fact, some images get reduced in size by 80 percent or more!

To take advantage of this yourself, just follow these easy steps:

1. After the files you want to compress are saved and closed (WinZip won't process open elements), launch WinZip using the desktop shortcut or the Start menu as appropriate, given your personal installation of the tool.

2. Click the New button on the WinZip toolbar. The New Archives dialog box opens, giving you the opportunity to move to the directory in which you'd like to save the newly created zip file.

3. When you reach the desired folder, you'll need to name the zip file you're about to create. Type the name into the File Name text box, and then click OK.

4. An Add dialog box similar to the one in Figure 24.8 appears. Click your way to the folder containing the files you want to compress.

FIGURE 24.8

Although it may look complex, you'll only need to acquaint yourself with a small percentage of the fields and options on this screen.

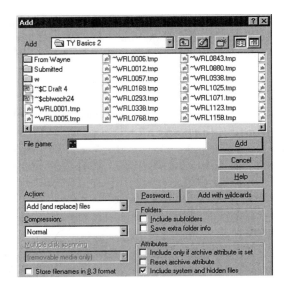

5. By default, WinZip packages everything in the chosen folder. You can handpick the files you want to including by using any of the following techniques:

   • To select a single file, simply click its name.

   • To select multiple contiguous files, click the top file's name on the list, press the Shift key, and hold it while you click the last file on the list to be included.

   • To select various files in the folder, click the first filename as usual, and then press the Ctrl key while clicking additional filenames. The order in which you select them really doesn't matter.

6. With all the files selected, click the Add button. WinZip puts all the files into a single, compressed zip file, making it easier and smaller to send via email or put on a floppy disk.

When you haven't got it together...   No insult intended here; I just wanted you to know what to do if the files you want to include in the zip file are stored in different folders. Before you close the WinZip window, click the Add button on the toolbar. The Add dialog box shown in Figure 24.8 appears again, giving you the opportunity to move to the new folder and select the desired files.

7. When the zip file is complete, simply click the Close button in the top-right corner of the WinZip program window. Your zip file will be safe because it was saved during the compression.

Finding the Goods

Although I hate giving lengthy lists of must-see Web sites because their addresses often change, I'm going to make an exception for this lesson. After all, what good is learning all these great file downloading tricks if you can't use them, right?

For your convenience, I've subdivided sites you may be interested in by category. To save some of the smaller treasures like animated .gifs or small sound bytes, you'll typically need to right-click over it, choose the Save Picture As (or Save Target As in the case of sound files) menu item, and then use the Save As dialog box to navigate to the folder in which you want to store the item. I also like to give the file a descriptive name so I can remember what it is. A Web site's proprietary numbering scheme does me no good when I'm in a hurry to construct a Web page.

What's mine is mine, what's yours is mine. When it comes to the treasures found on the Internet, that's not necessarily true. Many sites offer free Web design tools, but they occasionally ask that you place a link to their Web site from yours as a way of acknowledging their contribution. Before you exit a Web site from which you've downloaded design elements, be sure to consult the guidelines for using the items. In nearly all cases, items are free for personal use, but require payment (or at least permission) for you to use on a commercial Web site. Know what you're getting into before you use the design elements, and then take copious notes which you link to your given filenames so you can comply with any terms of use requirements.

When you've successfully saved the item on your computer, you'll be able to use them in documents and Web pages as described in the previous hour.

Programs: The Big Stuff

To track down software demos, shareware to try out, or even just plain free software, point your Web browser to some of these sites:

- www.download.com—One of the largest sites out there. If you can't find it here, it may not exist.

- www.shareware.com—Another huge, searchable site with oodles of goodies!

- www.gamespot.com—If your son is dying to test drive the newest computer game releases, here's a great place to do it.

Animated .gifs for Web Pages

Animated .gifs are a great way to add visual appeal to your Web site without dramatically affecting its download time. On the various Web sites listed here, you'll find thousands of these little gems—from cats to computers to clarinet players, you'll find it at one of these sites:

- www.animfactory.com—A collection of free, downloadable animated .gifs.
- www.developer.com/downloads—Still more animations for your viewing (and downloading) pleasure.
- www.fg-a.com/stateflags.htm—Show your loyalty to and pride in your home state by including one of these animated state flags on your Web site.
- www.rogersgifs.com/animaster/graphics.html—Another large site you'll have fun exploring. You should know, however, that you will need to type in a password to get to the animated gifs even though they are free. Don't worry, he gives you the password; it just prevents unauthorized people from linking to his page.

Web Page Backgrounds, Buttons, and Icons

There are so many Web design tool sites out there, you'll never have time to check them all out! Here are a few to get you started. If you're planning to design a themed Web page, I suggest you go to DogPile.com at www.dogpile.com, and search on Web design cats (or whatever your theme is). That should help you hone in on a few that have exactly what you're looking for.

- www.freeimages.com—Web graphics abound on this free site.
- www.coolarchive.com—More fun with Web page design!
- theboutique.org—A nice site with a lot of useful graphics.
- www.rogersgifs.com/index.html—Roger's gifs also has non-animated Web design elements you may want to make use of.

Sounds of the Internet

Want to give your Web page visitors some tunes to tap their feet to? Sounds good to me! (Get it? "Sounds" good to me? Okay, okay...)

To redeem myself for the bad jokes, I'll point you in the direction of some sound file sites you'll want to include on your travels for Web page design goodies.

- files.midifarm.com—I admit it; I got lost on this site for hours when I should have been writing. From the Backstreet Boys to Cher's newest hit, "Believe," it's all here. Many of the arrangements are also rated, so you know which ones are the best up front.

- `mmsound.about.com`—About.com is a super source of links and information, and sound effects are no exception. Just visit this link, and click the Sound Effects link on the left side of the page.
- `www.wavplace.com`—Sound bytes from TV shows and movies populate this site.
- `www.wavplace2.com`—An extension of the site above, WavPlace2 has sound files for people's names, holidays, and even takes requests for files. Think of all the fun you can have sending emails that literally say, "Hi, Mom!" (or whomever)!

Summary

Not only is there a lot of neat stuff to be found on the Internet, but now you can also retrieve it yourself with minimal hassles and disruptions. The resumable downloading of the Download Demon combined with the file compression capabilities of WinZip are a powerful combination when it comes to successfully saving the material you want to keep.

I hope you had as much fun learning about computers as I did writing about them! Hopefully you've come away from this book with newfound confidence and understanding of the technology that's become so fundamental in people's lives. I didn't attempt to bombard you with everything there is to learn out there, but you're armed with the essentials. You can decide what you want to learn more about later on. And when you do find a subject that interests you, there are plenty of great books in this same *Sams Teach Yourself in 24 Hours* series to guide you.

Happy computing!

Workshop

Now it's time to see just how much you learned in this lesson. I'll give you a short multiple-choice quiz to test what you learned, followed by a suggested activity designed to enhance the skills you acquired during the hour.

Quiz

Select the best answer to the questions from the choices provided, and then check your answers.

Questions

1. What does Netzip's Download Demon do?

   a. Chases away computer viruses.

   b. Allows you to resume lengthy downloads where you left off should your Internet connection unexpectedly terminate.

   c. It helps identify good programs to download versus bad.

2. What does it mean to zip a file?

   a. It's another word for emailing a file to someone, because email gets to its destination in a zip.

   b. It's what you do to your pants in the restroom after making a quick pit stop.

   c. It's a method of file compression that makes a file or group of files one small, quickly transferable and stored package.

3. What is a Midifarm?

   a. A modern day equivalent to the old "fat farms" you used to hear about.

   b. A mid-sized sedan car factory.

   c. A huge Web site of outstanding music files for your Web page.

Answers

1. B, and what an incredible tool it is!

2. The proper answer in this context is c; however b may be appropriate when it comes to daily life.

3. Okay, this one was a give-away. If you said anything other than c, boy, are you out of it!

Activity

I'm going to tie up the last lesson in this book with an easy (and fun) assignment.

1. Think of your most passionate interest, preferably one about which you'd like to create your own Web page.

2. Next, launch Internet Explorer, and surf on over to www.dogpile.com. I suggest this site because it searches multiple search engines at once.

3. Enter the name of your interest in the Dogpile search box followed by words like Web backgrounds, Web art, or Web design.

4. Visit the resulting Web sites, and download any items that appeal to you.

You'll probably stumble onto more stuff than you expected to; enjoy it, because that's how life is on the Internet—full of choices!

Part V
Appendixes

Hour

APPENDIX **A**

So You Want to Purchase a Computer

Many of the people who read this book will have already purchased a PC, but just in case you're still in the "thinking" stage, following are some things to consider before you make the big investment:

- **Know what you want to do with the machine**—What is your primary reason for purchasing a PC? Are you looking for a high-powered gaming platform? Do you want to surf the Web? Will you be bringing home work from the office?

  If it's the latest and greatest games you want, sink your money into the best machine you can afford. Games constantly push the technical envelope, so you'll want as much room to grow as you can possibly get. An upgraded video card may make a noticeable difference for flight simulators, racing games, and such. And, of course, you'll want a full multimedia setup and plenty of RAM. You can never have too much RAM!

For the net surfers among us, investigate the high speed Internet connection possibilities in your area before making a purchase. If, for example, you have cable modem service available at an affordable rate, you may very well want to consider getting that instead of a more traditional Internet connection. This means that the standard modem that comes with machines is virtually useless to you, so you may want to swap it out for more RAM. And again, a multimedia setup is a plus, but there's no real need for a fancy video card for the net.

If work is prompting you to make the purchase, then the software bundled with the PC may sway you one way or another. Obviously, if your company uses Microsoft Office 2000, you'll probably want to choose a machine that comes with Office 2000 (or at the very least Word 2000). No matter what the advertised retail value of a software bundle is, it has no real value for you if you can't make use of it.

- **When it comes to monitors, try before you buy**—It's tempting to go after the largest monitor on the market, but not only is that an expensive option, but it may not be the best one for you.

When it comes to monitors, there's a lot to consider. First off, there's the price. Upgrading to that fancy 21-inch monitor may cost you hundreds of dollars more. And the sheer size of some of these monsters is nothing to scoff at. You can't set these humongous hundred-pounders on just any old desk. They need a well-supported, commercial-rated surface, and a large one at that. Perhaps most important of all, the viewing quality/area gained by the increased monitor size may be a lot less than you think. For example, I tested various screen resolutions on 17-inch, 19-inch, and 21-inch monitors at a local store before ordering my newest PC. I opted for the 19-inch display. There was noticeable improvement over the 17-inch, and it was $600 less than the 21-inch. The 21-inch monitor just didn't offer $600 in value in my opinion, but your experience may differ. I strongly suggest you try out some monitors before making a final decision.

- **Read the fine print**—Offering a $99 PC with a three-year Internet service commitment has become quite the marketing ploy in recent times. While it may look like a great deal on the surface, it may not be what you're expecting.

Before you take advantage of such a deal, you should get the answers to the following questions: 1.) How much is the Internet service per month? $20 is pretty much the going rate for a basic personal account now. If it's more than that, beware. 2.) Are the fees paid monthly, or as one lump sum up front? 3.) What happens if you break your contract? Perhaps you may move within the three years, or maybe the constant inability to connect to the net because of busy signals frustrates you. At any rate, you should know your rights and any potential penalties.

- **When a deal isn't a deal**—Many electronic superstores offer PC packages complete with scanner and color printer. While these are both fun accessories, they may not be the model you want. Do some price checking of the individual components, too, because you may find the package deal isn't the financial bargain they'd like you to think it is.

- **The desktop versus laptop dilemma**—Unless you're on the road a lot and need to take your computer with you, a desktop will give you much more machine for your money. Additionally, laptops lag behind desktops in terms of how fast their processors are, so if you really need speed and performance, a laptop may not cut it. On the other hand, if you live in a tiny efficiency apartment, a laptop may suit you quite well since it doesn't take up much space. Just bear in mind that while the price of laptops has dropped dramatically, it's still not competitive with its desktop counterpart.

- **Know the warranty and availability of tech support**—When you buy your first computer, sometimes it helps you feel at ease to know that it's protected under a good warranty. Get the longest parts warranty you can find when choosing where to make your purchase. Also make sure their tech support is available to you during the hours you use your new PC most. If it isn't, it's of no value to you.

- **If you can only afford to upgrade one thing**—Put your money into RAM. That will give you the most noticeable difference performance-wise. Bumping up your PC's clock speed a notch or two may not return an impovement you can see for anyone but the power user or cutting edge game guru. Extra RAM will come in handy no matter what you're doing.

A

APPENDIX B

Getting Your New Computer Ready for Action

After you get your new PC home, there are some things you should consider doing to maximize both the life of your computer, and your comfort at the keyboard.

- **Save it!**—Computers generally come packed in large boxes with lots of padding, whether you mail order the PC or simply pick it up at your local wholesale club. While these boxes are unarguably cumbersome to store, there may come a time when you'd appreciate having the original packaging around. Suppose that your monitor dies and you need to send it back to the manufacturer for replacement or repair. Finding a box big and sturdy enough to do the job may be harder than you ever anticipated. Or what if you need to move cross-country—you certainly wouldn't want to send your computer into the moving van unprotected! Rather than throwing the boxes away, consider storing something in them along with the packing material. That way you have an extra place to stash your clutter, and you're ready to pack your PC up safely!

- **Chill out or do some warm ups!**—If your PC was shipped (or even if you just hauled it home in a cold car during the winter), you should give the console and monitor time to adapt to the temperature in your home before turning it on. A vast majority of CPU failures happen when a machine is turned on. Equipment that experiences extreme changes in temperature is especially prone to malfunction, so give it a little time. Even as little as two hours can make all the difference in the world.

- **Get some support!**—Before unpacking your PC, double-check the stability of the surface on which you plan to set it up. If it's a heavy folding table (such as a banquet table), make sure the braces are locked in place. If it's a desk, look underneath the desktop to help you find the sturdiest place for the monitor. Putting a huge monitor on a fragile, unsupported desk return could spell big trouble for both the desk and the PC, not to mention your feet and knees should they be underneath at the time of the big collapse!

- **Look at the big picture**—This is something you may even want to do before you get the new PC. Go to the desk/table on which you plan to put the computer to do a lighting check. What you're trying to determine is whether direct sunlight will hit the computer's screen. Checking the lighting at various times of the day is ideal, but it's most important that you check it at the time you think you'll be using the PC the most. Direct sunlight hitting your monitor can make it impossible to see the screen, so it's better you discover there's a problem before you hook everything up!

- **Check with the powers that be**—Take a look around your work area and make sure you have an adequate power supply. That is, try to have dedicated outlets for your PC instead of sharing the outlets with your hair dryer, VCR, and such. Overloading your home's wiring can result in blown fuses or, worse yet, an electrical fire.

- **Suppress the surge!**—Invest in one of those surge protectors for your new PC. That way you can plug the monitor, the console, and the printer all into one power supply which you can control with a single switch. And if you can, find a surge protector with a built in phone line outlet; that way you can protect your equipment from all angles. And whatever you do, make sure you're getting a rated surge protector. A simple power strip will do no good in an electrical storm. Sure you can get a plain old power strip for as little as $6, but a good surge protector goes for $30 on up. This is one item you may not want to risk penny-pinching on. If you have a TV tuner card in your PC that will be connected to a cable cord, you'll want to make sure that's run through a surge protector, too. Basically, any line from the outside going in to your computer should be attached to a surge protector to reduce potential damage to your equipment.

- **Room to grow**—Something else to consider when setting up your workspace is storage. You'll need to have a safe place to put all your software disks—a place where they'll be free from dust and close at hand while you work. You'll also want to have a special place for printer paper, spare ink cartridges, and computer books like this one. The documentation, receipts, and warranty slips that came with your machine should also be stored in a safe location.

- **Bottom's up!**—It may sound silly, but if you intend to spend large amounts of time at your computer, a good office chair is worth its weight in gold. Not only does it keep your backside from falling asleep, but a good one will support your back as you work, and you can adjust it to a comfortable height to reduce the likelihood of eye and wrist strain.

- **Ringing in your ears**—You'll want to make sure there's a phone line outlet close to your workspace as well. This is important for two reasons, the most obvious of which is you'll need it for your modem should you decide to connect to the Internet. But even if you don't intend to connect to the online world, having a phone that reaches to your computer will be invaluable should you ever need to call the technical support folks with a problem. That way, you're prepared when they try to walk you through the diagnosis or solution to the problem.

> **Going cordless?** You may want to reconsider keeping your cordless phone base/re-charger away from your hard drive since it can potentially wreak havoc with it. It's not a common problem, but one you should be aware of nonetheless.

- **The old fashioned way**—Sure, there are a lot of high-tech ways to remind yourself to do something. You could get Outlook 2000 and begin using the calendar and alarm functions, or you could do it the old fashioned way with a Post-It pad and a pen. I can guarantee you as soon as you get off the Internet, you'll think of three things you meant to check out; it happens to me all the time! With a Post-It pad, you can write it down as soon as you think about it and slap the note to the edge of your monitor. That way the information's there when you need it.

APPENDIX C

When Something Goes Wrong...

Just when you think you've got the hang of controlling this hunk of machinery, the unexpected will happen. Maybe your monitor doesn't flicker into action when you boot your machine, or perhaps your computer doesn't seem to recognize the new CD you just put into the disk drive.

In the pages that follow include some of the more frequently encountered problems, along with some possible solutions. Looking here may solve your problem before you spend hours on hold, waiting for tech support.

Computer Chaos

In this section, I've presented the most common problems encountered with a computer as a whole. Some solutions may seem overly obvious (translation: "Duh!"), but they're things you should double-check anyway.

My computer won't turn on! Before you panic, there are a number of things you can check that may remedy the problem.

1. Are the monitor and the console plugged in and turned on? They both have power switches, so it's possible the console is spinning up, but you can't tell that because the monitor is turned off.

2. Is your power strip in the "on" position? A pet can easily switch them off as can a falling object (you know, the ol' clutter on the desk syndrome), so it's worth a peek.

3. Is the power to your PC driven by a light switch as well? If so, verify that it is in the "on" position.

4. Still nothing? Then double-check to make sure all of the cables are securely in place.

5. Are all other electronics in the area working? If they aren't, you could have a blown fuse or a general power failure on your hands.

6. If you still get no response, try unplugging the computer and plugging something else into the power strip. If that "something else" works, you can assume the power strip is fine, but there may be a problem with the PC's power supply. That warrants a call to tech support because a blown power supply isn't repairable by an untrained person.

My computer froze! What now? Nothing's more unnerving than having your computer freeze on you. No matter what you do, nothing happens; even Ctrl+Alt+Del may fail. Before you start inventing new curse words as you shout at your PC, try the following:

1. If at all humanly possible, try to get into any open word processing documents or spreadsheets to save your work. The next steps you take may result in data loss if you don't. Of course, if your system is entirely frozen, you may not be able to get anywhere.

2. Next, try pressing Ctrl+Alt+Del, but *do it only once*!!! (If you do it twice, the system resets without giving you the chance to save anything.) The Close Program dialog box appears, listing all open applications. If an open application is causing the problem, you'll see the words "Not Responding" in parentheses behind the application's name. Click the name of the problem application, and then click the End Task button. How is your system running now?

> **Here today, gone forever.** Hopefully, the problem application wasn't one containing unsaved data. (Usually it's a Web browser with a memory leak or some other innocuous problem.) If it was an application like your word processor or spreadsheet program, there may be no way to recover your work. Office 2000 programs boast an AutoRecover feature which should, in theory, attempt to recover the active document during the crash when you re-launch the applicable application. I wouldn't count on this too heavily, though, as it seems to fail as often as it works.

3. If there's still a problem, repeat step 2 to see whether a second application is not responding.

4. Still frozen? Ctrl+Alt+Del again, and choose Shutdown from the Close Program dialog box. Hopefully Windows will shut itself down smoothly. If it doesn't, you'll have to turn the PC off, wait a few minutes, and then turn it on again. ScanDisk launches automatically to clean up any problem areas.

5. If you get repeated system lockups with a certain application, check the Internet to see if there's a patch or update to the program that may solve the problem. Many times, an update/upgrade will cure what ails your computer.

6. When repeated system lockups occur and you can't trace them to a specific application, there may be an underlying hardware problem. It may be worth a call to your computer's tech support department to see whether they can offer additional guidance.

Disk and Drive Dilemmas

Nothing lasts forever, and that includes disk drives. That's why people get all paranoid about backing up files. Disk drive failures don't happen often, but when they do, they can be catastrophic if you're not prepared. Likewise, you may be deceived into thinking your disk drive has failed when there's really a simple solution to the problem.

My floppy disk won't fit into the slot. Here again, there are several things you can try to isolate the problem. And please don't be offended by some of the more obvious suggestions; I know I've made some pretty basic mistakes while working late at night.

1. Verify that the disk you're trying to insert is the same size as the drive into which you're trying to insert it. An ancient 5¼-inch disk stands no chance of fitting into today's standard floppy drive.

2. Is the disk in the right position? A disk that is upside down or sideways will not fit into the drive.

3. Make sure you're really trying to insert the disk into a disk drive. I remember when I first started using a computer, I actually stuck a 5¼-inch floppy into one of the vents in front of the console!

4. Examine the disk for any abnormalities, such as warping, sticky spots, and so on, because any of these could potentially cause a problem for you.

5. If there's still a problem, you may want to have a qualified person check out the drive itself. Under no circumstances should you ever stick an object other than a disk into the disk drive, especially when it's plugged in.

I have a CD in the drive, but my computer doesn't recognize it. CD-ROMs can be very finicky, depending on the sensitivity of your drive. If you run into a glitch, try the following:

1. Open the CD drive, take out the disk, and blow any dust off of it. Also examine it for any scratches since they, too, can cause a problem. Replace the CD and see if the computer recognizes it now.

2. Trouble still? A more thorough cleaning may be in order. Cleaning methods vary depending on who you ask. There are plenty of commercial cleaning products on the market from which to choose. I'm too frugal to make such a purchase. If you want to try cleaning a CD from normal stuff you find in your home, start by finding a soft cotton rag. I use an old cloth diaper that was used for mopping up baby spit. It has been washed a gazillion times and is softer than just about anything else you'll find. Next, take out the CD and breathe hot air on the bottom of the disk—the hot, steamy air you exhale from your belly, not the cool air you generate with puckered lips. Finally, wipe the CD gently from the inside of the disk to the outside in a straight line, and retry it in the drive.

3. If that doesn't cure the problem, try putting another CD in the drive. If everything goes smoothly, you can attribute the problem to the CD itself. If it still doesn't work, you might want to try a third CD (perhaps a music CD if the problem CD was a data CD, or vice versa) before calling tech support.

Monitor Messes

A computer virtually is useless without a monitor (or a display in the case of a laptop), at least to you and me. Therefore, it's completely understandable that panic sets in whenever the monitor starts acting funky.

My computer's on, but I don't see anything on the screen. Don't write the monitor off just yet; try these things first.

1. If the monitor was on when it "died," check to see whether it's in Power Saver mode by moving your mouse or pressing a key. If it comes to life, you may want to consider either disabling or at least adjusting the power saving setting. Do this by clicking the Start button on the Windows taskbar, and pointing to Settings, Control Panel. Double-click the Power Management icon in the Control Panel, open the Power Schemes tab, and use the dropdown boxes to make the desired selections. Be sure to save your new settings by clicking OK.

2. Verify that the monitor was not shut off manually (as opposed to with the rest of the computer via power strip). You may not have shut it off that way, but on more than one occasion, my well-meaning son turned it off to save "'tricity," as he put it.

3. If that doesn't do it, check the monitor's connection to the console as well as double-check that the monitor is plugged in.

4. Still in the dark? If the monitor's LED power light is on, you might want to try tweaking the brightness and contrast on your monitor. Because the location of these controls can vary depending on your computer's manufacturer, consult the documentation that came with your system.

5. After all that, if it's still dead, it may be time to call your friendly tech support people. Be sure you have any warranty information with you when you call, as well as the information you wrote on the tear card at the front of this book.

Printing Problems

It usually happens when you're more pressed for time than normal. You send a document to the printer, go over to pick it up, and find nothing. What can you do?

Hey, where's my document? When you send a document to the printer and nothing comes out, consider the following:

1. First there's the obvious. Is the printer turned on and plugged in? Furthermore, is the printer securely attached to your PC?

2. Next, make sure the printer has enough paper to complete the job. This especially is true in the case of printers that are shared since you may not know who has printed what.

3. Is the printer online? Printers may unexpectedly go offline, which requires you to press the Online/Offline button on the printer to generate output.

4. If the print request is routed through a server (as may be the case with a computer attached to a network), contact the server's administrator to verify that the request actually made it. If it didn't, there could be a loose network connection.

C

5. If there's output but it's blotchy, disfigured, or totally black, it may very well be time for a toner/ink cartridge change.

6. If everything fails to remedy the problem, it's time to call a professional. Keep in mind that unless you purchased the printer from the company that manufactured and/or sold your PC, you'll most likely need to call a different tech support number.

Why did only part of my document print? This typically happens for one of the following reasons:

1. Obviously, if your printer runs out of paper part way through the print job, you'll end up with an unfinished product.

2. Go into the application's Print dialog box and make sure the "All Pages" option is checked.

3. Did you exit the application before the entire document could be downloaded to the printer's memory? Some older applications will abort a print job in this situation.

4. If the document was a frame-based Web page, you may not have gotten the frame you intended to print. Go into the Web browser's Print dialog box, select the applicable frame, and then resubmit the job.

5. Could there have been a power surge that interfered with the process? If so, simply resubmitting the job may be all you need to do.

Internet Irks

With something as massive as the Internet, complications can occur at any number of points. In fact, it may take significant amounts of time to isolate an Internet-related problem for that very reason.

The Internet is crawling at a snail's pace; what gives? Several things could be going on, including any of the following:

1. If you're surfing during the day and find Web pages loading at an excruciatingly slow pace, chances are the Internet is bogged down with traffic. And remember, just because everyone at your East Coast law firm has gone home for the day doesn't mean corporations in California also have called it quits. Given the time differences in the United States, combined with the millions of leisure surfers who log on from home, the net may very well be clogged into the early hours of the morning. The only thing you can do is surf at odd hours, plunk thousands of dollars into a high speed Internet connection to your home, or simply live with the sluggishness.

2. For those of you who have the opportunity to take advantage of cable modem service, go for it. You get super speed, and you don't even have to tie up a phone line! And if there's anything less than a 56K modem in your computer, seriously consider upgrading if you plan to do much surfing.

3. If things are crawling along into the wee hours of the morning, there may be a cut cable somewhere along the line. There's nothing you can do about it, mind you, because it's more than likely halfway across the country, but you will feel the effects of masses of rerouted Internet traffic.

4. Perhaps your connections are continually hit or miss. It could mean your Internet Service Provider doesn't have a high-speed link to the Internet. If they don't plan on upgrading soon, you may want to go shopping for better service.

Why does my connection keep getting dropped? If you keep getting those pesky "Do you want to reconnect?" messages, following are some things to look into:

1. Pick up your phone and listen to the dial tone. Is it crisp and clear, or do you hear crackles and static? Often times, a bad phone line can kill a connection. If the weather is stormy and windy, check the lines again when things settle down. If you've always had problems with your phone lines, there may not be much anyone can do about it until the phone company decides to upgrade or service its underground cables.

2. I've found that my Windows 98 machine has become almost hypersensitive to incoming calls. I don't have call waiting, but I do have voicemail through the phone company, which means the phone rings to the house and if the line is busy or goes unanswered, the call is forwarded to a mailbox at a phone company substation. Interestingly, when a call comes in and is forwarded to voicemail, I'll often get booted off the Internet. I wait a few moments, check for voicemail messages, and sure thing, there'll be one (unless, of course, it was a hang up call). The hassle may not be worth giving up voicemail, but you should be aware that such a situation could occur.

3. Check your modem's configuration. Many machines are set up to drop an Internet connection if it remains idle for a given amount of time. To learn whether this is the case for you, click the Start button on the Windows taskbar and point to Control Panel. Double-click the Modems icon, and click the Properties button (*not* the Dialing Properties button). Open the Connections tab and look for an option under Call preferences that reads: "Disconnect a call if idle for more than ___ mins." If this option is checked, you can either disable it by clicking it, or adjust the time as desired by clicking inside the text box and entering a new number.

C

4. If the disconnects persist even in the absence of either situation mentioned previously, check with your Internet Service Provider to see whether others have reported a similar problem. After you have the answer to this question, you should have a pretty good idea of whether the problem potentially lies with your modem or your ISP's.

I keep getting busy signals when I try to connect, and it's making me crazy! Here again I can offer some suggestions.

1. Get additional dialup numbers from your ISP to try in a pinch.
2. If that doesn't remedy the problem, call your ISP and ask what the user-to-modem ratio is. Someone once told me 7-to-1 was ideal, so if it's significantly higher than that, you may want to explore alternatives, or pressure them to add more modems.
3. For the night owls among us, surfing in the middle of the night may be all that's needed.

INDEX

WITHDRAWN